VISIBLE IDENTITIES

Studies in Feminist Philosophy
Chesire Calhoun, Series Editor

VISIBLE IDENTITIES

Race, Gender, and the Self

Linda Martín Alcoff

OXFORD
UNIVERSITY PRESS

2006

OXFORD
UNIVERSITY PRESS

Oxford University Press, Inc., publishes works that further
Oxford University's objective of excellence
in research, scholarship, and education.

Oxford   New York
Auckland   Cape Town   Dar es Salaam   Hong Kong   Karachi
Kuala Lumpur   Madrid   Melbourne   Mexico City   Nairobi
New Delhi   Shanghai   Taipei   Toronto

With offices in
Argentina   Austria   Brazil   Chile   Czech Republic   France   Greece
Guatemala   Hungary   Italy   Japan   Poland   Portugal   Singapore
South Korea   Switzerland   Thailand   Turkey   Ukraine   Vietnam

Copyright © 2006 by Linda Martín Alcoff

Published by Oxford University Press, Inc.
198 Madison Avenue, New York, New York 10016

www.oup.com

Oxford is a registered trademark of Oxford University Press.

Library of Congress Cataloging-in-Publication Data
Alcoff, Linda.
Visible identities:race, gender, and the self/Linda Martín Alcoff.
p. cm.—(Studies in feminist philosophy)
Includes bibliographical references and index.
ISBN-13 978-0-19-513734-7; 978-0-19-513735-4 (pbk.)
ISBN 0-19-513734-5; 0-19-513735-3 (pbk.)
1. Group identity.   2. Ethnicity.   3. Race awareness.   4. Gender identity.
I. Title.   II. Series.
HM753.A39 2005
305.8'0097—dc22   2005040614

3 5 7 9 8 6 4

Printed in the United States of America
on acid-free paper

For my sons, in admiration for the courage they've shown
in negotiating the complicated identities we have bequeathed to them,
and in gratitude for their ability to show me
the possibilities of a hopeful future.

Preface

Five months after the United States militarily invaded Panama in 1989, I flew back to see my family, and I brought my children, the youngest of whom had not yet been to meet his relatives there. My father, Miguel Angel Martín, drove us over to *Panama Viejo*, to the disheveled barrio where he grew up, and to the vacant lot where he used to play his favorite sport—baseball—which had by then been taken over for the greased-pole games (palo encebado) that young men like to play. To demonstrate his passion for baseball, my father loved to recount the story about the fire that destroyed his father's pawnshop in the late 1930s. A pawnshop was a lucrative business in those days, as small fortunes rose and fell around the turbulence of the canal-based economy, and the shop had gained a nice cache of gold jewelry over the years. My father worked there after school, and when the fire broke out, my grandfather called to him to get the jewelry, but my father first carried out two boxes of baseball cards.

My father no doubt loved the game for its pure sport, but there was also something of a colonizing effect in the way that baseball swept through Central America and the Spanish Caribbean in the early part of the twentieth century, just as cricket swept through the English West Indies. Later in life, after getting his Ph.D. in history at the London School of Economics, my father used to praise the orderly efficiency of British bureaucracy and unhappily compare it to the chaos of Panama. He was an anglophile all his life, spending every August in an apartment near the Old Curiousity Shop of Dickens fame, and naming his beach house "Chelsea." Though he did not marry an Englishwoman, he married first a North American (my mother) and then a Frenchwoman.

Still, like other colonials, he had ambivalent emotions in regard to his own country. Every single time we would pass Ancon Hill, the hill that overlooks *la Ciudad de Panama*, he would point out the Panamanian flag that has flown there since 1964, after a student struggle took down the U.S. flag that had symbolized U.S. dominance over the city. (Twenty-four Panamanians died in that event, which became a symbol of national resistance.) My father wrote his master's thesis

trying to prove that the coup that established Panama's independence from Colombia was not merely an imperialist-led plot to wrest control of the best land for
canal construction but was initiated by Panamanians themselves. No doubt in this
way he sought to establish, in effect, the dignity of the nation. And he was well
aware from having spent many years in Florida as a student and later as a professor
that his brown skin and Spanish accent did him no favors in the "land of the free,"
despite his accomplishments. With a master's degree, the only job he could find in
the 1950s was riding a bicycle delivering ice cream.

During that visit in June of 1990, my father drove us over to el Chorrillo, San
Miguelito and to the other poor neighborhoods in *Panama Viejo* that had taken
the brunt of First World weaponry during the invasion. He pointed out the bullet
holes peppered through porch walls, the piles of rubble where apartment buildings
had once been, and together we watched the U.S. Army Humvees that still pa-
trolled the area like vultures looking for scraps they left behind. Just as we turned
the corner to leave, an Army Jeep pulled us over. Two *solderos estadounidenses*
peered into our car, and then had my father get out and show them his papers. He
was not on U.S.-owned Canal Zone property, just in a neighborhood close to the
one he'd grown up in, stopped by two white foreigners in front of his daughter and
grandsons and asked to prove he had a legitimate right to be there.

That afternoon, my father's identity had nothing to do with the fact that he was
a professor of history at the *Universidad de Panama*, had published six books, or
even that he still loved and followed U.S. baseball. He was a brown-skinned man
driving a car with Panama plates. I knew he was humiliated to have this happen
in front of me, and I was wishing he would also be angry, but he betrayed no emotion as he stood there in the sweltering sun while the soldiers chatted with each
other in English while checking his car and papers.

This moment crystallizes for me the effect of social identity, precisely because
it is so obvious that global capital and neocolonial political formations had overdetermined that encounter between the U.S. soldiers and my father. My argument
in this book begins from the premise that structural power relations such as those
created by global capital are determinate over the meanings of our identities, the
possibilities of social interaction, and the formations of difference. Nonetheless,
the focal point of power most often today operates precisely through the very
personal sphere of our visible social identities. This should be no surprise, given
that capitalism was a racial and gender system from its inception, distributing roles
and resources according to identity markers of status and social position and thus
reenforcing their stability. Social identities such as race, ethnicity, and gender
remain the most telling predictors of social power and success, predicting whether
one works in the service sector, the trades, or the managerial class, whether and
how much profit can be had by selling one's home, how likely one is to be
incarcerated, how likely one is to suffer sexual or domestic violence, and even how
high one is likely to score on the SAT. Such facts do not displace the importance of
class; rather, they reveal that class works through, rather than alongside, the categories of visible identity.

Although my eyes and face are more from my father's side, I have my mother's
coloring, and that accident of fate has made a predictable world of difference in my

life. I was able to pass in places in Florida where my father would have been made to feel uncomfortable, especially when my voice and clothing helped me to blend in rather than stand out. In her comprehensive study of Latinos in the United States, Clara Rodriguez explains that "lighter Latinos...may be assumed to be white and consequently be better able to see how others are treated or that they are treated differently from those who are darker." But she also notes that "despite an individual's physical appearance as 'white,' knowledge of this person's Hispanicity often causes a readjustment of status...from 'I thought you were one of us' to 'You're an other'—and even an accent is heard where it was not before" (2000, 20). The ability to move across identities has been a useful but sometimes unpleasant experience, and the varied way in which different people view me is similar to the varied way in which my father was viewed as he moved from the university campus to the U.S.-patrolled neighborhoods of his hometown.

Though mixed identity and mixed families are normative in Latin America and the Caribbean, in North America, where racial identity is usually assumed to be unambiguous or "pure," mixed identity can cause cognitive dissonance and fragmented selves. This is a topic I will treat at some length in chapter 12. I raise it here only to indicate that the experience of having mixed or ambiguous identity teaches lessons early on about the fluid and at times arbitrary nature of social identity designations. A friend of mine has a son who is insightful even at the age of twelve about how visible features elicit different evaluative inflections: he has pointed out how the tone of voice his teachers use in speaking to him changes once they see him with his white mother rather than his African American father. As a "mixed race" boy in an integrated school, he also well understands how his choice of friends can alter his perceived identity. My goal in this book is to elaborate identity as a piece of our social ontology whose significance is still under-emphasized in most social theory, but I want to underscore the fact that I appre-ciate and have in fact some direct acquaintance with the contextual nature and fluidity of identity as well as the extent to which identity ascriptions can be op-pressive. My attempt to develop an ontology of identity is not meant to reify identities as unchanging absolutes but to understand their historical and contextual nature and, through this, to come to terms with their significance in our lives.

My own ambiguous identity has made me very conscious of the ways identity can open doors or shut them, yield credibility or withhold it, create comfort or produce anxiety. Just as Rodriguez claims for lighter skinned Latinos, those of us who have hybrid or mixed racial and ethnic identities have also generally under-stood the complex and problematic nature of social identity—its changeability and capricious social meaning—quite well. Identity designations are clearly the product of *learned* cognitive maps and *learned* modes of perception. Yet they operate through visible physical features and characteristics, and one cannot simply "rise above" or ignore them. As Frantz Fanon puts it, "I am the slave not of the 'idea' that others have of me but of my own appearance" (1967, 116).

There is growing concern over the political implications of social identities, especially ethnic, racial, and gendered identities, and this concern reaches beyond academic audiences to the larger public. Debates over multiculturalism, "political correctness," and affirmative action have at their center the question of identity's political relevance. Many are concerned today that the United States is heading down the same road as the former Yugoslavia and Rwanda, that is, toward intractable ethnic conflict. Academic attention to social identity is often accused of pandering to the selfish and divisive agendas of the practitioners of identity politics.

I fear that, in focusing on places such as the former Yugoslavia and Rwanda, we are missing the obviously different nature of the problems here in the United States. In our country, many millions of people can trace their relatives back to slaves, and millions of others are from families who were brought here by commissioned agencies as cheap labor to work in fields, mines, and on railroads. Millions more found their political identities and economic status changed overnight through the U.S. colonial expansion and annexation of their lands. Ours is not a society of multiple ethnic groups with longstanding border disputes, but a society of *forced* immigrants, forced by conditions in our countries of origin that in some cases the United States has fought against and in other cases has aggressively supported and even engineered. The manifestations and conflicts of identity *here* need their own analysis, and it will be an analysis that will have much more in common with the rest of our hemisphere and less with the rest of the world.

Racism and sexism in the United States are directly and primarily responsible for the absence of a viable "safety net" for the most impoverished in this country. The ideology of individualism, so effective in arguing against programs to redress poverty, is as influential as it is because so much of the poverty is associated with nonwhites, especially nonwhite women. Racism and sexism have also played a critical role in the low level of unionization and the lack of a viable left. The linchpin that maintains this status quo is the social, cultural, and political division between white workers and people of color. If these communities were mobilized and united in purpose, the current ruling oligarchy would be in trouble. There can be no significant social change, or change in the political structure of our economy, without the united support and leadership of these groups. This, I believe, is our only way forward. Yet the public discussion about "identity politics," which has spread well beyond college campuses to a larger discursive community, has worked effectively to discredit much antiracist and feminist work being done today and sowed confusion about the relationship between class, race, and gender. The "progressive" academic community has thus contributed once again, perhaps not surprisingly, to the divisions that keep us from moving forward.

These are my background political motivations and interests; make of them what you will. Politics does not work as a criterion for an adequate or plausible theory, but it can show us where we should be cautiously skeptical about existing dogmas and "common sense," where we need to press harder, and it can certainly guide our choice of topics.

One of the major problem with using personal experiences or histories is that one has the tendency to make oneself the heroine or at least sympathetic in every narrative. Especially where "identity matters" are concerned, where the stakes are high and misinterpretations are so frequent, this tendency is even stronger. There is not much that is personal in the following pages, but where there is I have tried to combat this tendency, no doubt with mixed success. I used as my guide and inspiration the *Black Notebooks* by Toi Derricote, a work that provides a model of honesty in this regard, even when the cost is quite painful. Having been born to parents of different races and ethnicities, and having grown up in the U.S. South during the era of civil rights, I do happen to have a history of such a sort that race figured prominently in my consciousness and in the consciousness of many of those around me. I have been privy to the kinds of "insider" conversations that occur on various sides of the racial border. And as a woman, and something of a "femme," I also feel privy to a space of experience many men do not know enough about to really understand: the double day, the ordinary stress and guilt of the working mother, the sexual harassment that is a constant aspect of the working environment, the epidemic of sexual terrorism that is neither named as such nor addressed with effective deterrents, the daily cultural assault of condoned instrumentalized reductions of women to their appearance. These life experiences have both motivated and informed my feminism, which I define simply as a nonfatalistic attitude toward "women's lot in life."

There is truly a huge gulf that separates races and genders in this country, one that only a minority of people have been able to bridge. This book is a bridging attempt, or maybe its just a rickety raft thrown on open seas. Whether it is seaworthy will be determined by its readers.

Acknowledgments

It is truly a fine skill as well as an intellectual virtue to be able to discern how to improve a project different from one's own, and I have been the beneficiary of many people with this excellent skill. Among them, I want especially to thank Robert Bernsaconi, Derrick Darby, Paget Henry, Lewis Gordon, Jorge Gracia, Eduardo Mendieta, Satya Mohanty, Paula Moya, Nancy Tuana, Karin Rosemblatt, and Bill Wilkerson, each of whom commented on significant portions of this manuscript.

In the decade since this project began, I have presented chapters of this book at institutions too numerous to list, and I have benefited greatly from the audiences, who asked critical and constructive questions. There are also specific scholars with whom I've had the benefit of continuing conversations over the years, conversations that have greatly influenced my work and expanded my intellectual horizons. These include Vrinda Dalmiya, Arlene Dávila, Elizabeth Grosz, Daniel Holliman, Chandra Talpade Mohanty, Sandra Harding, Susan Bordo, Margaret Himley, Leslie Bender, Tom Shelby, Ed Casey, Tony Bogues, Arindam Chakrabarti, Silvio Torres-Saillant, Lorraine Code, Juanita Diaz, Elizabeth Potter, Jorge Garcia, Sangmpan, Beverley Mullings, Iris Young, and Sally Haslanger. I owe a special and impossible debt to my former students, who responded to very fledgling versions of these ideas, especially Paula Moya, Raul Vargas, David Kim, John Draeger, Marianne Janack, Shishir Kumar Jha, Hayatun Nesa, and Michael Hames-Garcia. I am extremely grateful also to my department chair, Stewart Thau, for his steadfast material support.

Finally, I must single out for their extraordinary support: Eduardo Mendieta, whose dedication and generosity of spirit I have found so inspiring; Juanita Diaz, for her encouragement, for pushing me to do this work, and for her spiritual help; Leslie Bender, for her extreme kindness, undue praise, and steady friendship; Arlene Dávila, for her love, her guidance, her humor, and for being my role model; my mother, for the wellsprings of her love as well as for her unwavering confidence in me; my father, Ted Woodward, the one who raised and nurtured two 'Latino daughters' that he inherited through marriage, for all that his unguarded love and tolerance have taught me about the possibilities of human goodness; my brother and sisters Rafael Martín, Mimi Martín, and Aleika Martín, for their love and acceptance, which have changed my life; my sons, Sam and José Alcoff, for the inspiration of their own courage and commitment, and for their loving friendship; and Larry Alcoff, from whom I have learned so much about class struggle, identity, and community, and from whom I keep learning even after a quarter of a century in his arms.

Acknowledgments of
Previous Publications

Portions of chapters 3 and 4 were published in "Who's Afraid of Identity Politics?," in *Reclaiming Identity: Realist Theory and the Predicament of Postmodernism*, edited by Paula Moya and Michael Hames-Garcia (University of California Press, 2000).

A previous version of chapter 5 was published as: "Cultural Feminism v. Post-Structuralism: The Identity Crisis in Feminist Theory," *SIGNS* (spring 1988): 405–36.

A previous version of chapter 6 was published as "The Metaphysics of Gender and Sexual Difference," in *Feminist Interventions in Ethics and Politics*, edited by Barbara S. Andrew, Jean Kellor, and Lisa H. Schwartzman (Rowan and Littlefield, 2005).

A previous version of chapter 7 was published as "Toward a Phenomenology of Racial Embodiment," *Radical Philosophy* 95 (May/June 1998): 15–26.

A previous version of chapter 8 was published as "Habits of Hostility: On Seeing Race," *Philosophy Today* 44, *Selected Studies in Phenomenology and Existential Philosophy* 26 (SPEP Supplement 2000): 30–40.

A previous version of chapter 9 was published as "What Should White People Do?" *Hypatia* 13, no. 3 (summer 1998): 6–26.

A previous version of chapter 10 was published as "Is Latina/o Identity a Racial Identity?" in *Hispanics/Latinos in the U.S.: Ethnicity, Race and Rights*, edited by Jorge Gracia and Pablo DeGreiff (Routledge, 2000).

A previous version of chapter 11 was published as "Latinas/os, Asian-Americans, and the Black/White Paradigm," *Journal of Ethics* 7, no. 1 (2003): 5–27.

A previous version of chapter 12 was published as "Mestizo Identity," in *American Mixed Race: The Culture of Microdiversity*, edited by Naomi Zack (Rowman and Littlefield, 1995).

Contents

VISIBLE IDENTITIES

ONE

IDENTITIES REAL AND IMAGINED

Introduction

Identity and Visibility

Identity is today a growth industry in the academy. Generic "Man" has been overthrown by scholars and researchers who have realized the importance of taking identity into account— whether by taking gender into account in studies of cancer and heart disease or by taking race into account in studies of history and literature. The constitutive power of gender, race, class, ethnicity, sexuality, and other forms of social identity has, finally, suddenly, been recognized as a relevant aspect of almost all projects of inquiry. Yet at the same time, the concern with identity has come under major attack from many oddly aligned fronts—academic postmodernists, political liberals and leftists, conservative politicians, and others— in the academy as well as in the mainstream media. It may be widely conceded that generic "Man" was a rhetorical cover for the agency of a single subgroup, but many still pine for the lost discourse of generic universality, for the days when differences could be disregarded.

Against the critics of identity politics and those who see the attachment to identity as a political problem, psychological crutch, or metaphysical mistake, this book offers a sustained defense of identity as an epistemically salient and ontologically real entity. The reality of identities often comes from the fact that they are visibly marked on the body itself, guiding if not determining the way we perceive and judge others and are perceived and judged by them. The road to freedom from the capriciousness of arbitrary identity designations lies not, as some class reductionists and postmodernists argue, in the attempt at a speedy dissolution of identity—a proposal that all too often conceals a willful ignorance about the real-world effects of identity—but through a careful exploration of identity, which can reveal its influence on what we can see and know, as well as its context dependence and its complex and fluid nature.

Differences, it is widely believed, pose an a priori danger to alliance, unity, communication, and true understanding. As such, they are seen as a political threat for any political agenda that seeks majority support, given our increasingly diverse society. Differences can also be exaggerated, manipulated, and used opportunistically to coerce conformism and excuse corruption. Because differences are perniciously used in these ways *some* of the time, some jump to the conclusion that identity-based political movements will devolve into these tendencies *all* of the time. Some suggest that our differences—such as the differences between those who were brought to the United States as slaves, as indentured servants, as cheap labor, or who came as free immigrants—are relevant only to our past history, and that we have the power to choose the extent of their present and future relevance. Maintaining a focus on difference, according to some, will only get in the way of positive, cooperative, mutually beneficial action. Those persons who are seen to be "harping" on their difference and insisting on their identity are viewed as irrationally preoccupied with the past, or opportunistically focused on grievances with a goal of personal gain rather than justice.

In this book, my goal is to cast serious doubt on this suspicion of difference by explicating some of the important features of specific identities: race/ethnicity, sex/ gender, and the new pan-Latino identity. In this project I join with the new movement of scholars (often working in ethnic studies and women's studies) who argue that the acknowledgment of the important differences in social identity does not lead inexorably to political relativism or fragmentation, but that, quite the reverse, it is the *refusal* to acknowledge the importance of the differences in our identities that has led to distrust, miscommunication, and thus disunity. In a climate in which one cannot invoke history, culture, race, or gender for fear of being accused of playing, for example, "the race card," or identity politics, or "victim feminism," our *real* commonalities and shared interests cannot even begin to be correctly identified. When I refuse to listen to how you are different from me, I am refusing to know who you are. But without understanding fully who you are, I will never be able to appreciate precisely how we are more alike than I might have originally supposed.

Race and gender are forms of social identity that share at least two features: they are fundamental rather than peripheral to the self—unlike, for example, one's identity as a Celtics fan or a Democrat—and they operate through visual markers on the body. In our excessively materialist society, only what is visible can generally achieve the status of accepted truth. What I can see for myself is what is real; all else that vies for the status of the real must be inferred from that which can be seen, whether it is love that must be made manifest in holiday presents or anger that demands an outlet of violent spectacle. Secular, commodity-driven society is thus dominated by the realm of the visible, which dominates not only knowledge but also the expression and mobilization of desire and all sorts of social practices as well. The German film director Wim Wenders says, "People increasingly believe in what they see and they buy what they believe in" (quoted in Crystal 1997, 91).

Race and gender operate as our penultimate visible identities. Age can be surgically masked, homosexuality can be rendered invisible on the street, and class can be hidden behind a cultivated accent or clothing style, but when even these identities are mobilized in political movement, visible markers are generally highlighted, whether in styles of dress or bodily comportment. Social, cultural, and political affiliations, from orthodoxy to anarchism, must be marked by some form of visible dress code: a veil, a cross, *payos* (the side curls of the Hasidim), a tattoo, a particular hairstyle or hair treatment, or a strategically placed body piercing. Visibility is both the means of segregating and oppressing human groups and the means of manifesting unity and resistance.

Races and genders may have indeterminate borders, and some individuals may appear ambiguous, but in the case of gender, many people believe that if one could lift the person's skirt, or peer down their shorts, the matter would be closed. In the case of race, many believe—and this belief is widespread across races although not universal—that (a) there exists a fact of the matter about one's racial identity, usually determined by ancestry, and (b) that identity is discernible if one observes carefully the person's physical features and practiced mannerisms. In an infamous court case from the 1920s, the purported visibility of race served as the criterion of judgment. A wealthy white man sued for annulment on the grounds that his wife, Alice Rhinelander, had passed as white to marry him, after which he discovered that she was black. Her defense lawyer's strategy relied on the claim that the husband had to have known his wife's race when they had intimate relations before the wedding. To prove this, Rhinelander was asked by her lawyer and the judge to bare her breasts to the jury. The assumption operating here is that no one can completely "pass" because there will always be some sign, some trace, of one's "true" identity.[1]

The truth of one's gender and race, then, are widely thought to be visibly manifest, and if there is no visible manifestation of one's declared racial or gendered identity, one encounters an insistent skepticism and an anxiety. Those of us who are of mixed race or ambiguous gender know these reactions all too well. When the mythic bloodlines that are thought to determine identity fail to match the visible markers used to identify race, for example, one often encounters these odd responses by acquaintances announcing with arrogant certainty "But you don't look like . . ." or retreating to a measured acknowledgment "Now that you mention it, I can see . . ." To feel one's face studied with great seriousness, not for its (hoped-for) character lines or its distinctiveness, but for its telltale racial trace, can be a peculiarly unsettling experience, fully justifying of all Sartre's horror of the look.

When truth is defined as that which can be seen, there develops an uncanny interdependence between that which is true and that which is hidden. Besides its ubiquity, the visible also has the property of being endless, of never providing complete satisfaction. Foucault remarked that "this inexhaustible wealth of visible things has the property (which both correlates and contradicts) of parading in an endless line; what is wholly visible is never seen in its entirety. It always shows something else asking to be seen; there's no end to it" (1986, 110).

The visible is a sign, moreover, and thus invites interpretation to discern what is behind it, beyond it, or what it signifies. The "truth" of what we are is sometimes "as plain as the nose on my face" but sometimes it is hidden and must be brought into the light. It is an old practice of those with denigrated identities to hide them, by often ingenuous means and monumental effort: the light mulatto who eliminates all the contextual cues of his African ancestry; the southerner who drops her accent; the Asian American woman who has silicone injected around her eyes; the exertions of my mother to hide her childhood of homelessness behind a good vocabulary and an appreciation for high art. But the effort to pass as white or

WASP or normatively "normal" only turns what is hidden into the truth, the most "real" truth, about one's "real" self. When it is discovered, it is brandished by one's enemies as the true essence of one's character and murmured over by one's friends as a sad but insurmountable fate. And thus we get our familiar Western dogma about the necessary link between enlightenment and freedom: in the light, the dreaded thing can be seen for what it is, perhaps small and not all-powerful, or perhaps huge and central to one's life, but in any case more manageable in the "honest" light of day. Modern society strangely promotes both self-acceptance and self-transformation, though this is perhaps not so strange in a society that values freedom and therapy in equal measure. But our general belief in the creative autonomy of the individual is regularly tempered with the dictate to accept oneself, to know thyself, to be to thine own self true. I shall argue that the practices of visibility are indeed revealing of significant facts about our cultural ideology, but that what the visible reveals is not the ultimate truth; rather, it often reveals self-projection, identity anxieties, and the material inscription of social violence.

This book, then, explores race and gender as visible identities and seeks to uncover some of the mechanisms by which they are identified, enacted, and reproduced. In one sense, my aim is to try to make identities more visible, to bring them from their hiding places where they can elicit shame and obscure power. But my approach does not assume that there are ahistorical, transcultural truths about identities. My question is, rather, How are racial and gendered identities operating here, now? What is the best descriptive account of their current operations? How do they relate to subjectivity, lived experience, and what a given individual can see and know? And what are the implications of a fuller understanding of these identities on political practice?

Before exploring race and gender, this book addresses the general anti-identity trend of current (mainly white-dominant) public discourses, and develops a broad account of what social identities are. In the first three chapters, I offer an overview of the current critique of identity, showing its emergence from a broad variety of sources and summarizing its key claims. I unearth its implicit and implausible presuppositions, diagnose the cause of its emergence, and then develop a counter to the critique in the form of specific arguments against its claims. I have learned and benefited from the excellent critical analyses of the critiques of identity politics made in the last decade by an interdisciplinary group of scholars, especially the work of Robin Kelley, Silvio Torres-Saillant, José E. Cruz, Himani Bannerji, Richard Delgado, Satya Mohanty, Paula Moya, Renato Rosaldo, Gary Peller, Patricia Williams, Lani Guinier, and Gerald Torres, and I will reference many of their arguments in the second chapter (Kelley 1997; Cruz 1998; Bannerji 1994; Delgado 1995; Mohanty 1997; Moya 2002; Peller 1995; P. Williams 1997; Guinier and Torres 2002; Torres-Saillant 1992, 2000). I highly recommend these works to readers interested especially with identity politics. None of these scholars is a philosopher, although some of their arguments are deeply philosophical. But in fact, few philosophers have contributed to this work of critique, and thus this book attempts to provide primarily a philosophical analysis of the way in which certain specious assumptions about identity have functioned as a foundation for the critique of identity politics. I also offer a partial diagnosis of the critique of identity's more subterranean motivations in Western philosophical traditions. I explore the wide political and cultural anti-identity trend, but primarily focus on its manifestation in philosophy, politics, and current social theory. When the assumptions that motivate the aversion to identity are put to scrutiny, they often turn out to be a house of cards. But my main aim in this book is not critique but reconstruction. In chapter 4, I offer an account of identity superior to the account used by the critics of identity in its plausibility, relation to lived experience, and coherence with the ethnographic data from social movements. The central feature of this account is its ability to explain how social categories of identity—in this case, race/ethnicity and sex/gender—are related to the self, the lived experience of subjecthood, and what we can perceive and know. I argue that identities are grounded in social locations, and I make use of resources from hermeneutics and phenomenology to explicate the epistemic, the metaphysical, and the politically relevant features of identities that need to be taken into account in both social theory and practice. I make use of the concept of a hermeneutic horizon to suggest a way to visualize the epistemic effects of differences in social location. But hermeneutics tends to underplay the embodied features of subjective experience, and to correct this I use phenomenological accounts to flesh out more fully the ways in which raced and gendered identities are materially manifested. In the remaining chapters, I explore race/ethnicity, sex/gender, and Latino identity, take up various specific issues that arise in regard to these identities, and use the theory I develop in chapter 4 to address them.

Although I am making a general argument about the way in which social identities are manifest, in actuality I believe that the topic of identity is best approached in very specific context-based analyses. This locality and specificity is necessary because identities are constituted by social contextual conditions of interaction in specific cultures at particular historical periods, and thus their nature, effects, and the problems that need to be addressed in regard to them will be largely local. However, despite the need for context-based specificity, the critique of identity has been carried out as a general assessment and condemnation, and these general claims need to be countered with general claims, though the latter can take the form of denying that identities are generalizable! I do not at all imagine that the account I give of identity here is completely generalizable or universal, but I will argue that it is applicable to the social identities of race and gender in the United States, and that the specific problem topics I take up in later chapters represent local but significantly influential social phenomena, again mainly in the United States.

Moreover, let me say up front that this account is inadequate in a very important respect. Juan Flores notes, in his study of Puerto Rican culture and identity, that "the worldwide experience of diasporic displacement and realignment often appears dislodged from any causal connection to relations of disproportionate political and economic power among nations, as have the redefined cultural 'differences' among the newly interacting populations" (2000, 10). I share the view with him and others that many salient features of the current identity formations are the product of such diasporas and caused by colonialism as well as political and economic disparities between peoples, genders, and races. The difficulty of describing features of current identities is that they are dynamic and that these global economic realities will continue to affect their formation and constrain their transformation. No significant transformation of identities can happen in the absence of redressing the disparities of wealth and resources. Still, Flores himself has contributed excellent work that precisely describes and characterizes specific identities in Puerto Rican communities without reifying them or obscuring the colonial context of identity formation. In contrast to Flores's work, my work as a philosopher is more general and abstract and thus perhaps more vulnerable to a decontextualized interpretation. However, I believe that there remains some significant utility in a general approach that is conscious of its limitations, since one can then focus on the general epistemological features of at least a wide set of identity positions, as well as on some common metaphysical features of social identities as they are currently lived in a certain broad locale.

The account that I develop here does have a certain specificity: it is one that restricts its focus to raced and gendered identities, and I don't claim that it applies equally well to other forms of identity. Social identities operate in very specific ways, utilizing and invoking different features of social realities, practices, and discourses, and therefore they require analyses that will not lose sight of these particularities. Partly for that reason, I focus in this book only on race and gender, and the bulk of the chapters explore various issues that arise in relation to these two identities, or to specific forms of them, such as female identity, Latino/a identity, mixed race identity, and white identity. I try to suggest the best way to understand and characterize how these identities work in North American societies here and now, not as timeless entities but as temporal, historically and culturally located ones. I consider various possible ways to make sense of the existing social reality of racial designations and gender identity, how they correlate to different possibilities for knowing and judging, and what possibilities currently exist for their transformation.

At times I will address race/ethnicity and sex/gender as if these each represent a common entity. This is because, as I shall argue, race and ethnicity often slip into one another's shoes, as some ethnicities (or cultural identities) are perpetually and relentlessly raced even while race (as bodily identity) is made to stand in for ethnicity. Similarly, many feminists have critiqued the sex/gender distinction from a variety of positions, arguing that it replays a nature/culture schema that is more of a hindrance than a help in social research. I shall argue that a materialist account of gender cannot separate it from sex. So although my primary focus is race and gender, I will take note and at times explore the fluid and partially constitutive relations that exist between race and ethnicity and between gender and sex.

It goes without saying that my own horizon of visibility is not the Absolute—but I hope what is visible to me will prove interesting and useful to others.

The Pathologizing of Identity

The ethnic upsurge...began as a gesture of protest against the Anglo-centric culture. It became a cult, and today it threatens to become a counter-revolution against the original theory of America as "one people," a common culture, a single nation.

Arthur Schlesinger, *The Disuniting of America*

There is too much group identification in our society and too little human identification.

Rudolf Giuliani, mayor of New York City, at a press conference on May 19, 2000, in answer to a question about whether his administration would change its attitude toward blacks and Hispanics in light of charges that it favored white racist police over their victims.

When Al Gore announced his choice of running mate in his ill-fated 2000 campaign for the presidency, the very first sentence aired on National Public Radio and CNN news was: "Al Gore has chosen a Jewish vice president." Before many of us knew Joseph Lieberman's name, we knew his ethnicity. And his identity was a topic of discussion for several weeks while news analysts and political pundits discussed whether his strongly felt Jewish identity would hinder his ability to lead a Gentile nation, and whether his Saturday Sabbath observance could be a liability for national security. Even within various Jewish communities there was criticism of Lieberman for emphasizing his Jewish identity too much: Abraham Foxman, national director of the Anti-Defamation League, was reported in the *New York Times* as saying that "hearing repeated professions of faith from a Jewish candidate" made him very uncomfortable. Fearing that his public profession of faith would incite anti-Semitism, the Anti-Defamation League advised Lieberman to "play it down."[1] In effect, Lieberman got it from both sides, not just in the sense of having both Jewish and Gentile critics, but in the sense that he was criticized for announcing his identity as if it *were* relevant, even while its *real* relevance was precisely what some were worried about. Lieberman's identity was taken as relevant to politics on the grounds, in part, that it might skew his political judgment; in light of this one could well interpret Lieberman's frequent reference to his Jewish identity as an attempt to put his own spin on the relationship between his heritage and his political office. In his view, being Jewish was relevant because it gave him insight into practices of exclusion and oppression and because it provided him a moral compass to temper and guide the necessities of pragmatic politics. Thus, in essence, Lieberman invoked his identity as a means of bringing universal considerations to the table.

As the Lieberman case might suggest, the critiques of identity politics that warn of separatism, particularism, and narrow group interest often exhibit a weird disconnection with the actual ways in which identities figure into political discourses and practices. There is often a significant disparity between the way in which identity is characterized by the critics of identity politics and the way in which identities are generally lived or experienced as well as how they actually figure in political movements.

There is also a strange contradiction between the amount of attention social identity is receiving today in academic inquiry—compared with the scant attention it received in previous eras, when it was all but ignored outside of anthropology and sociology departments—and the increasingly negative assessment identity is given in the academy. Identity is certainly enjoying a growth period in the academy, across the humanities and social sciences, reaching even into law and communication studies. There are sociological accounts of the work histories of various ethnic communities, political analyses of the voting patterns of racially defined groups, art and literature studies focused on the cultural production of marginalized groups, all meant to be correctives to previous practices of academic exclusion. It has been generally recognized that neither medical studies nor psychological studies nor virtually any other discipline of inquiry can claim universal application to all social identity groups when they are based in the experiences of, or experiments on, a single identity group. Thus, many theorists in diverse fields now understand that identity needs to be taken into account before one can claim reliable, general knowledge, whether it is a claim about nutrition, political participation, or poetics. And this has led to an increased study of identities themselves: alongside ethnic studies and women's studies, there are now whiteness studies and men's studies. Thus, it may seem as if identity is "in."

However, simultaneous to this focus and, one might say, commodification of identity, there is also an increasing tendency, especially in contemporary social theory, to view strongly felt identities as a political danger for democracy as well as a metaphysically erroneous view about the true or fundamental nature of the self. Some have even argued that the very belief in identity is a kind of social pathology. To an extent, this is an old idea, a remnant of universal and disembodied accounts of the self in modernism, and a continuation of longstanding suspicious and hostile attitudes toward nonwhite ethnic communities. But, as I shall shortly discuss, this suspicion of identity has received new formulations in recent work that takes into account the emergence of identity studies from the 1960s and thus provides a more sophisticated and putatively plausible critique. The upshot is that, today, even while identity is receiving more theoretical focus than ever before, many theorists are troubled by the implications of the claim that identity makes a difference.

Our cultural anxiety about identity is revealed by the way in which identity is sometimes brought center stage inappropriately. The debate over racism in the United States, for example, has come to be formulated largely as a question about the appropriate or inappropriate relevance of identity. Debates over affirmative action have been reformulated as debates over the question "Is it ever legitimate to take into account identity categories of, say, race and gender in assessing job qualifications or district boundaries?" As a result, what could be a debate over alternative methods of reducing race discrimination, which would be a comparative analysis, is transformed into a decontextualized argument about the justifiability of taking identity into account under any circumstances. In this reformulation it is identity that takes center stage as the focus of political argumentation rather than race and sex discrimination, and the court is asked to rule on what is partly a metaphysical question about the salience of identity.

After I gave a talk recently on the issue of identity politics, an African American student came up to me and spoke passionately about Eurocentrism in the academy. Standing next to me was a white professor, who responded to the student with the sort of non sequitur that one finds extremely common today when discussions of race occur in mixed white/nonwhite groupings. The exchange went roughly as follows:

> *Student*: Eurocentrism is a huge problem in the university here, in the selection of required courses as well as the content of courses.
> *Professor*: My family was extremely poor, and I had a very difficult time even getting to college.

Obviously, the student's remarks had no connection whatsoever to the issue of the white professor's class background or the racial exclusivity of suffering. But the professor's response indicates that this is the way such charges of Eurocentrism are evidently heard, nonetheless, as if they imply that white identity is monolithically privileged in all respects.

Such responses are a constant problem besetting discussions of racism, inside and outside the academy. One tries to raise a reflective discussion concerning various forms of racism and cultural imperialism, and one is heard as assuming homogeneity, total culpability, and a whole variety of things about all people designated white. A parallel phenomenon still besets feminists routinely when a discussion of the oppression of women is heard as trashing all men or entailing a biologistic determinism about masculinity. Discussions about sexual violence and sexual harassment, in particular, at least in my experience, evoke charges of "male bashing" even when no causal analysis is even broached, much less developed and defended. In one lecture I gave to a religious group, my very reporting of the FBI statistics on rape was characterized as being anti-male. Such responses make us disinclined to speak about racism or sexism in any form unless we are in the mood for a fight. The statement made by Rudolph Giuliani that was quoted at the beginning of this chapter also indicates this strategy: in response to a question about the charges of racism made against his administration—charges based especially on his unconditional support for a police force that had gunned down unarmed black and Latino men—Giuliani deflects to humanism. But clearly, a concern with racism is not antithetical to humanism and should in fact be an integral part of any humanism.

Despite these clear cases of strategic obfuscation, I want to acknowledge that the anxiety about identity has at times some legitimate motivations. That is, there have been unfair attributions and unrealistic ascriptions of homogeneity, to be sure, coming from within progressive social movements. The problems of enforced conformism within identity groups, and of what the left used to call narrow na-tionalism or narrow group politics, do exist and deserve critique. And essentialist constructions of cultural, ethnic, racial, and gendered identity are on the upswing, found on both left and right, not only among the less educated but among the highest academic elite, as in the work of Samuel Huntington, Peter Brimelow, Charles Murray, Allan Bloom, and many others. But my principal interest in this chapter and throughout this book is with the idea that social identity itself is an a priori problem, that identities, under *any* description, pose dangers and commit one to mistaken assumptions when they are believed to be real and/or acted upon politically. I want to differentiate this formulation of the problem of identity—as an a priori problem—from other kinds of formulations of the problem that express a concern *only* with overly homogenizing, essentialist, reductive, or simplistic con-structions of identity. In my view, there are certainly serious difficulties with *some* constructions of identity, but I have been curious about the claim that identity itself, under any construction, is a problem and even a kind of mistake.

Identity Politics

If identity has become suspect, identity politics has been prosecuted, tried, and sentenced to death. Like "essentialism," identity politics has become the shibboleth of cultural studies and social theory, and denouncing it has become the litmus test of academic respectability and political acceptability. A partial list of the main liberal or progressive critics would include Todd Gitlin (1995), Eric Hobsbawm (1996), Nancy Fraser (1997), Betty Friedan (1996), Frances Fox Piven (1995), Paul Berman (1996), Arthur Schlesinger (1992), Richard Rorty (1998, 1999), Robert Hughes (1993), Jean Bethke Elshtain (1995), Wendy Brown (1995), and Jean-Luc Nancy (2000), but there are many others. In contrast, there has been a noticeable thaw regarding the concept of essentialism which has sustained such widespread feminist critique since the early 1980s. Christine Battersby, Elizabeth Grosz, and Teresa de Lauretis have pointed out that only the Aristotelian concept of essence has been used in the feminist debates—that is, the idea of a fixed and stable feature common to all members of a natural kind (Battersby 1998; Grosz 1995; de Lauretis 1990). On such an account, an essence is something "real" in a prelinguistic sense. But modern philosophers criticized Aristotle's concept precisely because it would seem to require us to know something that by definition we cannot know: the real as it exists hidden from perception and thus description (this is hardly, then, a con-temporary critique). Hobbes and Locke then proposed a concept of nominal es-sences wherein "the essence of a thing is its verbal definition: it is no more than 'an accident for which we give a certain name to any body, or the accident which denominates its subject'" (Hobbes 1655, quoted in Battersby, 28). In this way, as Battersby argues, "a feminist advocacy of 'nominal essences' could deal comfortably with linguistic, historical, and cultural variations in the way that the female is de-fined" (Battersby, 29). Susan Babbitt has gone even further to defend a nondeter-ministic naturalist (and thus non-nominalist) account of essentialism as consistent with feminism's liberatory aims as well as with the heterogeneity of women's experiences (Babbitt 1996). She suggests that the problem for feminism is not the concept of essentialism but the deterministic account of gender, and neither essentialism nor naturalism commit us to a hard determinism about gender identity. On scrutiny it turns out, then, that the denunciations of essentialism were based on an inadequate exploration of the concept, its history, and its variable meanings. I believe it is time we reassess identity politics in the same light.

One of the problems is that identity politics is almost nowhere defined—nor is its historical genesis elaborated—by its detractors. Identity politics *is blamed* for a host of political ills and theoretical mistakes, from overly homogenized conceptions of groups to radical separatism to the demise of the left. But what are its own claims? In what is undoubtedly its locus classicus, the Combahee River Collective's "A Black Feminist Statement" of 1977, identity politics emerges as a belief in the general relevance of identity to politics: "We realize that the only people who care enough about us to work consistently for our liberation is us. . . . This focusing upon our own oppression is embodied in the concept of identity politics. We believe that the most profound and potentially the most radical politics come directly out of our own identity, as opposed to working to end somebody else's oppression" (365). Such a claim does not assume that identities are always perfectly homogeneous or that identity groups are unproblematic. The very formation of the Combahee River Collective was motivated by the founders' concerns with the racism in the white-dominated wing of the women's movement, the sexism in the male-dominated wing of the black liberation movement, and heterosexism that was virulent everywhere. They knew that social identities are complex entities and that identity groups are always heterogeneous, but they argued that, in their experience of political work, identities *mattered*.

The Combahee River Collective argued that African American women needed to develop some organizational autonomy at that time in order to develop their analysis of the particular forms of subordination they faced as well as to articulate an effective agenda for change. Members of the collective did not see this call for autonomy as in any way rejecting the simultaneous need for coalition. They state, "We feel solidarity with progressive black men and do not advocate the fractionalization that white women who are separatists demand" (Combahee River Collective, 365). They also declared themselves to be socialists who believed that overcoming oppression will require a movement of solidarity against capitalism and imperialism, but they argued that "although we are in essential agreement with Marx's theory as it applied to the very specific economic relationships he analyzed, we know that this analysis must be extended further in order for us to understand our specific economic situation as black women" (366). Thus, the collective was not supportive of a general separatism but simply insistent on the need for specific analyses.

Nonetheless, for many theorists today, the belief articulated by the Combahee River Collective that identities are relevant to one's politics has had a devastating impact on progressive and democratic politics. Identity politics is often called "balkanization" and arguments are made that even the atrocities of ethnic cleansing we have witnessed elsewhere will become a reality in the West if we don't trounce this trend once and for all.[2] The eminent French philosopher Jean-Luc Nancy, for example, offers an amazing list of all the "places, groups, or authorities that constitute the theater of bloody conflicts among identities" (Nancy 2000, xii). His listing of identity-based conflicts run from the struggles for autonomy in Chiapas to the Islamic Jihad to the military conflict in Chechnya to "Chicanos" (without explanation), as if these struggles are essentially caused and motivated by clashing identities. In his analysis, it doesn't matter whether identities are religious, ethnic, cultural, mythical, historical, transnational, "independent or 'instrumentalized' by other groups who wield political, economic, and ideological power": he proposes to offer one analysis that can address the conflicts among the groups on this "endless list" (Nancy, xii–xiii).

My question is, How did the legitimate concern with specific instances of problems in identity-based movements become a generalized attack on identity and identity politics in any and every form?

Schlesinger's "America"

To begin to answer this question, we should surely look at one of the most powerful early salvos in the war on identity: the publication of Arthur Schlesinger's *The Disuniting of America* in 1991. In this short, readable book, Schlesinger paints a picture of a past "America" happily moving toward the melting-pot nation that Hector St. John de Crèvecoeur first described in the 1700s in his widely read *Letters from an American Farmer*. Crèvecoeur imagined a United States where individuals lost their old identities and formed a "new race of men." This was a good thing, not simply because a homogeneous nation would be a stronger nation, but because what these individuals left behind included "ancient prejudices and manners" or backward ways of life, in favor of a more advanced set of rules based on democratic ideals (Schlesinger 1991, 1). Schlesinger is well aware that nonwhite ethnicities were not initially included in this imagery of the new nation, but he argues that, by the 1800s, a new trend toward inclusiveness had emerged and was manifest in some of the most important representations of the "new race," such as the writings of Herman Melville and Ralph Waldo Emerson. There was also a nativist and racist countertrend, to be sure, such as the "American Party" of the 1850s, which opposed immigration and "political rights for the foreign-born" (9). But Schlesinger's principal narrative is one of constant, steady movement toward an inclusiveness in which ethnic differences would be left behind, and he neglects to consider the implications of the divergent treatment received by Northern European, Southern European, and non-European ethnic groups.

Schlesinger's main thesis is that the 1960s "cult of ethnicity" derailed this steady progress. He suggests that this cult had a precursor in the early 1900s, which was not a product of the grass roots but of intellectual elites who presumed a right of cultural and political leadership as "ethnic spokesmen" (34). These intellectual ethnic spokesmen were actually alienated from the groups for which they spoke but were "moved by real concern for distinctive ethnic values and also by real if unconscious vested interest in the preservation of ethnic constituencies" (34). Thus, their opposition to assimilation was neither an expression of the spontaneous will of the masses nor was it wholly motivated by their own selfless concern with principles of fairness. This is a charge that he continues to maintain against the political leadership of minority communities today.

Schlesinger considers Congress's passage in 1974 of the Ethnic Heritage Studies Program Act to be a key moment in the culmination of the identity problem. This act applied "ethnic ideology to all Americans" and thus "compromised the historic right of Americans to decide their ethnic identities for themselves," ignoring those millions who refused ethnic identification of any sort (he claims this latter group must surely represent the majority of Americans, but he does not consider whether there is a difference between white and nonwhite Americans in this regard) (17). Here, then, is the picture Schlesinger paints: authoritarian elites ramming ethnicity down the throats of gullible citizens for their own narrow purposes. And here is the effect:

> The ethnicity rage in general . . . not only divert[s] attention from the real needs but exacerbate[s] the problems. The recent apotheosis of ethnicity, black, brown, red, yellow, white, has revived the dismal prospect that in happy melting-pot days Americans thought the republic was moving safely beyond—that is, a society fragmented into separate ethnic communities. The cult of ethnicity exaggerates differences, intensifies resentments and antagonisms, drives ever deeper the awful wedges between races and nationalities. The endgame is self-pity and self-ghettoization. (102)

Schlesinger believes that whites in the United States have shed their European legacy, that they have given up their European identities out of rational and progressive motivations, but that nonwhites are now refusing to follow suit. However, we also find him arguing against the multicultural agenda on the basis of what he calls the "facts of history": that "Europe was the birthplace of the United States of America . . . [and] that the United States is an extension of European civilization" (122). Like Huntington, Schlesinger gives the values of democracy and inclusiveness a European cultural identity, and on these grounds criticizes multiculturalism. Although he supports some of the multiculturalist proposals for a more inclusive history—for example, teaching children to imagine how it was to be on both sides of the Conquest—Schlesinger argues that the "crucial difference" between the Western tradition and other traditions is that the West produced antidotes to its problems. Every culture "has done terrible things," he claims, but "whatever the particular crimes of Europe, that continent is also the source—the *unique* source—of those liberating ideas . . . to which most of the world today aspires. These are *European* ideas, not Asian, nor African, nor Middle Eastern ideas, except by adoption" (127, emphasis in original). So much for the transcendence of old ethnic identities.

Schlesinger, like Huntington, Pat Buchanan, Peter Brimelow, and other opponents of multiculturalism, falls into the contradiction of arguing that we should oppose the "cult of ethnicity" because, on the one hand, "America" is a melting pot where originary cultures are dissolved in favor of a new unity, but on the other hand, because it is the specifically European customs and values that have made this nation great and must remain dominant. Thus, his argument is baldly in favor of maintaining European American cultural hegemony. As Huntington points out (2004), this does not require maintaining the numerical or political dominance of European American people, but whoever becomes numerically dominant must accept and promote European cultural values and practices.

The remainder of *Disuniting America* "documents" the curricular battles fought out in U.S. educational institutions in the wake of the Ethnic Heritage Studies Program Act. Schlesinger quotes anti-bilingualism Latinos such as Richard Rodriguez and cites anecdotes reported by neoconservative Dinesh DeSouza (whose nickname in the days when he edited the infamously conservative *Dartmouth Review* was "Distort DeNewsa"). Schlesinger then takes the most extreme forms of Afrocentrism as propounded by Leonard Jeffries and contrasts these with the more moderate political views of Frederick Douglass and W. E. B. Du Bois, neither of whom saw the need for school curricula that would teach black children about Africa (Cf. Eze 2001, chap. 4). Clearly, Schlesinger is not representing the pro-multicultural arguments in their strongest light or in their diversity. He contrasts reasonable-sounding, rational-minded critics who charge multiculturalists with monolithic portrayals of Europe with discredited ideologues who propound ahistorical deterministic theories of human difference, as if these represent our exclusive options. He quotes liberally from conservative people of color who attack multiculturalism. And he presents dire predictions of the effect of "the cult of ethnicity" run amok: balkanization and tribalism. This is a polemic, not a serious argument. Hence one should be curious about why Schlesinger's book became a bestseller and why the views he propounds seeped so quickly into the discourse of the mainstream public sphere.

Schlesinger is no Republican; he is one of this country's most well-known and well-respected liberals. But this is a liberal attack on multiculturalism.[3] This work and others like it have contributed centrally to the formation of the near consensus that identity is a problem. In the next chapter I will offer a rational reconstruction of the principal arguments against identity, endeavoring to put them in their best light by referring to some of their strongest and smartest adherents.

Schlesinger's arguments usefully demonstrate that the critique of identity politics often manifests ambivalence about the relevance of identity to politics. He does not really want to eradicate all identities, but to keep non-European identities from dominating American identity. Given this, one might think that what we need is simply a more consistent opposition to identities, pursued with equality across both the dominant and the subaltern. I will argue that such a plan is neither wholly possible nor necessary for social justice. In my view, the real danger is not the likelihood of balkanization resulting from identity politics but the split that results from a wholesale critique of identity that then perceives minority agendas as a threat to progressive politics. It is this mistaken idea that is endangering the future of progressive alliances. After all, the political movements based on identity politics have themselves been organized precisely against our own homegrown versions of ethnic cleansing, in the form of the histories of racist terror and disenfranchisement, differential police treatment and arbitrary immigration policies, and the ongoing, widespread, and severe political and economic disempowerment of many minority communities. The real challenge that identity politics must address in my view is the need to articulate its precise relation to class, a topic I address in chapter 2, and the need for a decolonized version of humanism that can ensure universal rights while conceptualizing justice across cultural difference, a topic I will address in the conclusion.

In the following two chapters, I divide the critiques of identity into two groupings, one primarily political, the other primarily philosophical. After assessing each of these critiques, in chapter 4 I develop a hermeneutically based account of identity and identity formation that I argue has greater plausibility and explanatory value in light of the actual ethnographic data of social movements. This different account is also less vulnerable to the charges made by the critics of identity and yet also demonstrates the critical relevance of identity to political mobilization, movements, and understanding.

My analysis and counterarguments are not put forward as exhaustive or fully adequate, given the complexity of this topic and enormity of the discussions that have taken place. But I do believe I can disable the most important lines of critique and convince the reader that there are serious grounds for doubting the widespread trend toward viewing identity in any form as a political problem and metaphysical mistake. Overall, then, my project is to critique and diagnose the fear of identity and to develop a more plausible understanding of what identities are. Only when we understand identities more accurately can we see where our true challenges lie.

The Political Critique

Any man who carries a hyphen about him carries a dagger which he is
ready to plunge into the vitals of the Republic.

Woodrow Wilson, 1918

Not everyone is male, white, hearing, heterosexual. Very well. But what
is a Left if it is not, plausibly at least, the voice of a whole people? ... If
there is no people, but only peoples, there is no Left.

Todd Gitlin, *The Twilight of Common Dreams*

Political concerns about the importance of social identity are voiced equally
across left, liberal, and right-wing perspectives. Moreover, the suspicion of
identity is not relegated to the discourse of intellectuals but is also manifest in the
mainstream as a widespread public attitude, and not only among white communities.

Without doubt, the critique of identity has worked effectively, and justifiably,
against some of the problematic interpretations of identity politics, where identity
is construed in reductionist and simplistic fashion and where its link to politics is
rendered overly determinist. Nonetheless, I believe the more significant effect of
the critique has been a negative one in discrediting all identity-based movements,
in blaming minority movements for the demise of the left, and especially in
weakening the prospects for unity between majority and minority groups, contrary
to the beliefs of such theorists as Schlesinger and Gitlin. Although the critique
purports to be motivated by just this desire for unity, it works to undermine the
credibility of those who have "obvious" identities and significantly felt identity
attachments from being able to represent the majority, as if their very identity
attachments and the political commitments that flow from these attachments will
inhibit their leadership capabilities. It also inhibits their ability to participate in
coalition politics as who they fully are. In this way, the critique of identity has
operated to vindicate the broad white public's disinclination to accept political
leadership from those whose identity is minority in any respect: Catholic or Jewish,
black or Latino, Asian American or Arab American.

The suspicion against ethnic identity has a long tradition in U.S. history, as
Silvio Torres-Saillant has shown. In the early 1900s, the new immigrants from

southern and central Europe who were less easily assimilated to the dominant Anglo culture were seen as a threat to the nation. Teddy Roosevelt declared that cultural assimilation, and the demise of the specific cultural ways of these ethnic groups, was a condition of patriotism: "The man who becomes completely Americanized...is doing his plain duty to his adopted land." This view gained strength during the First World War, when many in the United States expressed concern, sometimes violently, about the European allegiances of U.S. citizens who were of German or Austrian extraction. By 1916, when the United States was beginning to enter the war, Roosevelt insisted that the country's "crucible" ought to turn "our people out as Americans, of American nationality and not as dwellers of a polyglot boarding house,...we have room for but one loyalty and that is a loyalty to the American people." Woodrow Wilson even pressured his party in 1918 to condemn ethnic associations as subversive, and went so far as to state that "any man who carries a hyphen about him carries a dagger which he is ready to plunge into the vitals of the Republic" (quoted in Torres-Saillant, 1992.; see Dicker 1966, 35; Stubbs and Barnet 1966, 677; McClymer 1982, 98).

Wilson's and Roosevelt's concerns that ethnic identity would inevitably create conflicting loyalties were based on the assumption that ethnicity and nationality are permanently coextensive or co-determining, that is, that one's ethnicity determines one's nationality. This is a mistake few theorists or politicians would make today. However, strongly felt identities are still blamed for increasing conflict among various social groups by emphasizing differences at the expense of commonalities and thus weakening the prospects for an inclusive nationalism. And as the Wen Ho Lee case recently illustrated, certain ethnicities, especially Asian American ones, are still suspected of harboring a primary loyalty to their countries of origin—no matter how many generations back. Wen Ho Lee, a naturalized U.S. citizen, came here in 1964 as a student at Texas A & M University, met his wife at the Rose Bowl, got a job at Los Alamos, and for more than thirty years enjoyed bridge, classical music, and reading Charles Dickens before he was racially profiled and arrested for suspected treason (Wu 2002, 178). Lee's arrest occurred shortly after the House Select Committee on U.S. National Security issued a report in May of 1999, which argued that every individual of Chinese ancestry in the United States is a "potential spy" (Wu 2002, 179). Here, racialization mediates ethnic identity and national origin to produce the specter of an identity that is viewed as beyond assimilation or even rationality. As Frank Wu shows in his comprehensive study of contemporary anti-Asian prejudice, the idea that ethnicity determines nationality continues to operate in some cases—mainly for Asian Americans and Latinos—where ethnic identity has been racialized.

The Liberals

Why would liberals, though, who advocate in favor of individual freedom, oppose the expression of ethnic attachments? In classical liberal political theory, the initial state of the self is conceptualized as an abstract individual without, or prior to, group allegiance. It is from this "initial position" that the self engages in rational deliberation over ends and thus achieves autonomy by freely choosing, rather than blindly accepting, its doxastic commitments, including its cultural and religious traditions. As Kant developed this idea, a person who cannot gain critical distance from and thus objectify his or her cultural traditions cannot rationally assess them and thus cannot attain autonomy. In Kant's view, an abstract or disengaged self is for this reason necessary for full personhood. Moreover, the process of modernity, which was conceptualized as analogous on the societal level to the process of individual maturation, became defined as just this increased ability to distance oneself from one's cultural traditions. In this way this distancing ability also became a key part of the global, European-centered teleology of intellectual and moral development, defining the terms by which societies were to be labeled advanced or backward.

The norm of rational maturity, then, required a core self stripped of its identity. Groups too immature to practice this kind of abstract thought or to transcend their ascribed cultural identities were deemed incapable of full autonomy, and their lack of maturity was often "explained" via racist theories of the innate inferiority of non-European peoples. But liberal social theorists attempted to develop nonracist explanations for the inability or unwillingness of some to let go of their identities.

In the 1960s an influential account of ethnicity was developed by Nathan Glazer and Daniel Patrick Moynihan according to which people develop a strong sense of ethnic identity as a result of being excluded from the melting pot and from political participation (Glazer and Moynihan 1963). According to this account, if individuals are shunned or segregated off to themselves, whether because they are Italian, Irish, or African American, they will develop a powerful sense of group identity and internal solidarity as a defense mechanism. Glazer and Moynihan thought that social steps toward inclusion, then, would work as the "solution" to ethnic identity. A kind of analogous position has more recently surfaced in feminist theory, suggesting that gender identity is also something produced entirely by conditions of oppression that would wither away under conditions of equal empowerment. For these feminists, feminism is the "solution" to gender identity.

Why is it assumed that social identities require a "solution"? This only makes sense given the liberal conception of the self as requiring autonomy *from* identity in order to exercise rationality. After all, the fact that a social identity was created under conditions of exclusion or oppression does not by itself entail that its features are pernicious: oppression can produce pathology without a doubt, but it can also lead to the development of strength, perseverance, and empathy. Moreover, the desire to be free of oppressive stereotypes does not necessarily lead to the desire to be free of all identity; it can just as easily lead to the desire to have more accurate characterizations of one's identity and to have the collective freedom to develop the identity through developing culture and community as well as the individual freedom to interpret its meaning in one's own life.

Nonetheless, strongly felt social identities are considered by many to harbor inherent political liabilities. Liberal political theorists such as Arthur Scheslinger (1991), David Hollinger (1995), Jean Bethke Elshtain (1995), and others have argued that a strong sense of group solidarity and group identification endanger democratic processes and social cohesion; that they will inhibit the ability to form political coalitions; that they will ground "knowledge and moral values in blood and history" (Hollinger, 3) and in this way substitute the determination of group membership for critical reflection, thus producing what Cornel West (1994) calls "racial reasoning."

Elshtain provides an especially clear articulation of the argument that identity politics derails democracy, and her account shows how this view is connected to the conception of rational autonomy sketched above. She holds that when

> private identity takes precedence over public ends or purposes ... the citizen gives way before the aggrieved member of a self-defined or contained group. Because the group is aggrieved—the word of choice in most polemics is *enraged*—the civility inherent in those rule-governed activities that allow a pluralist society to persist falters. This assault on civility flows from an embrace of what might be called a politicized ontology—that is, persons are to be judged not by what they do or say but what they *are*. (52–53)

Elshtain contrasts, as if they were mutually exclusive, (a) the citizenry that advances public or common purposes and (b) self-defined identity groups or "private identities" that are concerned with group-related grievances. She holds that the determination of public ends should not or cannot be developed through associations or actions that are organized around identity. In her view, public citizens and private identities are two separate kinds of things, even though instantiated in the same individual. Insofar as that individual reasons and acts as a citizen, it cannot be thinking of itself primarily in terms of this private identity, and one that has been aggrieved and is enraged. Identities must be left aside so that individuals can enter the arena of public debate and action as anonymous or dispassionate reasoners, weighing evidence on the basis of its merit no matter its implications for the future of one's own social group.

Elshtain's argument that "only behavior, not identity, should be criticized" (53) is persuasive as an argument that one should not be criticized merely for one's identity. This is precisely the argument against racial profiling, which put identities themselves into suspect categories independently of behavior. Thus, she is correct insofar as she is asserting that, in assessing someone's behavior or ideas, we should never *reduce* the assessment to a mere question of identity. However, rejecting a reduction to one's identity does not require or imply rejecting the salience of identity under any circumstance. A police officer, for example, might legitimately take a person's apparent identity into account, not for the purposes of assuming criminal behavior, but for the purposes of ensuring that the person can understand the officer's commands given in English.

In the kinds of cases Elshtain is considering—public spaces of deliberation or debate—the question is whether judgment can be realistically disentangled from identity. We appear in public spaces just as much fully identified persons as we do in the private sphere, although because we are known less well in public than in private relationships, those identity categories may loom even larger in public. As anthropologist Renato Rosaldo has argued: "Can women disguise their gender in the public sphere? If they must appear as women, and not as universal unmarked citizens, then one can ask, who has the right to speak in public debates conducted in the square? Are men or women more likely to be interrupted with greater frequency? Are men or women more likely to be referred to as having had a good idea in these discussions?" (1997, 28). The point is that identities are constantly used to lend or withhold credence from participants in almost any public exchange. Ideas are assessed in relation to who expresses them, and indeed, will be expressed in variable ways depending on the speaker and the context. For example, we can sometimes gain a clearer interpretation and assessment of someone's claims by understanding it in relation to their identity. A young athlete tells me in-line skating is easy to learn, and I take his words with a grain of salt. In an argument over how easy the United States is on foreigners living here, an Anglo claims its very easy while a foreigner claims it is not; their identities don't prove their points, but they are relevant to consider as I assess their likely knowledge on the matter. Foucault recommends that we reconceptualize discourse as an *event*, which would incorporate into the analysis not only the words spoken but also the speakers, hearers, location, language, and so on, all as a part of what makes up meaning. This neither reduces meaning to identity nor assumes a priori that it is in every case irrelevant.[1] Thus there are good reasons to contest Elshtain's claim that it is possible to separate private identities and public citizens as well as the claim that it would always be desirable to do so. I will return to this issue to develop this argument further at the end of this chapter.

Elshtain's and Schlesinger's views represent a common liberal understanding that ethnic attachments are legitimate only when circumscribed to the private realm. If one's ethnicity is allowed to be the site from which to launch grievances or antagonisms in public debate, liberals think this will reduce the latter to polemic and "war by other means." Thus, for liberals, a strong sense of ethnic or racial identity poses an a priori problem for a democratic state: for Elshtain because it conflicts with the development and assessment of public ends, for Glazer and Moynihan because it has been created by exclusion and thus is the obverse of democracy, and for Roosevelt and Wilson (and the House Select Committee on U.S. National Security) because it threatens the security of the United States. From this point of view, the movement toward a more perfect union is by definition a movement away from social and ethnic identity. Identities may be championed and their right to exist defended by political policies but they are not to play a constitutive role in policy formulation without risk of derailing the possibilities for rational deliberative democratic procedures.

The Left

In recent years the left has also played a prominent role in the critique of identity politics. Leftist writers such as Todd Gitlin, Immanuel Wallerstein, Richard Rorty, Nancy Fraser, and others have criticized what they see as the turn to identity politics that occurred sometime after the New Left revival of progressivism in the 1960s. It is important to remember that this position has not been uniform among all left-wing, socialist, or communist organizations here or elsewhere. For example, the Communist Party USA of the 1930s demanded "Self-determination for the Afro-American Nation" in its basic party platform, and supported black nationalist demands even unto the right of separation (Haywood 1976, 1978; Foner and Shapiro 1991). In the early 1970s, a major difference between the groups that evolved out of Students for a Democratic Society was over the question of whether race and gender should be emphasized in present-day organizing or held off until "after the revolution," and several groups vigorously criticized the latter position.[2] And worker's parties in Latin America have differed sharply over their attitude toward *indigenismo* and black consciousness movements, with the very successful Brazilian Worker's Party strongly supporting the struggles of ethnic groups. Even the labor movement in the United States has come around to recognizing the importance of addressing ethnic and gender differences, and leading unions such as the Service Employees International Union (SEIU) have adopted diversity quotas for national conventions, put out multilanguage newsletters, and now hold regular workshops for union stewards on questions of racism, sexism, and homophobia.

Nonetheless, most prominent (white) leftists in the United States today are critical in varying degrees of movements that make identity their organizing basis, and are worried about "overemphasizing" difference. The debate over multiculturalism that raged throughout the 1990s was instructive in this regard. Most leftists wanted to carefully distinguish good and bad forms of multiculturalism, and were very critical of forms that they felt reified identity and promoted a politics of visibility without an agenda of class struggle. The forms of multiculturalism that they approved of were defined as those that characterized ethnic, racial, gender, and cultural differences as produced or created by structures of oppression (Kanpol and McLaren 1995). To avoid the pejorative label "liberal," a form of multiculturalism needed to argue not only for the inclusion of diverse cultural groups but also for the inclusion of narratives explaining the relations of exploitation and oppression that existed between dominant and subordinate groups. That is, it needed to explain the relationship between identity formations and power structures. This brings out the most radical implications of identity struggles, showing the incoherence of an all-inclusive pluralism that would equate identities forged as tools of domination (whiteness, masculinity) and identities created to target populations for exploitation (blackness).

Few would contest the link between identity formation and power structures, given the historical context of colonialism in which all of our identities have been shaped. The issue of contention here is whether identities that have been historically subject to oppression are reducible to that oppressive genealogy. Many leftists insisted that cultural differences can be explained *mainly* in reference to oppression, thus suggesting that without oppression, difference might well wither away. I will take issue with this view in what follows.

Leftist concerns with identity politics have been in many cases the same concerns that the liberals have, such as Schlesinger and Elshtain, but they also have some of their own worries. In his book *The Twilight of Common Dreams: Why America Is Wracked with Culture Wars*, Gitlin echoes many of the liberal worries listed earlier: that identity politics fractures the body politic; that it emphasizes difference at the expense of commonalities; and that its focus on identity offers only a reductivist politics, one that would reduce assessment of political position to the process of ascertaining identity. But as a leftist, Gitlin worries primarily that the focus on identities and thus differences inhibits the possibility of creating a progressive political majority based on class. Rather than building from common interests, identity politics, he thinks, makes "a fetish of the virtues of the minority." And in his view this is not true of just some versions of identity politics, but of all. "*All* forms of identity politics" are reductive: they are all "overly clear about who the insiders are . . . and overly dismissive of outsiders"(Gitlin 1995, 127). He thus finds the emphasis on identities "intellectually stultifying and politically suicidal." If we want to make genuine social revolution, he argues, ethnic- and racial-based political organizing must be minimized.

Similar to Glazer and Moynihan, Gitlin attempts to offer a kind of therapeutic diagnosis to explain the current attachment that so many in our society have to their identities. "The contemporary passion for difference is . . . the consequence of unsettled psychological states. The American pace of change constantly eats away at identity . . . The search for hard-edged social identities is surely an overcompensation" (160). In other words, identity-based movements are forms of resistance against capitalism, which has caused a fragmentation of the extended family, the breakup of community, and the lost significance of history and tradition. Americans are pining for fixities of identity to cure the vertigo produced by so much postmodern disarray. For the participants of identity politics, "the benefits of the pursuit of identity [are] manifold: a sense of community, an experience of solidarity, a prefabricated reservoir of recruits. . . . Try telling someone who feels . . . the hunger for wholeness that this is a totalitarian principle, that he or she had better get used to the overlap and complexity of attachments" (147). Gitlin thus tries to sympathetically explain the motivations for identity attachments, even while he critiques the construction of identity as a kind of mistake. He believes that a strong sense of group identification may be understandable but that an insistence on identity's political salience is ultimately irrational, often opportunist, and strategically disastrous.

Gitlin's account thus returns us to an outdated view of class as an essentially homogeneous entity rather than a cluster concept with internal contradictions. By separating class demands from identity struggles he implies that there are generic class demands rather than the demands of skilled or unskilled workers, of the trades or the service professions, of minority workers, of women workers, of immigrant workers, and so on, that is, of groups whose interests sometimes coincide and at other times collide. Gitlin implies that the labor movement can only maintain a united front if it ignores internal differences.

In my experience, maintaining unity requires a careful attending to difference. For example, in a recent contract negotiation that I observed at a hospital in Syracuse, New York, the issue of preferences for internal hiring or in-house advancement came up for discussion among members of the SEIU bargaining committee, each of whom was an elected representative from a particular sector of the hospital. In the process of preparing the negotiating points that the union will put forward to management, priorities have to be set and some issues must be left aside, and the question on the table was, How much of a priority would the union give the issue of in-house advancement in its negotiations? The members of the professional trades—electricians, plumbers, and so forth, who are almost entirely white men—initially saw no reason to fight for this provision in the contract or to make it a priority. However, an African American woman on the bargaining team spoke up for the importance of in-house advancement, pointing out that almost all of the minorities in the hospital worked at the relatively lower skilled and lesser paid jobs. Given the difficulty minorities still have in entering the trades, the outside hiring of minorities is a slim bet. It is much more likely that a minority person will be hired into housekeeping or dietary departments, for example, but be stuck in those departments unless preferences are given for in-house hiring into the trainee positions available in the more lucrative departments. In this particular bargaining subcommittee, if the tradesmen had voted as a bloc against this woman's proposal, and if the mostly white male union leaders had supported them, then the conditions of work for nonwhite workers at that hospital would continue to be unrelievedly at the bottom of the hierarchy during the next three- or five-year contract period. Fortunately, in this case the white workers united in supporting in-house advancement because they came to recognize the relevance that racial difference made to union members' work lives.[3] These kinds of discussions are an everyday occurrence in labor organizing and contract battles. It is no accident that SEIU is today the largest union in the United States, the fastest growing, and that it has the most proactive policies in support of racial and gender democracy.

Thus, one cannot either imaginatively or practically pursue "class demands" as if the working class has one set of united and homogeneous material interests. It makes neither political nor theoretical sense to imagine an undifferentiated working class demanding a larger share of the pie, to be divided among them with the same ratios of remuneration as currently exist based on racism and sexism. Just as black workers cannot stand in for the whole, neither can skilled white workers. Each group is exploited in a specific manner, and to different degrees. Certainly, there is a motivation for unity, but unity will have to be negotiated in piecemeal terms, such as the bargaining committee in Syracuse discovered. Redistribution demands will either reproduce or subvert the inequalities among workers, or, as is often the case, do some of both.[4] Thus, neither class demands nor class identity can be understood apart from the differences of social identity.

The very possibility of unity that Gitlin aims for will require that, for example, the minority members of a union feel connected to it and feel that it is addressing their conditions of work. But this requires the exploration and recognition of difference, as well as making a space in union meetings for sometimes extensive discussions about the different situation of the various workers and accommodating their different demands, interests, and needs.

In her recent books, Nancy Fraser offers a less polemical and arguably more persuasive critique of identity politics that tries to accommodate a recognition of difference. Though she is very critical of identity-based politics, she is also critical of those who use the excuse of its failures to retreat from the struggles against racism and sexism, turning back to class reductionism, economism, or the old-fashioned kind of unselfconscious universalism that existed prior to social struggles around identity.

Fraser develops a broad mapping of contemporary social struggles and political movements with many points of reference but essentially one major divide, that between struggles for recognition (women, oppressed minorities, gays and lesbians) and struggles for redistribution (labor, the poor, welfare rights). She argues that there is an analytical as well as a practical distinction between these types of movements because struggles for recognition tend toward promoting "group differentiation" while struggles for redistribution tend to "promote group dedifferentiation." In other words, gays and lesbians, for example, are fighting for the very right to exist free of violence and discrimination, while the poor would rather eradicate their identity as poor.

Fraser explains that "recognition claims often take the form of calling attention to, if not performatively creating, the putative specificity of some group and then of affirming its value. Thus they tend to promote group differentiation. Redistribution claims, in contrast, often call for abolishing economic arrangements that underpin group specificity. . . . Thus, they tend to promote group dedifferentiation. . . . Thus, the two kinds of claims stand in tension with each other; they can interfere with, or even work against, each other" (Fraser 1997, 16). She views this conflict of aims between recognition and redistribution as one of the central problems of political mobilization today. Unlike other leftist critics such as Gitlin, Fraser holds that we should attempt to bring these two sorts of struggles together, and that both kinds make legitimate political demands. But, like Gitlin, Fraser is highly critical of the effects of interpreting the need for recognition in terms of a recognition of identities.

Fraser's critique of identity politics is the most perspicuous and clearly articulated to date, and thus well worth a careful reading.[5] Her account is also worth addressing because, unlike many others, she not only sympathizes with the aims of recognition movements but attempts to reformulate them in such a way so as to lessen what she considers their problematic effects. In what follows, I will explore Fraser's arguments in some detail. After this, I will summarize the main points of the political criticism of identity, tease out the assumptions behind these criticisms, and then offer counterarguments that address each major point.

Fraser's Critique

Fraser divides the forms that struggles for recognition can take into two camps, the first involving the struggle for an affirmation of identity, and the second involving the struggle for equal participation (Fraser 2000, 2003). Her main criticism is directed toward this first form, which she calls a "culturalist" struggle that aims at self-realization. It is this form of the struggle for recognition that she associates with identity politics. Identity politics by her definition, then, is a struggle in which the political goal is articulated as an affirmation, including self-affirmation, of previously denigrated identities.[6]

In part because she is critical of this form of recognition struggles, Fraser endeavors to develop and articulate the second form (the struggle for equal participation) and in this way to salvage the project of recognition from the deleterious effects of identity politics. I will consider this second option in a moment, but I will turn first to her concerns with the struggle to affirm identities.

Fraser argues that a politics that understands itself to be aiming at the affirmation of identities will have the following effects, even if unintended: (a) displacing redistribution struggles, (b) tending toward separatism and away from coalition, and

(c) reifying identities, which she objects to not on metaphysical grounds but on the grounds that it leads to a policing of authenticity, the promotion of conformism, and some form of, again to use West's phrase, "racial reasoning." The struggle to affirm identities will tend toward these effects because, according to Fraser, these struggles tend to view identity-based forms of discrimination as "free standing" rather than caused by a complex array of social institutions.

> Largely silent on the subject of economic inequality, the identity model treats misrecognition as a free-standing cultural harm; many of its proponents simply ignore distributive injustice altogether and focus exclusively on efforts to change culture.... [It] casts misrecognition as a problem of cultural depreciation. The roots of injustice are located in demeaning representations, but they are not seen as socially grounded.... Hypostatizing culture, they both abstract misrecognition from its institutional matrix and obscure its entwinement with distributive justice. (Fraser 2000, 110)

Neither here nor elsewhere does Fraser provide examples of groups that hold such views.

Here one might be tempted immediately to argue that the real problem is just these mistaken views about cultures and identities rather than identity politics per se. Identity-based political organizing will not divert attention from redistribution, as she predicts, unless it also imagines that identity-based hatreds occur within a completely autonomous cultural sphere. But it is not at all clear that such beliefs are an intrinsic feature of identity politics or of identity-based political organizing that aims at the affirmation and self-affirmation of identities. One could desire to affirm identities even if one held nonhypostasized accounts of cultures and identities. Nor does the affirmation of identities itself entail a commitment to a particular social theory about oppressive causes. For example, the various watch groups that report on minority representation in the media and that demand more and better representation are organized simply around media representation, and offer no full-blown theory about social change; nor do they imply that this reform will have a greater impact on society than other reforms. Yet they are clearly motivated by the goal of affirming presently denigrated identities.[7]

Fraser seems to accept that some forms of identity politics entail no commitment to a monocausal culturalist theory of identity-based forms of oppression. But she says that even when the proponents of identity politics "appreciate the seriousness of maldistribution and genuinely want to address it" they still result in "displacing redistributive claims" through an orientation of practice toward recognition rather than redistribution (Fraser 2000, 110). I suspect many more people share her concern with recognition struggles on these grounds, that is, because they believe that redistribution is a more important goal, and because they believe that redistribution has a more lasting value on society when its goals are achieved.

But we should note that if the problem here is one of *relative* weight or importance, this is not an *intrinsic* problem with identity politics itself. The problem of relative weight arises only if one puts more importance on recognition than redistribution. One could also ask, if one truly believes that both the redistributive and recognition struggles are warranted, as Fraser claims she does, why is it that the recognition struggles are problematic because they may divert energy and attention from redistribution struggles, but not vice versa?

More important, we need to question the assumption that recognition *can* be separated from redistribution, which is an assumption necessary to generate the question Fraser addresses of whether it *should* be. In fact, identity-based political organizing does not exist in necessary opposition to the struggle for redistribution of resources because redistribution demands are part and parcel of virtually all identity-based organizing. African American political organizations like the NAACP and the Black Radical Congress have called for reparations for slavery; women's organizations like NOW have demanded an end to gender-based pay inequities; and NARAL (the National Abortion Rights Action League) has demanded access to abortion for poor women. The National Council of La Raza has organized for welfare rights, home loans for Latinos, and improvement in public schools, and the National Gay and Lesbian Task Force has fought for an end to job and housing discrimination and universal access to AIDS medication as well as health insurance for domestic partners. These are demands that would effect significant redistributions of income and resources and would benefit not only middle-class individuals marked by these identities but also the working-class and poor members. Moreover, the organizing among immigrant women garment workers, as recounted in the wonderful book *Sweatshop Warriors* by Miriam Ching Yoon Louie, has largely developed from ethnic-based community centers, such as the Asian Immigrant Women Advocates organization, Korean Immigrant Workers Advocates, both in California, and the Chinese Staff and Workers Association in New York (Louie 2001). The languages and cultural backgrounds of immigrant workers significantly affect not only the possibility of communication but also the possibility of developing the high levels of trust required in organizing efforts that could lead to job loss and deportation. In these cases, identity-based organizing is simply a necessity and has in no way blocked the coalition efforts made between these ethnic organizations of workers and various labor unions. These examples may not establish a logical necessity to the connection between recognition and redistribution demands, but they establish the historical fact that in the leading groups organized around identity, redistribution demands are their raison d'être. Identity-based organizing is one way, and sometimes the only way, to mobilize and frame demands for redistribution and is an integral part of class transformation.[8]

Fraser may wish to characterize these sorts of groups as aiming not at the affirmation of identities but at equal participation, and thus to place them in her "safe" category distinct from identity politics. In this alternative approach, she says, "recognition is a question of social status" and "what requires recognition is not group-specific identity but the status of individual group members as full partners in social interaction" (Fraser 2000, 113). The language of recognition used here is meant to apply to the individual capacity and right of moral reasoning and political participation, both of which are denied by identity-based forms of discrimination. But in her view, instead of focusing on getting recognition *for an identity* that has the right of full participation, we should be focusing on the right of full participation directly. By articulating the demand in this way, Fraser argues, we will put the focus where it really needs to be.

Thus, the key aspect of Fraser's alternative approach to recognition is clearly its ability to decenter and even efface any concern with identity. Identities may enter in only insofar as they affect participation; otherwise we will be on the slippery slope toward affirming identities for their own sake, and this promotes further differentiation rather than dedifferentiation. Rather than seeing the attainment of equal status as bound up with identity, Fraser *contrasts* the recognition of identity with the recognition of status, as when she explains that on her model a claim for recognition should be "aimed *not* at valorizing group identity *but rather* at overcoming subordination" (2000, 114).

On the face of it, this alternative formulation may be persuasive in that it seems to be going after the real target and thus avoiding all the problems of the identity approach. But it is essentially a mischaracterization of the nature of class oppression and a proposal that will risk making it very difficult for group differences or group interests to be articulated in the public sphere. Let me explain.

In Joel Olsen's critique of her argument, he reminds us of Du Bois's demonstration in *Black Reconstruction* that addressing antiblack racism is not a *diversion* to class struggle but, in the context of the United States, *centrally* necessary for the very possibility of class struggle. White identity was created as a recompense and distraction to white workers for their economic disenfranchisement. Class consciousness has been stymied in the United States more so than in any other industrialized country through the racial ideology of white supremacy. This is precisely why, Olsen argues, that "the great American struggles for 'recognition'—Abolition, Reconstruction, and the civil rights movement—have inaugurated the nation's most significant efforts toward redistribution" (2001, 175).

In separating redistribution from recognition, Fraser implies, just as Gitlin did, that class can be conceptualized apart from identity. Thus, she provides as an example of a "pure distribution demand" the case of a white male skilled worker who becomes unemployed because of a factory closing resulting from a speculative corporate merger. In this case, she tells us,

> the injustice of maldistribution [that is, the worker becoming unemployed] has little to do with misrecognition. It is rather a consequence of imperatives intrinsic to an order of specialized economic relations whose *raison d'etre* is the accumulation of profits. To handle such cases, a theory of justice must reach beyond cultural value patterns to examine the structure of capitalism. It must ask whether economic mechanisms that are relatively decoupled from structures of prestige and that operate in a relatively autonomous way impede parity of participation in social life. (2003, 35)

But the reality here is that it is profitable to transfer production (or outsource it) from one class segment to another—from, for example, white male workers to a lower paid segment either within a given nation or outside of it—because of the segmentation of the labor market by race, ethnicity, gender, cultural identity, nationality, and geographic location. Corporate reorganization increases profit when it lowers labor costs, and labor costs are lowered by transferring production to a different labor segment. Without an account that can couple an analysis of "cultural value patterns" with the "structure of capital," we have no way to explain why certain labor segments are thrown out of work, even if, as in this case, it is the segment of white male skilled workers.

National minorities often form, willingly or unwillingly, an "ascriptive class segment," which the Berkeley economist Mario Barrera defines as a "portion of a class which is set off from the rest of the class by some readily identifiable and relatively stable characteristics of the persons assigned to that segment, such as race, ethnicity, or sex, and whose status in relation to the means and process of production is affected by that demarcation" (Barrera 1979, 101). Besides developing the general concept of ascriptive class segments more than two decades ago, Barrera also developed concepts of colonized class segments in which segmentation in the labor market is based on race and ethnicity. Barrera defines colonialism as "a structured relationship of domination and subordination, where the dominant and subordinate groups are defined along ethnic/racial lines, and where the relationship is established and maintained to serve the interests of all or part of the dominant group" (1979, 193). Neither race nor gender determines class position; such identity groups almost always include persons from multiple classes. Yet this fact in no way obviates Barrera's point that social identities operate to organize and segment the working class, differentiating its structure of wages and benefits as well as its condition of work. Picturing class formations as ideal types without race or gender disenables our ability to use the concept of class as an explanatory concept in social theory.

Fraser's hope that the demand for equal participation can bypass questions of the value of cultural and social identities is in vain. The reason why certain social actors are denied full participation in this context is their identity, as Fraser herself acknowledges when she says that "To be misrecognized . . . is not simply to be thought ill of, looked down upon or devalued in others' attitudes, beliefs or representations. It is rather to be denied the status of a full partner in social interaction, as a consequence of institutionalized patterns of cultural value that constitute one as comparatively unworthy of respect or esteem" (2000, 113–14). Thus, the denial of equal status is organized around and justified on the basis of identity. It is therefore unworkable to struggle for equal social status without contesting the *basis* upon which such status has been denied.

There are actually two separate reasons used to justify denying full partnership because of group identity: (1) because the particular group that the individual belongs to is argued to be inferior in some significant and relevant way, and/or (2) because *any* strongly felt group identity is argued to be an obstacle to reasoned judgment, since it will conflict with the individual's autonomy. If we can eliminate, in a utopian thought experiment, the occurrence of sexism and racism and thus (1), this in no way decreases the possibility that (2) will continue to obstruct full participation. That is, one might have a strong attachment to an identity that is not denigrated, being Norwegian, for example, but on some constructions of nationality, this very attachment will itself be viewed with suspicion as likely leading to a distortion of judgment. Such an argument may even seem to be a much more rational concern, more rational than the simple denigration of their Norwegian specific identity, and for that reason may be even harder to dislodge. Thus, even if the individuals are saved in the struggle for equal social status, their identities will remain outlawed from the public realm of deliberation. This solution is no different from the liberal approach Sartre excoriated in *Anti-Semite and Jew* when he said that the liberal wants to save the man but leave the Jew behind.[9]

The goal of redistributing resources, which Fraser claims to be her main concern, requires addressing all of the causes of the problem of maldistribution, which include (a) structural and institutionalized based forms of discrimination, (b) ideologies among dominant groups that legitimate their exploitation of, or inattention to, the plight of the subordinate groups, but also (c) the internalization of such ideologies among the oppressed themselves, among the effects of which is the reticence to demand redistribution. Internalizations of self-hatred and inferiority cannot be solved after redistribution, but must be addressed and at least partially overcome in order to make possible effective collective action. Every successful progressive and revolutionary movement has known this, and has then given expression to artistic, literary, and other forms of positive self-images as well as ways of working through and beyond the internalizations, from Soviet social realism to first world feminist art to the Mexican muralists to the AIDS quilt.

Consider Fraser's analysis in light of the recent battle at the University of North Dakota over the name of the school mascot, the "Fighting Sioux." It is not only the use of the name that has been opposed, but the highly demeaning images used around the local sports events, including portrayals of American Indians performing fellatio on buffalo. Although similar battles have occurred across the country for nearly three decades now, the battle at North Dakota had some unusual aspects. First, this is a university that houses 25 American Indian programs, including a quarterly student magazine, a program on American Indian life and culture, and a program in medicine that reportedly trains a fifth of the American Indian doctors in the United States. Thus, one might argue that here is a case that was truly about the affirmation of identities rather than redistribution, since the demands of redistribution seem to have already been met.

But the second unusual aspect of this case reveals that there is more to the story. The battle came to a peremptory climax when a donor who pledged $100 million gift to the university for a new sports arena threatened to withdraw his gift and close down construction if the school logo or slogan were changed to omit the Indian name. If one is tempted to think, like some of the white students were reported as saying, that this is a trivial issue, a returned check for $100 million would suggest that for some it is indeed not trivial at all.

I would suggest that the identity politics at play in this case is white identity, in which whiteness is associated with the privilege to name others, to choose one's own form of discursive banter with total autonomy, as well as with vanguard narratives of Anglo-European cultures that portray the rest of the world as existing in various stages of "backwardness." Can we really make a neat separation between racial ideology, psychic processes of internalized superiority, and the economic hierarchy of resource distribution? Clearly these are bound up together, mutually reenforcing. Eurocentric vanguard narratives are critical tools used to justify the existing hierarchies of ascriptive class segments. According to Fraser, the Sioux need to understand their long-term goal as a deconstruction of their identities. But this is simply an extension of the privilege associated with whiteness to name and signify difference and to determine its place in a progressive narrative of united struggle. Thus the lesson I take from the struggle at North Dakota is that redistribution and recognition demands are interwoven not only at the level of the resource allocations for the marginalized groups, as evidenced by the redistribution demands made by identity-based political groups, but also at the level of the resources under the control of dominant groups. The struggle for redistribution requires a critique not only of negative ascriptions, but also a critique of at least some positive ones.

Fraser certainly does not deny the need to combat negative images, but on her view, given the inherent problems associated with struggles organized around the affirmation of identities, the better strategy is still to fight for equality as persons rather than for respect as groups. Given her critique of the affirmation of identities, individual group members can only achieve equal status by *transcending* their group membership, at least in the domain of social interaction. To divorce identity affirmation from a struggle for social redemption is to encourage a move from group to individual interpellation. It appears then that, like Elshtain, Fraser would have the participants of public deliberation act and be seen primarily as individuals without their social identity, which is also suggested by her description of the future form of socialism: "For both gender and 'race,' the scenario that best finesses the redistribution-recognition dilemma is socialism in the economy plus deconstruction in the culture. But for this scenario to be psychologically and politically feasible requires that all people be *weaned* from their attachment to current cultural constructions of their interests and identities" (Fraser 1997, 31; emphasis added).

Thus far I have argued that recognition struggles do not necessarily pull against redistribution struggles, and that Fraser's preferred alternative—the fight for equal status—can not be successful without paying careful attention to identity. Her "solution" leads away from groups and toward individualism despite the fact that she has not shown that group identities per se are problematic. Her two main remaining arguments against identity politics are its tendency toward separatism and toward reification. These two issues can be found across the literature on identity politics, and I will address them in some depth in the following section. But I want first to turn briefly to one fairly idiosyncratic argument Fraser uses that is independent of the arguments about separatism and reification but that is also representative of some of the common concerns about identity politics.

Fraser claims that identity politics, though it is generally theoretically grounded in a tradition of social theory that understands identities as the product of social interaction, operates with a "monologic" approach to identity affirmation. In other words, Fraser charges identity politics with the view that those outside the designated identity have no right to say anything about it:

> Paradoxically, moreover, the identity model tends to deny its own Hegelian premises. Having begun by assuming that identity is dialogical, constructed via interaction with another subject, it ends by valorizing monologism—supposing that misrecognized peoples can and should construct their own identity on their own. It supposes, further, that a group has the right to be understood solely in its own terms—that no one is ever justified in viewing another subject from an external perspective or in dissenting from another's self-interpretation. (Fraser 2000, 112)

Here Fraser is referring to the sort of view that says that only African Americans can define African American identity or that only Jews can say who counts as a Jew.

Fraser's argument concerns two distinct claims designating two different processes: one is the widely agreed upon fact that identity is constructed through recognition from another at a kind of deep psychological level; the other is the claim that the process of reassessing and reconstructing identities that have been denigrated and misrecognized should be done by those so misrecognized themselves. Fraser claims that, if one holds the first of these claims, one cannot hold the second. But this doesn't follow. One can hold both claims without contradiction, as, for example, Frantz Fanon did when he argued that black people need to redirect their gaze from the white man and instead toward each other in seeking recognition, that they needed to give up on winning recognition from the imperialist forces and instead work on developing a sense of identity that can yield self-respect because it is recognized as worthy of respect by other black people (Fanon 1967). Fanon did not believe that individuals can go about identity construction by themselves; if they could, withstanding racist insults would be much easier. But he did believe that the social interactions necessary for identity formation need not be dominated by the oppressor culture. Having a more accurate and loving recognition from within one's community can bolster a strong sense of self and a positive sense of identity, as many people have experienced.

I doubt that Fraser would hold, against Fanon, that oppressed groups require recognition from oppressor groups. I suspect that her concern is with group solipsism, in which all open critical dialogue with those outside the group is preempted. But it is clear that group solipsism does not follow from Fanon's position. In fact, in the utopian last lines of *Black Skin, White Masks*, Fanon himself holds out the hope for an "authentic communication" between whites and blacks. He says: "Superiority? Inferiority? Why not the quite simple attempt to touch the other, to feel the other, to explain the other to myself? ... At the conclusion of this study, I want the world to recognize, with me, the open door of every consciousness" (1967, 231–32).

Fraser's argument takes a familiar form of the slippery slope. First we repudiate the right of oppressor cultures to define us, and then, she surmises, we end in group solipsism impervious to outside input. I agree that group solipsism is to be avoided, but this does not require a repudiation of the political salience of identity. Solipsism can be avoided by the recognition that all group identities are internally heterogeneous, that group members will belong to a diversity of other groups as well, and thus that dialogical encounters across group differences occur always *within* groups. Further, solipsism can be argued against on the grounds that other groups besides my own have experienced oppression also and may well have wise counsel. In the positive reconstruction I will give of the concept of identity in chapter 4, it will become clearer why solipsism is not only avoidable—it is, strictly speaking, impossible, no less for groups than for individuals.

What about the favoring of intragroup processes of identity construction and recognition? Is this either feasible or a good idea? It does not preclude productive intergroup interactions around common political goals, or in other words, political coalition. And favoring intragroup processes makes a lot of sense within a climate of intense, daily denigration of one's cultural identity by the dominant society. But, again, rejecting the goal of gaining recognition from oppressor cultures does not require rejecting input from any and every external source.

Fraser's concern with identity politics is not simply based on intergroup relations but also, and equally, intragroup dynamics. She argues that identity politics "encourages the reification of group identities" (2000, 113), which in turn leads to "conformism, intolerance, and patriarchalism" (2000, 112). There is no doubt that these problems can occur, as well as defining authenticity arbitrarily (e.g., as male, straight, etc.), and discouraging open debate by casting aspersions on the authenticity or loyalty of internal critics. But are such problems intrinsic to identity-based political movements? Will identity-based political organizing inevitably devolve in these ways? Or are such problems more likely under certain kinds of contextual conditions that we might identify? For example, it might be the case that identity politics tends toward reification when the group is so embattled that a mistaken trust could cost lives. It is well known that social movements operating under conditions of intense state repression and surveillance are prone to paranoia and commandist forms of leadership. In order to analyze when, and why, social movements go wrong, we need careful attention to contextual conditions, specific histories, economic analyses, and so on, rather than a blanket condemnation of identity-based movements.

The question that remains is why identity itself is taken to be the problem here when one might seek out other explanations about the development of the problems Fraser and others identify. We can all agree that the internal policing for conformity, dehistoricized and rigid accounts of identity, the refusal to consider the possibility of coalition across differences, and the separation of cultural from economic processes are mistakes and can present serious problems in political struggle. But do these mistakes follow necessarily from taking the political relevance of identity seriously, or from the desire to affirm identities, or from a notion of utopia in which social identity still exists?

The argument against identity launched by Fraser and others clearly has some missing premises, since the conclusion does not follow from the evidence presented. We need to see more precisely what the assumptions are behind the wholesale critique of identity. In the following sections I will summarize the key arguments, the assumptions behind these arguments, and then examine the plausibility of each claim.

The Key Arguments

The political arguments behind the critique of identity can be boiled down to the following three:

(1) Strongly felt ethnic or cultural identities will inevitably produce a problem of conflicting loyalties within a larger grouping, such as a nation, in which many such identities are included; Schlesinger, for example, targets what he calls the "cult of ethnicity" because it "exaggerates differences, intensifies resentments and antagonisms, drives ever deeper the awful wedges between races and nationalities" (1991, 226). If identity by itself intensifies conflict, then identity-based movements

Key arguments
problems of id

will weaken the possibility of coalition and lead to separatism. Call this the separatism problem.

(2) Identity politics "encourages the reification of group identities," as Fraser argues, which in turn leads to "conformism, intolerance, and patriarchalism" (2000, 112–13). While the separatism problem worries about relations between groups, this criticism worries about the kinds of problems that exist in intragroup relations: the policing for conformity, the arbitrary defining of authenticity, the de-emphasis and discouragement of internal differences, and the preempting of open debate by castigating internal critics as less authentic and disloyal. Thus, identity politics curtails the ability to creatively interpret one's identity and to determine its degree of relevance, or irrelevance, in one's life. Because it reifies identity, then, identity politics constrains individual freedom. Call this the reification problem.

(3) Identities pose major problems for rational deliberation, especially over public ends. Rationality mandates that we must be able to subject the claims embedded in cultural traditions to rational reflection, and this requires achieving enough distance from our social identities that we can objectify and thus evaluate them. Individuals need to be able to enter the arena of public debate and action as dispassionate reasoners, weighing evidence on the basis of its merit no matter its relationship or implications for the future of one's own social group. Call this the reasoning problem.

These three problems involve (at least) three important corresponding assumptions, without which the above claims would not be convincing. I am classifying these as assumptions because they are deep-seated beliefs in the Western philosophical and political traditions rarely given explicit articulation or defense. I will list them here and then examine them more carefully in the final section.

(1a) The separatism problem follows from the assumption that strongly felt identity is necessarily exclusivist. This is what is behind Roosevelt's and Wilson's arguments against the hyphenated citizen, but it is also behind more recent claims that identity politics exacerbates differences. Identities are thought to represent a set of interests and experiential knowledge or perspective that differentiates them from other identities, thus creating difficulties of communication and political unity.

Call this the assumption of exclusivity. This assumption is also operative in the reification problem, but the main assumption behind the reification problem is somewhat different:

(2a) The reification problem follows from the assumption that whatever is imposed from the outside as an attribution of the self is necessarily a constraint on individual freedom. Social identities, by the very fact that they are social and thus imposed on the individual, inherently constrain individual freedom. Even if the individual is allowed to interpret the meaning of their identity, they are forced to do so, insofar as they are forced to engage with the identities imposed on them by the arbitrary circumstances of their birth. We are generally born into social identities; after all, we don't choose them. Many thus believe that even those who are given identities involving privilege are made less free by this despite the fact that their privilege increases their options vis-à-vis others; privileged persons are forced to have privilege whether they want it or not, and this constitutes a constraint. If one considers identities associated with oppression that carry the weight of discrimination, fear, and hatred, and that did not even exist prior to the conditions of oppression (like black identity), it can seem even more odd that anyone would willfully choose to be constrained by such an identity.

On this view, then, identities are constraining, *tout court*, no matter whether privileged or oppressed. The problems of conformism and so on that are associated with reification follow from identity per se, and not only some forms of it. Conformism is itself a kind of social imposition; one cannot be a conformist in a class of one. Given this, if a political organization or movement is based on and therefore emphasizes identity, those constraints will be emphasized and even maximized for the individuals involved in that organization or movement. Call this the assumption of the highest value being individual freedom.

(3a) The reasoning problem associated with identity follows from the assumption that identities involve a set of interests, values, beliefs, and practices. Therefore, the sort of reasoning that one is called on to do as a political leader or simply as a citizen engaging with public issues of concern requires transcendence of one's identity, or as much transcendence as possible, in order to be able to weigh the evidence rationally and without prejudice, interpret the relevant data, and give order to conflicting values. Reasoning, since the Enlightenment, is defined by just this sort of objectivizing, reflective operation, in which one detaches oneself from one's assumptions, or "foreknowledge," in order to put them to the test of rationality. To the extent that identities are like containers that group sets of beliefs and practices across categories of individuals, and to the extent that a strongly felt identity is defined by its commitment to these beliefs and practices, then it follows that the strength of identity will exist in inverse proportion to one's capacity for rational thought. Call this the objectivizing assumption.

These assumptions—that identities are exclusivist, imposed from outside and therefore constraining on individuals, and that their substantive content provides a counterweight to rationality—are hardwired into Western Anglo traditions of thought; by that I mean that they are rarely argued for or even made explicit. In the remainder of this chapter, I will provide some reasons that should, at least prima facie, call these assumptions into question.

A More Realistic View

The critique of identity politics is based on a certain picture of what identity is, a picture that begins to become visible from the three assumptions listed above. This picture, however, does not actually correspond to the lived experience of identity or its politically mobilized forms. In this section I will begin to develop an alternative account of identity, which I will further develop in the following two chapters. This alternative account will be used to show the inadequacy of the assumptions behind the critique of identity.

Let's start with the assumption that identities are inherently exclusive and thus tend toward separatism. When one goes beyond the anecdotal to the empirical, there is simply not sufficient evidence for the absoluteness with which the critics of identity have assumed that strongly felt identities always tend toward separatism. Of course there are problems with essentialist constructions of identity and overly narrow formulations of political alliances, and there are serious problems with the view that identity itself constitutes innocence or culpability or that only those sharing an identity can unite together in common cause. But these positions are the result of certain kinds of construals of identity rather than the automatic effect of a strong sense of group solidarity and group cohesiveness.

In the National Black Politics Survey conducted in 1993–94, the first survey of mass political opinion among African Americans conducted in the United States, one of the most striking findings was a very high degree of belief in what political theorists call "linked fate": the belief that what generally happens to people in your identity group, in this case your racial group, will significantly affect your life. (Dawson 1994; Holliman and Brown 1997). An individual who believes that their fate is linked to others in their group will tend to use group data as a kind of proxy to understand how a given event might affect them or to predict how a given choice might work out for them. Researchers found that more than 80 percent of respondents felt a strong sense of linked fate with African Americans as a whole.

A belief in linked fate has obvious political ramifications for alliances, organizing, and one's ability to trust the analyses of political leaders. Yet researchers also found that less than 40 percent of their respondents agreed with such proposals as "Blacks should control the economy in mostly black communities" or "Blacks should control the government in mostly black communities." Even fewer than this (by about a third) agreed with the proposal that "Blacks should have their own separate nation." Thus, the very high level of group identification that exists among African Americans showed no evidence of having a correlation to a racially separatist political approach or a tendency to reject coalition efforts.

Political scientist José E. Cruz conducted an important ethnography of Puerto Rican politics in Hartford, Connecticut (1998). In particular, he analyzed Hartford's Puerto Rican Political Action Committee as a case study of identity politics in action, in relation both to PRPAC's effect on the Puerto Rican community and on that community's relationship to the dominant Hartford political scene. The Puerto Rican community in Hartford is the oldest and largest concentration in the United States, and by 1990 they comprised more than 25 percent of the city's population. Yet they had almost no political representation in city government. The PRPAC took up ethnic mobilization as "a way of achieving representation and a means to negotiate individual and group benefits" (Cruz 1998, 6), once again uniting the demands for recognition with the demands for redistribution. And in fact, identity-based organizing led not toward separation but was precisely the key to the enhanced political mobilization and involvement of Puerto Ricans in Hartford politics (12).

Cruz concludes from his study that the focus on their Puerto Rican identity was not a rejection of "Americanism" but "a code that structured their entrance into mainstream society and politics" (6). Identity politics did not "reify victimization" but "encouraged individuals to overcome passivity" precisely through a rearticulated "self-image" and the demand of "equal access to positions of responsibility within the civil and political society" (12). Although identity politics there as elsewhere had its problems, according to Cruz these "should be seen as cautionary

rather than invalidating" (19). On balance, he argues that the identity-based political organizing of the PRPAC resulted in significantly increased voter turnout and
in political representation for Puerto Ricans not only in the city but in the state. The
very possibility of coalitions with the black and white communities of Hartford
requires this political mobilization and involvement. Cruz concludes that

> the view that identity politics balkanizes the political landscape and threatens the
> viability of the political order is more in tune with simplistic and misinformed
> apprehensions about the role of conflict in politics than with the more reasoned
> and well-established political science axiom that societal integration and political
> power are inextricably bound. As Philip Gourevitch suggests, the threat of conflict
> often lies in the inability of those who feel threatened to ascertain what the conflict
> is exactly about. This is, in no small measure, true of identity politics and the
> feelings of distress that it causes among those who see only chaos and instability in
> its wake. (19)

Cruz's study provides further support for the argument of "cultural citizenship" advanced by anthropologist Renato Rosaldo and developed by the interdisciplinary group of scholars involved in the Latino Cultural Studies Working
Group, who have led research teams in California, Texas, and New York (see
Flores and Benmayor 1997). The concept of cultural citizenship is meant to
counter a model of the abstract individual citizen who participates in civil society
as a rational agent imagined to have no gender, race, or cultural background.
Rosaldo argued that this model is ineffective in addressing the prejudices that beset
white women and people of color when they enter the public arena, such as the
interrupting of their speech, dismissal of arguments, and peremptory rejections. In
actuality, the public arena is a space where women and men of various races and
cultures negotiate with one another, and the concept of the cultural citizen allows
us to understand those specific identities as an integral part of one's activity as a
citizen—the basis, in some cases, of the knowledge they bring and very rights they
are claiming, rather than that which must be "left at the door." Rosaldo points out
that part of the problem here has been a view that "regards culture as a relic, an
inert heirloom handed down wholecloth from time immemorial" rather than as a
kind of social practice always involving "innovation and change" (1985, 2). A more
accurate understanding of what cultures are will yield a more realistic account of
cultural identity and its effect on politics.

Another relevant study is being conducted by Omar Encarnacion on civil
society and the effect of identity-based organizing in South America. Encarnacion
(2000) argues that in Brazil, which since the 1960s has seen a virtual explosion of
identity politics in the form of the black consciousness movement, there has at the
same time been an expansion of popular participation in politics, of notions of citizenship, of the boundaries of the policy arena, and of political associations. This
has visibly empowered civil society vis-à-vis the state. Rather than crippling the
progressive movement, then, identity politics has expanded its base, its agenda, and
its effectiveness.[10]

Encarnacion has hypothesized that identity politics had these effects in Brazil—
which has not been the case in every country where identity politics has emerged

in South America—because of the existence of what he calls a "progressive left" in the form of the Brazilian Worker's Party, which has consistently emphasized classic concerns of social liberalism such as women's equality, environmental protection, and an end to racial discrimination. Thus, the critical factor for an effective left was not whether there were identity-based political movements, but whether the left labor organizations understood these movements as a diversion from or an integral part of their own struggle for a better society.

These empirical findings clearly suggest that we need a better account of the nature of identity itself than the sorts of accounts one finds among the critics. Strongly felt identities *in reality* do not uniformly lead to the political disasters the critics portend because identities *in reality* are not what the critics understand them to be. What we need to understand, then, is how it is possible that identities that are strongly felt and considered to have political relevance can be such that they do *not* lead to separatism.

The notion that identities lead to separatism or mutually exclusive political agendas seems to be based on the idea that identities represent discrete and specifiable sets of interests. Identities, it is assumed, must therefore operate on the model of interest-group politics: a specific set of interests is represented by lobbyists or movement leaders in order to advance that specific agenda. That agenda may, naturally, come into conflict with other agendas put forward, or even with the "majority's interests," and thus there will be a conflict that can be addressed through compromise but never completely resolved. The notion of interest groups has gotten a very bad reputation in U.S. political discourse, in which special-interest groups are viewed as single-mindedly advancing one agenda and as incapable of considering other points of view or a larger frame of reference in which the "common good" is considered. Special-interest groups have particular preset agendas for the promotion of which reason becomes attenuated to the instrumental calculation of advancing that cause, without the possibility of calling the cause into question or of modifying it in light of larger public concerns. Minority constituencies have often been characterized as being like special-interest groups in these ways.

Social identities can and sometimes do operate as interest groups, but that is not what identities essentially are. On the basis of analyzing a wide sample of identity-based movements, sociologist Manuel Castells describes identity as a generative source of meaning, necessarily collective rather than wholly individual, and useful as a source of agency as well as a meaningful narrative (1997, 7). This account accords with the research by Cruz, Encarnacion, and Rosaldo. In analyzing identity-based political movements, Castells offers a typology of identity constructions corresponding to a variety of political agendas and historical contexts. His work provides a model for the kind of contextual analysis I called for earlier that would analyze the operation of concepts within contexts rather than assuming that concepts operate uniformly across contexts. I will turn to Castells later on for more help in developing an empirically adequate description of identity, but here it is enough to note that Castells's work also strongly counters the view that identity politics always tends toward the same political forms or that the political relevance of identity always is cashed out in similar fashion.

In a more philosophical account based in his readings of contemporary literature, Satya Mohanty argues that identity constructions provide narratives that explain the links between group historical memory and individual contemporary experience, that they create unifying frames for rendering experience intelligible, and that they thus help to map the social world (Mohanty 1997). To the extent that identities involve *meaning*-making, there will always be alternative interpretations of the meanings associated with identity, Mohanty explains, but he insists that identities refer to real experiences.

Of course, identities can be imposed on people from the outside. But that is more of a brand than a true identity, or more of an ascription than a meaningful characterization of self. Identities must resonate with and unify lived experience, and they must provide a meaning that has some purchase, however partial, on the subject's own daily reality. Supporting Mohanty's realism about identity, Anuradha Dingwaney and Lawrence Needham explain identity's lived experience as that which "signifies affective, even intuitive, ways of being in, or inhabiting, specific cultures. . . . [I]t is perceived as experience that proceeds from identity that is given or inherited . . . but it is also, and more significantly, mediated by what Satya Mohanty calls 'social narratives, paradigms, even ideologies'" (Dingwaney and Needham 1996, 21). In other words, although experience is sometimes group-related (and thus identity-related), its meaning is not unambiguous. Dingwaney and Needham go on to say, following Stuart Hall:

> What we have are events, interactions, political and other identifications, made available at certain historical conjunctures, that are then *worked through* in the process of constructing, and/or affiliating with, an identity. However, to say that identity is constructed is not to say that it is available to any and every person or group who wishes to inhabit it. The voluntarism that inheres in certain elaborations of the constructedness of identity ignores, as Hall also notes . . . "certain conditions of existence, real histories in the contemporary world, which are not exclusively psychical, not simply journeys of the mind"; thus it is incumbent upon us to recognize that "every identity is placed, positioned, in a culture, a language, a history." It is for this reason that claims about "lived experience" resonate with such force in conflicts over what does or does not constitute an appropriate interpretation of culturally different phenomena. (20–21, quoting from Hall 1987, 44–45)

This is an account of identity that holds *both* that identity makes an epistemic difference *and* that identity is the product of a complex mediation involving individual agency in which its meaning is produced rather than merely perceived or experienced. In other words, identity is not merely that which is given to an individual or group, but is also a way of inhabiting, interpreting, and working through, both collectively and individually, an objective social location and group history.

We might, then, more insightfully define identities as positioned or located lived experiences in which both individuals and groups work to construct meaning in relation to historical experience and historical narratives. Given this view, one might hold that when I am identified, it is my horizon of agency that is identified.

Thus, identities are not lived as a discrete and stable set of interests, but as a site from which one must engage in the process of meaning-making and thus from which one is open to the world. The hermeneutic insight is that the self operates in a situated plane, always culturally located with great specificity even as it is open onto an indeterminate future and a reinterpretable past not of its own creation. The self carries with it always this horizon as a specific location, with substantive content—as, for example, a specifiable relation to the Holocaust, to slavery, to the *encuentro*, and so on—but whose content only exists in interpretation and in constant motion. The Holocaust is one dramatic example that exists as an aspect not only of every contemporary Jewish person's horizon but of every Christian European's. But there will be a difference in the way that these two groups are situated vis-à-vis this narrative: the one as knowing that he or she could have been the target of the Final Solution, and the other as knowing that this event occurred within the broad category of their culture. Each must react to or deal with this event in some way, but to say this does not presuppose any pre-given interpretation of the event or of its significance in forming a contemporary identity. There is even a vibrant debate over the degree of significance the Holocaust holds for Jewish identity today. But obviously, for some time to come, it will remain a central feature of the map of our collective Jewish and Gentile horizons.

In what sense are identities grouped then, if they are to be a meaningful political category, if not by mutual interests and shared experiences that must form each individual at least to some extent in the same way? Although meanings are made and remade, the "internal" agency of the individual to judge, to choose, or to act operates within and in relation to a specific horizon, and thus one is open to an indeterminacy but from a specifiable position. Recognizing the openness of identity and historical experience to interpretation must be tempered, however. There remains a certain amount of uniformity of experience within an identity group, though only in regard to a more or less small sector of their experience, for example, that sector involving being treated in the society as a certain identity, or having a common relationship to social power and specific historical events.

There is also an important epistemic implication of identity, which Mohanty describes as follows: "Social locations facilitate or inhibit knowledge by predisposing us to register and interpret information in certain ways. Our relation to social power produces forms of blindness just as it enables degrees of lucidity" (1997, 234). On this account, identity does not determine one's interpretation of the facts or constitute a fully formed perspective; rather, to use the hermeneutic terminology once again, identities operate as horizons from which certain aspects or layers of reality can be made visible. In stratified societies, differently identified individuals do not always have the same access to points of view or perceptual planes of observation. Two individuals may participate in the same event but have perceptual access to different aspects of that event. Social identity is relevant to epistemic judgment, then, not because identity determines judgment but because identity can in some instances yield access to perceptual facts that themselves may be relevant to the formulation of various knowledge claims or theoretical analyses. As Mohanty and others have also argued, social location can be correlated with certain highly specific forms of blindness as well as lucidity. This would make sense if we interpret his account as correlating social identity to a kind of access to perceptual facts: to claim that some perceptual facts are visible from some locations is correlatively to claim that they are hard to see from others. Social identity operates then as a rough and fallible but useful indicator of differences in perceptual access.

This kind of hermeneutic descriptive account of social identities is more true to lived experience and more helpful in illuminating their real epistemic and political implications. As a located opening out onto the world, different identities have no a priori conflict. Aspects of horizons are naturally shared across different positions, and no aspect comes with a stable ready-made set of political views. What is shared is having to address in some way, even if it is by flight, the historical situatedness and accompanying historical experiences of a given identity group to which one has some concrete attachment. Because of this, and because identities mark social position, the epistemic differences between identities are not best understood as correlated to differences of knowledge, since knowledge is always the product in part of background assumptions and values that are not always grouped by identity categories. Rather, the epistemic difference is in, so to speak, what one can see, from one's vantage point. What one can see underdetermines knowledge or the articulation of interests, but the correlation between possibilities of perception and identity mandates the necessity of taking identity into account in formulating decision-making bodies or knowledge-producing institutions. Such an idea is implicit in the concept of representative government.

The second assumption at work in the identity critique that I listed in the last section was the idea that social identity is inherently constraining on individual freedom because it is imposed from the outside. Judith Butler makes this point in *The Psychic Life of Power*: "Vulnerable to terms that one never made, one persists [i.e., continues as a subject] always, to some degree, through categories, names, terms, and classifications that mark a primary alienation in sociality" (1997, 28).

Western thought has developed two sharply conflicting lines of argument over the last 200 years. On the one hand, the Enlightenment calls on individuals to think for themselves, and holds that autonomy and thus the capacity of reason (which requires autonomy) necessitates that the individual be able to separate from all that is externally imposed in order to evaluate and consider these imposed ideas. To the extent that one has features that are dependent on others (in the way Butler describes, for example), this is necessarily a weakening of the self and a loss of freedom. On the other hand, since Hegel every major psychological account of the self has placed its dependence on the other at the center of self-formation. For Hegel, one needs the Other to recognize one's status as a self-directing subject in order to create the conditions for the self-directing activity; one's self-image is mediated through the self-other relation not only in terms of its substantive content but also in terms of the self as bare capacity. For Freud, the Other is internalized to become a central organizing principle for one's desire, one's needs, and one's life plans. Feminist and postcolonial theories have emphasized the deformations of the self in hostile environments. Thus, on the one hand freedom requires reason, which requires the ability to separate from the other, while on the other hand, the self is ineluctably dependent on the Other's interpellations. If both of these traditions are broadly correct, it would seem that we are doomed to unfreedom, because freedom is defined as precisely that which we cannot have. I will look at these traditions in some detail in the next chapter.

A hermeneutic account again has advantages here. The Other is internal to the self's substantive content, a part of its own horizon, and thus a part of its own identity. The mediations performed by individuals in processes of self-interpretation, the mediations by which individual experience comes to have specific meanings, are produced through a foreknowledge or historical a priori that is cultural, historical, politically situated, *and collective*. In this sense, it is less true to say that I am dependent on the Other—as if we are clearly distinguishable—than that the Other is a part of myself. Moreover, one's relation to this foreknowledge is not primarily one of negation; it makes possible the articulation of meanings and the formulation of judgment and action. One's relation is better characterized precisely as absorption, generation, and expansion, a building from rather than an imposition that curtails preferred possibilities.

Whether this fact about the self necessarily limits our capacity for reason brings us to the final assumption I listed, that the capacity of reason requires a transcendence of identity. One way to approach this would be to say that transcendence is simply impossible, and there is abundant evidence that because reasoning in all but deductive arguments (and even those have to start with a premise) involves *phronesis* or a judgment call that invokes background assumptions and values, identity is always operative in reasoning. The wholesale repudiation of identity attachments is often itself a form of tribalism under cover, as in Schlesinger's argument against multiculturalist "cults of ethnicity" on the grounds of Europe's unique cultural values. When Teddy Roosevelt painted a contrast between "Americanness" on the one hand, and polyglot hyphenated ethnic associations on the other, he failed to realize that his view of "Americanness" was just as ethnic as those he opposed.

However, the very notion that transcendence of identity is necessary for reason is itself a mistake. Elshtain argues that social identities are and should be private, even though they are obviously constructed largely through social relations. And she assumes that private identities cannot follow rules of civility or pursue public ends but are reduced to narrow self-interest group calculations. For Elshtain, the importance that Lieberman attaches to his identity might well render him a problematic political candidate.

But the reason why identity is argued to be in conflict with reason is because identity is conceptualized as coherent, uniform, and essentially singular, as if what it means to be Mexican American is a coherent set of attributes and dispositions shared by all members of the group and essentially closed or stable. If this were the case, and to the extent there are people who believe this to be the case and who act on that belief, there is indeed a conflict, since the closed nature of such an identity would close one off to the new possibilities that rational deliberation can make evident. But once one understands identity as horizon, an opening out, a point from which to see, there is no conflict. How could there be reason without sight, without a starting place, without some background from which critical questions are intelligible?

The mistake made by Richard Rorty and some others like him, who do accept the importance of cultural identity in setting out background for thought, is to think that because horizons can be mapped onto identities, we are bereft of communication across the expanse, doomed to incommensurable paradigms; in short, we will never be able to understand one another, and therefore we will never be able to resolve conflict through dialogue. This is simply a profound mischaracterization of culture and of identity, as if they were closed systems with no intersections. Of course there will always exist some common ground from which to chart a disagreement. Of course understanding across wide differences will never be complete, but of course it will always be partially possible. Moreover, given the dynamic nature of identity, existing gulfs are not likely to remain forever. The true route to understanding across difference is a literal movement of place, which will require a change of social institutions and structures.

I have endeavored to make a case in this chapter that there is yet a case to be made about the nature of identity and its political and epistemic implications. It is certainly not the case that the work we need to do is finished; there are numerous "authentic" problems of identity that need attending, but we don't need to overcome identity as much as to more deeply understand it.

Let me end with another example that illustrates the practical implications of my claim that the recognition of the political relevance of identities is *required* for, rather than opposed to, unity and effective class struggle. The attempt to form a Labor Party in the United States in the 1990s was heralded by many of us who maintain hopes in deconstructing the two-party bloc on U.S. electoral politics. But I decided not to work for the party for the following reason. The national leadership organization of the party was being organized exclusively through union membership. Thus, it would be composed only of representatives from unions.[11] This might appear to make sense for a party calling itself a Labor Party. But in reality, less than 20 percent of U.S. workers are organized, and a number of nonwhite workers do not see their union as the most reliable spokesperson for their needs. They may see the local NAACP chapter, their church, or other community organization based around a shared ethnic identity as more reliable and also as a place where they have more of a voice. By refusing to seat such groups at the top, the Labor Party was not effective in breaking from the traditional white dominance of the Labor movement. By refusing to recognize the salience of social identities like race and gender, it undermined the possibility of unity, and it weakened class struggle in the United States.

The Philosophical Critique

> The Other *looks* at me and as such he holds the secret of my being, he knows what I *am*. Thus the profound meaning of my being is outside of me, imprisoned in an absence. The Other has the advantage over me.
>
> Jean-Paul Sartre, *Being and Nothingness*

> Called by an injurious name, I come into social being, and because I have a certain narcissism that takes hold of any term that confers existence, I am led to embrace the terms that injure me because they constitute me socially. The self-colonizing trajectory of certain forms of identity politics are symptomatic of this paradoxical embrace of the injurious term.
>
> Judith Butler, *The Psychic Life of Power*

The political critique of identity has had a public impact beyond the academy, especially in regard to the concern with minority movements. But no less important has been the widespread trend away from identity in academic social theory and political philosophy. This philosophical critique, moreover, has in many ways grounded the political critique, though the relationship in reality is more one of mutual reenforcement.

Some philosophers express a worry that the very concept of identity presumes sameness and thus excludes difference, because the identity of a thing refers to its *haecceity* or unique, intrinsic essence. In modern philosophy, the concept of identity was thought to involve a conundrum, the discovery of which is credited to Leibniz, given that (a) to share an identity is to be indiscernible or to share every property, but (b) two entities that are thus indiscernible cannot be individuated. Thus, separate entities can never have a relationship of identity, since at the very least they will not share the same space-time coordinates.

However, this idea of identity as entailing indiscernibility is not the ordinary language understanding of identity used in relation to social groups, in which it is common to talk about national identity or ethnic identity even while one assumes that there are also differences between the individuals who might share such an identity as well as similarities that such individuals may share with those in another identity group. Identity in this sense is conceived as something which delimits a group, and thus something that each member of the group shares, but what this something is need not be based on the Aristotelian notion of a stable and inherent feature but could also be something that is socially and historically contextual. For example, individuals could come to share an identity on the basis of being subject to a certain kind of treatment. Another common approach, especially for ethnic, cultural, and religious identities, is to use ancestry as the criterion of identity, for example, the idea that all those with Jewish mothers count as Jews. But ancestry hardly yields a uniformity in political view, religious belief, or cultural practice. Even if one were to add self-identification to the criterion of Jewish identity, so as to leave out those with Jewish mothers who neither feel nor practice a relation to other Jews, there will still be a variety of interpretations of what Jewish identity means. Thus, the worry that identity *entails* an ahistorical essentialism or that it posits an absolute sameness seems to me to be the sort of worry Wittgenstein said philosophers develop when we let language go on holiday. It is based on a conflation of contextually based meanings and standards.[1]

But there is a more plausible worry about whether group categories of identity pose an inherent constraint on individuals, curtailing, for example, the variety of ways in which they might establish a meaningful life. If identities pose prima facie constraints on individuals, then one might indeed wonder at the reason for their construction in the first place, and why groups that have been systematically oppressed through the use of identity ascriptions would want to hold onto these identities.

Such questions bring us to the issue of the self, and its relationship to social identity. Is identity separable from the self, or can we make it so? Although there have been predictably voluminous debates over the nature of the self by philosophers the world over, there has been much less discussion about how the self is affected by social identities such as gender, ethnicity, or race. Certainly, Western philosophy's sustaining assumption has been that its domain covers only the universal and generalizable; particulars are left to the lowly sociologist. Nonetheless, the Western philosophical corpus has included many debates that have strong implications for a theory of social identity, and some of the more recent philosophical work (over the last 200 years) has addressed these implications directly.

In the last chapter I very quickly described the modern view of the self that motivates the current suspicion against identity, a view in which rationality increases the more one is able to obtain a critical distance from, and thus to objectify, one's cultural traditions. To be rational requires autonomy, and thus autonomy is not seen as a *possible* attribute that a self can sometimes have but *essential* to even having a human, as opposed to animal, sort of being. Social ascriptions of identity, cultural traditions that include beliefs and practices, unquestioned loyalties to communities, are therefore all in conflict with achieving a self in any full or meaningful sense. And so identity is inherently problematic, not just in some formulations, but in all. As we will see, however, there is much more than this notion of the necessity of autonomy for rationality involved in the philosophical critique. Also involved are particular conceptions of self-other relations, the nature of embodiment, the critique of ocularcentrism or vision-centered cognition, and more issues besides.

In order to understand the current aversion to cultural identity, then, one would need to retrace the development of the philosophical treatment of the self in modern, Western philosophy, a much larger task that I can accomplish here. Charles Taylor's *Sources of the Self* (1989) is undoubtedly the best recent attempt to do this, and I will begin with an overview of some of the main ideas in his philosophical history that relate to the questions of identity I am concerned with.[2] From there and from my own readings of Hegel, Sartre, and other key figures, I will develop a genealogy of the philosophical critique of identity, finding its more fundamental basis not actually in the Western concept of rationality but in the modern Western treatments of the Other developed in the context of the European colonialism. Finally, I will show how this legacy lives on today in some aspects of postmodern philosophy.

Taylor characterizes his project as an attempt at historical retrieval: to retrieve those forgotten or less well remembered aspects of modernity's thinking about the self such as, for example, modernity's critique of atomist notions of the self, notions that later grounded the ideologies of individualism. Taylor hopes to complicate our understanding of the modern period and thus save it from some of the distorted caricatures that are unfortunately abundant in critical postmodern social theory. Taylor also sets out to reveal the philosophical background or hermeneutic horizon that lies behind our contemporary universalist, or antiparticularist, moral intuitions. Because of his effort to go "behind the scenes," in effect, of contemporary beliefs about the self, and to uncover the founding presuppositions and historical basis of current ideas, Taylor's approach is ideally suited to understand the current critique of identity. But we can delimit our attention even further than Taylor's broad focus on the self to his discussion of the relationship between self and other, since, as the quotations used at the start of this chapter reveal, the problem of identity has been formulated as a problem of the individual self's relationship to group categories and therefore to public interpellation or recognition. I will argue that the treatment of self-other relations is actually fundamental to the concept of rationality and of autonomy that has been so central to the critique of identity. Thus we must begin with the question of rationality.

Substantive versus Procedural Rationality

One of Taylor's central claims is that rational deliberation over broadly moral aims (broad enough to encompass all kinds of claims about what makes life worth living) always occurs within a cultural and historical context that frames the inquiry, · produces the central questions, and provides the range of relevant evidence. It is in this sense that we should understand the claim that reason is culturally and historically embedded. What makes sense to us and thus what facts or views are actually operative or efficacious in processes of deliberation, always makes reference to the cultural moment, to our particular histories. The naturalism some believe to be at the root of our moral intuitions, inclining us against torture, for example, because it is experienced as distasteful, is compatible with this view as long as it acknowledges that moral intuitions *also* "involve claims, implicit or explicit, about the nature and status of human beings" (Taylor 1989, 5). Thus we distinguish between legitimate and illegitimate violence done to humans versus animals, and to various types of human beings, based on claims about who is made in God's image, what kinds of things have souls, and who has the rational capacity of self-determination and who does not. In this way, natural disinclinations can sometimes be overcome.

The claims about what counts as human and inviolable are developed through complex reasoning processes that involve our cultural traditions, which contribute to determine how we make qualitative judgments between, for example, the pain inflicted on a chicken in a processing plant and the distress of a hungry child or between the distress of a child and an adult. This does not mean that what we call reason actually isn't, as some postmoderns would have it. Taylor argues repeatedly throughout the book for his view that the postmodernist skepticism on morality and epistemology is a performative contradiction, since normative commitments are implied in the very critiques. On his view, an embedded reason—that is, a reason that is framed by, and thus dependent on, specific cultural and historical contextually produced concepts and assumptions—is still reason. But the broadest and most common type of reason—*phronesis*, or practical reasoning—always works through comparative judgments: arguing in defense of an account through showing its qualitative advantages over the previous account. And what counts as a qualitative advantage will refer to the horizon we are in at the moment. This is not simply an expression of need or desire or a game determined by force: rational deliberation operates on the basis of intelligible reasons, and the reasons are no less reasons because the conditions of their intelligibility involve a cultural locatedness.

Taylor's main target, or the view that he most wants to discredit, is the widely influential proceduralist approach to moral and political philosophy, an approach one finds across very divergent theoretical traditions. The proceduralist approach denies that reason has any cultural or historical content, and holds that procedures transcend their location because moral deliberation does not always have to presuppose metaphysical commitments about the nature of the self or, indeed, any substantive moral metacommitments, nor does scientific reasoning always entail ontological commitments about the universe. The proceduralist view, in other words, avoids the problem of cultural difference by portraying reason as having only formal rather than substantive content. The hermeneutic approach that Taylor adopts argues that the proceduralists are only fooling themselves. Rationality and moral agency require a framework of substantive commitments in the form of qualitative discriminations, and "stepping outside these limits would be tantamount to stepping outside what we would recognize as integral, that is, undamaged human personhood" (1989, 27):

> To be a full human agent, to be a person or self in the ordinary meaning, is to exist in a space defined by distinctions of worth. A self is a being for whom certain questions of categoric value have arisen, and received at least partial answers. Perhaps these have been given authoritatively by the culture more than they have been elaborated in the deliberation of the person concerned, but they are his in the sense that they are incorporated into his self-understanding, in some degree and fashion. My claim is that this is not just a contingent fact about human agents, but is essential to what we would understand and recognize as full, normal, human agency. (3)

Even the philosopher, who embodies the vanguard of rationality, is, as Hegel says, "a child of his time; so philosophy too is its own time apprehended in thoughts. It is just as absurd to fancy that a philosophy can transcend its contemporary world as it is to fancy that an individual can overleap his own age, jump over Rhodes" (Hegel 1975, 11).

It is important to note that Taylor's account provides counterpoint not only to the assumptions behind proceduralism concerning the nature and capacity of agency, but also to the inner/outer ontology that is so strong in modern cultures, or the belief that our thoughts, beliefs, and feelings are "inside" while objects we might consider and deliberate over are "outside" (Taylor 1989, 111ff.). What is considered inside is thought to be, and experienced as, interpretation free; we have direct, immediate knowledge of our internal state. Interpretation only enters in when we begin to perceive, categorize, and evaluate things outside of us. Following the Hegelian tradition, Taylor views this bifurcation as false and misleading, since what we feel inside of us, which *feels* as if it were unable to be any other way, is at least partly contingent on our horizon or framework, or that which is (supposedly) outside. Taylor then defines personal identity in relation to these frameworks: "My identity is defined by the commitments and identifications which provide the frame or horizon within which I can try to determine from case to case what is good, or valuable, or what ought to be done, or what I endorse or oppose. In other words, it is the horizon within which I am capable of taking a stand" (27).

I will return to this account of identity in the next chapter, and will argue that it is very useful as a starting place from which to understand raced and sexed identities in particular. The inner/outer ontology of the self will be especially relevant. In this chapter, however, my focus is the development of our current framework of substantive assumptions, and in particular that aspect of it that has to do with the value of disengagement and the assumed relationship between the capacity for disengagement on the one hand and human autonomy, self-governance, and dignity on the other.

Starting in ancient Europe, Taylor finds three sources of human dignity given in various accounts: power, self-sufficiency, and positive attention from others. Sometimes all three are operative, but they are given different amounts of value. The honor ethic that Plato criticized placed the highest value on the third source: positive attention from others. To achieve dignity through honor requires no deliberation on the part of the individual, and in particular no deliberation over what values he should pursue. As long as the individual seeking honor pursues those values valued by the society, he will attain dignity in this sense. Plato criticizes this form of dignity on the grounds that rational behavior requires that one gives *one's own* reasons for one's actions, but the man seeking honor above all else cannot do this.

However, Plato's ideal rational self is not the disengaged independent thinker of modernity. That concept comes much later and emerges from a radically different ontology. Plato's ideal rational self is, rather, he who can discern the nature and contours of the intrinsic good in the existing cosmic order. Plato is not here relying on an inner/outer bifurcation of the sort previously mentioned; for him, the relevant, intelligible oppositions are those between body and soul, material and immaterial, and eternal and changing (see Taylor 1989, 121). He neither relies on nor articulates a concept of an interior mental life of beliefs and feelings to which the individual alone has privileged access, as it were, or an image of the individual standing apart though surrounded by the objects of the world. For Plato, rationality is not essentially an inner process of deliberation because rationality is defined not via its procedure but via its content: he who sees the truth is rational, pure and simple. Thus, Plato's account of rationality is substantive rather than proceduralist.

A substantive account of rationality can sound very counterintuitive today, given the dominance of a proceduralist understanding of reason as a set of operations. But it is useful to note that the substantive view lingers on even in our own horizon of framing assumptions. Consider the insanity defense. A woman who kills her own children is almost always considered insane by the very act itself; in our society today, if a mother believes that she has the right to kill her children, that she ought to kill her children, then she is generally thought to be incapable of rationality. She may have deliberated about it for weeks, months, even years, written out the pros and cons, calculating their likely happiness to unhappiness quotient. But we will still call her irrational because of the *content* of her beliefs.

Plato has a substantive account of the rational self that has the consequence of affording less power to the individual to think whatever he likes and still be called rational. The individual must think a certain way, within at least some broad parameters, to be considered rational. Augustine's concept of the self is similar to Plato's in this one respect: for Augustine, the self is internally structured by God in such a way as to be capable of seeing the Good. Augustine was a pivotal figure for the West in inaugurating a conception of an interiority to the self, through the detailed self-examinations of his *Confessions*, but for Augustine this interiority of the self is determined by God not only in its set of capacities but also in its substantive knowledge. Again, such an account conceptualizes the self as less powerful, and less autonomous, than the modern self, and autonomy is in fact not only valued less but sometimes taken to be the sign of one's sinfulness and disorder.

Descartes's ideal rational self is different in just this way: it has the capacity to construct the order that it then will live by. The mechanistic universe beginning to emerge in modern Europe is emptied of intrinsic moral order. Taylor explains:

> Descartes' dualism of soul and body [is] strikingly different from Plato's. For Plato, I realize my true nature as a supersensible soul when I turn towards supersensible, eternal, immutable things. This turning will no doubt include my seeing and understanding the things which surround me as participating in the Ideas. For Descartes, in contrast, there is no such order of Ideas to turn to, and understanding physical reality in terms of such is precisely a paradigm example of the confusion between the soul and the material we must free ourselves from. Coming to a full realization of one's being as immaterial involves perceiving distinctly the ontological cleft between the two, and this involves grasping the world as mere extension. (1989, 145)

Where Plato's and Augustine's counsel might be read through contemporary eyes as moving toward opening oneself up to determination from the outside (although they do not have this concept of outside) in order to be "attuned" to the Good that orders the cosmos, Descartes's counsel in contrast is to objectify the world and to see it functionally. The Cartesian self is more like Adam in the Garden of Eden, naming the animals according to his own preference, than like Job bewailing his fate until he comes to accept its moral validity, no matter whether he can fully understand the ground of its validity. The difference involves an assumed relation of mastery between man and world.

Although not until Descartes do we have a self defined in terms of its ability to determine the good for itself, Taylor traces elements of the modern moral ideal of autonomy or of the disengaged self as based on a different kind of mastery: the ancient ideal of "mastery of self," found in both Plato and the Stoics. Mastery over the world was not to appear until the modern period and, not surprisingly, was coincident with Europe's new sense of itself after its conquest of the Americas, which is one reason one might take Taylor's account, as Dominick LaCapra criticizes, to be overly "celebratory" (see La Capra 1994, 186; see also Dussel 1995). In contrast with this concept of mastery of the world, mastery of self was the central criterion of moral virtue the Stoics believed to be worthy of citizens, and it consisted in the rational part of the self gaining mastery over the desiring self (Taylor 1989, 21). They believed desire to obscure one's ability to see the truth, and thus one's ability to be rational (which, remember, Plato defines as seeing the truth). But mastery of self also precludes mastery by another and thus here intersects with a more modern concept of autonomy. When one is mastered by another, one cannot know whether that other is operating on the basis of his own reason or from desire, and in a relationship of mastery, this criterion would not in any case be used to justify obedience. Thus, one cannot submit to another's domination if one wants to attain moral virtue when moral virtue is defined as the mastery of the rational self over the desiring self.

In the modern period this ethical motivation for autonomy is largely replaced by an epistemological one, however, as rationality comes to be redefined as disengagement rather than truthful belief. The ideal of autonomy becomes a cornerstone aspect of the scientific worldview's ideal of the "disengaged self, capable of objectifying not only the surrounding world but also his own emotions and inclinations, fears and compulsions" (Taylor 1989, 21). Those most likely to attain such disengagement were thought to be gentlemen of independent means, the males of the bourgeois and petit-bourgeois classes, who were thus not beholden to anyone for their livelihoods (see Shapin 1994).

Against the background of this framework, the aversion to cultural identity can be explained as a result of its conflict with reason: if people cannot disengage from their culture, even if this amounts only to an imaginative disengagement for the purposes of reflective critique, then they cannot gain the critical distance necessary for rational judgment, and thus even their allegiance to their culture cannot be rational. One's allegiance to one's cultural traditions may be based on the desire for honor in the sense of respect and acceptance from others, but this too is a motivation that Plato does not find honorable. The bottom line is that if one simply follows one's cultural traditions because they are what one knows and has grown up with, one cannot know that one is operating from reasons rather than from desires; the traditions of one's culture may have been arrived at rationally, or they may be irrational and based on desire. But if one makes an independent or autonomous judgment about the validity of one's cultural traditions, then even if one continues to embrace them, this is not *because* they are one's traditions, but because one finds them rational. For moderns in the West, rationality requires that we maintain no a priori attachment to, or even presumptive favor for, our substantive cultural identity.

Cartesian versus Hermeneutic Rationality

The story that Taylor tells presents us with two alternative ways to understand the relationship between cultural identity and the self, meaning the rational self, based on the two different accounts of rationality he develops. According to the view characteristic of modernism and initially formulated so clearly by Descartes, and the view that is still dominant today in much of political thought, one's cultural or social identity must be objectified and judged *before* a loyal attachment to it can be rational. If one grows up Catholic, never considers an alternative to being Catholic, and is never exposed to any alternatives, then, on this account, one's attachment to a Catholic way of life would not be rational.

But the second account of rationality that Taylor presents, the one that he calls a hermeneutic account, holds that such objectifications and disengagements cannot be requirements for rationality under all conditions. On this view, even the ideal of rational judgment borrows from or relies on previously held qualitative discriminations, such as, for example, that an examined life is more valuable than an unexamined life. It is possible to engage in some amount of self-reflection about one's framing assumptions of this sort, and to submit these assumptions to thoughtful examination, but the judging that is going on even in *this* process of examination requires the operation of qualitative discriminations or, in other words, a context within which the reasons one gives for one's conclusions will be intelligible as well as plausible. Even if one were to go through the procedure of examining a way of life, and were to develop reasons to defend or reject it, the reasons that one person will find effective as a defense will not be so to everyone.

For example, in U.S. society, it is extremely difficult for parents of almost any persuasion to comprehend why their sons or daughters might want to join a close-knit religious sect that has extensive behavioral rules and little substantive interaction or communication with the outside world, such as the Amish or the Hare Krishnas, members of the Waco community led by David Koresh, or other such groups. Unless one were to grow up in such a community, few parents could be made to understand the reasons their child might prefer such a life, no matter how much the child tried to explain it. Their child might give such reasons as "David Koresh is Christ resurrected" or "The Amish way of life is how God intended us to live," but these would be reasons that most contemporary parents could not accept or really comprehend as conceivable examples of rational belief on anyone's part. There would exist a gap of intelligibility between the reasons the child gives and what their parents can comprehend, in which case they might then opt to hire an agency that promised to kidnap their child and behaviorally modify his or her beliefs and desires. Without the possibility of intelligible communication, the parents might feel justified in the use of force in the belief that their child is acting irrationally. Structurally similar but secular cases might involve a child's declaration of homosexuality, or feminism, or communism, which could elicit similar responses from those parents for whom these represent fundamentally wrong ways of life.

Sometimes, familial relations can be held intact only by concealing certain things or agreeing never to discuss them, precisely because generational or other differences make it impossible to accommodate the political, sexual, religious, or other conflicts within one relational unit that understands itself to have a shared moral dimension or identity.

This example shows that all reasons cannot be transmitted across major differences in framing assumptions or value commitments. Before one could believe that a person might make a rational choice to enter a Waco-like cult or a closed society such as the Amish, one would need to previously hold, or to be open to holding, certain values that most Anglo-Americans in the United States find hard to understand: the value of community and having a well-ordered, morally and spiritually meaningful life over the value of individual freedom, autonomy, integrity, or self-determination, and perhaps even over rationality itself.

Of course, many U.S. parents *could* understand their child's desire to go into a convent or monastery, and thus to enter a life that is not very different from the ones we have been discussing. The parents themselves may not prefer such a life, and they may not even share the extensive religious beliefs that those entering religious orders generally have, and yet they may be able to recognize the choice as a rational one. But this is only because such a choice exists *within* the frames of intelligibility that most Christians assume, rather than outside. The strong value commitments many have to autonomy, individual freedom, integrity, and self-determination would in this case be sacrificed for the greater good of service to God and to the cause of religion. Here, a comparison of goods in which service to God is given the highest value is viewed as rational. But of course such a judgment will make sense only within a substantive frame of reference or horizon of intelligibility.

Those inclined toward the Cartesian account of rationality may be tempted to say here that if Taylor is right, this proves merely (and regrettably) that our capacity for rationality is seriously circumscribed rather than that we should redefine rationality. To the extent that cultural identity inculcates certain qualitative orientations that cannot be dislodged through disengaged rational deliberation, this simply proves once again that cultural identity is an obstacle to rationality. I think Taylor's response might be something like this: the all-important criterion of disengagement that the Cartesian considers absolutely inherent to the very concept of rationality has, itself, a history and a cultural location. And it is precisely this history that he traces in *Sources of the Self* in order to help us *disengage* from and reflect upon *that very belief*. The idea that the examined life is the highest good is itself a substantive cultural value, which then motivates the ideal of disengagement. Taylor himself supports the value of critical reflection and thus disengagement. But the disengagement that Taylor aims at is not an attempt to transcend our hermeneutic horizon but works, rather, through expanding our conceptual imagination such that reasons that were heretofore unintelligible become intelligible. This is the way the genealogical method of Nietzsche, Foucault, and, at least in this instance, Taylor works: to show that the route we took to arrive at one of our absolute commitments might have gone another way, that we might believe differently and still be rational, though perhaps we would no longer be who we are now.

Thus, on the hermeneutic account of rationality, just as on the Cartesian account, change and critique are possible. We are not caught ineluctably within the prison house of our current cultural traditions. But on the hermeneutic account, change does not happen through a complete disengagement from all value commitments and framing assumptions but through the ability to imagine life under the terms of more than one set. The bounds of our imaginative abilities are themselves affected by the particular horizon in which we live, which is perhaps why the concept of mastery over the world evolved in the colonial centers. But our hermeneutic horizon is not a tightly sealed, perfectly coherent, closed set, nor are framing assumptions or value commitments ever such that they can be made consistent with only one form of life. And the juxtaposition of alternative horizons, less easy to ignore with the increasing resistance to colonialism, has become a persistent feature of Western life with a similar effect as genealogical histories in extending our imaginative capabilities toward new possibilities.

Let me summarize this excursus on the relationship of rationality, cultural identity, and the self. Only if rationality is understood to be some sort of process that occurs ex nihilo will cultural identity prove to be an a priori obstacle to rationality—that is, only if rationality must perform its operations of judgment without benefit of any stable background belief. To the extent that rationality can be defined as comparative judgments made from within a given substantive horizon, and one allows that even the criteria of judgment itself—such as whether consistency is made more important than explanatory value, say—is constituted only within a given horizon, then cultural identity is no a priori threat to rationality. Consistency is not, after all, always the overriding concern; sometimes a theory has little internal consistency but great simplicity and predictive power, such as the theory of quantum mechanics; or in a case where one is looking for an appropriate partner for a friend, perfect consistency with their preferences and priorities is often less important than physical chemistry and emotional compatibility. If consistency itself cannot be considered an a priori necessity for adequacy or intelligibility or compatibility, then there is no decontextualized algorithm of rationality. Rational deliberation always occurs within a field of meanings and practices, and it is only within this field that the rational character of a deliberative judgment can itself be judged.

If rationality cannot be made sense of independently of a given horizon, then the dictate to completely disengage one's prior commitments can never be followed. I will return in the next chapter to the interesting puzzles about rationality that such a hermeneutic account might seem to engender, because this is clearly a critical motivation for the suspicion against identity. But a fuller discussion will require a fuller treatment of the concept of horizon.

The current philosophical discourses that distrust identity are not restricted to those that follow the Cartesian and, later, Kantian traditions in which autonomy, or complete disengagement, is a necessary condition of rationality. Butler and Foucault, for example, follow the Hegelian break with this tradition, which scoffs at the very possibility of a total disengagement from culture or history. And yet they end up with just as much of a suspicion against identity as the Cartesians, portraying it as alienating and oppressive and counterposed to freedom. It is this trajectory of theoretical development that I would now like to trace in more detail. I will begin with a review of the Hegelian critique of modernist notions of the self and of rationality, and then explore how some have united with this critique and yet still ended up sharing what amounts to the same view about identity as those from whom Hegel broke.

Identity in the Hegelian Tradition

Hegel provides an early formulation of the critique of the ideal of disengagement, essentially on the grounds that it cannot operate as a norm for a self that is necessarily dependent on the Other, whether that Other is understood individually, collectively, or structurally. For Hegel even the most well-developed self has this dependence. Self-knowledge, in fact, requires confirmation from the Other, on Hegel's view, from which it follows that both epistemic and moral forms of agency require a certain structure of possible intersubjective relationships.

This view represents a radical break within modernism. But what is especially interesting about Hegel in this regard is that his formulation of the relation between self and Other succeeds at both contradicting and confirming the value of autonomy. On the one hand, Hegel moves away from a self-enclosed conception of identity—of an identity that is fundamentally the product of an autogenous process—to a conception of identity as dependent on recognition, and this transformation inaugurated a new problematic of identity that I would argue is still framing Western thinking about the self. But on the other hand, Hegel also portrayed the need for recognition as leading inevitably to a death struggle between self and Other, as each seeks to receive recognition and resists reciprocation.

Before I turn to a brief look at Hegel's account of recognition and the social self, I think at least as important as this is another shift that Hegel initiated in our thinking about the self, and that is the shift toward becoming over being, toward understanding the self as a kind of process rather than as a substance in the early modern sense of an unchangeable essence. In *The Phenomenology of Spirit* Hegel attempts to describe the moments of the shifting, evolutionary trajectory of the self as it is manifested simultaneously in Geist and in the historical human self. Though Hegel imagines this process as exemplifying a discernible, developmental teleology, he makes an important departure from the previous pursuit of timeless substances. For Hegel, the appearance of discrete stable objects is epiphenomenal on a more fundamental metaphysical state of incessant change which inheres in all that is real. Geist itself is a process of advancing self-knowledge and self-realization; its essential nature is not to be found in an originary moment or final end state but in the very movement itself. Here he describes perfectibility, which is the key feature of Absolute Spirit and that toward which reality aims, as "something almost as undetermined as mutability in general; it is without aim and purpose and without a standard of change. The better, the more perfect toward which it is supposed to attain, is entirely undetermined" (1953, 68).

Hegel's famous description of the developmental trajectory of "man's" subjectivity, which moves through stages of consciousness in which the core is fundamentally altered through its negotiations and struggles with an external environment, is based on his claim that there exists an explicit parallelism between the unfolding and indeterminate circuit of activity that constitutes life in general and that which constitutes self-consciousness (Hegel 1977, 108). But the human self has the potential to participate *consciously* in this open-ended, undetermined formative process that constitutes the rational Real. Alexandre Kojève brilliantly captured Hegel's idea in this way: "The very being of this *I* will be becoming, and the universal form of this being will not be space, but time. . . . Thus, this *I* will be its own product" (Kojève 1969, 5).

Hegel thus makes self-determination parasitic upon a process ontology within an open dialectic. If man is to be self-determining, he cannot be the mere unfolding of an inner logic or expression of inherent tendencies, but must have the capacity to exist within a dynamic context that is itself indeterminate. In this move from being to becoming, Hegel moves radically away from Kant's theory of constitutive categories and even from Hume's psychologistic account of the self, and lays the groundwork for a more thorough concept of self-determination and of freedom. However, since self-determination comes at the cost of indeterminacy, Hegel's account also manifests a tremendous anxiety about the formlessness of our inner essence. To the extent that Hegel then goes on to give a larger role to the social in the formation of the self, the potential harm or interference of that social realm on the self is all the greater. We must remember that the self Hegel conceives as self-determining is not the individual, but the collective subject. Although this super-subject is not determined by things external to it, such as a Calvinistic God's eternal plan, individual subjects may well be highly determined by their social or inter-subjective context. Thus, the combination of the open-endedness or indeterminacy of subject formation with this external dependence has threatened the key concepts of individual autonomy and the myth of individual autogenesis and self-control still popular in the West today.

Anticipating Sartre, one might say, Hegel describes the process of development that self-consciousness undergoes as primarily one of negation, the negation of the independent object that confronts it, and he makes this a necessary step toward its own self-certainty and thus its being for-itself. The negation that inaugurates the process by which self-consciousness develops is only the initial moment toward the sublation of the Other, where sublation—what Richard Miller translates as "ambiguous supersession"—has a double meaning and is a kind of double gesture, involving both the repudiation of the Other and its absorption. Self-consciousness "must proceed to supercede the *other* independent being in order thereby to become certain of *itself* as the essential being; secondly, in so doing it proceeds to supercede its *own* self, for this other is itself" (Hegel 1977, 111, emphasis in original).

What is curious about this account is that, on the one hand, the self is presented as fundamentally social: an individual can achieve self-consciousness and thus become a subject and a moral agent only after recognition from the Other and thus, in a certain sense, after it has been absorbed by the social. "Self-consciousness exists in itself and for itself when, and by the fact that, it so exists for another; that is, it exists only in being acknowledged" (Hegel 1977, 111). This represents an important turn in Western metaphysical accounts of the self; to know oneself is no longer a solipsistic affair. "Each [self-consciousness] is for the other the middle term, through which each mediates itself with itself and unites with itself" (Hegel 1977, 112). Agency here is possible only in unison: "Action by one side only would be useless because what is to happen can only be brought about by both. Thus the action ... is indivisibly the action of one as well as of the other" (Hegel 1977, 112). But on the other hand, Hegel goes on to describe the attitude of self-consciousness as a negation and sublation of the other who *is, or has become, one's self.* The potential power that the Other may have to constitute the self, in that self-consciousness or subjectivity requires recognition, is thereby dissolved. As Allen Wood puts it, without any apparent qualms, Hegel's account holds that otherness "can be overcome" (Wood 1990, 45).

Thus, on Hegel's view, we are dependent on the other only to the extent that achieving our independence requires a certain process of engagement with the other and cannot be achieved by "Stoical aloofness" or an attempt to flee (Wood 1990, 45). The necessary process of engagement as Hegel describes it works ultimately to separate rather than to entwine. "Through the supersession," he tell us, self-consciousness "receives back its own self, because, by superseding *its* otherness, it again becomes equal to itself" (Hegel 1977, 111). In the "trial by death," which immediately follows the initial encounter with the other, "the two do not reciprocally give and receive one another back from each other consciously, but leave each other free only indifferently, like things" (114). The victor becomes the lord, a position precisely defined by making the other "inessential" to itself. Thus, Hegel's model of the genealogy of the self is a model of only temporary engagement with the aim of separation and an overcoming of dependence through achieving domination. As Mitchell Aboulafia says, "Hegel's self-consciousness ... attempt[s] to use the strategy of negating that which is other in order to deny the intrusion of otherness" (1986, 109). The presence of the other is the occasion or prompt of the development of self-consciousness; it is not its ground nor does it make a substantive contribution to the content of one's self. Hegel seems clearly anxious to avoid such an outcome: the dependence of self-consciousness on the other is dissolved almost immediately after it is acknowledged.[3]

Relational Accounts of the Self

This characterization of self-other relations as merely a kind of prompt for self-actualization is manifested in several influential and contemporary relational accounts of the self, and seems to be the main way in which the self's dependency on the Other is explained in contemporary social theory. I want to take a close look at it here because it may well seem to promise a more substantive account of self-other relations than the typical modernist individualist model. But it too reveals the tendency we saw in Hegel to immediately cordon off the power of the other over the self as quickly as it is acknowledged.

For example, in Ricoeur's recent book *Oneself as Another,* as well as in the work of feminist philosophers Lorraine Code and Susan Brison, and in the pragmatic traditions of thinking about the self, as developed (differently) in Peirce and in Mead, the self is presented as a narrative which is produced through a reflexive movement that can only be performed in interaction with another (see Ricoeur 1992, esp. chaps. 5 and 6; Code 1995; Brison 1997; Colapietro 1989; Mead 1934 and

1982; and Aboulafia 1986). Thus, the Other is necessary not to provide an accurate or confirming reflection of the self, or as someone whose recognition can yield true information about the self that it cannot obtain by any other means, but as the mere stage, in effect, or prompt by which the self's *own* reflective narratives can be produced. In the presence of the Other, one perceives oneself as an object for the Other, and having gained this perspective one can then go on to engage in the narrativizing or meaning-making activity of self-constitution. To the extent that one can be said to be constituted by the Other on this account, the constituting process is more formal or procedural than substantive. What the Other contributes is the initiation of a process the self engages in essentially alone rather than the substantive recognition of who one is.

Susan Brison and Lorraine Code have independently made arguments in favor of intersubjective, rhetorical selves that come into existence through dialogic communities (Code 1995; Brison 1997, 2002). Code argues that "persons are essentially 'second persons' who realize their 'personhood' in addressing one another as 'you' "(183). Brison argues that autonomy is a "function of dependence on others" (1997, 28) but only because "In order to construct self-narratives...we need not only the words with which to tell our stories but also an audience able and willing to hear us and to understand our words as we intend them" (21). Thus in each case, the Other's role is limited to what pop psychologists would call "effective listening" or the ability to elicit self-narratives and confirm their meaningfulness. The Other is not the source of our substantive self-knowledge.

The thrust of Brison's and Code's feminist revision of traditional philosophical accounts is to argue that the Other is necessary rather than expendable to a full self, and Brison makes an especially powerful argument that the dependence on the Other is vital to autonomy rather than contradictory with it. These are persuasive and important arguments with which I agree; my concern here is to argue against a view that would see this as the only role the Other plays in the self. It is unclear whether Code or Brison restricts the role of the Other in this way, but they don't discuss further ways in which the Other figures into the self.

Ricoeur's account might on the face of it seem stronger than this; his title, after all, is *Oneself as Another*, not *Oneself through the Other*. But it is essentially a rhetorical account of the self that he builds up through some selective borrowing from Aristotle, Dilthey, Parfit, and others. Ricoeur's argument for the rhetorical account of the self is, briefly, this: human action is a form of subjective practice involving a level of organization that gives it a "prenarrative quality" or "narrative prefiguration" (1992, 155–57). To bring this prenarrative condition into narrativity requires a higher level of subjective ordering given to one's sequence of actions, and this in turn requires the development of meaning-attributions such as might be given in a "life plan" or the "narrative unity of a life." One's life plan is mobile and changeable through the ongoing consideration of various ideals as well as the advantages and disadvantages of particular choices (1992, 157–58). The process of consideration always involves an external orientation because the act of narrativizing itself inherently brings one to view oneself as an "other" or objectivized self as seen from the outside. Meaningfulness can be achieved only in regard to a unitary conception of a life, that is, of a life that has an order or organization and is not a random sequence. Though actions are imbued with subjectivity, as it were, from the inside or lived experience of them, true meaningfulness is not possible if one stays only in this first-person orientation toward oneself and one's experiences.

Ricoeur likens identity to character, or that set of features and dispositions by which the Other knows me and which he comes to expect and to depend upon. But the "narrative constructs the identity of the character, what can be called his or her narrative identity, in constructing that of the story told. It is the identity of the story that makes the identity of the character" (1992, 147–48). Thus, otherness enters only as the perspective required for a development of identity; in this sense Ricoeur's title presents the Other as a mere imaginative extension of myself. Indeed, this allows him to read even Descartes's account of the self as a narrative account, wherein Descartes imagines God as the Other who determines the certainty of his own cogito (1992, 8–9). From within his own subjective orientation, "the 'I' of the cogito is Sisyphus condemned, . . . fighting the slope of doubt" (1992, 9). From the perspective of God, the idea of myself gains certainty and permanence, that is, the order and stability that only narrative can provide. So on this account, one does not even need a real, material Other in order to have an identity or to develop fully one's self; one can but imagine the Other in order for the process to work.

Hegel's treatment of the self/Other relation in *The Phenomenology of Spirit* prefigures a rhetorical account like Ricoeur's insofar as he restricts the importance of the Other to a temporary engagement. He neither conceptualizes an ongoing interdependence nor privileges in any way the (actual) Other's opinion of one's self. The Other is required to provide confirmation for our beliefs, before we can name them as knowledge; as Elliot Jurist reminds us, "it is important to understand that the concept of 'recognition,' introduced in the Self-Consciousness chapter, is itself a form of cognition" (2002, 23). But the Other's role in making possible one's knowledge of oneself is quickly overcome and dispensed with through the death struggle. However, the *Phenomenology* is arguably an immature work: it was written early in Hegel's career and very quickly, without much revision, and famously completed on the very eve of Napoleon's invasion of Jena. It is not a work of political philosophy as much as a phenomenology of knowledge and of philosophical history, despite the fact that it contains moments of radical political tendencies and insight.

In Hegel's mature political philosophy and ethical theory there emerges a different and arguably better account of intersubjective relations that, in fact, "shreds . . . the subjectivistic, atomistic, and moralistic foundations of modern liberalism" and promotes "communitarian principles," as Wood puts it (1990, 258). Hegel at this stage develops the idea that individual self-actualization is best maximized through collective institutions and the pursuit of shared goals, a clearly more robust account of interdependence than the one he gives in the *Phenomenology*: "Universal self-consciousness is the affirmative knowing of oneself in another self, so that each self has *absolute self-sufficiency* as free individuality; . . . each is thus universal [self-consciousness] and objective, and has real universality as reciprocity, in such a way that it knows itself as recognized in the free other, and knows this other insofar as it recognizes it and knows it as free" (1971, paragraph 436, quoted in Wood 1990, 89).

Only in this sphere of reciprocal relations with others does one become a moral subject or a subject with moral agency; only insofar as one is constituted by the Other does one acquire specific social identities, both objectively and subjectively, on the basis of which collective interests (i.e., the universal) that motivate rational action and judgment can even be developed.

This is much more robust than the position in the *Phenomenology* that self-consciousness is produced by a negation or an overcoming of the Other's otherness. And the role of the Other is certainly stronger here than in the narrative account that portrays the Other as a mere prompt for the self's own self-constitution. In the *Philosophy of Right*, the otherness of the Other is to be neither negated nor feared. It is my relations with specific others that constitute my social identity as mother, citizen, worker; these are objective and not merely the product of internal narra-tivizing or meaning-making. Within collective institutions in which my social identity is manifest, I have interests and can operate as a rational and moral agent. And freedom of action and of decisions is not counterposed to the social but made possible by it:

> This subjective or "moral" freedom is what a European especially calls freedom. In virtue of the right thereto a man must possess a personal knowledge of the distinction between good and evil in general: ethical and religious principles shall not merely lay their claim on him as external laws and precepts of authority to be obeyed, but have their assent, recognition, and even justification in his heart, sentiment, conscience, intelligence, etc. (Hegel 1971, 249)

This returns us to Taylor's claim that agency and rationality operate through the making of qualitative distinctions that are internal to the self but are historically and culturally bound. It is interesting to note also that Hegel locates this positive ac-count of freedom as "European," despite its outright opposition to the liberal Eu-ropean tradition that viewed the self as completely independent.

Thus, in his mature work Hegel begins to displace the classical liberal core/periphery model of the self with a more holistic model in which the self's very internal capacities are preconditioned by external relations. Consciousness itself becomes an emergent entity of a social and historical process rather than a kind of presocial thinking substance that could conceivably exist entirely on its own (e.g., as a brain in a vat). The locus of agency, in particular, is not simply internal to the self. Given Hegel's other views about the importance of cultural location and historical moment in the particular formulations of ideas—political and otherwise—the self's dependence on the Other and on collective institutions would suggest that under-standing self-formation will require understanding it in a cultural and historical context. In my view, Hegel's account of the self as open-ended, dependent on the Other, and contextually grounded would be an excellent place to start a serious reflection about identity as well, and I will pursue this in chapter 4.

Psychoanalysis

Despite the positive characterization of self/other relations in Hegel's mature work, his influential legacy contains both the original claim of a constitutive self/Other relation but also manifests an anxiety about this very dependence and the integration of the self with the Other. The chapter of the *Phenomenology of Spirit* on lordship and bondage has surely been one of his most influential, if not the most, in his entire corpus. As I intend to show, this double gesture of acknowledgment/anxiety about our dependence on the Other can be traced out through subsequent developments in Western thought. What is also clear is that Hegel's fear of otherness has had a stronger influence than his subsequent embrace of the holistic model of the self, at least outside of Marxism.

There are several traditions of social theory since Hegel that have taken as one of their founding premises the idea of intersubjective interdependence. Two of the most influential are psychoanalysis and post-Husserlian phenomenology. Marxism also begins with a notion of the individual as constituted through collective praxis, but most of the classical Marxist tradition neglected intrapsychic dynamics (the main exception is Marx's "On the Jewish Question," but this essay still discusses identity primarily in the context of public political discourse). Only the theorists who attempted to creatively fuse Marxism with psychoanalysis or phenomenology addressed self/other relations in any substantive detail, such as the Frankfurt School and the Marxist existentialists, but since these are working heavily in the psychoanalytic and phenomenological traditions I would group them accordingly under those rubrics.

I will divide the post-Husserlian phenomenological treatment of the social self into two subtraditions, one that views intersubjective interdependence as tantamount to inescapable oppression, and another that views it in a more positive light. My own account of social identity will be heavily based on this more positive side of the phenomenological work, and I will critique the negative account in this chapter. But first, I have a few remarks to make on the psychoanalytic tradition, which, although it too has multiple strains, has overwhelmingly portrayed the self as recoiling from its dependence on the Other with various forms of psychopathologies.

In classical psychoanalysis, the Other is not merely the prompt for the process of self-constitution, but also provides much of the content of the self's interior, substantive life. Freud offers what is in some respects an expansion of Hegel's account of self/Other dependency, but Freud emphasizes the individual or microlevel process and avoids presuming the inevitability of a higher synthesis or a sublation or, indeed, any necessary outcome. The ego develops through negotiations between multiple, conflicting inner drives on the one hand and the outpouring of stimuli from the external world on the other (Freud 1995, 1962). The self or subsequent identity which develops through this process contains sedimented features that are in some sense internal, but Freud does not take these features to be intrinsic, presocial, or ontologically self-sufficient. Rather, he portrays them as generated through interpersonal interaction, especially during infancy.

The central constituting Other for psychoanalysis has always been the mother, despite the power of the phallic father. It is the mother with whom the child first experiences a self/other relationship, who is first recognized in her "otherness," whom the self is completely dependent on in every sense, and who, because of this felt dependence and vulnerability, elicits the negative aggression Hegel represented as a desire for the death of the other. Psychoanalysts noted that the human infant is, much more so than all other animals, helpless at birth, totally dependent on the mother, and that it initially does not even recognize its separation from the mother's body. When it is finally forced to acknowledge this separation, it recoils with a terrible anguish and anxiety manifested in a split self, a self that cannot simultaneously accept its dependence and its separation. The child responds through processes of identification, object-cathexis, and introjection, all involving an internalization of the Other.

The self cannot then develop a true image of wholeness, or of coherent identity, which both Freud and Lacan assume to be an identity that is corporeally autonomous, self-standing, and without fluidity or flux. The mirror image of the self is what it wants, a third-person perspective of wholeness and separation, but this is impossible to maintain from the internal perspective. Identity is then broken down, ruptured from reality through its process of imagistic introjection of the m/other and the external world into itself in the form of its phantasmatic interior life. The wholeness of identity can only be achieved by internalizing the Other who can see the self in its static image of wholeness, so this Other's viewpoint must be incorporated and then controlled. Our self-image is necessarily produced via our projection of how we are seen by others.

Psychoanalysis thus portrays the subject as projecting his or her own meanings onto external Others, objects, and events, rather than merely reflecting imposed meanings. One tries to maintain the illusion that one is not in fact dependent on the Other, and this can again take the form of incorporating the necessary Other into the self, seeing it not as Other but simply as one's self, which is an attempt to create an illusion of independence or self-sufficiency. In actuality, the self can maintain a self-image only through mediation by the Other, but in phantasmatic or imaginary life, one attempts to control this self-image by incorporating the Other on which it depends into the self, as if it is a mere part of oneself. Throughout one's life, imaginary figurations of those early Others will continue to provide the protagonists for one's psychic life, the internal Others whose perspective on the self is necessary for it to have any sense of calm. But these internal Others are really mere projections based on Others and events that the self has experienced in early childhood, though only as these experiences are filtered through the self's psychic fantasies. The bottom line is that self-other relations with reciprocating acknowledgment and mutually supportive freedom are essentially impossible; hence the persistent charge of fatalism that has continued to dog psychoanalytic approaches to social theory. Against such criticisms, some seem to merely present this fatalistic account as "realistic," as one that must be faced up to if one is rigorous, without ever considering the possible cultural and historical locatedness of such a political orientation to the world.

Despite his theory's primary base in individual family dynamics, Freud used psychoanalysis to explain some macro social tendencies, notably in *Totem and Taboo*. But as Anthony Storr puts it, Freud was writing "in the era of 'armchair' anthropology," when Eurocentric interpretive schemas were rarely put to an empirical test and certainly were never made open to external critique by the "natives" (1989, 84). Despite this, what is interesting about this portion of his work is the strength of Freud's confidence in his claim that civilization constitutes a major repression of the natural drives or tendencies of the self. Here we can see an echo of

Hegel's double gesture, in that Freud both makes dependence on the Other inescapable and yet views that inescapability with great consternation. For Freud, civilization, or the forcible accommodation of individual desires to social rules, is both a positive and a negative. The difference between Freud and Hegel is that Freud counsels us to desire our own repression; he was no fan of the unchecked drives of the libido, unlike some of his recent French followers for whom these represent a space of freedom and subversive tendencies that can lead to revolution or at least *jouissance*. Freud was no revolutionary, and distinguished "primitive" and "civilized" cultures precisely in relation to their degree of repression. Although Freud's analysis was completely wrong here, for example in his characterization of non-Western cultures as less repressed than Western cultures, what is important to note is that Freud equated the individual's inculcation in a social domain with repression.

The equation between civilization and repression has never been left behind in future developments of psychoanalysis, with the sole exception of some feminist work (notably Kristeva). Lacan's linguistic development of psychoanalysis had the effect of integrating wider cultural and historical forces into the processes in which the self is generated primarily through his emphasis on the importance of language. But the bearer of language, who brings to the process of infantile ego-formation these wider cultural elements, is the father, whom Lacan equates with the law of prohibition, the threat of castration, and the check on the unbridled flux of drives that constitute mother/child relations. Feminists such as Kristeva have taken up precisely the mother/child relationship as a possible resource for beginning to rethink self/ other relations in a nondominating way, but they have had to do theoretical somersaults to overcome the tendencies in all Freudian-based theory to conceptualize self/other relations as either violently repressive (through the father) or identity-obliterating and smothering (through the mother) (see esp. Kristeva 1984, 1986).

The Frankfurt School theorists also extended the Freudian account of the unconscious and of the subject-in-process in order to describe and explain collective, cultural phenomena, but their primary use of it was precisely to seek explanations for the desire for authoritarianism that they witnessed in Germany, Spain, and Italy (Jay 1973; Adorno and Horkheimer 1987; Horkheimer 1972). Early on, however, some of the members, most notably Erich Fromm, were critical of Freud's account of the death drive, and the importance he attached to it in the formation of society, as being too biologistic and determinist (Jay 1973, 92). In effect, their critique was that Freud dehistoricized social relations and narrowed the possibilities of social transformation. In the spirit of this, Marcuse took up the concepts of eros and pre-oedipal sexuality as possible sources for new and positive relations between subjects, not based on the repressive tendencies of the death drive but on the desire to "merge and expand" in the drive toward life and experience (Marcuse 1969a, 1969b). Marcuse's conception of this utopia, however, is open to the critique that although he holds out the possibility of positive forms of intersubjective relations, his portrayal of these relations mirrored the "free love" ideology of the 1960s, which were hardly based on mutual recognition and accountability to others and in fact generally resulted in the denial of full sexual subjectivity to women. Women who resisted "merging" whenever and wherever they were asked were labeled uptight, frigid, and politically conservative. Thus, whether one emphasized the eros or thanatos elements of Freudianism, it seemed that truly reciprocal, accountable, and supportive self-other relations could not be reached.

In one of the most interesting recent psychoanalytic accounts of intersubjectivity, Teresa Brennan develops an analysis based on a foundational fact about the subject: that its ego receives its identity from the other (1992, 1993). Only the Other can give a reified portrait of the self's identity as not only whole but as fixed, with a stability and continuity the self can never truly achieve. The role of the other, then, is to provide "an image which remains still or constant in relation to the movement of life" (1993, xii). Brennan argues that we are inclined toward the other's image of ourselves because, "psychically, we need these fixed points" but, she believes, "they also hold us back" (1993, xii). Brennan's theory views identity similar to Butler, whose views we will discuss shortly, in that, for her as for Butler, identity is a social necessity that is also a social pathology, and, moreover, that although identities are necessary, they are always inaccurate representations.

In a useful departure from this tradition, however, and one that factors in its social location, Brennan diagnoses the current pathology of Western consciousness as the foundational fantasy of absolute autonomy, the very attempt to control one's environment both physically and psychically. This is a pathology that Butler's work seems to exhibit in the sense that it is the desire for such autonomy that structures and motivates her critique of social identities; they are imposed on the individual, necessarily escaping our control, and thus constitute repression in her view. By contrast, Brennan, rather than pining for this impossible autonomy, analyses the source of the pathological desire for it and historicizes these dynamics within very specific material conditions.

Brennan also suggests an expanded sphere of application for this theory that follows the Frankfurt School move from interfamilial dynamic to structural social explanation. She suggests that the psychical need for fixed points of reference that will allow us to maintain a sense of individual identity also usefully explains the current fanatical pursuit of commodities, which, as material entities, can serve as the fixed reference points even the other cannot provide. In new, modern, technologically wondrous or simply luxurious commodities, we can see our selves reflected back as if we now have the attributes we impute to them. But here, Brennan notes that the dangers of this process for individual agency are powerful indeed, since we are investing not the intersubjective collectivity but the fetish with the power to constitute selves. As fetish, commodities are far less susceptible to openness or transformation than intersubjective negotiations that operate directly, without mediation through a reified substance.

Overall, then, psychoanalytic theories about the formation of identity offered a significant challenge to previous accounts of a rational, free, and self-determining subject. Freud knew he was overturning the illusionary metaphysical foundations of bourgeois society, and, on his first trip to the United States to introduce his theories, he registered surprise at his audience's positive response, remarking to Jung, "They don't realize we're bringing them the plague" (quoted in Grosz 1990, 11). Even if the unconscious is to some extent the sedimentation of my own projections, it operates on my lived experience and behavior in such a way that I have no direct control over it. After Freud, the liberal, rational, essentially independent self was no more.

But Freud and Lacan were no more happy about the loss of this self than their bourgeois critics. In losing its autonomy and its self-control, the self lost its freedom, in their view, hearkening back to the ancient view that we are free when we act on the basis of our *reasons* rather than on the basis of our *desires*. Thus the Freudian tradition consigns us to determinism, and the more *social* directions in which some have taken psychoanalysis has often simply exacerbated this tendency toward determinism in the Freudian model. If the individual projects meanings onto relational objects and events, something like free will seems still compatible with such an account. But what sense of free will could be consistent with a collective process of projection or a collective unconscious? And what account of individual agency could possibly be efficacious in a subjectivation process dominated by the external and by macro social structures like commodity fetishism? The problem of determinism has thus loomed large in theoretical debates over the self in the twentieth century, creating various positions both within and between structuralism, Marxism, and existentialism, and inspiring new free will debates in Anglo-American philosophy. Earlier, the problem of "free will" had been primarily a theological concern, but in the last century it became reformulated within the domain of the social and psychological sciences.

The most radical alternative to this determinism was developed in the wing of post-Husserlian phenomenology that developed into what became known as existentialism. Existentialism worked better than the classical liberal accounts of the self to thwart the determinist tide because it went a long way toward acknowledging the power of the other and the desire of the self for an illusory fixity and stability. The self imagined by existentialism was not an essentially rational being; nor could it boast of total self-knowledge. These acknowledgments made existentialism a more plausible theory than classical liberalism, especially in light of the debacle of the European-based world wars that strained credulity in regard to rationalist models. In the next section, I explore the most influential and extreme of the existentialist theorists, Jean-Paul Sartre. I shall argue that his early model of self-other relations, despite the fact that it has received widespread criticism since the 1960s and was revised by Sartre himself in later work, is nonetheless precisely exemplary of the anxiety Hegel expressed in 1806, an anxiety which has in no way left Western thought.

Sartre's Solution to the Other

Sartre's account of the self in his early work, though enormously at odds in different respects with both Hegel's and Freud's, is also continuous with the Hegelian tradition in that he acknowledges the Other's power to give or withhold recognition and even characterizes the interrelationship of self and Other as a kind of death struggle. Sartre's early work is famous for its defense of radical freedom, but even here he recognizes that the self must operate within a situation that constrains the scope of its possible choices, and that one of the most important of these constraints involves the look of the Other and the subsequent felt alienation of the self. The only limits he acknowledges on freedom come from our facticity—our mortality and our inability to repudiate our freedom—and from our being-for-others, that is, on the meaning and valuation of one's self within domains of projection configured by the Other. Thus, one of the most important aspects of human existence is the look of the Other and the subsequent alienation of one's own self by the Other, who in effect has a privileged perspective over certain truths about one's self.

However, Sartre developed an ingenuous answer to this problem of the Other's power. In his ontology of conscious existence (that is, the for-itself), Sartre sharply separated the "real" self—which is simply the ability to nihilate the given—from the ego or more substantive self, which consists of the historical sedimentation of states through which we have built up a substantive self and by which we would ordinarily identify a specific individual. (In this, he is certainly following in the Cartesian tradition, or reviving that tradition from where Hegel had undermined it, in terms of minimizing the self to its capacity for thought). That is, in one sense for Sartre the self is a mere capacity to negate or go beyond whatever is presented to consciousness, including the given material environment, social context, and one's own individual history. The substantive self or ego is formed through such acts of nihilating the given. But the essential feature of *être-pour-soi*, that which thankfully distinguishes it from the unfree, inert *être-en-soi* but which also causes all of its existential difficulties, is its absolute freedom to negate the given.

Thus, against Freud, Sartre erects an impenetrable border between the substantive self or ego, which consists of the pattern of one's past choices, and the core capacity of the for-itself to nihilate the given. This distinction allows Sartre to hold onto a strong version of agency while recognizing the facticity of our unchosen situations, since the capacity to negate remains unaffected by the substantive self and even by its particular social environment.

In Sartre's ontology, then, what we would call identity is positioned outside the real self. "But what *are we* then," he asks, "if we have the constant obligation to make ourselves what we are, if our mode of being is having the obligation to be what we are?" (1956, 101). Identity must be a feature of the ego, which is coextensive with one's past, or in its public manifestation identity is a feature of one's situation, which imposes limited and often oppressive categories and is subject to a total negation. It is bad faith—a kind of moral failing motivated ultimately by cowardice—if we conflate our real selves with our identity or our publicly interpellated self. "It is not that I do not wish to be this person or that I want this person to be different. But rather . . . [i]t is a 'representation' for others and for myself, which means that I can be he only in *representation*. But if I represent myself as him, I am not he; I am separated from him as the object from the subject" (1956, 103, emphasis in original).

What I want to highlight here is that the distinction Sartre draws between identity and the for-itself allows Sartre to hold, in effect, the Other at bay, such that the recognition by the Other vital to the development of subjectivity has purchase only on the ego or past self, and not on the real or core self. Sartre believed that the Other knows me in a way I cannot know myself, and this view, as much as Hegel's, acknowledges a critical and unavoidable dependence on others. However, by separating the for-itself from the ego or substantive self, the power that the Other has over me is deflated. The Other knows only the object that I act to represent, but I can negate this at will. Thus the Other is not in a position to know me as subject, or to constitute *me*, in the sense of my fundamental project which aims toward future choices, but only that past self from which I am already separated. "For man to put a particular existent out of circuit is to put himself out of circuit in relation to that existent. In this case he is not subject to it; he is out of reach; it can not act on him, for he has retired *beyond a nothingness*" (1956, 60).

As in Hegel's *Phenomenology*, the defining activity of the for-itself, and the criterion of differentiation between the for-itself and the in-itself in Sartre's ontology, is the ability to negate, to destroy, to change, and to imagine what is not, capacities that constitute the *negatités*. Sartre claims that the essential character of the for-itself is to be remote-from-itself (1956, 55), and he develops a transcendental argument to prove that the for-itself "must be able to put himself *outside of* being, and by the same stroke weaken the structure of the being of being" (59).

It is striking that there is no mention of absorption, augmentation, expansion, or generation as other modes of relating to the given with equal ontological significance in the structure of the for-itself. In this early account, Sartre provides no theoretical description for the manner in which individuals are augmented in positive ways by their intersubjective interactions, or of the nondamaging ways in which the self absorbs the other, and although in his later work he acknowledges more fully the boundedness of our choices by real situations and the interiorization within the self of its intersubjective environment, he still portrays these without positive value.

What can account for this valuation of the ability to negate and separate over the fact of our constitutive connections? The overwhelming individualism of Sartre's early work certainly reminds one of the modernist predisposition toward the private and away from the social, understood as if these were not mutually constitutive. That which is given to me, which by definition is not something I myself have made, must be challenged, thwarted, and rebuffed precisely in order to establish my own reflective consciousness, my own power. "Man's *relation* to being is that he can modify it" (1956, 59–60). Without that ability, "man," as "Man," does not exist.

Although Sartre's individualism and modernism have been widely repudiated, it is this sort of ontology of the self, in its broad strokes, that is presupposed in the philosophical and political critiques of identity that take it to be an a priori political danger and a metaphysical mistake. These critiques are suspicious of identities because they involve the individual in social categories, which are understood to be outside the core self, to be public, imposed, and never a wholly fair or adequate representation. It is this ontology that makes all substantive representations of the self inadequate and even equates the very attempt to represent with the attempt to oppress. The excess that escapes all representation is, fundamentally, one's real self, one's capacity to negate, and the seat of purposeful action and choice. It is only the excess that is undetermined by external forces and therefore free, uncontainable, indeterminate, too fluid to be characterized in substantive terms. The excess is called an "excess" precisely because it is transcendent of identity. But the idea of transcending one's identity, of never being fully contained within it, returns us to a Sartrian for-itself that is itself defined as transcendence.

Thus, from Hegel's inaugurating moment of recognizing the constitutive power of recognition itself, of bringing the Other center stage into the formation of the self, Western philosophy has struggled with this alien internal presence, has struggled to find the means to offset its power of determination. The Other, from Hegel to Althusser to Foucault, is accorded the power to recognize, to name, even to constitute one's identity. This is why the look of the Other produces nausea and even terror, as our own capacity of determination drains away in Sartre's famous metaphor. In the extreme valuation accorded to negation by this account, in which the self that resists and is free is only the self who negates, it is as if even contemporary philosophers continue to desire the ontological self-sufficiency Hegel imagines in the following description of how self-consciousness tries to present itself in the moment before the death struggle: "The presentation of itself, however, as pure abstraction of self-consciousness consists in showing itself as the pure negation of its objective mode, or in showing that it is not attached to any specific *existence*, not to the individuality common to existence as such, that it is not attached to life" (1877, 113). Hegel, however, was himself under no illusions that this is either possible or truly desirable. Sartre, Derrida, Butler, and Foucault, however, as I shall argue, seem to express only Hegel's longing for a self of pure negation rather than his more mature acceptance of the Other within the self.

Although I take issue with many aspects of this account, as I shall develop in the following chapter, I do not take issue with the potency of the Other's recognition, or of the ways in which this can sometimes be experienced as a threat that reaches to the very core of the self. We need, however, a material and historical accounting of *when* the look of the Other poses a threat rather than an existential universalizing of this threat to every self/other relationship, and we need an account that can take note of the real differences in the extent and manner of the threat. For example, as Lewis Gordon has argued, racism's attempt to constrain, imprison, and deny nonwhite subjectivity is precisely motivated by this desire to deflect the look of the nonwhite Other. "The white body is expected not to be looked at by black bodies. . . . There was a period in the American South when, for blacks, looking a white in the eye carried the risk of being lynched" (1995, 102). If the look of the Other generally has a potentially terrifying power, the look of the Other whom one has colonized and enslaved is a special threat, and must be deflected at all costs. A white identity that has been grounded on racist, vanguard narratives—an identity that gains its very coherence through supremacy—can literally not survive the look of the colonized Other whose recognition must necessarily be accusatory of white identity. Irigaray has shown a similar effect of female presence in a masculine order where masculine subjectivity is predicated on the erasure of women. The power of the Other to constitute the self must lead, in such situations, precisely to the death struggle that Hegel envisioned. These examples suggest that it is white and male identity—or the dominant identity—that is threatened by the power of the Other to name it and confirm or disconfirm its beliefs about the world and itself. The problem for the dominated, by contrast, is, as Hegel said, their *lack* of recognition: they are caricatured but never truly seen.

The problem in accounts of identity has occurred, however, when the threat of the Other to the self is decontextualized, dehistoricized, and then universalized. In classical liberalism, developed against the backdrop of European colonial expansion, that which originates outside of me must be fought against, it is assumed, else my very selfness, my ownness to my self, will be at stake. The human self is essentially a reasoning self, but according to liberal ideology, reason requires autonomy or the ability to gain critical distance and to pass independent judgment on anything external. The idea of being constituted by others threatens such a self with dissolution. The tradition we have just retraced starts from a different place but effectively ends in the same view. To submit to our being-for-others as if this were an inescapable truth about ourselves is to commit bad faith. The essential self is the capacity to resist, to transcend and to exceed all attempts at representation. I suggest that this is a Western pathology written into a phenomenological ontology of being, and it has unconsciously constituted the very meaning of "autonomy" and "freedom" in Western political traditions (see Hartsock 1985; Lloyd 1984).

Postmodernism's Other

We find a similar scene, in a very different play, written into more recent treatments of identity given by Althusser, Foucault, Derrida, and Butler. For them, as for Sartre, resistance to identity is both metaphysically and politically mandated, insofar as it is possible (which in their estimation is far less than Sartre imagined). The difference between modern and postmodern accounts is simply in their degree of optimism about the extent to which the individual can negate the given and resist an external power. But in both cases negation, resistance, and destabilization are the privileged tactics because what comes to the individual from the Other is assumed to be ultimately both inaccurate and oppressive.

Given its generally determinist account of discourse and its repudiation of intentionality, postmodernist philosophy is in many respects diametrically opposed to existential phenomenology and Sartre's work in particular. However, there are striking similarities when it comes to their attitude toward social categories of identity. Foucault has probably been the most influential figure among the postmodernists on this topic, and a close look at his treatment of the self reveals that, like Sartre's distinction between the identifiable ego and the anonymous for-itself, Foucault enacts a very similar separation between identities, which are discursively constituted and have substantive characteristics, and the basic capacities of self-transformation that he takes as the cornerstone of his ethics of the self. Foucault even privileges resistance—and especially resistance to identity—as the central feature of contemporary political struggles in his call to replace and resist any form of sexual identity with bodies and pleasures.

What is striking about Foucault's account is that there is no identity that is not a form of subjugation (see esp. Foucault 1978, 1979, 2000a). For Sartre, identity offers a representation of the ego or the self's past, and as such is always, but only, inaccurate when attributed to the self in the present, which, given the centrality of consciousness for Sartre, is the core or "real" self. In contrast, Foucault's account seems to go beyond the charge of misrepresentation to assert a more active form of subjugation itself, albeit without ascribing intentionality to the Other who enacts the subjugation. For Foucault, identity is a form of subjection and subjugation in which the individual is interpellated within structures of discourse. Becoming a subject, that is, capable of self-reflective agency, of articulating one's intentions, one's rights, and one's interests, is always also to be subjected to power. The notion that there is a deep truth about one's identity, such as an innate and stable sexual orientation or a set of amoral tendencies that must be thwarted, promotes the self-policing disciplines endemic to the modern form of power. Unlike in classical liberalism, Foucault does not posit the existence of a self prior to subjection, a self that is then subordinated to the constraints of social life. Rather, he figures the process of subjectivation—of becoming a subject—as having an irremediably ambivalent political valence: it makes possible both agency and resistance to power as surely as it enfolds the individual into power's embrace.

Famously for Foucault, the moment of subjectification—the moment at which we attain the status of subject—is simultaneously the moment of subjection. It was the disciplinary practices of Christian confessionals and, later, prison procedures that produced the inward reflection necessary for a sense of self as an interior, stable entity. But such selves were the product of dominant power/knowledges involved in the regulation and dissemination of bodies. Only as subjects can we be made subject to the disciplinary strategies that produce docile bodies. Only when we conceive of ourselves as possessing a "self" can this self become the focal point of the self-monitoring practices embedded in the Panopticon (i.e., that Panopticon we call "modern living"). "Selves" as such—as the sort of entities that can be characterized, trained, pathologized, and thus identified—are the effect of power.

Foucault was particularly concerned with substantive categories of identity that work to produce individuals as they currently exist: "I don't think we should consider the 'modern state' as an entity that was developed above individuals, ignoring what they are and even their very existence, but, on the contrary, as a very sophisticated structure in which individuals can be integrated, under one condition: that this individuality would be shaped in a new form, and submitted to a set of very specific patterns" (2000, 334). This set of "specific patterns" operates through self-analysis and the development of a conscience that pursues the "salvation" of the individual through detailed knowledge of their innermost thoughts. Thus the modern identities that we name, differentiate, group, and consider the expression of our true selves, such as "gay," are products of the state. And despite his attempt in his late work to develop an account of an ethical relation to one's self, Foucault apparently never explored or considered the possibility of refashioning an ethical relation with a collectivity of others, presumably because he believed such collectivities to be dangerously useful for power.[4] Collective categories of identity produce a similar opportunity for disciplinary mechanisms by working through groups rather than individuals. Thus his politics of identity called for the following: "Maybe the target nowadays is not to discover what we are, but to refuse what we are.... The conclusion would be that the political, ethical, social, philosophical problem of our days is not to try to liberate the individual from the state, and from the state's institutions, but to liberate us both from the state and from the types of individualization which is linked to the state" (2000a, 336).

There have been important debates over whether such statements as these should be interpreted as denying the existence of a subject who has agency and an interior life (see Allen 1999, Halperin 1995 for recuperative arguments). But there seem to be no debates over whether Foucault could sanction the persistence of a social identity as the basis of political organizing, or whether, in other words, he could have accommodated a politics of recognition aiming at the "affirmation" of identities. Foucault's main target is clearly normalization, but his account strongly implies that social categories of identity are always the product of normalization, or so many of his interpreters assume. One way to reopen the debate would be to distinguish the processes of normalization from the processes by which we adopt or adapt to social identities.

Derrida's writings have manifested a similar distrust of identity by raising concerns that to make demands in the name of a subject (say, woman) will replicate structures of domination because such demands must be predicated on a concept of the substantive self (i.e., with characterizable content). In regard to women in particular, Derrida has suggested that any concept of woman remains in the logic of phallocentrism by positing a pretheoretical given about which one can seek a final truth. There is a violence in this attempt to fix indeterminacy and mandate an essential criterion or core of identity. Because reality will never actually accommodate itself to the claims of a fixed identity, Derrida points out that we will have to engage in violence *on* reality, in effect, in order to force its fluidity and variability into the determinate essence we can predict and thus control. This means that building a politics based on the defense of any given identity collaborates with the empire of the law.

Of course, it is entirely plausible that Derrida is motivated here to avoid having women's lives forcibly constrained through ahistorical and nondynamic interpretive schemas. But what is curious is why Derrida thinks that any representation will have an equal effect in this way or, in other words, why he takes this worry about a final truth about gender to counter even historical and dynamic conceptualizations of gender identity. Trying to champion a feminism without "women," Derrida echoes Nietzsche in some of his more thoughtful and less misogynist moments, in suggesting that because "woman" has existed entirely at the anterior to "man" as the subject of history, without a teleological narrative of her own, woman signifies only disruption and subversion, an inherent destabilizing force (see Oliver 1995).

Irigaray holds a similar view about the inherent subversiveness of the category "woman," but she grounds her argument on a corporeal sexual difference whose disruptive potential is based in its *substantive* difference from a masculinity grounded in the erasure of women. For Irigaray, it is not because women are "pure" difference that they are subversive, but because our specific, substantive difference is unrepresentable in the terms of present masculine-based philosophy and conceptions of subjectivity. The gendered binarisms that structure Western logos, being/becoming, having/lacking (the phallus), logos/silence, are, she says,

> interpretive modalities of the female function rigorously postulated by the pursuit of a certain game for which she will always find herself signed up without having begun to play. Set between—at least—two, or two half, men. A hinge bending according to their exchanges...Off-stage, off-side, beyond representation, beyond selfhood. (1985a, 22)

> Woman, in this sexual imaginary, is only a more or less obliging prop for the enactment of man's fantasies. (1985b, 25)

But what if, she asks, woman started to speak, to participate, to slide out from behind the mirror reflection of man? Woman's true representation or visibility will come at the price of the validity of the existing meaning of "man."

In contrast, Derrida maintains a rigid opposition to substances, conflating the difference between ahistorical and historical conceptions of substance to such an extent that the only way to undermine the essentialism of substance-concepts is to destabilize and deconstruct any concept with content. One can have form, it seems, as in "pure difference," but not content, though in this way Derrida re-instantiates an old binary. *Differance* works as a kind of liberatory interruption from the oppressive solidity of substance precisely by its nonbeing, because it lacks meaning or content. To the extent that identity concepts of any sort attribute content, they require deconstruction. Identity thus imposes the lie of being onto indeterminacy and as such colludes with the law. Derrida does not hold that this precludes the use of identity claims in all cases, but he does suggest that at best we should approach identity as a strategy, through a strategic essentialism, a temporary utilization rather than a deep commitment, and/or with an ironic attitude. We should use identity categories only in ways that will work ultimately to subvert them (see Gates 1992; Derrida 1982a, 1982b; Feder, Rawlinson, and Zakin 1997; Steele 1997).

Where Derrida's and Foucault's antipathies to identity are motivated by metaphysical arguments and political concerns with the strategies of power, there are also numerous postmodernists who follow Freud's view discussed earlier that identity attachments are based in psychological pathologies and are the symptom of a certain ego dysfunction. That is, when the ego is incapable of maintaining equilibrium in the face of loss or disturbing stimuli, it may compensate by collapsing the distinction between the ego and the ego ideal to posit an imaginary identity whose esteem will then be unassailable. As Ernesto Laclau puts it, "the psychoanalytic category of identification" explicitly asserts that there is "a lack at the root of any identity; one needs to identify with someone because there is an originary and insurmountable lack of identity" (1994, 3). The more one expresses an insistence on identity, then, the more one is manifesting this lack.

Many postmodernists also make use of psychoanalysis to explain the social dynamics of the belief in identity. Given that only the master has the power to name, naming is a kind of imaginary fixing of the Other and is an expression of aggression. From the perspective of the subordinate or the self that is named, accepting one's name is based on the narcissistic desire to be seen, the delusional fantasy of wholeness, but as such is doomed to failure and only makes one dependent on the master who names (Brennan 1993; Seshadri-Crooks 2000). Thus, the effort to overcome the unavoidable disunity of the self through a collective identification or group solidarity is seen as the sign of a pathological condition.

Butler's Synthetic Constructivism

Judith Butler's work will bring us up to the present in the postmodern critique of identity. Her impressive and influential writings have from the beginning sought to apply the theory of social construction to every element of the self and even, using

Foucault, to the body. She has taken up postmodern theory and made it her own, fashioning it to reflect on feminism's problematics and to etch out an exhaustively anti-essentialist progressive politics. Because her account of the self is relentlessly antinaturalizing, I call her approach a synthetic constructivism, to highlight her view that even the very basic elements of the body and subject are made of, so to speak, synthetic materials.

I am motivated to address Butler's work not only because of her enormous influence in feminist theory, but also because hers is one of the relatively few political analyses of identity that addresses it as an issue of interiority or lived experience (though these are not terms she would probably choose). She does not address identity simply as an issue of political effects or political struggles in the public domain, which, for example, is largely true of Habermas's work on identity and even Laclau and Mouffe's. This latter approach is important but limited by exploring the politics of identity only from the outside in, so to speak, and never from the inside out. One thus loses essential features of the problem that play an important role in the formulation of political positions and judgments. Butler's *The Psychic Life of Power* (1997) sets out as one of it main aims precisely to bridge the external and internal approaches, which is why she brings together Freud and Foucault despite the fact that their views about the self are so often contradictory: Freud offered an account excessively internally focused, while Foucault brackets subjective agency to focus instead on discourses and institutions.

Nonetheless, in *The Psychic Life of Power*, Butler fashions a synthesis between the political analysis of Foucault and the psychological theories of the Freudian tradition, notably Lacan. By bringing these two approaches into contact, she proposes to offer a psychoanalytic account of power as it is manifest in the formation of political subjects. Such attempts to combine these traditions represent a growing trend in contemporary Western theory, especially but not exclusively by feminists, who are unhappy with the politics of orthodox psychoanalysis but find Foucault's analytics of power—the most influential new theory of power in the last quarter century—too inattentive to the psyche or the interiority of the subject (see, e.g., de Lauretis 1994; Cornell 1995; Brennan 1992, 1993).[5]

Butler, building on Althusser as well as Freud and Foucault, argues that social naming is a form of primary alienation whose source is power. From Althusser she takes the claim that interpellation never identifies that which existed before, but calls into existence a subject who becomes subject only through its response to the call (Butler 1990, esp. part 1; and 1997, esp. the introduction and chaps. 3 and 4). Identity, in other words, comes into our consciousness through a second-person invocation rather than from our first-person experience of ourselves. Althusser says: "Ideology 'acts' or 'functions' in such a way that it 'recruits' subjects among individuals (it recruits them all) by that very precise operation which I have called *interpellation* or hailing, and which can be imagined along the lines of the most commonplace police (or other) hailing: 'Hey, you there!'" (1971, 174). Though he adds "(or other)" it is not insignificant that Althusser chooses the police in this example in which he gives his first and most general definition of the interpellation of the subject, because the ultimate source of interpellation for Althusser is always ideology and thus the power of the state.

Foucault differed from Althusser famously on the topic of ideology and the centrality of the state, but like Althusser he viewed the process of becoming a subject as simultaneous to "the process of becoming subordinated by power" (Butler 1997, 2). Subjectivation produces a subject who then can act, for example in making demands in his own name, but at the same time it misnames that subject and inscribes it into power. As Butler puts it, power not only *"acts on* a given individual as a form of domination, but also *activates* or forms the subject"(1997, 84). In his most persuasive example of this process, Foucault describes the rehabilitative regimens of the prison as not only constraining the prisoner but also producing the prisoner's interior reflexive attitudes and motivations, and thus not only fashioning but even bringing forth the prisoner's self, a self in the modernist mode of exhaustive self-consciousness. Unlike either the phenomenologists or the psychoanalysts, both Althusser and Foucault retreated from universal ahistorical claims about the processes of identity formation that they studied, and both located their analyses within the modern period of Western societies.

Butler adopts this account of subjectification as given by Althusser and Foucault, but like the psychoanalysts she tends to portray the process of subjectivation as if it would unfold in just this way no matter the historical context.[6] Thus, she makes a "psychoanalytic criticism of Foucault" because in her view neither the generation of the subject nor its capacity for resistance can be accounted for with the thin analysis he provides (1997, 87). Psychoanalysis is necessary to explain, among other things, why the subject chooses its own subjection. But she also wants to critique the tendency in psychoanalysis toward "romanticized notions of the unconscious defined as necessary resistance" (1997, 87). Rather than naturalizing resistance, or portraying it as a necessary given, Butler suggests that we understand the resistances manifested in the unconscious as themselves produced in power relations. Thus, her ultimate position will be a combination between Foucault and psychoanalysis, supplementing Foucault's inattention to issues of interiority with a psychoanalytic account of subject formation. The combination she develops, however, surprisingly retains Lacan's fatalism rather than Foucault's pessimism (which was not fatalistic). By making power formative of resistance, Butler helpfully undercuts those theories in which the unconscious has an inherently revolutionary potential, theories that romanticize, dehistoricize, and decontextualize the unconscious. But by offering a psychoanalytic rather than historical account of subject formation, she renders inevitable and ahistorical the link between subjection and subjectification. Agency is largely an illusion (see Benhabib et al. 1995).

Butler also criticizes Foucault for his insufficient explanation of agency (1997, 89ff.). In one of the central arguments of the book, she offers her own explanation in an account that is interestingly close to Jean-Paul Sartre's. She hypothesizes that because identity is never adequate to that which it names, there always remains a psychic excess beyond that which is named and which is ultimately the source of individual agency. This is not to say (as Sartre would) that agency preexists the process of subjectivation; on Butler's account the appearance of an excess itself is made possible only by the process of naming, which tries to accurately and fully identify the self. In other words, interpellation, or naming, creates an identity the inadequacy of which produces the excess, and it is only on the basis of this excess or disjuncture between the identity and the individual that the latter can resist, critique, and thus exercise agency. It is on the basis of the excess that one resists the imposition of the identity, but it is only because one has an identity that one can act.

I agree with Butler that Foucault's own account of agency is underdeveloped, but it is still interesting to note the different conclusions between their accounts. For Foucault, agency and resistance require power but they do not require subjectivation or becoming a subject in the terms of modernity, replete with a deep self, an essential truth about the self that can be named, and so on. Modernity makes possible certain kinds of social acts, in which one can claim unassailable rights, for example, on the basis of this deep self with its inherent needs and desires and orientations. Thus subjectivation is necessary for certain forms of agency. But Foucault also envisions agency outside of modernity—and even a kind of self-fashioning without the naming or "true" identities modernity would impose—in his exploration of ancient Greek problematics of the self and the possibility of certain elements of this different discourse being made use of today. Subjectivation is necessarily subordination, but subjectivation is not the only route to agency. Thus, like Amy Allen (1999), I suspect that Foucault's view of the subject is complex and not merely deconstructive, given his call for the reformulation of subjectivities. Butler's account, by contrast, is more than pessimistic given the necessary connection she makes between agency and excess and between subjection and subjectivity. This difference affords a much greater role for social naming, since it is this naming that always produces an excess.

Butler is unequivocal about the oppressiveness of interpellation or social naming:

> The desire to persist in one's own being requires submitting to a world of others that is fundamentally not one's own (a submission that does not take place at a later date, but which frames and makes possible the desire to be). Only by persisting in alterity does one persist in one's "own" being. Vulnerable to terms that one never made, one persists [i.e., continues as a subject] always, to some degree, through categories, names, terms, and classifications that mark a *primary alienation in sociality*. (1997, 28, emphasis added)

Social categories of identity make resistance possible but always fail to identify accurately, and thus by this very fact create the need for resistance. Accepting identities is tantamount to accepting dominant scripts and performing the identities power has invented. Identities are not and can never be accurate representations of the real self, and thus interpellation always in a strict sense *fails* in its representational claim even while it succeeds in inciting and disciplining one's practice. It is useful to compare Butler's analysis of identity and its excess with what we saw about Sartre's distinction between the for-itself and its ego (a comparison also made by Schrift 2001). Remember that for Sartre, when we are identified as, for example, "the homosexual" or "the heterosexual," we are recognized by our past choices, which can be transcended in the future. Thus, identifications in a sense never hit their mark; they never identify the real self but only its historic trail.

The question Butler then poses in this book is, when we are interpolated in this way by power, why do we respond? Why do we turn toward the identifying source, rather than away from it? This question is especially troubling to Butler in regard to oppressed identities—for example, racial and sexual identities—in which the turn is even more evidently pathological. Following Freud here, she holds that interpellation is the price for recognition.

Let me pause at this point to compare the two concepts at play here in Butler's account: identity and subjectivity. Butler generally uses these terms to distinguish between social categories and interiority. Thus, identity is one's public self, based on publicly recognized categories, whereas subjectivity is one's lived self, or true self, or thinking self, and so on. However, this neat separation doesn't quite apply to any post-Hegelian social understanding of the formation of the subject in which social interaction plays the constitutive role. Social interactions take place in a public arena organized by identities (such as lord and bondsman) but are also and by this very interaction constitutive of subjectivity or one's interior life. Thus, Butler herself unapologetically critiques identity and subjectivity (i.e., the modernist account of subjectivity) in the same breath, because on her view they are created simultaneously. There remains a possible way to use the conceptual distinction between identity and subjectivity, even if the distinction is never pure, to illuminate some of the political problems that we are all familiar with, such as when one's public recognition differs sharply from one's lived sense of self. In this way, one could use the distinction just as Gadamer counsels the use of the binary subject/object, as long as one does not take it too far or too literally. *Pace* the liberals, one cannot have a subjectivity that can transcend the effects of public identification, but even so, it can be useful to focus on identity and subjectivity as two different aspects of the self.

One might argue here that for Butler the move toward recognition is a move toward oppression precisely because recognition assumes a completeness in its interpellation of the subject that never obtains. It is that completeness that would deny the excess Butler emphasizes as the seat of agency, analogous to Sartre's rejection of the identification between substantive ego and nonsubstantive consciousness. Social identity collapses the distinction, denies the excess, and portrays me as just that social identity.

But this reading of Butler, if right, is no more persuasive as a critique of identity. It is tantamount to the referencing of Leibniz's problem with identity (mentioned at the beginning of this chapter), or the assumption that when we speak about identity we always imply, project, or assume absolute indiscernibility. This is just nonsense as a characterization of meaning in everyday discourse or common experience. I would not claim that identity ascriptions attain a completeness, but the question is whether that sort of absolute completeness is required of an interpellation that we would say is accurate or successful. I can say it is accurate to portray me as a woman even though I would resist the claim that such an interpellation exhausts who I am, as would most (nonfundamentalist) women. Given that some interpellations can be accurate, it then follows that interpellations do not in every case require or motivate resistance. So what needs to be explained, then, is not the pathological attachment to always inaccurate and oppressive identity categories, but the increasing consensus in social theory that identities are always inaccurate and oppressive.[7]

The bottom line for the postmodern approach to identity is that identities are subjugating and cannot be a cornerstone of progressive politics. Wendy Brown represents the most extreme example of this position, and her concern as a political scientist is primarily politics rather than metaphysics. In her view, when we organize on the basis of social identities we are unwittingly, naively, remaining caught in power's clutches. In *States of Injury* Brown argues that the assumption some feminists have made that we need a coherent concept of woman in order to advance feminist demands is a dangerous error. She says "this truth" some feminists think we need "has been established as the secret to our souls not by us but by those who would discipline us through that truth" (1995, 42).

Moreover, when we organize around identity, or what she names our "wounded attachments," we are compulsively repeating a painful reminder of our subjugation, and maintaining a cycle of blaming that continues the focus on oppression rather than transcending it. Brown makes use here of Freud's theory that a compulsion to repeat traumatic events from the past is motivated by our desire to gain control over and thus master the event. But this repetition compulsion maintains the power of the event over us by making it the organizing focus of our actions and choices. Brown suggests that identity-based political organizing is a manifestation of such a repetition compulsion by its focus on the sources of oppression, which are, precisely, social identities.

Brown also makes use of Nietzsche's claim that "man" would rather will nothingness (or nihilism) than will nothing at all to argue that those who embrace their identity categories are saying in effect that they prefer oppression to what they fear will be annihilation if they relinquish their attributed identities. Butler makes an identical argument when she characterizes the passionate attachment to identity as a form of saying, "I would rather exist in subordination than not exist" (1997, 7). Like Brown, she does not condemn the desire that motivates the passionate attachment; it is not a desire for subordination, but a desire simply "to be" or to be a subject, a desire that is then realized through accepting the imposition of coercive identities as the means "to be." But this means for Butler that the movement toward life and toward survival, what Nietzsche might have called the movement of the will toward life itself, is a movement in which the subject turns back on itself, since "the subject is the effect of power in recoil" (Butler 1997, 6). Butler concludes unsurprisingly from this that subjectivity itself is thus irretrievably bound up with melancholia.[8]

Summarizing the Critique

The difference between modern and postmodernist accounts is simply in their degree of optimism about the extent to which the individual *can* negate the given and resist an external power. Postmodernists are much less sanguine about the efficacy of individual agency. But in both modern and postmodern accounts it is striking that negation, resistance, and destabilization of what comes to the individual from the social—whether that social is discourse, disciplinary mechanisms, the Law of the Father, or cultural traditions—are valorized as the privileged, most important capacities of a rational self given the prior assumption that what comes to the individual from the social is necessarily constraining and pernicious. And this is simply to say that what comes to the individual from the Other is never to be acknowledged as accurate.

Although identities are, then, according to these theorists, both pernicious and metaphysically inaccurate, in another sense they are, or seem to be, unavoidable. As we've seen, many of even the most severe critics of identity acknowledge that identities are needed in the political arena so that movements can make demands "in the name of" and "on behalf of" women, people of color, gays and lesbians, and other groups of people who have been stigmatized precisely because of identity attributions. They allow that the natural reaction to hateful characterizations of one's identity is to try to overturn those characterizations and replace them with positive or at least innocuous ones. And there is also a need to redress discrimination through targeted policies of reparations and antidiscrimination laws.

But the critics of identity that we have reviewed here worry that these movements organized around the defense of stigmatized identities may do more harm than good, or may have come to that point now even if initially their identity-based political work was necessary. The political critics worry that differences will be emphasized at the expense of commonalities, divisiveness will increase, and an irrational tribalism will grow. The philosophical critics worry that movements "in the name of" social identities reinscribe their importance and reinforce the harmful illusion of their substantial reality. It is obvious that straights, whites, and men have been the primary groups left out, respectively, of movements against sexual, racial and ethnic, and gender discrimination, and some of the books tell tales of frustration at incidents where the straight, white, male authors were the target or witness of attacks that they saw as entirely unreasonable and unfair. But generally their criticisms of identity-based movements are meant to show that these strategies are harmful for the marginalized groups themselves because, in the long run, their own aims will backfire.

We can summarize the basic lines of the philosophical critique of identity in the following way:

(1) Identities are artificial and oppressive constraints on the natural indeterminacy of the self.
(2) Identities are the product of oppressive practices such as self-disciplining mechanisms, and the desire for their "affirmation" is a manifestation of a repetition-compulsion complex.
(3) Identities are pathological and unproductive, even doomed, responses to lack or ego dysfunction and instability.
(4) Identities are never accurate representations.
(5) Identities are manifestations of a primary alienation in which categories are imposed from without.

What follows from these claims is that:

(6) Freedom in any sense must be a move away from identity.

At bottom, the critique of identity follows from some major metaphysical assumptions or claims, specifically, that the true nature of the self is indeterminate, a claim we found starting with Hegel, and that freedom is the ability to resist all that comes to the self externally, a view that is also in evidence at least in early Hegel. It also assumes a description of identity formation as having a necessary link to Power. But is this claim truly convincing? Of course, if we try to resist it some would have a ready diagnosis of our resistance: we are pining for a lost fixity and compulsively focused on the source of our own victimization (see esp. Brown 1995 and Gitlin 1993, 1995). Identities are foisted on the weak; a truly free self would be one free of social identity.

But why assume that the source and effect of identity claims are nefarious? Why assume that the parent/community/society or the discourse/episteme/socius is, in every case and necessarily, psychically pernicious and enabling only at the cost of a more profound subordination? Why assume that if I am culturally, ethnically, sexually identifiable that this is a process akin to Kafka's nightmarish torture machines in the penal colony? My diagnosis in this chapter points to a fear of the power of the Other as providing the missing premise to make this argument compelling. It is implausible that the simple mistaken equation of identity categories with absolute reductive essentialist identity categories can explain the volume of theory devoted to the critique of identity. The problem for the critics is with identity in any form, because it is foisted on the self from the outside by the Other. But the need to deflect the Other is not a universal feature of the for-itself, but a very situated need. The colonizers and dominant need to deflect the reflection in their victims' eyes, and the victims themselves need to be able to transcend the oppressors' representations. However, these do not exhaust the possible relationships that can exist between self and Other. Nor do they exhaust the genealogies of social categories of identity.

Hegel brought Western philosophy face to face with the crucial fact of our dependence on the Other for our very identity, the very quality and form of our subjectivity and affective life. But the exact form and nature of this dependence is not by any means clear. The political implications of our dependence on others will change depending on the characterization of this dependence. I want to end this chapter, and anticipate my discussion of the metaphysics and politics of self/other relations in the next chapter, with a brief discussion of a pair of contrasting implications that follow this dependence on the other.

As we've seen, one possible formulation of self/other interdependence that has already been discussed here is the relational theory of self, as developed, for example, by Ricoeur, Code, and Brison. Ricoeur takes up the issue of the political implications of this account most explicitly in his suggestion that recognizing our dependence on others will yield more ethical intersubjective relations. Remember that Ricoeur conceptualizes the self as created in a process of reflection performed in interaction with the Other. Thus, the Other is necessary not as itself an accurate reflection of the self, but as the stage, in effect, or prompt by which our own reflective narratives can be produced. Thus, Ricoeur's argument for the ethical implications of this account follows his assumption that if one recognizes one's necessary dependence on the other, a more ethical, humane relationship will result.

However, dependence on the Other pure and simple entails no particular normative effects, nor does its acknowledgment ensure against xenophobia. This is because one's dependence on the Other can be nicely dealt with, as Fanon,

Gordon, and Irigaray have shown, through a subjugation and even erasure of the Other's subjectivity in order to force it to reflect a flattering self. If woman can be made to reflect men as Gods, or masters of meaning and of history, and if the colonized can be forced to reflect only the superiority and justifiable dominance of their masters, then dependence on these Others bodes no disadvantage but quite the reverse. Slavery, colonialism, racism, and patriarchy have all developed masterful mechanisms toward this end. Dependence does not go away, but structures of domination can ensure the virtual ubiquity of positive representations and nonreciprocal recognition.

Such mechanisms can work because the relational theory's characterization of self/other dependence is far too limited, which becomes clear when it is compared with the Hegelian formulation. Where Ricoeur sees the self as created in a performance prompted by interaction with the Other, Hegel's model suggests a more significant and more constitutive relationship: it is not that I create myself only in dialogical interaction with the Other, but that the Other's view of me—that is, my identity in the Other's presence—is internalized and thus is constitutive of my self. My self emerges in interaction with the Other because the Other's perspective gives substance and content and constitutes the horizon from which I perceive and act.

Thus, the relational theory of self seems to hold little promise, at least as represented in these examples, to develop the idea of a constitutive relation between self and Other that would yield a politics of equality or reciprocal relations of respect. Other aspects of the hermeneutic approach, however, which Ricoeur is drawing from, hold more promise. The hermeneutic insight is that the self operates in a situated plane, always culturally located with great specificity even as it is open onto an indeterminate future and a reinterpretable past not of its own creation. Given this view, one might hold that when I am identified, it is the horizon itself which is identified. No "internal" movement, judgment, choice, or act by an individual can be made intelligible except within this specific horizon which is constituted by Others. Thus, the Other is not here the mere prompt for subjectivating processes that are essentially performed by the self; rather, the Other is internal to the self's substantive content, a part of its own horizon, and thus a part of its own identity. The mediations performed by individuals in processes of self-interpretation, the mediations by which individual experience comes to have specific meanings, are produced through a foreknowledge or historical a priori that is cultural, historical, politically situated, *and collective*. In this sense, it is less true to say that I am dependent on the Other—as if we are clearly distinguishable— than that the Other is a part of myself. (Such concepts of collective subjectivities seem to me to be part of what Deleuze and Guattari began to think through, which thus indicates the complexity of poststructuralist philosophy; see esp. Deleuze and Guattari 1987). Moreover, one's relation to this foreknowledge is not primarily one of negation; it makes possible the articulation of meanings and the formulation of judgment and action. One's relation is better characterized precisely as absorption, generation, and expansion.

Arguably, the political implications of such an account of self/Other relations would necessarily yield better results than the relational account. An example of this can be found in an article on racial identity and multiculturalism by Robert

Gooding-Williams (1998). Gooding-Williams suggests that the motivation of multiculturalism is inaccurately represented as cultural relativism or the belief that all cultures have something important to say (which is Charles Taylor's account of it and, on some readings, Du Bois's). Such an account provides arguments for multiculturalism as if selves can *choose* to recognize others or not. Against this, he argues that the motivation behind and aim of multiculturalism is more accurately understood as self-recognition, or a "knowledge of one's [own] community in its multifaceted complexity. Recognizing who *we* are, as distinct from recognizing that *they* have something valuable to say, is the critical element" (1998, 35). Such recognition, he concludes, "will move us to change our views of ourselves" (36). As Adrian Piper has powerfully argued, this is the true test of antiracism: not what one might *do* for the Other, but whether one can contemplate *being* the Other (1992– 93). This might involve acknowledging one's own nonwhite forebears, which is Piper's focus, or acknowledging more generally the Other within the self, the Other or external elements that help constitute one's own identity. My argument in this chapter has been that antirealist accounts of identity that would allow one to avert the power of the Other need to be reconsidered in this light.

Real Identities

These questions, which have engaged so many, have troubled all of my work. How to be both free and situated; how to convert a racist house into a race-specific yet nonracist home. How to enunciate race while depriving it of its lethal cling? . . . The defenders of Western hegemony sense the encroachment and have already defined the possibility of imagining race without dominance — without hierarchy — as "barbarism." We are already being asked to understand such a world as the destruction of the four-gated city, as the end of history. We are already being asked to know such a world as aftermath — as rubbish, as an already damaged experience, as a valueless future. Once again, the political consequences of new and threatening theoretical work is the ascription of an already named catastrophe. It is therefore more urgent than ever to develop non-messianic language to refigure the raced community, to decipher the deracing of the world. It is more urgent than ever to develop an epistemology that is neither intellectual slumming nor self-serving reification.

Toni Morrison, "Home"

The sweeping anti-identity trends that have come to dominate the U.S. academy and parts of the culture at large collude with the "defenders of Western hegemony" that Morrison names above, that is, those who have called a barbarism the project to create a "race-specific yet nonracist home" or the project of imagining a liberal polity whose price of inclusion does not demand erasure through assimilation. I have argued that the a priori repudiation of identity is based on mistaken assumptions about the nature, source, and lived experience of social identities, an understandable mistake given that, as Morrison says, the task of developing a refigured discourse of identity is not yet complete. But the repudiation may also be based, I have suggested, in the fear of living in a world where the point of view of one's own social identity does not hold hegemony over meaning, value, or creative institutions, where the Other, in some cases, holds the epistemic upper hand even over some truths about oneself.

Up to this point my argument has taken primarily a negative form. I have argued that we should be wary of the unscrutinized assumption that social identity is innately pathological or politically pernicious, or that social categories of identities *necessarily* mischaracterize the individual or diminish individual agency. I have suggested that at its core, in its common usage, identity does not entail an ascription of sameness that elides group difference, but it does imply a constitutive relation of the individual to the Other, as well as between self and community, and that the refusal of identity is nothing less than the futile hope of avoiding the Other's power to name, to characterize, and to judge. However, my intention has been to target only the a priori critiques of identity, those that would reject or view as highly dangerous any and all formulations of identity, and those that assume that in a progressive future social identities will ideally wither away.

Such refusals and preemptive strikes against the work of refiguring identity delay difficult theoretical work that needs to be done. In this and in the remaining chapters of this book, my aim is to contribute toward the project of creating a new kind of epistemology and metaphysics of identity that is neither "intellectual slumming nor self-serving reification," one that can begin to make sense of how identities work today and thus how they might realistically be transformed in the near future. Although the concern of this book has primarily been with the charge of "barbarism," or the a priori repudiation of identity, there is an equally troubling danger from the other direction, when identities maintain a "lethal cling." Where the salience of identity is affirmed, it is sometimes all too easy to then concretize identity's impact, to assume clear boundaries, and to decontextualize and dehistoricize identity formations. In reality, identities are much more complex than any of these caricatures will allow.

Critics of identity are sometimes responding to the overplaying of the salience of social identity, for example, when social identities like ethnicity or race are mistakenly taken as sufficient causes for political orientation. Shortly before he was murdered by the FBI, Fred Hampton, leader of the Black Panthers, recouped from such a mistake when he said, "Our ten point program is in the midst of being changed right now, because we used the word 'white' when we should have used the word 'capitalist'" (1970, 143). I take it that Hampton did not mean to deny that it is fair to characterize the dominant order in the United States as a "white power structure," or, as bell hooks comprehensively calls it, a white capitalist patriarchy. But to characterize whites as the enemy of black liberation occludes white poverty and class oppression, upon which a coalition might be built, and misnames the structural dynamic. Thus I would say that the fact that mistakes can be made in formulating *how* identities figure into power dynamics is not to say that identities do *not* figure. Workers in the United States are fundamentally racialized, taking up their position in the labor pool as largely determined by their race, gender, and immigration status as much as by their class genealogy. Thus, in the struggle against the social destruction wrought by private profiteering, we need a more precise and realistic articulation of what identities are in order to produce more precise and realistic social theories of oppression and strategies of liberation.

We need also to recognize the diversity of identity constructions and processes of identity formation. We cannot assume that the process of constructing "whiteness," for example, which has involved strict border control, illusions of purity, and a binary opposition to nonwhiteness, is analogous to all other processes of identity formation. Identities need to be contextualized and processes of identity formation need to be historicized. Manuel Castells, who has written probably the most comprehensive study of identity-based movements globally, concludes that "no identity can be an essence, and no identity has, *per se*, progressive or regressive value outside its historical context" (1997, 8). Stuart Hall has charted the developments and permutations of black identity in England, and argues that there has been a recent shift in black consciousness and in the politics of representation, or identity politics, specifically, "a new cultural politics which engages rather than suppresses *difference*" (1996, 446). Hall himself has critiqued the construction of English ethnic identity as "closed, exclusive, and regressive" (1996, 446). But in his account of the new developments in black cultural politics in Britain, he gives an account consistent with Morrison's goal of a nonreductionist yet still salient identity. Hall writes:

> We all speak from a particular place, out of a particular history, out of a particular experience, a particular culture, without being contained by that position as "ethnic artists" or film-makers. We are all, in that sense, *ethnically* located and our ethnic identities are crucial to our subjective sense of who we are. But this is also a recognition that this is not an ethnicity which is doomed to survive, as Englishness was, only by marginalizing, dispossessing, displacing and forgetting other ethnicities. This precisely is the politics of ethnicity predicated on difference and diversity. (1996, 447)

The specific context in Britain has been a racial ideology that has similarly targeted ex-colonized subjects from diverse countries, thus spawning a uniquely broad permutation of "blackness" that merits its own specific analysis.

Rather than attempting a reconstruction of identities in a generic and general sense, my focus will be on contemporary raced and gendered identities. There are too many specific differences in the ways in which various identities are formed, operate, and lived to warrant general analyses (see Alcoff and Mendieta, 2002). Class and nationality are also embodied identities, but their relationship to the body is less intimate and more easily alterable than the relationship with one's race or one's gender. Class and nationality profoundly affect the shape and condition of the body, but the physical effects can often be overcome when class and national identities are changed. Class and nationality are primarily manifest as behavior, whereas race and gender affect, and reflect, less easily alterable physiological features (and, in the case of gender, significant physiological features). Race and gender operate similarly in Western societies as visible marks on the body, though even here there are important differences to explore in the ways in which these two identities have developed. The increasing plasticity of social identities does not preclude there being a qualitative difference between varieties of identity categories. In this chapter, then, my task is to offer an account of identity applicable to race and gender, though it may well have some application to aspects of other forms of identity. In later chapters I will address more specific issues that arise in regard to race and gender, such as the material basis of gender, the link between race and visibility, and the issue of racial "mixes."

The various positions people take on identity depend heavily on the account one gives of identity's relation to the self, that is, the relationship between ascribed social categories and the lived experience of consciousness. Those who take identity to be an a priori problem assume a certain understanding of what consciousness is, or what the core of the self is, such that social ascriptions can operate only oppressively. The alternative to this account that will be developed here aims to explain why the willful attachment to raced or sexed identities, identities created in conditions of oppression, is *not* necessarily pathological. It will also explain how strongly felt identities can coexist with democratic politics and solidarity across difference. Most important, it will explain how raced and sexed identities can be compatible with a plausible concept of autonomy and agency. From this account, we can then begin to see what kind of identity politics makes sense.[1]

The Epistemological Question

> Although personal experience is not necessarily a good starting point—it is often limited and very obscure—it is however a good test if one can manage to integrate it into critical work; for the contrary is definitely a bad sign, not only where feminist thinking is concerned, but in any kind of philosophy. And particularly when one is seeking a form of philosophy which can grasp realities that need to be made appreciable, if only so that one can fight against them.
>
> Michéle Le Doeuff, *Hipparchia's Choice*

What justifies a claim about identity? To bring philosophy into the *social* arena poses new epistemological questions about the claims of philosophy itself, because it requires departing from the usual method of justifying metaphysical arguments that rely on logical entailments from ordinary concepts or that are based heavily on intuitions or from theorizing about the necessary character of entities across possible worlds. I acknowledge that I am engaged in philosophical speculation to a certain extent here, although it is not unconstrained speculation but one based on my interpretations of identity theories, ethnographies of social movements, and my social experience. This does not add up to an empirically adequate sample of evidence. And although my intuitions will be engaged here, I take intuitions to be rife with ideological and culturally specific content, and far from irrefutable tests of universal truth. Intuitions sometimes reveal truths only after we engage in symptomatic readings of them, to reveal their ideological preconditions, rather than taking them at face value. Like LeDoeuff, then, I think personal experience is necessary but not sufficient for the development of practical theories.

I will bring some empirical and ethnographic data to bear, but primarily my method will be to draw from two long-developed traditions of philosophy—hermeneutics and phenomenology—to devise a coherent account of raced and gendered identity as they operate in our world today, and one that is at least comparatively better than the accounts assumed by the critics of identity in its ability to cohere with the variability shown in the ethnographic record. To be plausible, an account of social identity must be able to account for historical fluidity and instability, as well as the differences within identities, and yet also account for the powerful salience and persistence of identities as self-descriptions and as predictors for how one is treated and what one's realistic life options are. Thus, the justification for such an account as I will offer here is based on its comparative standing vis-à-vis other existing accounts in cohering with these facts.

But justifications of new ideas often come more from the future rather than from a grounding in current and adequate bodies of evidence. That is, the test of a philosophical account comes after it is written, when and if it is taken up as a meaningful and helpful explanation for the experiences and phenomena that its readership widely shares. For example, the seventeenth-century Cartesian theory of the rational, doubting self helped to make sense of the seventeenth- and eighteenth-century revolutionary, antiaristocratic movements, since Descartes's account made greater sense of their rejection of tradition and convention than either the Platonic or Augustinian accounts could with their rigid hierarchies of human capabilities and their belief in received wisdom (Bordo 1987). Later on, the Hegelian dialectical and dynamic concept of the self as an ongoing process-in-formation made sense of the dramatic cultural transformations and the historical, social, and political changes that beset Europe throughout the nineteenth century (Solomon 1983). In the twentieth century, phenomenological accounts of the self, especially de Beauvoir's and Merleau-Ponty's, helped to make sense of the nonrational aspects of selfhood that came to be accepted more widely in a post-Freudian world, offering an explanation that did not devolve into a counterintuitive, hopeless determinism (which most Westerners in the modern era reject) but which acknowledged the complexity and limitations of intentionality. More recently, the performative account of the self developed by Erving Goffman and Butler has proved useful as a way to understand the plasticity of sex/gender, a plasticity many people have been forced to recognize at least since the uprising of the women's movement and the gay and lesbian movement. My belief is that a somewhat rewired hermeneutic and phenomenological account of the self, one that builds from a pluritopic rather than the traditional monotopic hermeneutics, will help us begin to make sense of the claims of identity politics and of some aspects of the political clashes between culturally defined groups, as well as filling in some of the features of gender identity that the performative account cannot address. This portrayal of how philosophical claims are judged recognizes that philosophy is always situated, in both the problems it addresses and the answers that make sense, but this need not sacrifice our ability to claim truth. Philosophy can successfully clarify and explain without those explanations needing to be transcendentally true for all time or completely adequate to all aspects of the object it studies.

The remainder of this chapter will be divided into five sections. In the first section, I consider some of the central ways of thinking about identity and the self in the Western philosophical tradition, and how the present study departs from these traditions. In the second section, I consider the concept of interpretive horizon as discussed by Gadamer and Charles Taylor as a way to understand the effect of social location on the self, what is visible from this location, and thus what the self can know. While important, the sphere of visibility operates only metaphorically in the hermeneutic account; what is seriously lacking is a sustained attention to the body, and thus in the third section I supplement the hermeneutic approaches with a phenomenological account, attending especially to the role of vision and visibility.

In the fourth section, I summarize what the hermeneutic and phenomenological accounts say concerning the self-other and self-community relationship, relating this to the work of George Herbert Mead, whose account of the social self coordinates well with both approaches. In the concluding section, I draw out the specific implications of the approach I have developed for conceptualizing race and gender, which will be elucidated further in subsequent chapters.

Identities and Essences

> I think, therefore I am.
>
> Descartes

> I am because my little dog knows me.
>
> Gertrude Stein

The debates around identity are embroiled in a long philosophical tradition of thought involving organizing concepts of intrinsic or essential versus context dependent and nonessential, as well as the modern distinction made between the mind versus the body and between the interiority of the self versus its exterior (so that, for example, one's sexual subjectivity may not "match" one's anatomical sex [see A. Davidson 2001]). Generally, if a property is context dependent, it is considered inessential.

The Western philosophical canon has generally been concerned with *haecceity*, or that which makes a thing the thing that it is and distinguishable from other things. *Haecceity* is that without which a thing is no longer identical to itself, and thus said to consist of only intrinsic, nonrelational properties. The relational properties of a thing are contingent and subject to change, and thus, so many have thought, *those* properties cannot be essential to a thing's *haecceity*, properties sometimes called essential or primary rather than inessential or secondary. Essential properties for Aristotle are timeless and necessary, or therefore they are those a thing would have in any context or possible world. If there are some properties that a thing could have in one context, and another set of properties that it could have in another context, then those contextually dependent properties cannot be that which makes the thing the thing that it is, or it would no longer remain the same thing across contexts. Descartes's example was a piece of wax, which might take liquid or solid form depending on the temperature of its surroundings, but which will always have extension. Therefore, its status as a liquid or solid is not essential in the same way that its status as a thing with extension is. The identity of a thing, on this account, or what makes the thing the thing that it is, is determined only by its intrinsic and nonrelational properties.

Famously for Descartes, one knows what one is—a thinking substance— because one has immediate, private knowledge of this act of thinking, knowledge that requires no external corroboration and which is thus independent of the happenstance of one's context. Gertrude Stein's famous send-up of Descartes—"I am because my little dog knows me"—is not only poking fun at the pretensions of philosophical thought, but also making a claim about the necessary relational character of one's essential identity. Since at least Hegel there is now a long tradition within the West of arguing that basic human capacities—such as critical rationality and moral agency— are made possible only within social contexts in which such capacities can be developed and their options made intelligible. In the case of social identities such as race and gender, however, even some Hegelians, as we saw in the last chapter, consider these aspects of selves inessential, even illusory, and certainly dispensable.

I would argue that social identities are relational, contextual, *and* fundamental to the self. Some relational properties, such as being a parent, are fundamental. One might be a parent today and then lose one's child or children, yet continue to exist, and thus it is not an essential property of a person in the sense of *haecceity*. Moreover, in one context parenthood might be profoundly life altering, and in another context, as for a sperm donor, it might be inconsequential. Yet in most contexts being a parent is fundamental not only to one's daily life, but also to one's orientation toward the world, one's concerns about the future, one's relationship to her or his community, one's social standing, one's potential life choices, one's understanding of one's *own* parents and to some of one's political and intellectual dispositions.

Our relational properties can be fundamental to who we are when they have causal determinacy over our epistemic and political orientations to the world— what we notice, what we care about—but also when they profoundly affect how we are seen and interacted with by others. Learning that someone is a mother produces unconscious or conscious reactions in people, involving assumptions that may involve one's intellectual state, one's emotional state, one's ability to achieve detached objectivity on certain matters, one's maturity, or one's moral status as a working mother. Similarly, racial and ethnic identity often engenders unconscious assumptions about one's past experiences, one's authority to make certain claims, or about one's vested interest in certain beliefs. The revelations that I made in the introduction about my own identity may well have engendered assumptions that will bear on readers' assessments of my claims in this book, the amount of credibility or presumption they will accord in my favor, and the interpretation made of some of my arguments and philosophical commitments. My use of the phrase "mixed race" may have elicited the question in some readers' minds about what I look like, whether I look like one or another race, or whether I look like an amalgam, and these conjectures are motivated by the need to decide how much credibility I will be accorded in regard to my claims to certain kinds of knowledge, although there are often wide differences in the conclusions that different people draw from a person's identity in regard to how credible they are and what they are considered to be credible about.

Such assumptions, as I shall argue, however various, vague, and semiconscious they are, are yet an unavoidable feature of the present-day operations of social identities. In societies where we encounter too many people too quickly to come to know them as individuals, we have to make educated guesses all the time. We all make assumptions based on social identities, whether we are aware of this fact or not, and I shall argue that they are not in all cases unwarranted or politically pernicious. Many women are skeptical of men who make absolutist claims about abortion; many people of color take whites' claims to "not see color" with a large grain of salt. In trying to assess the difficulties of life as an immigrant in the United States, we need to consult immigrants themselves, and we may even want to see how immigrant researchers interpret the data. Although some group-related assumptions are legitimate insofar as they are used as one factor, and never the sole factor, in assessing someone's claims, we need to become more reflective about how such assumptions operate, especially those that confer or deny epistemic authority to make certain sorts of claims or to analyze certain kinds of topics. But my main point here is to argue that our social identity is profoundly significant in determining the state of the "world" (or worlds) that each individual inhabits: whether they experience that world as hospitable, friendly, judgmental, skeptical, intrusive, or cold. Habits of expectation are engendered by patterns of experience, and in this way is created our unique self.

One might agree to these points yet hold that race and gender attributes are not context dependent. Anatomical features are physical properties less amenable to change than a piece of wax. However, it is the meaning of those properties that determine one's identity category. As Amilcar Cabral writes:

> The identity of an individual or a particular group of people is a biosociological factor outside the will of that individual or group, but which is meaningful only when it is expressed in relation to other individuals or other groups. . . . Therefore the identity of a being is always a relative quality, even circumstantial, for defining it demands a selection, more or less rigid and strict, of the biological and socio-logical characteristics of the being in question. (1973, 79)

Identities are relational both in the sense that their ramifications in one's life are context dependent and that the identity designations themselves are context dependent; the latter is evident in, for example, the tribal percentages required by law for claiming native American identity in some contexts, informal acceptance of the one-drop rule, or social recognition of only two or of more than two sexual categories. Whether one's identity as Chinese American or Puerto Rican will confer advantages or disadvantages depends upon one's immediate context.

Racial identity especially is a patently non-intrinsic and context dependent feature of a person. As many people travel across countries, cultures, and sometimes even neighborhoods, their racial identity can change from mulatto or Cuban to black, from Mexican to Latino, even from white to black (for both analysis and first person accounts, see Domínguez 1997; Harris 1995; Haney López 1996; G. Williams 1995; K. Johnson 1999; Derricotte 1997). This is especially true for those who are mixed race, but it is also true of others who are "pure"; systems of racial classification differ across cultures, and aspects of racialized identity singularly salient in some locations—such as skin color—are secondary to other aspects in other locations. For example, in some parts of the Caribbean, hair type is as or even more important than gradations of skin color in determining identity, making beauty salons that can process and lighten hair a very profitable business from the Dominican Republic to uptown Manhattan. The case of gender is not analogous in all respects to race on this point, as I shall argue in chapter 6. Whether transsexuals retain their previous identity in all respects is today being debated in the courts, as if the legal system could determine the metaphysical validity of a person's claim about themselves.

Social identities may be relational, then, as well as contextually variable, but they remain fundamental to one's experience of the world and to the development of one's capacities. One's racial and gender identity is fundamental to one's social and familial interactions. It contributes to one's perspective on events—to one's interpretation of conversations, media reports, and social theories—and it determines in large part one's status within the community and the way in which a great deal of what one says and does is interpreted by others. Thus, our "visible" and acknowledged identity affects our relations in the world, which in turn affects our interior life, that is, our lived experience or subjectivity. If social identities such as race and gender are fundamental in this way to one's experiences, then it only makes sense to say that they are fundamental to the self.

One might agree with the arguments just presented, and yet hold that there is still a way to talk about *basic human capacities*, such as critical rationality and moral agency, that are independent of race and gender identity in the sense that they can be defined, described, and analyzed independently of social identity markers. Thus, some might argue, race and gender may well be significant but they are not fundamental to the self. In response to this, I am open to the idea that there are commonalities in human capacity. But the question is whether those capacities can be fairly described as processes without substantive content, in which case they are shared among all human beings, or whether they involve some content, which must be given in their specific context. In other words, is there a method of judging rationality that is acontextual? This is not a question that I can give a definitive answer to within the scope of this book. However, I will argue in this chapter that social identities are correlated to certain kinds of perceptual practices and bodily knowledges that, as such, may fall below the cracks of the sort of explicit beliefs and assumptions that can be assessed in rational debate. Moreover, the operations of rational thought necessarily involve making *qualitative* judgments, judgments that by their nature are influenced by one's experience because they are neither deductive nor clear-cut. My goal, however, is not to contribute to the debate over the universality of a given description of rationality so much as to show the positive and constructive relevance that identities sometimes have for reasoning, rather than merely as drags and hindrances from the realm of the particular on the otherwise rational operations of the universal "mind."

I have thus far argued that the categories of social identity are fundamental, even while they are contextual and relational. Whether or not they are essential to the self, they are certainly essential to the way the self experiences the world. Thus, the categories of intrinsic/non-intrinsic and essential/inessential confuse more than they clarify in thinking about the nature of the self. Nonetheless, the distinction between the interior and the exterior of the self may be useful to retain for the purposes of distinguishing between one's subjectivity and one's public identity. Let me clarify how I will distinguish these terms.

There are two aspects of selves that are involved in social identity. By the term identity, one mainly thinks about how we are socially located in public, what is on our identification papers, how we must identify ourselves on Census and application forms and in the everyday interpolations of social interaction. This *public identity* is our socially perceived self within the systems of perception and classification and the networks of community in which we live. But there is also a *lived subjectivity* that is not always perfectly mapped onto our socially perceived self, and that can be experienced and conceptualized differently. By the term subjectivity, then, I mean to refer to who *we* understand ourselves to be, how we experience being ourselves, and the range of reflective and other activities that can be included under the rubric of our "agency." These terms—public identity and lived subjectivity—are generally seen as corresponding to "interior" and "exterior" aspects of selves, without always taking note of the constant interplay and even mutually constitutive relations between each aspect. The problem with using such terms as "interior/exterior" is the danger of these invoking the longstanding tradition of thinking about the self in Western philosophy that has tended to posit an interiority as ultimately distinct and cut off from, and certainly not constituted in its essential nature by, external social reality, whether this refers to the interior and exterior of selves or of objects in the world (on this see Grosz 1994). A more plausible account of the self, or one with more explanatory value and coherence with everyday experience, would hold that neither public identity nor lived subjectivity are separable entities, fundamentally distinct, or entirely independent from the other. One of the tasks of analysis, then, is to explore the interrelationships between a public identity and a lived subjectivity.

But however potentially misleading, there persists a need to characterize the way in which a public self may not match a lived self, and to consider the manner in which we manage to separate ourselves from our public interpellation. Those with denigrated public identities have long resisted oppression precisely by maintaining a distance between how they are seen by others and how they see themselves, by asserting, "How you portray me is not who I really am." One can indeed experience oneself significantly differently from how one is publicly characterized. Thus, maintaining such a distinction is important in order to be able to critique the inaccuracy of some representations. As with most concepts and philosophical traditions, the political effects of imagining a mind/body split have been various, reminding us once again of Castells's point that "no identity has, *per se*, progressive or regressive value outside its historical context" (1997, 8).

However, the problem with explaining the experience of a felt separation between how I am seen by others and how I see myself via a metaphysics of mind/body differentiation is that it allows one to say, "I am not really my body," as if one were actually housed elsewhere and only there as a tenant. Moreover, it is not the only possible explanation: alienation from one's public identity can also be explained through a monistic discourse of embodiment, utilizing first- and third-person points of view and how these affect body image and body posture, as I shall show in what follows through drawing from the phenomenological tradition.

The philosophical project today, then, is to rearticulate the picture of the "inner" self in such a way as to maintain its correct core intuition—that these disparate aspects of the self are not always perfectly mapped onto each other in our lived experience—while simultaneously critiquing the traditional binary form of the description that ossified the distinction into totally separate and mutually exclusive oppositions between interior/exterior, mind/body, and essential/inessential. Accordingly we need also to explore the ways in which the substantive and particular nature of a given subjectivity is constituted *through* its publicly recognized identity. What are the implications of this mutual dependence between subjectivity and identity for our understanding of reason, belief formation, and cognition?

Identities as Interpretive Horizons

> The reef on which [the bourgeoisie] foundered was its failure to discover even a theoretical solution to the problem of [economic] crises. The fact that a scientifically acceptable solution does exist is of no avail. For to accept that solution, even in theory, would be tantamount to observing society *from a standpoint other than that of the bourgeoisie*.
>
> Lukács, *History and Class Consciousness*

To attain knowledge in most cases we must engage in a process of reasoning, and to engage in most kinds of reasoning—practical reasoning, moral reasoning—we must engage in a process of judgment. As Taylor shows, judgment involves a *qualitative* weighing of the evidence; it is not simple deduction, but more akin to an interpretation. Identities correlate to experiences that are influential on our judgments, such as judgments of who is telling a plausible story or how a person is likely to act under certain circumstances. This is the basis for supporting jury diversity: not just to appease political interests but to enhance the likelihood of an *epistemically* reliable decision.

Interpretations are discernments of meaning and are always performed in a particular place and time by a particular person whose individual experiences, and the interpretations the person has made of these, will have formative influence. Hermeneutics is the study of interpretation, and within the tradition of hermeneutics, there is generally a rich appreciation for the importance of the interpreter's background and particular perspective. We can look to this tradition, then, for a discussion about what we might today call situated reasoning.

It is the knower's very embeddedness in the world, with its attendant concerns and aims, that reveals the world to us. Heidegger distinguished three modes of understanding by using the example of a hammer. In the first mode, while we are actually *using* the hammer, we have a form of knowing how, an unreflective practical form of knowledge of the sort described well by Aristotle, Ryle, and Wittgenstein. In the second mode of knowledge, we stand at a distance from the hammer and approach it as a thing or object, perhaps noting its weight and dimensions. This is the Cartesian approach, which is useful in a limited respect but is hardly exhaustive or even representative of the ways we interact with the world. The third mode is Heidegger's favorite. This mode simply occurs—we cannot force it—just at that moment in our use of the hammer when we are interrupted or it breaks, a moment in which we are still close to our engaged relation with, or use of, the hammer yet are forced to become more *reflectively* aware of it *but as it exists in the context of our world*. Thus, the third mode is the most reflective mode. The second, Cartesian mode has a certain reflexivity but without the context necessary for understanding because it is detached from that which it seeks to know. Richard Palmer calls this "a hermeneutical principle: that the being of something is disclosed not to the contemplative analytical gaze but in the moment in which it suddenly emerges from hiddenness in the full functional context of world" (1969, 133; see also Heidegger 1962, esp. part 1, chapters 3, 5, and 6). That "world" is the "life-world," which Gadamer says is the "antithesis of all objectivism," that is, the world of bare existents, and refers rather to "the whole in which we live as historical creatures" (1991, 247). Thus the life-world is simply the lived or experienced world, a world that is intrinsically meaningful but whose meanings can change as they are interpreted within the lives of historically situated persons.

In the philosophical hermeneutics developed by Heidegger's student Hans-Georg Gadamer we probably find the best account in the Western tradition of a situated reason as an interpretive process involving the social location of the knower (see Palmer 1969, Weinsheimer 1985). "Reason," Gadamer says, "exists for us only in concrete historical terms—i.e. it is not its own master but remains constantly dependent on the given circumstances in which it operates" (1991, 276). The very process of trying to reach an understanding of something brings to the forefront one's personal experience, from which one draws in order to make sense of the thing. Time, place, and individual experience give rise to what Gadamer calls prejudgments through which the self deliberates, and as such are contributions rather than mere obstacles to the knowing process. "The very idea of a situation means that we are not standing outside it and hence are unable to have any objective knowledge of it. We always find ourselves within a situation, and throwing light on it is a task that is never entirely finished" (301). Thus, we can strive toward what he calls "effective-historical consciousness" or a reflective awareness about the horizon of our situation, recognizing it to be dynamic and not the only element determining our eventual understanding.

Gadamer defines the horizon as "the range of vision that includes everything that can be seen from a particular vantage point" (302). The horizon of our cultural tradition, then, is not a mere instrument of vision, but the condition in which vision occurs. Gadamer explains: "Our usual relationship to the past is not characterized by distancing and freeing ourselves from tradition. Rather, we are always situated within traditions, and this is no objectifying process—i.e. we do not conceive of what tradition says as something other, something alien. It is always part of us" (282). But it has content as well as location: one cannot see the sun if one's horizon is located underground, but one might take the subterranean shadows for a kind of sun if one is so disposed. The horizon is a substantive perspectival location from which the interpreter looks out at the world, a perspective that is always present but that is open and dynamic, with a temporal as well as physical dimension, moving into the future and into new spaces as the subject moves. The idea of a closed horizon, Gadamer says, is merely an "abstraction": "The historical movement of human life consists in the fact that it is never absolutely bound to any one standpoint, and hence can never have a truly closed horizon" (304).

The concept of horizon helps to capture the background, framing assumptions we bring with us to perception and understanding, the congealed experiences that become premises by which we strive to make sense of the world, the range of concepts and categories of description that we have at our disposal. It is thus useful in elucidating cultural, or group-related, and personal differences that affect interpretation. "In a conversation, when we have discovered the other person's standpoint and horizon, his ideas become intelligible without our necessarily having to agree with him" (Gadamer 1991, 303). The horizon is just the individual or particular substantive perspective that each person has, that makes up who that person is, consisting of his or her background assumptions, form of life, and social location or position within the social structure and hierarchy. Just as a servant has a different experience, perception, and perspective of the queen's castle, knowing intimately its back passageways, its pantries and cupboards, and viewing its fine rooms and furnishings primarily in terms of their degree of required maintenance, so the queen herself will have a different experience, perception, and perspective, perhaps having little knowledge of the underground rooms and no awareness of what her requests cost the servants in work time; she views her fine rooms and furnishings in terms of their ability to hold large numbers of guests, to provide her with comfort, or to please her aesthetic senses. We are not left with a dysfunctional relativism by acknowledging such perspectival knowledges: we can note the limitations of each, the different ways in which each is positioned epistemically, and then argue that one or the other has the epistemic advantage depending on what our project is. For emancipatory and egalitarian projects, clearly the servant's horizon will be the most valuable.

This concept of horizon thus offers an account of knowledge that links experience and identity as constitutive features for understanding without making them all-determining, and thus provides a *realistic* approach to explaining the relevance of identity to understanding while allowing for the mediated nature of experience and the fluid character of identity. The mediations performed by individuals in processes of interpreting their experience and the world are produced through a foreknowledge or historical a priori that is cultural, collective, historical, and politically situated. Social location is the site of mediations and is itself indexed to a particular (rather than universal) ethical engagement or interest with the issue at hand as well as a particular foreknowledge operative for certain persons in certain contexts and not for others. Reflective rationality requires, perhaps above all, the capacity to *doubt*, a capacity which has been said to be the basis for all inquiry. But as C. S. Peirce argued, doubting requires prior content and context: true or real doubt comes only when we have *reasons* to doubt, reasons that are by necessity substantive beliefs (Peirce 1940). Doubting does not guide inquiry as an abstract operation that would be equally applied to any and every claim; such a universal doubt that made no distinctions between predictions about the weather and the idea that your partner might really be a robot would be irrational. The doubting that is the basis of rationality is *prompted* by a specific experience, a *feeling* of anxiety and uneasiness. This *feeling* is based on an incoherence between our actual beliefs and beliefs that we have had proposed to us. Thus, the background foreknowledges that one holds are what makes possible the operation of critical reason, providing the context within which a claim will appear either plausible or inspiring of doubt. We cannot, therefore, stand completely outside of all traditions, freely choosing what will be preserved and what will be relinquished. Our ability to negate, and even to reflect on and identify, aspects of the traditions within which we stand is always and necessarily partial. This also accords with Wittgenstein's idea that justification's ultimate bedrock is not an epistemically grounded foundation or self-presenting state but a form of life, a complex, interrelated network of practices and perceptual orientations within which we navigate the world and function. And there certainly exists more than one possible, and functional, form of life.

The main problem with this kind of account of reason, and why some prefer the modern, contextually transcendent account, is that it apparently opens the doors to a dysfunctional relativism. Horizons yield different conclusions, yet how can we claim that a horizon is "wrong"? To admit the salience of horizon, some think, is to condemn us to a relativism without recourse. Another way to put this problem is that knowledges constituted by horizons will be unrelievedly ethnocentric.

It is no overstatement to say that the specter of ethnocentrism haunts the Western academy in these times.[2] If social location cannot be transcended, if the standards of justification are themselves in some sense contextual, and if identity therefore has epistemic salience, we fear the possibility that our diverse worlds of meaning, or forms of life, are truly incommensurable, without an overlap of shared belief and experience from which to communicate effectively and adjudicate debates. I suspect this crisis has been brought on more by the critique of Eurocentrism—revealing the purported universals emanating from the West as no more than particulars all along, and thus shaking faith in the universal—than by clear reasoning, because it takes only a moment of reflection to see the absolute falsity of the claim that horizons of justification are truly incommensurable, with no shared content from which to begin the work of clarifying disagreements. We may have varied "lifeworlds" but we do share an environment, as well as biological dependencies of various sorts, and even a history in broad terms. Edward Said, scholar of comparative literatures and comparative knowledges, wrote that "far more than they fight, cultures coexist and interact fruitfully with each other" and that "cultures are intertwined and can only be disentangled from each other by mutilating them" (2004, xvi and 52). In an interview he explained further:

> We have before us endless examples of, not the dialogue of culture but the clash of cultures, which can sometimes, as Samuel Huntington, alas, is right about, be very bloody. And a lot of people like Huntington have made a universal out of this, and have said cultures or civilizations today are so different that we have to accept the idea they are going to clash, that they cannot communicate except through opposition, sometimes through exterminatory relationships. I deeply disagree with that. I think the history of cultures, if you take the long view of them, suggests that cultures are really not impermeable, they are open to every other culture. . . . And, therefore, it seems to me, one of the prime motivations of a lot of my own work . . . is to try to expose the historical roots of clashes between cultures *in order* to promote the possibility of dialogue between cultures. (2001, 271)

Said's view, then, was that there is a historical rather than metaphysical or linguistic basis for conflict among cultures and that those conflicts can be overcome and do not prove the incommensurability of cultures.

In developing his influential theory of radical interpretation, Donald Davidson imagines an encounter with a species so alien that we have no common reference points and therefore we must guess their language from their truth ascriptions, but this is not the actual experience of cross-cultural encounters. Nor was it the experience of any of the parties to perhaps the most dramatic clash of lifeworlds since recorded history began: the *encuentro* of 1492. It may be helpful to flesh out what the idea of the hermeneutic horizon has to offer by looking for a moment at this most powerful example of a challenge to communication.

The actual obstacles to communication at that time did not result from incommensurable worlds or a lack of foundation upon which to debate conflicting values, but, on the side of the Europeans, greed, arrogance, and, to put it mildly, inadequate interpretive approaches, though this last problem was no doubt overdetermined by the first two. As new research reveals, Mesoamerican cultures did indeed share much with their contemporaries in Europe: a tradition of literacy, theocratic governance systems, and rigidly hierarchical and collectivized forms of social life (see, e.g., Boone and Mignolo 1994; Dussel 1995; Leon-Portilla 1990; Stannard 1992; Todorov 1984; Parkes 1969). Western cultures today would have much more difficulty accepting Aztec social relations than the fifteenth century Spaniards should have had: neither culture had concepts of democracy or equality, neither treated most women better than chattel slaves, and neither had religions in which there was a direct relationship between individuals and their God. Moreover, each had an extensive history of cross-cultural relationships in which differences of religion, language, and custom were productively negotiated, and for the Spaniards at least, these relationships crossed over what we today would call racial lines, or perceptible differences in appearance. Thus, there was much in common from which they might have had a very rich conversation, perhaps a debate, but more fruitfully an exchange of ideas.

There is some evidence that this is what the Aztecs and Incas themselves endeavored. In the initial period of the encounter, when the Europeans were far outnumbered, the Amerindians did not take them as prisoners or execute them but conducted some bartering and even held banquets and arranged at least a few "summit meetings" between leaders from both sides.

In one of these meetings, the clash of horizons was recorded. When the Franciscan missionaries came to the New World in 1524 to initiate spiritual conversion, they presented Christianity, as it was then presented in Europe, as pure dogmatic doctrine without rational defense or explanation (Dussel 1995, 52). They interpreted any resistance to the catechism as intolerable pride and the sign of the devil's temptation. Some of the people that the Europeans encountered, however, had a different tradition of discourse. When the Spanish insisted that the Amerindians accept the doctrine of Christianity in place of their own religion, they replied that just as the Spanish had a God, so too did they have Gods. The implication was that each must allow for, and respect, the different beliefs of the other, because the important thing, perhaps, was that they each had theological beliefs.

The famous Incan Garcilaso de la Vega, one of the first mestizos, recounts that when the Spaniards made their way to Atahualpa and related the catechism to the Incans, the latter responded thus:

You listed five preeminent men whom I ought to know. The first is God, three and one [a reference to the Trinity], which are four, whom you call the creator of the universe. Is he perhaps our Pachacamac and Viracocha? The second claims to be the father of all men, on whom they all piled their sins. The third you call Jesus Christ, the only one not to cast sins upon that first man, but he was killed. The fourth you call pope. The fifth, Carlos [king of Spain], according to you, is the most powerful monarch of the universe and supreme over all. However, you affirm this without taking account of other monarchs. But if this Carlos is prince and lord of all the world, why does he need the pope to grant him concessions and donations and make war on us and usurp our kingdoms? And if he needs the pope, then is not the pope the greater lord and most powerful prince of all the world, instead of Carlos? Also you say that I am obliged to pay tribute to Carlos and not to others, but since you give no reason for this tribute, I feel no obligation to pay it. If it is right to give tribute and service to all, it ought to be given to God, the man who was Father of all, then to Jesus Christ who never piled on his sins, and finally to the pope.... But if I ought not give tribute to this man, even less ought I to give it to Carlos, who was never lord over these regions and whom I have never seen. (Quoted in Dussel 1995, 53)

De la Vega then recounted that, immediately after this impressively well-argued response, the Spaniards "jumped from their seats and attacked the Indians and grabbed hold of their gold and silver jewels and precious stones." The Spaniards quickly moved, in other words, from an intellectual encounter, for which they were indeed ill-equipped, to a physical encounter, for which unfortunately they were quite well-equipped.

In dialogues in which one's only concern is with the reality of the object under discussion, or the reference of the terms used, communication is often stalled and even disrupted. This was the Spaniards' approach: they didn't reflect on how the Incans themselves approached religion; their only concern was whether the Incans accepted the Christian God as the true and only referent of the word "God." They apparently could not imagine a referent for the Incan god, so this belief was summarily dismissed. They could only hear the Incans say "yes" or "no" to the demand for tribute; they couldn't hear, or understand, an alternative response made possible by an alternative interpretive horizon or set of beliefs.

Obviously, the Spaniard's greed for gold surely overdetermined their hermeneutic obtuseness, but there is clear evidence here also of a difference in interpretive horizons. The problem for the Spaniards was not just that their attitude toward their own religion was unquestioning, but also that Christianity presumed universal application. Thus Las Casas had to spend decades in debate with Sepulveda and creatively develop a case using unheard-of concepts to show that the Indians deserved self-determination despite their refusal of Christianity. This was, apparently, a difference it had from Aztec and Incan religious beliefs. In this the latter groups were perhaps similar to the early Hebrews, for whom Yahweh was understood to be *their* God (see Genesis 17).

This example should also help to make apparent why it is that interpretive horizons are constitutive of the self. It is easy to intuit the vast difference between worlds in which either religion or science is dominant. It is also easy to realize how profound a difference it would be to view others' religions as equally legitimate rather than as forms of barbarity and/or absurdity. These differences would have significant effect on one's self, how one understood one's own beliefs, how one understood one's own practices vis-à-vis those of others different from oneself, how one looked out at the world, and what one saw there.

An interpretive horizon is not analogous to a magnifying glass by which any pair of working eyes could see any small object in more detail. The magnifying glass is a mere tool, without constitutive relation to either its object or its user. The interpretive horizon, on the other hand, may be thought of as constitutive of both: it constitutes the self in representing the point of view of the self, and it also constitutes the object which is seen in the sense that it is seen as what it is from the frame of reference and point of view that the horizon makes possible, looking at it, for example, from above or below, close up or from a distance.

This account of interpretive horizons does entail some relativism, but this does not require a suspension of judgment across differences of horizon. As Gadamer noted, the discovery of an interlocutor's horizon can enhance the intelligibility of his claims for us, but intelligibility does not entail acceptance. No horizon of a human being living on earth will be incommensurable with ours or lack a single element in common, because we share a material life and a planet, but there is a nonetheless relativism in the valuation of social practices brought on by the significant variations in horizon. Moreover, absolute relativism also is ruled out because no horizon is closed or incapable of movement. In some cases understanding and respect for a different form of life occur when *our* social location and form of life changes, when we have new sets of experiences through new practices, or when we take action. Relativism and incomprehension can be addressed through making physical changes in one's location and in one's practices.

There is, however, one argument against hermeneutics which I find important to address before moving on to phenomenology.

The hermeneutic tradition is not widely influential in contemporary philosophical work, in comparison to, say, Derridean deconstruction or Habermasian discourse ethics, despite the fact that it has played a crucial role in the development of philosophical thinking about the relationship between meaning and history and the nature of interpretation, and indeed, in the development of deconstruction and discourse ethics themselves. But it has been tarred with the tag of being too "subject-centered," to adopt Habermas's useful phrase, by those who wish to disassociate themselves from the Cartesian tradition of the intentional subject, which would include poststructuralists as well as all those influenced by the linguistic turn (see Habermas 1987). This criticism of hermeneutics, then, needs to be addressed.

To be subject-centered is roughly conceptualized as an approach in which what the subject wills and intends in his or her linguistic and practical action is key to his or her understanding as well as key in assessing it in either epistemological or axiological terms. Language and social practices, on this view, are essentially tools for human use, to be directed as we will. Given Heidegger's and Gadamer's intensive and sweeping critique of the Cartesian tradition, it may well seem odd to worry about whether hermeneutical philosophy is too subject-centered, but the worry is motivated by the fact that, although hermeneutics reduces the efficacy of individual *intention* to determine meaning, it does not reduce the *centrality* of the subjective perspective in the creation of meaningfulness. In Gadamerian hermeneutics, for example, it is the subject who carries prejudgments into the interpretive process, and thus the subject is still the locus of interpretive action rather than an anonymous language in which the embedded norms and meanings do not vary across different subjectivities.

There is contention over whether Heidegger in particular is truly susceptible to such a charge; the telos of his entire corpus, after all, involves a move away from man and toward that which is precisely not man: being. In Heidegger's work, man is not the lord and master of being, the giver of names, but more properly thought of as the shepherd who accompanies, appreciates, and stands in ek-static relation to being. This theme in his work is less relevant to the issue at hand, however. It may be that if subject-centered means epistemic mastery, then Heidegger's is not a subject-centered hermeneutics. But more to the point in this critique of subject-centered theories is the concern that the subject is taken to be the central figure for whom the interpretation must make sense or who serves as the reference point from which interpretive meaningfulness arises, and indeed, is indexed. Thus, there are two possible formulations of the subject-centered charge: one about epistemic mastery, or the claim that the subject controls interpretation, and a second about the centrality of the subject in interpretation, or the claim that the adequacy of a given interpretation can be judged only when it is indexed to the horizon of a particular knower.

This distinction between the ways in which the concern with subject-centeredness can be understood is very important for the assessment of the subject in hermeneutic thought. The critique of subject-centeredness fails to note the importance of Gadamerian hermeneutics' radical anti-Cartesianism, which is at bottom a critique of the idea that the subject can distance herself from her tradition in order to pass judgment on it. This assumption of a potentially complete epistemic mastery is not part of the hermeneutic tradition. And I would argue that, in the two possible senses of the subject-centered charge as given above, the first concern—about epistemic mastery—is the only issue that actually needs to be addressed. The second criticism—about the centrality of the subject in interpretation—actually can be ignored, since this feature carries none of the disadvantages of the Cartesian account of the subject that we should be legitimately concerned about. The centrality of the subject does not preclude the subject's imbrication in ideology or discourse.

Clearly for Gadamer, although the subject is important, the subject is not the master over interpretations or the attributions of meaning. "*Understanding is to be thought of less as a subjective act than as participating in an event of tradition*" (1991, 290 emphasis in original). When reading a text, understanding occurs when one places oneself within the tradition of which the text is a part, thus opening oneself up to what the text has to say. It does not involve a method to be used by a knower to force reality to yield her secrets. The method-focused legacy of Cartesianism puts an almost exclusive emphasis on the knower's epistemic performance, her acts of intellectual virtue, the reliability of her process of belief formation, or her ability to provide justifying reasons for her beliefs. The idea of epistemic mastery thus leaves aside an examination of what lies beyond their performance but makes it possible, that is, its constitutive conditions. Thus, by using the concept of interpretive horizon we are not then saddled with a problematic assumption of epistemic mastery but, quite the reverse, can articulate the substantive context and location from which a given subject develops understanding. The concept of interpretive horizon is essential to explain situated reasoning, the way in which one's context of horizon affects how one experiences the world and one's perceptions and interpretations. Horizons are open-ended, in constant motion, and aspects of our horizon are inevitably group-related or shared among members of a social identity. The significance of the group-related aspects of a horizon will vary depending on the subject matter at hand; they will not be all-determining, but they may become very significant in some contexts. Thus their significance is historically variable and contextual. But we need to understand the situatedness of horizons as a material and embodied situatedness, and not simply mentally perspectival or ideological. The hermeneutic concept of horizon signifies a locatedness that in reality is a metaphor for the body, but it is often conceptualized as an abstract body without attributes other than its location in a specific time and place. In the following section I will try to correct this abstraction by supplementing the hermeneutic concept of horizon with a phenomenological account of the link between embodiment and rationality.

Identities as Visible and Embodied

> I shall regret the absence of your keen mind. Unfortunately, it is inseparable from an extremely disturbing body.
>
> Gary Cooper to Barbara Stanwyck in *Ball of Fire*

The concept of identity in everyday usage, much more so than subjectivity or even the self, implies a recognition of bodily difference. We can imagine subjectivity as mind or imagination, merely mental, and thus as transcending its necessary physical base. But the social identities of race and gender operate ineluctably through their bodily markers; they do not transcend their physical manifestation because they *are* their physical manifestation, despite the fact that the same features can support variable identities depending on how the system of marking works in a given culture. Both race and sex are social kinds of entities in the sense that their meaning is constructed through culturally available concepts, values, and experiences. But to say that they are social is not to say that they are some kind of linguistic rather than physical thing or to imply that meanings are conceptual items pasted over physical items. They are most definitely physical, marked on and through the body, lived as a material experience, visible as surface phenomena, and determinant of economic and political status. Social identities cannot be adequately analyzed without an attentiveness to the role of the body and of the body's visible identity.

Racial and gender identities that are not visible create fear and consternation. Children born with ambiguous genitals are routinely given reconstructive surgery to make the genitals conform to what we expect males and females to look like, even when the surgery will result in their inability to have pleasure in sex. Marilyn Frye describes the discomfort most people feel when we don't know the sex of the person we are meeting: the discomfort comes not just from some abstract conceptual block but because we don't know how to greet or interact with them, so gendered are our gestures (Frye 1983). Census takers used to mark down racial identity based on what they thought the person looked like rather than by asking persons to self-identify, a procedure that assumes that the process of perceiving racial identity is objective and invariant. The Nazis were determined to find perceptible, objective means to find out who was Jewish, and developed a whole science toward this end complete with outlandish instruments. In the film *Europa, Europa* the young, closeted Jewish hero is chosen by his teacher to model Aryan facial features before a classroom of boys. His teacher ironically but terrifyingly got it wrong, ironically in mistaking his Jewish student as a paradigm of Aryan looks, but terrifyingly in bringing the boy to the front of the class for inspection. Despite the teacher's mistake, the modeling nonetheless conveys the importance of visibility within the Nazi regime: Jews *had* to be visible, and thus were measured carefully, from nose to ear, and navel to penis, in the attempt to establish a reliable and perceptible means of identification.

One might well argue that it is the very ideology of visibility that is the problem here; if race and gender could be divested of their purported visible attributes, they might be transformed to better reflect people's subjective sense of themselves—their actions, choices, their *humanity*—rather than mere physical attributes that were accidents of birth. In chapter 8 I will explore the question of the link between racism and the visibility of racial identity.

In our society today, however, race and gender operate without a doubt as visible identities; their visibility is key to the ideological claims that race and gender categories are natural, and that conflict is understandable because of our fears of what looks different. Visibility is also vital to how race and gender operate in the social world to allocate roles and to structure interactions. Thus, the experience of embodiment is in important respects a racialized and gender-differentiated experience.

It is important to add this embodied dimension to the account of interpretive horizon I sketched from the hermeneutic tradition. Although hermeneutic approaches maintain that the subject's location in any analysis of knowledge and experience cannot be eliminated, that location is conceptualized abstractly, without attention to any of its physical features. But "location" is a mere metaphor here for the body, the real locus of horizon. Western philosophy continues largely to operate with a kind of schizophrenia in regard to the philosophical importance of the body. On the one hand, body types differentiated by race and gender operated to determine epistemic status and thus philosophical ability, and philosophers such as Hume, Kant, Aristotle, and even John Stuart Mill were unabashed about this, claiming that dark skin was a sign of an inferior intellect (Hume and Kant), that all women have by their nature an intellect different in kind and inferior to men's (Hume, Kant, Aristotle), and that nonwhite societies are incapable of self-government (Mill) (see Eze 1997; Goldberg 1993; Bell 1983). Thus bodies mattered enormously to mental capacity. But on the other hand, despite the requirement of a particular embodiment for rational capacity, those deemed to have philosophical ability could then extrapolate from their embodied experience and location to make universal, even transcendental claims about the nature of human experience, as if their own experiences were unmarked and unlimited by their bodies.

In reality, our rational faculty is indeed embodied, and there is a wealth of implicit or tacit nonpropositional knowledge carried in the body. In a series of fascinating books and articles, Mark Johnson and George Lakoff have been trying to convince the cognitive science community for more than a decade that concepts, metaphors, imagination, structures of meaning, the interior experience of subjectivity, and rationality itself are fundamentally dependent on the particularities of the human body (Lakoff and Johnson 1999; M. Johnson 1987; Lakoff 1987). Concepts in particular are generally taken by philosophers and scientists alike to be objectively independent and in correspondence to the nature of a reality as it is in itself, or from a "God's eye view." Rationality is supposed to be capable of, and in fact is thought to require, transcending the body and its various limitations. To contest this Lakoff and Johnson cite empirical studies of mental operations and their own theories of cognition based heavily on the study of commonly used metaphors to argue that there is no such thing as a "fully autonomous faculty of reason separate from and independent of bodily capacities such as perception and movement." We therefore need "a radically different view of what reason is" that can accommodate the fact that "our bodies, brains, and interactions with our environment provide the mostly unconscious basis for our everyday metaphysics, that is, our sense of what is real" (Lakoff and Johnson 1999, 17). One example Johnson develops is the pervasive metaphor of "up" for "more," or the tendency to understand an increase in quantity by an increase in verticality. We say "prices keep rising," "the number of books published is going up each year," and "their gross earnings fell." Johnson explains:

> There is a good reason why this metaphorical projection from up to more is natural, and why more is not oriented down. The explanation has to do with our most common everyday bodily experiences and the image schemata they involve. If you add more liquid to a container, the level goes up. If you add more objects to a pile, the level goes up. More and up are therefore correlated in our experience in a way that provides a *physical* basis for our *abstract* understanding of quantity. (M. Johnson 1987, xv)

Thus, Lakoff and Johnson provide some suggestive evidence that the structure of our rational activity operates within and through systems of metaphors that arise out of embodied experience. They discuss many more examples in depth, including causation, essence, similarity, and importance, showing the ways that our formulation of these concepts has been based on embodied experiences. They argue that conceptual metaphors such as these are (a) *necessary* for abstract reasoning and (b) formed *only* through the body. Our conceptual system includes our fundamental metaphysical categories, the ways in which we experience and articulate our inner lives, even our understanding of morality, all of which are "crucially shaped" by our bodies. These conceptual systems are largely unconscious, since they are correlated with sensorimotor experiences that are so common that they become, Lakoff and Johnson imaginatively argue, "neurally linked": "Primary metaphor is the activation of those neural connections, allowing sensorimotor inference to structure the conceptualization of subjective experience and judgments" (1999, 555). Thus conceptual metaphors exist as tacit bodily knowledge, but they permit the operations of abstract reasoning that rely on constant qualitative comparisons and the structural analysis of relations. Our lack of consciousness about the strength and ubiquity of these conceptual metaphors, and their correlation with embodied experience, means that conceptual change is very difficult.

Drawing from research by Eve Sweeter and others, Lakoff and Johnson also show that "there is an extensive subsystem of metaphors for mind in which the mind is conceptualized as a body" (1999, 235). We conceptualize thought as motion (e.g., "My mind was racing"), thinking as seeing (e.g., "I see what you are saying"), ideas as locations (e.g., "I see your point of view"), and communicating ideas as manipulating objects (e.g., "You are putting ideas into my head"). We imagine our memory as a storehouse full of filing cabinets; we talk about an idea that "smells fishy" or is "half-baked"; we speak of "straying away from" and "returning to" a topic. And to know something is to perceive it: we say, "Do I have to draw you a picture?," "He pulled the wool over their eyes," "That is clouding the issue," and "She pointed out that...." Although this metaphor as well as others works at a mostly unconscious level, the fact that we conceptualize the mind and the operations of thought in bodily terms means that the body is always present in our perception and assessment of our own and others' intelligence. I would suggest that this could explain part of the recalcitrance of sexism and racism, as we conceptualize variously marked bodies very differently, with different "natural" movements and abilities.

Although Lakoff has looked at metaphors involving gender (see esp. Lakoff 1987), neither he nor Johnson has ventured to hypothesize the effects of different cultural, racial, and gendered embodiments on conceptual structures. In their 1999 study, *Philosophy in the Flesh*, Lakoff and Johnson give a few examples of Japanese metaphors just to be "provocative and tantalizing" because, they say, "very little research has been done on the metaphoric systems of inner life in other languages" (284). Therefore, although they argue that most metaphorical structures are apparently universal, they don't have the evidence to make this claim. In fact, even from their small Japanese sample, they suggest there is a radical difference not in the Japanese conception of inner life, which is the Western stereotype, but in the Japanese conceptualization of the self's relation to the other. If there are radical differences between *some* of the common conceptual metaphors used in different cultures, this would indicate that the basic shape and biological constitution of the human body are not in all cases sufficient to determine the specific metaphors we develop; there may well be more than one set of metaphors that can accommodate the vagaries of human physical experience, even if most metaphors are in fact universal. Philosophers do need, as Johnson says, to put the body back into the mind, but we also need to attend to the differences between bodies and embodiment.

Feminist phenomenologists, notably Simone de Beauvoir, Iris Young, and Sandra Bartky, have produced convincing descriptions of varied gendered experiences of embodiment (Young 1990; Bartky 1991; de Beauvoir 1989). One might begin to worry that this could get dangerously close to a vulgar Freudianism such as Camille Paglia sometimes descends into, where the arc of urine emanating from a penis is used to explain male projections into space, or the sophistries about women thinking in circles and men thinking in linear terms. The problem with such "explanations" is that they take the body out of its social context, moving directly from organ shape to cognitive approach. De Beauvoir, Young, and Bartky resist such binary demarcations of rational thought based on gender differences and instead focus on specific experiences that have been made gendered through cultural practices—such things as "throwing like a girl," or the kind of compact as opposed to expansive sitting that females are trained to do—and on experiences that can't help being gendered, such as "breasted embodiment." The former category makes for an exceptionally long list. There is not only throwing and sitting, but standing, walking, running, patterns of conversation involving interruptions and dominating the topics, perceptual orientations that can encompass sideline issues so as to notice household dirt, distressed children, bored interlocutors, and so forth, as well as the very interior experience of one's own emotional subjectivity. Mothers were the original "multitaskers," of course, and the need to keep "one eye" on the children while fixing dinner or writing poetry has debilitated many of us from that capacity to achieve the singularity of concentration produced by transcending the distractions of one's context, although this has become an equal-opportunity problem in the age of simultaneous media input and overload. Lakoff and Johnson develop a useful analysis of metaphor as tied closely to perception and movement, but to the extent that some perceptual habits and practiced movements tend to vary by sex, we might imagine the development of a more diversified account.

Young and de Beauvoir also venture into accounts of embodied experience that are less marked by socialization than by morphological difference, such as the experience of breasts, menses, lactation, and pregnancy. Whereas Freud focused more on the unconscious in hypothesizing an isomorphism between internal, unfelt bodily organs, such as the womb and imaginative projections, Young, Bartky, and de Beauvoir focused on conscious physical experiences, which have a less deterministic implication. Conscious experiences are readily subject to cultural interpretation and variation, such as shame or pleasure, and are bounded also by required social practices surrounding these physical attributes and activities, such as the necessity to conceal one's breasts. To note these differences in experiences and in practices in no way consigns us to the thesis "anatomy is destiny." Young argues this point in regard to physical strength: "There are indeed real physical differences between men and women in the kind and limit of their physical strength. Many of the observed differences between men and women in the performance of tasks requiring coordinated strength, however, are due not so much to brute muscular strength as to the way each sex *uses* the body in approaching tasks" (1990, 145). Feminists have been understandably skittish about talk of a physical basis for the behavioral differences between men and women, based on an eon or more of experience with deterministic theories hatched to justify patriarchy. In chapter 6, I will look at this issue in more detail.

Whatever analysis we make of how it gets there, the interpretive horizon that constitutes our identity is undoubtedly constituted in turn by a wealth of tacit knowledge located in the body. Perhaps the most general way to characterize this knowledge, as Gail Weiss suggests, is in the term invented by Sir Henry Head. Head names the "postural model of the body" that nonlinguistic imaginary position of the body that manifests its imagined relation to its environment and to other bodies (Weiss 1998, 7–8). Women's practiced movements and mannerisms, as well as the specific attitudes we take about our female features, all flow from this postural model of the body and its imagined conception of the proper, or necessary, relationship between women and men, women and children, and women in public versus domestic spaces. This body image is reflective not only of tacit bodily knowledge, but also of a perceptual orientation and a conceptual mapping that determines value, relevance, and imaginable possibilities. The gendered characteristics in women's bodily comportment indicate a very clear and coherent meaning for female embodiment, as Young's descriptions show especially well:

> Reflection on feminine comportment and body movement... reveals that these... are frequently characterized, much as in the throwing case, by a failure to make use of the body's spatial and lateral potentialities.... Women generally are not as open with their bodies as are men in their gait and stride. Typically, the masculine stride is longer proportionally to a man's body than is the feminine stride to a woman's. The man typically swings his arms in a more open and loose fashion than does a woman and typically has more up and down rhythm in his step.... [W]omen still tend to sit with their legs relatively close together and their arms across their bodies. (1990, 145)

The examples she describes continue for several pages, but the clear theme of all of these habits is that women assume less of a right or freedom to take up and move through space.

Now recall the importance that Lakoff and Johnson accord to "moving through space" in our conceptual metaphors for human thought. Just as we tend to take up less space in subway seats, do we move more gingerly, and with much less range, through the "spaces" of the history of philosophy and the broad theories of human experience? It is certainly not clear that male subway riding habits are *better* than female ones, so perhaps our reduced sanguinity about our ability to universalize and generalize could be, in some respects, an advantage.

No doubt Young's and other feminist analyses of female embodiment would require a cross-indexing by cultural and ethnic specificity. De Beauvoir claims that women tend to view their bodies as objects to be seen rather than tools for their own use, but Fanon argues that for all black people in the colonial world, it is precisely this self-consciousness about being a body-for-others that dominates black consciousness in public settings, perhaps eliminating the gender differences on this point for colonized peoples. He says:

> I came into the world imbued with the will to find a meaning in things, my spirit filled with the desire to attain to the source of the world, and then I found that I was an object in the midst of other objects.... The real world challenged my claims. In the white world the man of color encounters difficulties in the development of his bodily schema. Consciousness of the body is solely a negating activity. It is a third-person consciousness... assailed at various points, the corporeal schema crumbled, its place taken by a racial epidermal schema. (1967, 109–12)

Here, one's interpretive horizon, the space from which one looks out to understand and make meaning in the world, becomes doubly inhibited and self-conscious. The state of one's clothes and one's body becomes more important when one has a heightened awareness of one's object status for others. Every image imparted will be imparted for the whole race (or I would add gender); every gesture will reflect on the whole race (or gender); every failure will prove the preordained conclusion.

Michael Omi and Howard Winant describe the formation of racial identities as occurring within a dynamic historical context bound by macrostructures of political economy but also affected by the microinteractions in which resistance can influence the particular forms that race can take. Thus, the individual operates within a domain not of his or her choosing and yet still operates *on* that domain. Omi and Winant develop a description of "racial etiquette" that they define as "a set of interpretive codes and racial meanings which operate in the interactions of daily life. Rules shaped by our perceptions of race in a comprehensively racial society determine the 'presentation of self,' distinction of status, and appropriate modes of conduct" (Omi and Winant 1986, 62). This is a productive way to explore how race operates preconsciously on spoken and unspoken interaction, gesture, affect, and stance, to reveal the wealth of tacit knowledge carried in the body of subjects in a racialized society. Greetings, handshakes, choices made about spatial proximity, tone and decibel level of voice, all reveal the effects of racial awareness, the assumptions of solidarity or hostility, the presumptions of superiority, or the protective defenses one makes when one routinely encounters a misinterpretation or misunderstanding of one's intentions.

Merleau-Ponty's concept of the habitual body is also useful here. The habitual body he describes is the default position the body assumes when performing various commonly experienced circumstances that require integrated and unified movements, such as driving a car. While driving a car for a month in Australia, I came to realize the multitude of small dimensions I knew implicitly about driving on the right that I immediately lost when having to drive on the left—the knowledge of how to turn smoothly into the proper lane, of how to judge the distance of the curb when parking on the street, and of how to judge the distance of oncoming cars on a two-lane road. As Heidegger suggested, only such disruptions of normalcy bring us face-to-face with the wealth of knowledge we take entirely for granted, knowledge lodged in our bodies and manifest in its smooth mannerisms and easy movements. Similarly, race and gender consciousness produces habitual bodily mannerisms that feel natural and become unconscious after long use; they are thus very difficult to change.

Merleau-Ponty's development of a phenomenology of embodiment remains one of the most sophisticated treatments to date for describing embodied experience and bringing unconscious habits to consciousness. Phenomenology was the first Western philosophical tradition that attempted to deflate the abstract metaphysical approaches to knowledge in favor of a method of descriptive psychology that would discern the outline of consciousness by attending closely to the way the world actually appears to it. Thus phenomenology foregrounded a human consciousness first conceptualized as universal but soon understood to be richly indexed by its time, its place, and its particular corporeal foundation. The phenomenological tradition, extending from Hegel's project to theorize knowledge as it appears to consciousness, and developed further through the work of Husserl, Sartre, Heidegger, and especially de Beauvoir, Fanon, and Merleau-Ponty, has itself struggled to formulate an account of knowledge and the cognitive aspect of experience without separating mind from embodiment or reifying the object world as completely separable from subjective, corporeal experience.

Husserl conceptualized consciousness not as a passive receptor, as it was for many modern philosophers, but as positional, intentional, inherently and incessantly open to the world, and yet constitutive of the meaning of that world and of our experience within it. Perceptual experience is indubitable not as a means to know an object world separate from human existence, but as a means to know the lived world and to disclose the necessary structures of consciousness. Thus, despite its focus on immediacy of perception, Husserlian phenomenology did not accept without challenge the naturalness of experience or of what consciousness encounters; one of the purposes of the transcendental phenomenological reduction he invented is to suspend the natural existence of what I perceive, to distance myself from the familiarity of the world, and to transform the world from the realm of the actual to the realm of the phenomenal—that whose validity is not yet determined. Despite Husserl's heavy investment in the Cartesian project of providing a foundation for certainty, for him experience is not a clear datum or transparent fact, as it was for Moritz Schlick and some of the early logical positivists, but a complex of elements in need of clarification and reflection. Thus, for Husserl, "experience" is a complex object that exceeds sensory perception to include cognitive and interpretive faculties as well.

Husserl's epistemology remains, however, too wedded to the goal of establishing certainty and too confident about the possibility of the transcendental reduction. The reduction attempts to achieve through philosophical means that interruption of familiarity that one gets from driving on the opposite side or entering a foreign culture, but can such an interruption be achieved by philosophical reflection alone without a change of location or of practice? Husserl's concept of the transcendental ego remained in important respects disembodied, with its valorization of critical detachment as the route to a reasoned assessment of immediate experience. Merleau-Ponty's development of Husserlian phenomenology more successfully transcended the legacy of mind-body dualism that still operates in Husserl's epistemology, and shifted emphasis away from a foundationalist project and toward acknowledging the fact that knowledge is always unfinished and incomplete, precisely because of the open-ended and located nature of experience and of meaning.

For Merleau-Ponty, the purpose of existential phenomenology was not to ground absolute knowledge but to describe what exists in this here-now space, this present, which is a dynamic and developing synthesis incapable of total consistency or closure precisely because of our concrete, fleshy embodiment. Whereas poststructuralism bases its claims about the inevitability of incomplete understandings, about the absence of closure, and about the deferrals of meaning on the nature of language, phenomenology bases its account primarily on a reflective description of lived human experience as a corporeal being in the world. Lived experience is open-ended, multilayered, fragmented, and shifting not because of the play of language, but because of the nature of embodied, temporal existence. The world is laden with a depth of meaning without total closure or consistency not because deferral is the inevitable structure of linguistic meaning, but because the temporal texture of experience folds the absent and the past into the present moment.

As Iris Young explains, for Merleau-Ponty:

> Consciousness has a foundation in perception, the lived body's feeling and moving among things, with an active purposive orientation. Unlike a Cartesian materialist body, the lived body has culture and meaning inscribed in its habits, in its specific forms of perception and comportment. Description of this embodied existence is important because, while laden with culture and significance, the meaning embodied in habit, feeling, and perceptual orientation is usually nondiscursive. (1990, 14)

Here note that nondiscursive experience is not taken as uncontestable, like the logical positivists' notion of an experiential datum, because this would presuppose that a world not imbued with language is determinate and coherent, without layers of conflicting meanings already embedded. Such is not the case. The phenomenal world constantly folds back on itself, adding to what has come before and what remains still in the background of the present moment; the past is that which has been surpassed, yet remains within. There are no complete breaks or total separations, only folds within a continuous cloth, pregnant with latent meaning.

> When we speak of the flesh of the visible, we do not mean to do anthropology, to describe a world covered over with our own projections, leaving aside what it can be under the human mask. Rather, we mean that carnal being, as a being of depths, of several leaves or several faces, a being in latency, and a presentation of a certain absence, is a prototype of Being, of which our body, the sensible sentient, is a very remarkable variant, but whose constitutive paradox lies in every visible.... What we call a visible is, we said, a quality pregnant with a texture, the surface of a depth, a cross section upon a massive being, a grain or corpuscle borne by a wave of Being. Since the total visible is always behind, or after, or between the aspects we see of it, *there is access to it only through an experience* which, like it, is wholly outside of itself. (Merleau-Ponty 1968, 136, emphasis added)

Like structuralism and poststructuralism, and to a much greater extent than Sartre's thought, Merleau-Ponty's account of subjectivity allows us to understand how it is constituted by and through historically specific cultural practices and institutions. However, he is consistently critical of the objectivist descriptions of the self found in some versions of structuralism. He says that in a phenomenology-based descriptive psychology, "I am not the outcome or the meeting-point of numerous causal agencies.... I cannot conceive myself as nothing but a bit of the world, a mere object of biological, psychological, or sociological investigation" (1962, viii). However tacit and unconscious, we have agency in the constitution of our experience. At the same time, contra Descartes and Kant, phenomenological description also shows that my subjectivity is never detached from the world, never standing free and clear, capable of providing its own foundation, or merely "housed" in a mechanical body. On phenomenological grounds, Merleau-Ponty rejected the traditional

European transcendental accounts of the self imbued with masculinized autonomy and exaggerated self-control. Because subjectivity is not an object or mere epiphenomena of something more basic, it cannot be theorized apart from its lived, embodied experience. Thus he attempted to walk a line between structuralist accounts that recognize the importance of social influence and individualist accounts that allowed for meaningful intentionality. Toward this end, he strived to develop a new language of ontological description that could avoid invoking the dualisms of subject and object, body and world, past and present, perception and imagination.

Merleau-Ponty's account of embodiment provides a nondeterminist, nontransparent account of experience. Experiences matter, but their meaning for us is both ambiguous and dynamic. We are embodied, yet not reduced to physical determinations imagined as existing outside of our place in culture and history. This account helps to capture the dialectics of social identities, in which we are both interpellated into existing categories as well as making them our own.

The idea of an embodied, visible identity that operates as an interpretive horizon highlights the capacity of the body to see, which has been centered in Western epistemology as the basis for mastery through a detached, objectifying gaze. In contrast, for Merleau-Ponty sight is grounded in the body's own visibility. "To say that the body is a seer is, curiously enough, not to say anything else than: it is visible. When I study what I mean in saying that it is the body that sees, I find nothing else than: it is 'from somewhere.' . . . More exactly: when I say that my body is a seer, there is, in the experience I have of it, something that founds and announces the view that the other acquires of it or that the mirror gives of it" (1968, 273–74). Thus, in one sense, it is our own objectification, our embodiment in the world, and thus the very opposite of mastery, that grounds the possibility of our seeing. There is an ontological interdependence between being seen and seeing. This does not mean that reciprocal or egalitarian politics are likely or necessary, but that nonreciprocal constructions of visible identities are always based on an ontological lie. In Merleau-Ponty's unfinished notes, he began to explore another useful concept in this regard:

> The idea of *chiasm*, that is, every relation with being is *simultaneously* a taking and a being taken, the hold is held, it is *inscribed* and inscribed in the same being that it takes hold of. Starting from there, elaborate an idea of philosophy: it cannot be total and active grasp, intellectual possession, since what there is to be grasped is dispossession—[i]t is not *above* life, overhanging. It is beneath. (1968, 266, emphasis in original)

Knowing is a kind of immanent engagement, in which one's own self is engaged by the world—touched, felt and seen—rather than standing apart and above. One not only changes but is always changed as well. The key to this reconceptualization is his phenomenological insistence on embodiment, which structures and organizes the relational and epistemic possibilities.

These elements of Merleau-Ponty's analysis will be used to develop more specific accounts of race and gender in following chapters. The most important implication of the phenomenological approach for the question of social identity is to reject the dualist approaches that would split the acting self from the ascribed identity. It is just such dualist assumptions that lead to the view that identities must of necessity always fail as representations, that there is an "I" that always exceeds my identity. Identities gain their meanings always in a social context rather than simply from intrinsic features, yet they can be "true" of one nonetheless. The excess that may remain beyond an identity category, unnamed by it, is not the fluid, ephemeral, and pure capacity of negation or of flight. Identities themselves—meaning not the mere representation but the lived bodies—are fluid, complex, open-ended, and dynamic, which is why reductive and overly homogeneous characterizations of identity are inaccurate. The excess that may remain beyond any given identity category is not my "real" self, more true of me than any social interpellation, or the active core which creates the substantive self that can then be identified. It is simply an aspect that is relatively unconnected to multiple identifications. It makes no sense to locate the "I" only in that imagined active, negating core. Moreover, there is no ultimate coherence between anyone's multiple identities; there will always be tensions between various aspects. But this does not mean that there is an "I" that can stand outside of identity, or that can completely negate any of the identities that are true of it in a complete negation. Moral agency, subjectivity, and reasoning capacities are made possible within social networks of certain types. There is no amorphous substance or pure capacity lying pristine below the layer at which social constructions of identity take hold.

The absence of mastery in Merleau-Ponty's account of consciousness has important implications for intersubjective relations. To some extent Merleau-Ponty is developing his account in opposition to the early work of Sartre, whose famous pessimism about human relationships, as we saw in the last chapter, was based on his ontological picture of the configuration between selves and world, in which each consciousness posits its own system of meanings and values and posits the Other as a mere value to be configured within this schema. In Sartre's view, conflict arises inevitably over whose system will prevail, in effect over whose mastery will dominate to organize the social and symbolic field. By contrast, in Merleau-Ponty's picture, neither consciousness can effect such mastery, either over the meaning of the world or of the Other. "The other is no longer so much a freedom seen *from without* as destiny and fatality, a rival subject for a subject, but he is caught up in a circuit that connects him to the world, as we ourselves are, and consequently also in a circuit that connects him to us" (1968, 269). There are two points made here. One is that we cannot objectify the other any more successfully than we can objectify the visible world, the world that sees us in our seeing of it. There is no position of mastery that can be won or lost, though we might well fight foolishly over an imagined hope of mastery. The other is not an "object" for us, as a thing over and against us that we can see as if from above; we are, rather, beneath the other, in the same way that we are beneath being generally. A second point is that we are primordially, ineradicably, connected to the other. In both Hegel's and Sartre's ontology of self-other relations, it is possible to theorize the self prior to the other, prior to that moment of encountering and being shaken by the other's competing existence. For Merleau-Ponty, our connection to the other is inscribed in our being, our capacity to see, to touch. We are fundamentally an "openness," he says, a "stage" where something takes place (1968, 263). Our consciousness of this fact may not be explicit in our spoken characterizations of our existence—and in our pronouncements, say, of our "autonomy" and our "freedom"—but is revealed in our comportment in the world, our gestures or what might be called "body language."

In this section, I have presented philosophical work that shows the relationship between embodiment and perception, rationality and knowledge in order to argue that the interpretive horizon we each bring with us should be understood not simply as a set of beliefs but as a complex (meaning internally heterogeneous) set of presuppositions and perceptual orientations, some of which are manifest as a kind of tacit presence in the body. The work of Lakoff and Johnson builds on a large body of research mostly in cognitive linguistics to produce what they call "a new view of the person" in which the concepts we use in everyday functioning are presented as largely unconscious embodied conceptual systems. The work of Young, de Beauvoir, and Bartky describe the variability of bodily comportment and postural body image, again a kind of tacit knowledge and orientation toward the world and toward others. I then introduced the phenomenological approach to embodiment, and in particular Merleau-Ponty's work, in order to further develop an understanding of embodiment in relation to our concept of the self and of subjectivity. Merleau-Ponty develops an account of the person in his or her context that is thoroughly distinct from the modern, liberal picture of the separate, autonomous self, a picture almost all of us carry as unconscious conceptual assumptions. If we consider the idea of embodied interpretive horizons in light of Merleau-Ponty's work, we can avoid imagining horizons as totally discrete, impermeable, or situated at a distance from "the world." Thus, we can build up a concept of identity closer to reality.

The final ingredient for an adequate general account of identity, beyond its hermeneutic and phenomenological dimensions, is its relation to the other. Many people seem to think that socially ascribed identity categories impose a kind of external constraint on self-representation. Thus social identities are thought to involve a self-other relationship that is oppressive or disciplining. If this were true, the salience of identity and the attachment to identity could only be political trouble. In the following section, I will draw out how we might reunderstand self-other relations and self-community relations so as to explain social identities—our experience of them, our attachments to them—in a different way.

Identities and Self-Other Relations

> I borrow myself from others.
>
> Merleau-Ponty, *Signs*

The two main concerns that the critics of identity politics voice about identity both involve its connection to self-other relations, but the concerns come from opposite sides. On the one hand, critics are concerned that identities are a form of imposition of the other onto the self, unchosen and therefore unfree. Given this assumption, fighting to maintain one's identity is irrational. On the other hand, critics are concerned that an emphasis on identities will increase mistrust, conflict, and isolation, and that they will inhibit cooperative and integrated self-other relations. The first concern is that individuals will be too susceptible or open to the influence of others, while the second concern is that group identities create unnecessary conflicts or closed attitudes toward others.

These concerns are actually not in logical conflict: in the first case, it is the individual who is seen as the target of imposition from the group, and in the second case, it is group constructions of identity that create conflicts among individuals. Thus in both cases, groups are the problem. And this is simply to say that the realm of the social—or the collective or the community—is assumed to be at odds with individual autonomy, rationality, integrity, and self-determination. And notice that it is not *some* versions of the social here, but all. I have suggested that the hermeneutic and phenomenological traditions can help us see the implausible assumptions that generate these concerns. Social identities are part of our interpretive horizon and have an effect on what we perceive or notice, but it is incoherent to propose that horizons be "overcome." At least some of the perceptual practices and tacit knowledge that make up our interpretive horizons are actually located in the body, that is, below the level of conscious articulation. However, the body as conceptualized in contemporary phenomenology is neither simply natural nor the effect of determinism nor the location of *transparently* meaningful or *stable and fixed* meanings. The body is not a cage or mere canvas for social meanings foisted on us from society. As is clear in Lakoff, Johnson, Merleau-Ponty, and others, it makes more sense to think of the body as, oddly enough, a kind of mind, but one with a physical appearance, location, and specific instantiation. (This at least makes more sense than imagining the mind as a body.) We perceive and process and incorporate and reason and are intellectually trained in the body itself. This helps us to understand why race and gender are integral to the self: bodies are positioned and located by race and gender structures and have access to differential experiences, and may also have some differences in perceptual orientations and conceptual assumptions.

The question that remains is how selves or horizons can operate in a condition of plurality or reciprocal recognition. What is the self's relation to the other, individual or collective? The essential question is whether the other dominates the self, or threatens, oppresses, constrains its freedom, and so on. What I have shown in the previous two sections may help to establish the political importance of identity, but how does this situation come about? If identity necessarily involves the individual in a collective, what is the dynamic of that relationship and that process?

One important way to understand the relationship of identity to the other is through the necessity of history to the articulation of an individual's life. Stuart Hall says very simply that "identities are names we give to the different ways we are positioned by, and position ourselves within, the narratives of the past" (1990, 225). Identity categories always signify historical relationships and processes, and as Satya Mohanty argues are at least sometimes actual *explanations* of history. The identity "Chicano," for example, signifies a colonial history with a present-day reach into the political economy of the labor market. A historical narrative in this sense can also be thought of in terms of the concept of "tradition" developed by Gadamer. It is not that a historical narrative operates as a macroforce imposing its will on the individual; rather, it lives through individuals who interpret it and operationalize it into a set of social practices. Individuals have agency over interpretations of their history but they cannot "choose" to live outside history any more than they can "overcome" their horizon. The praxis of the past has formed the practico-inert of their environment, to use Sartre's terminology, within and against which they build their lives. The practico-inert may appear natural and inevitable, consisting just of found objects, but in reality it is the sedimentation of human praxis in the physical world around us. Thus too, history is dynamic and unstable, but its meanings are not completely indeterminate or infinitely flexible, and they are not forged by any individual alone.

It is important to be reflective about the different attitudes toward our embeddedness within history. Himani Bannerji says: "Those who dismiss so disdainfully all projects of self-naming and self-empowering as 'identity politics' have not needed to affirm themselves through the creative strength that comes from finding missing parts of one's self in experiences and histories similar to others. They have no project for change. They would prefer to forget their history, for whatever reason" (1994, 9–10). The descendants of those who dominated previous societies have a reason to forget, so that their current material wealth can be imagined to have come through their own, or their forebear's, hard work rather than unfair advantages taken in the past. The descendants of the oppressed may well have an interest in either remembering or forgetting: remembering, because this is a way to make sense of the present frustrations; or forgetting, because one hopes thus to avoid trauma and avoid being reminded of the humiliations and defeats of one's forebears. (This latter interest is often ignored by those who think everyone from oppressed nationalities to rape victims like to wallow in victimhood; in reality, acknowledging that one or one's family has been victimized can be extremely painful and humiliating, and out of the fear of one's own inability to deal with the emotional effects of acknowledging such experiences one may well just want to avoid the subject.)

Thus, we need to become reflectively aware of how our own historical and social positioning may be affecting our feelings about public acknowledgments of historical events. Identities may be playing a role over whether we feel the past is being "dredged up again for no good purpose" or whether we view it as a necessary facing up to responsibilities. Adorno and Horkheimer pointed out that "the destruction of cemeteries is not a mere excess of anti-Semitism—it is anti-Semitism in its essence" (1987, 183). We may debate various interpretations of our shared history, including the significance of various events, but we cannot and must not give in to the belief that its effects can be summarily erased or that the present is unrelated to the past.

The individual's embeddedness in what is always a collective, and contentious, history is one important way to understand self-other interdependence. Not only are the historical narratives that claim us collective processes, their intelligible meanings emerge only in light of substantive cultural values and available discourses. The process of interpreting history, and not just making it, is always collective.[3]

Part of what the collective praxis creates are aspects of the self. Our preferences, our dispositions toward certain kinds of feelings in certain kinds of situations, what typically causes fear, anxiety, calmness, anger, and so on, are affected by our cultural and historical location. Sometimes people take such internal feelings as proof of a natural origin, as when a homosexual kiss elicits feelings of disgust. The feelings may well be quite real, but this is not proof that homosexuality is unnatural; physical reactions can be altered by knowledge and acquaintance. This example suggests the most powerful role that the other plays in self-formation: the character of the other determines in no small part the self, as Hegel surmised, but, as Freud amended, this requires only an *attribution* of a certain character to the other, not the reality. Ortega y Gasset beautifully reveals the dialectic of sexism when he explains:

> This patent characteristic of weakness is the basis of woman's inferior vital rank. But, as it could not but be, this inferiority is the source and origin of the peculiar value that woman possesses in reference to man. For by virtue of it, woman makes us happy.... Indeed, only a being inferior to man can radically affirm his basic being—not his talents or his triumphs or his achievements, but the elemental condition of his person. The greatest admirer of the gifts that we may have does not corroborate and confirm us as does the woman who falls in love with us. (in Bell 1983, 452–53)

The inferior Other does not affirm us because they can judge our talents, triumphs, and achievements, but because their very presence alters how we judge ourselves. When one keeps regular company with a person whom one thinks of as having "inferior" intelligence, morality, athletic ability, strength, and so on, one's self-confidence in all these respects will increase. These are no mere surface feelings; the confidence they give creates the courage to try, to work at developing one's abilities, which then has a positive effect on the person.[4]

Thus, one way that the self depends on the other is for their very substance, their characteristics, their sense of themselves in relation to the world. The other gives content to our self, and also affirms that our self-estimation is real and not just imagined. The other provides empirical proof, in her own form, as well as sometimes by her judgment in cases, unlike the one Ortega y Gasset describes, where we consider her a fit judge. Hegel has a much more simple explanation of this than Freud's claim of a pathological desire to see oneself as whole through one's objectification in the other's eyes: Hegel suggests that we simply need epistemic confirmation of who we think ourselves to be, of how we understand the world and what we value in it. I prefer Hegel's theory to Freud's because it does not depend on a questionable claim about the overwhelming desire of the self for perfect coherence, wholeness, stability—that objectivist view of ourselves we can only get from the other because we certainly cannot get it from lived experience. Many persons happily and functionally compartmentalize their lives, having one self at work and another at home, thus suggesting that Freud's claim is not universal. On Hegel's view, our dependence on the other is primarily for confirmation, guidance, an insight into our behavior, or an interpretation of our history, and not always or simply to fill some pathologically projected "lack."

What is clear is that individual agency does not require separation and independence from others but actually the reverse. Individual agency is not intrinsic but made possible through certain kinds of social relations; to claim otherwise is a mere abstraction. As Merleau-ponty says, I borrow myself from others, that is, my confidence, self-assurance, my sense of who I am in the world. Moreveor, only in the context of something like a civil society, where one's opinions will be heard and respected, and where one has the capacity to act in such a way as to make a difference, can one then exercise moral agency by developing and exercising his moral judgment. A minimal level of respect from others, and from those others whose judgment counts in both figurative and physical terms, will create the possibility of personhood.

Since Hegel, one of the most powerful and influential accounts of the self's dependence on the other was developed by the social psychologist George Herbert Mead, who developed a theory of the social self in the early part of the twentieth century. Mead's analysis has numerous advantages, especially in its ability to explain some of the phenomena we can observe today in regard to identity conflicts. Mead's formulation takes up Hegel's belief that the self develops in the context of its relationship with other selves, but Mead turns Hegel's philosophical speculations into a more empirically based social psychology.

On Mead's account, the subject is born into a perspective that involves general, shared meanings which, because they are intersubjectively shared, have attained objective status, or in other words have been confirmed, as Hegel argued. He explains:

> What goes to make up the organized self is the organization of the attitudes which are common to the group.... Consciousness, as frequently used, simply has reference to the field of experience, but self-consciousness refers to the ability to call out in ourselves a set of definite responses which belong to the others of the group. Consciousness and self-consciousness are not on the same level. A man alone has, fortunately or unfortunately, access to his own toothache, but that is not what we mean by self-consciousness. (1967, 162–63)

Thus, in a formulation highly evocative of Gadamer and Merleau-Ponty, for Mead it is less correct to say that the individual self "has" a perspective than that it is "in" a perspective: the perspective, and thus group meanings and practices, precedes the individual and makes possible self-consciousness or self-knowledge. The group is not extraneous. "Social consciousness is organized from the outside in. The social percepts which first arise are those of other selves" (1982, 53). This is what yields Mead's idea of "objective relativism," that the shared meanings which make up our world and our subjectivity are broadly group-related and thus variable but also objective in that they exist in the world, not merely in our (collective) heads.

Mead does not describe this, however, as a deterministic process; the individual has agency, but its agency operates from the beginning in a collective context. "The child fashions his own self on the model of other selves. This is not an attitude of imitation, but the self that appears in consciousness must function in conjunction with other selves" (1982, 54). It is not that the self develops by a "blueprint" mapped out for him, but that its formative process occurs through a reality constructed and maintained by the social collective. This community perspective is captured in Mead's concept of the "generalized other" which is not meant to signify a sort of Big Brother that inflicts surveillance on the individual, but more as a communal perspective through which the individual self perceives and understands the world and which thus makes up the self's own experience. In other words, the generalized other comes into play when the individual abstracts from its own particular position in the social space to assume a perspective on the whole, as one does in watching a baseball game, for example, while operating within an understanding of the rules of the game and the roles set out for participants. One's perspective on the display is not organized by one's own individual reactions, about the aesthetics of a good run or physical feat, for example, but by reactions dictated by the symbolic system of the game. With this concept, Mead transforms Hegel's absolute self-consciousness into the irreducible relativism of multiple consciousnesses, but he retains Hegel's account of the larger perspectival domain not as a mere collection of individual perspectives but as an organization of the field of conscious experience.

Mead himself did not offer a theoretical analysis of a situation in which multiple perspectives are organized hierarchically, or a political analysis, in other words, of how these domains are structured. But some of his concepts can be applied to this more realistic picture. Self-consciousness in the more restricted and familiarly experienced sense is produced through social contexts, which affect not only an individual's sense of the world but also the individual's sense of self: "The child's consciousness of its own self is quite largely the reflection of the attitudes of others toward him" (1982, 54). Moreover, Mead argues, self-consciousness is heightened by social disapproval in any form, or by being treated as if one is operating outside the norm (1982, 17). We get more attention by being significantly better than our peers, or alternatively, by being significantly worse, or simply by behaving badly.

Children of course often strive for greater attention in one of these ways, but we can also gain attention without intending to if we are *perceived* as outside of any given norm, either a norm of behavior or of appearance. And such heightened attention from others draws our own attention toward those "abnormal" features. This could help to explain the commonly perceived lack of reciprocity between white and nonwhite self-consciousness, or self-awareness, about their own racial identity. Only recently have whites in large numbers felt self-conscious as white, aware of themselves as not only having a gender, a nationality, an occupation, perhaps an ethnic origin, but also as having a race. When nearly every cultural image in entertainment or politics was uninterruptedly white, that very attribute receded into the background of consciousness, because it was so shared and normative as to escape reflective awareness.[5] It received no attention either from the self or from their relevant others, that is, other whites. On the other hand, as Fanon describes in searing detail, nonwhites have very much been made to feel their racial identity, and to be aware of a generalized other in which their own identity was peripheral. Though gender identity is more diffused throughout the social space, in specific domains a similarly heightened self-consciousness could beset women when they occupy masculine-majority locations, as de Beauvoir describes at length. One then watches oneself performing, operating through a double perceptual relation to the environment: one which is first person but without integration into the dominant generalized other, and one which is third person from the point of view of the dominant generalized other, which is a part of one's own perspective or self but which involves a marginalization of one's identity.

Women in such masculine domains and persons of color in majority white contexts are not operating strategically or opportunistically when they note their minoritarian status or act so as to call attention to it; their identity calls attention to itself, a call that communicates both to them and to others. Mead's claim that our self-consciousness is produced through the reactions of others makes sense of this phenomenon, and recognizes it as an effect not of the minority group's own actions but simply of the shared meanings of the collective space. Ofelia Schutte's phenomenological descriptions of being Latina in a white male academic environment illustrates this very well.

Schutte argues that those individuals who operate in more than one culture will necessarily have to leave part of themselves behind each time they cross over. She provides a rich phenomenological description of how this feels that is reminiscent of de Beauvoir's description of the inherent conflict between what is signified human and what is signified feminine, but Schutte's focus is ethnicity. To be recognized in North American contexts, Schutte explains, "I must show that . . . I can perform, in my North American voice, a public erasure of my Latina voice. . . . My white Anglo-American counterpart is not called on to perform such a feat with respect to her own cultural background." She goes on to acknowledge that her white counterpart may have to erase a working-class or lesbian background, but "she does not need to combine her cultural background with, say, that of Middle Eastern, Asian, African, or Latin American people before being accepted as an important contributor to society and culture" (2000, 59). Schutte thus describes the alienating self-consciousness of Latina subjectivity and agency when we are forced to operate in terms that are weighted toward the dominant culture. In order to gain recognition, "I need to be knowledgeable in the language and epistemic maneuvers of the dominant culture, the same culture that in its everyday practice marks me as culturally 'other' than itself." It is thus only when we make our own selves "other" that we gain recognition, or when we become split subjects. And for those whom the dominant group represents as inferior, this means participating in self-denigration. De Beauvoir says that the characteristics of *woman as other* in male dominant society "have all too evidently been dictated by men's interest" (1989, xxxiii).

The price for this self-denigration is predictably high:

> The local metanarrative exists in tension with what the Latina knows and experiences, . . . the former shuts out the latter. This is why sometimes, when some interlocutor responds to me (say, at the office) in reference to the self I perform there as a speaking subject, I get the sense that this colleague is not speaking to me at all; that my interlocutor is missing something, because the "me" that is culturally different is ignored, shut off, or bypassed. (Schutte 2000, 60)

In other cases Latinas may be valued for their very ability to represent Latino culture in an Anglo-American world, which requires exceeding "the category of the national" and incorporating "two or more cultures into our way of being." But she points out that this is always accompanied by the demand to "demonstrate that the way we bring such cultures together can benefit the Anglo-American public" (2000, 59).

The general point here is that the self does not exist prior to these operations but becomes manifest through them, even in cases of incoherence and internal disjunctive heterogeneity. This again shows that race and gender are fundamental, rather than peripheral, to the self. Mead argues:

> The given individual's membership in several of these abstract social classes or subgroups makes possible his entrance into definite social relations (however in-direct) with an almost infinite number of other individuals who also belong to or are included within one or another of these abstract social classes or subgroups cutting across functional lines of demarcation which divide different human social communities from one another, and including individual members from several (in some cases from all) such communities. (1967, 157)

Here Mead recognizes the multiplicity of the groups that constitute a given self and argues that it is nonetheless one's group identity that makes social interaction possible, although he doesn't consider the power relations that may determine the ways groups interact and how these affect the formation of a given individual who operates in differentially empowered communities. This passage also resonates with the study by José E. Cruz, discussed in chapter 2, of the Puerto Rican community's political involvement in Hartford city politics. Cruz argued that the political par-ticipation of Puerto Rican individuals in Hartford politics was made possible by identity politics or group political action. Mead's account helps to explain why this is the case. Unless the Puerto Rican group-based generalized other became oper-ative in the city's political discourse and practice, Puerto Ricans' subjectivity would have to be left behind when engaging in political action. On Mead's account this is impossible, but if we follow Schutte's description of the split self we might imagine it as happening at the expense of bringing in a Puerto Rican agenda. Without their group identity being recognized, and thus being a player, in the larger political scene, Puerto Rican individuals would have to exert just the kind of self-alienation that Schutte describes in order to participate. This is more than just putting aside for the moment one's ethnic habits; it is having to attempt to at least temporarily erase and even denigrate a fundamental aspect of one's self.

This analysis makes clear that selves are affected by others in that they are constituted in and through collectives or groups; it is not that I am constituted in terms of only intentional attitudes that originate in the other but in terms of the collective meanings, roles, and modes of perception made possible within a given context, implicitly agreed upon as are the rules of a game everyone is playing. The binarism of self/other breaks down with this account, as does the idea of the other *inflicting* categories on the self, and the assumption that individuals are clearly and neatly demarcated. The other is, rather, in or a part of the self, and this can be true even of others who have been repudiated. Alain Locke wrote in 1924:

> It must be increasingly recognized that the Negro has already made very substantial contributions, not only in his folk-art, music especially, which has always found appreciation, but in larger, though humbler and less acknowledged ways. For generations the Negro has been the peasant matrix of that section of America which has most undervalued him, and here he has contributed not only materially in la-bor and in social patience, but spiritually as well. The South has unconsciously

absorbed the gift of his folk-temperament. In less than half a generation it will be easier to recognize this, but the fact remains that a leaven of humor, sentiment, imagination and tropic nonchalance has gone into the making of the South from a humble, unacknowledged source. (1992, 24)

Locke is suggesting that the selves of white and black southerners are inextricably entwined, if not necessarily politically, then psychoculturally. Nonblack Americans have imbibed linguistic patterns, food preferences, and other aspects of a mode of life from hybridized African sources. The power relations involved in this are of course not to be taken lightly, and the ongoing problems of commodifying and expropriating the "exotic" cultures within deserve serious critical analysis. But it is not the case that whites stand fully apart and outside minority cultures, choosing when and where to adopt ideas or be influenced by them. Power does not operate solely by separating, but by determining the conditions under which hybridizations will be formed, acknowledged, and who will benefit from them. This is also echoed in Gooding-Williams's claim quoted previously that multiculturalism is about recognizing the diversity within, rather than simply the diversity without.

Thus, the other is in the self in the sense that the self internalizes a variety of group attitudes as well as congruent characteristics. Moreover, it is not always useful or necessary to theorize affect, unconscious dynamics, desire, or psychological states in general as located in individuals, certainly not as wholly caused by or originating in individuals. Naomi Scheman developed this argument in relation to psychological states and subjective experience, arguing that, while being five feet tall or having pneumonia is an individual state, "being the most popular girl in the class or a major general or divorced are not individualistic states; nor, I want to argue, are being in love or angry or generous, believing that all eels hail from the Sargasso Sea, knowing how to read, intending to be more honest, or expecting an explosion any minute now" (1983, 226). Such states are not properly individual because how we learn to identify them, grouping experiences together and interpreting them—all of which will affect how we *feel* them—requires the developed social consciousness of just the sort Mead described. The rich and complex texture of what we think and experience as our inner lives is frequently beyond our individual intention and understanding.

Group identities can be misnamed, misrecognized, or misrepresented, but they are real entities, and thus are not *inherently or inevitably* incorrect descriptions. They are not illusions, or reducible to the machinations of power, or stable and fixed with closed borders and clear criteria of inclusion. To recognize the importance of one's group identity is not necessarily to be opportunistic, essentialist, or to be committed to separatism. It is to recognize the reality of the social basis of individual selves. Mead's account enriches the notion of horizon I drew from the hermeneutic tradition: each individual's horizon is significantly incorporative of social dimensions or shared features. The practices and meanings that are intelligible to me are ontologically grounded in group interactions, which are themselves structured by political economies of social structures. For example, the way in which aspects of an African American diasporic identity was absorbed generally in the South by whites and others without acknowledgment cannot be explained apart from the political economy underpinning southern cultural practices and social relations.

Mead's account thus needs to be supplemented by an exploration of hierarchies, power differences, and the material determinations that contribute to the construction of a generalized other or the rules of the game. But this needs to be done as a very particular and specific analysis in particular and specific cases. There are no grounds to assume that the generalized other is always oppressive. It seems to me that the modern ideal of autonomy understood as disengagement assumes as a default or general starting position that the other is hostile, oppressive, or at least less rational, and this assumption is the key to unraveling the Western resistance against the dependence on and constitution of the self within a social domain. For Plato, we must use our own reasons because the other may not be guided by reason at all but by emotion; for Hegel, the other desires my death; for Lacan, the other's impositions are the impositions of the Law of the Father, an irrational claim of force; for Sartre, the other wishes to imprison me in the in-itself; for Foucault, the other is the means of normalization and discipline; for Butler, the social categories by which I am identified in the social domain impose a profound alienation. Contrast these accounts with Fanon, who specifies the problem as the *colonizing* other, or Mohanty and Scheman, for whom the other is a source of knowledge. The dominant Western tradition of thinking that self-reliance and disengagement are the best and surest route to rationality, moral rightness, and integrity requires the missing premise that the other is guilty until proven innocent. But why assume one is always smarter than the community?

Epistemology is as involved here as metaphysics: for Plato and the early moderns, metaphysical autonomy is the basis of the capacity to reason; for Hegel, self-consciousness and knowledge are entwined; for Sartre and Butler, categories of identity are in an important sense false claims. But the fact is that nearly every truth we learn we learn from others. We routinely go to friends, family, therapists, religious leaders, books, and newspaper articles for help and guidance on every life trouble (and those who don't are foolhardy). And sometimes we accept the advice we receive even when we don't fully understand it or believe in it. I experience a traumatic event and am beset by nightmares, flashbacks, and panic attacks. I try desperately to gain control of my emotions but find it impossible, and so seek help. I am advised to "feel my feelings," to let myself feel what comes without worrying about feeling it or attempting to control it. I think this is crazy and frightening advice but try it. It works: I spend my energy more productively learning to cope with my trauma than unproductively trying to make it disappear. By letting myself feel I can discover what triggers the feelings and work to avoid them. And when the feelings come no matter what I do, I let them go, even nurture them along, and after a while find I feel refreshed. Here I learn that self-mastery comes when I let down my guard to others as well as myself, when I follow another's lead and give up my insistence to do only what I can fully comprehend and agree with. I gain self-determination by embracing my emotions and embodiment rather than seeking to transcend them, even emotions caused by the destructive acts of others. Instead of retreating from all others after a traumatic event, my salvation from destructive acts lies in opening myself up to others, even leaning on them. We have experiences over and over in life in which we rely on and are rewarded by the knowledge and guidance of others. So why not assume the other is innocent until proven guilty, rather than the other way around?

Although many strains of Western philosophy can be found also in other philosophical traditions, this individualist assumption that underlies much of Western metaphysics and epistemology appears not to be. Arindam Chakrabarti, in his comparative study of Anglo-American and classic Indian epistemology, argues that the knowledge analyzed in the Nyāya tradition is always assumed to be within a social world (1994) . In the modern tradition of Western epistemology, and still today in mainstream Anglo-American epistemology, from Hume to Keith Lehrer, testimony is hardly theorized at all. But when it is, it is considered a legitimate source of knowledge only if the claim has been independently verified. Thus, assessing the epistemic reliability of others requires assessing the epistemic justi-fication of their claims, in which case the fact that a claim is testimony is like an unnecessary middleman: it adds no epistemic value (see Alcoff 2001, 56–57). The reasons given for this are the same as those used to require individual autonomy for rationality: we cannot be certain as to whether the other is leading us astray, so we must rely only on ourselves. In contrast, Chakrabarti explains that testimonial knowledge is considered very important, entirely legitimate, and, most interest-ingly, it is characterized as *not distrusting* the source. In other words, to say that I trust Lorenzo is to say that I have reasons for believing Lorenzo to be epistemically trustworthy. When I distrust Lorenzo it will also be on the basis of specific reasons. But the default position, before those reasons are manifest, is the absence of distrust, which is thus an openness to the other. In the Nyāya tradition, Chakrabarti explains, it is understood that cognition normally operates without either distrust or doubt, but through a disposition toward acceptance.

To repeat, the issue here is mastery, not rationality. Rationality does not require us to assume before there is any evidence that the other is hostile, ma-nipulative, or untruthful. However, once we alter our orientation, and enact consciously, and articulate philosophically, what is in reality *already the case*—that we are dependent on the other—we lose the conceit of mastery and domination, of being in total control.

Of course, besides the worry about the other's hostility or untruthfulness, there is also the worry about the irrationality of one's whole culture or community in which one is ineluctably embroiled. If we accept uncritically the normative ideas and practices of our society, we may be accepting immoral, unjust, and irrational ideas. Some of the arguments I have made here may seem to take the form of criticizing the culture of the West as it is manifest in Western philosophy, or criticizing Western philosophy because it manifests some problematic aspects of Western culture that are hard for us to see. Thus I am critiquing my own culture, which might be seen as a performative contradiction. One might also trace the excess of hostility toward the other to the devolution of human relationships produced in market-driven societies, in which so many of our relationships are such that we know the other person—whether salesperson, banker, advertiser, job competitor—is either lying or withholding the whole truth in order to maximize his or her advantage. Such cynicism grows apace with the penetration of the market in social life: few people now believe politicians, believing them to be strategically motivated as well, and increasingly we become skeptical of religious leaders and even health professionals, who are driven by insurance and management concerns rather than our health alone. If this problem is rooted in our shared culture, then doesn't this prove that rationality would counsel the individual to seek escape? Wouldn't it be better to gain some distance, to aim at just thinking for ourselves?

But this formulation of the problem assumes that one is interpellated in a neatly coherent form of identity, hardly the contemporary reality. The worry about grounds for resistance and critique dissipates quickly when one acknowledges the multiple resources we have for alternative forms of life and the open rather than closed nature of cultural and identity formations. Indeed, the incoherences are intense enough to produce their own problems, but it is an advantage to have contrasting assumptions from which to generate dialogue and in some cases repudiations of aspects of cultural knowledge one has grown up with. Every social identity, from Latino to white to Asian American, and certainly female identity, has wide rifts and contra- dictions within, and the many forced migrations of the transnational economy have made cultures increasingly heterogeneous, even as commodities become more homogeneous.

Here I find the Western hermeneutic and phenomenological traditions as well as Mead's social psychology seriously deficient, not because they assume the jus- tification of our existing beliefs but because they tend to portray our situation as if it were coherent, monocultural, and internally consistent in all respects. A nec- essary complication for the account of identity arises when we consider the in- coherences, multiplicities, and hybrid aspects of selves, cultures, communities, and horizons. Again, I am less concerned with the fracturing of the self that Freud hypothesized, and his portrayal of an inevitable conflict between life and death drives—an internalized Hegelianism—than with the plurality of cultural tradi- tions that make up the contemporary individual. We need to reformulate the account of the formation of identity as well as the theorizing of self-Other relations in an increasingly hybridized, multicultural frame. The complexity, inevitable cultural hybridity, and multiplicity of the contemporary self requires what Rai- mundo Panikkar, Enrique Dussel, and Walter Mignolo call a pluritopic, rather than monotopic, hermeneutic (Panikkar 1988; Dussel 1985; Mignolo 1995). As Mignolo and others have pointed out, the Western tradition of hermeneutics is itself monotopic and monologic; it presupposes a single coherent tradition that is dynamic through history but unchallenged by alternative horizons competing in a given space or time frame. This is of course key to colonial ideology as well as patriarchal conceit. As one of the founders of postcolonial theory, Edouard Glissant, put it, "One of the most disturbing consequences of colonization could well be this notion of a single History. . . . The struggle against a single History for the cross-fertilization of histories means repossessing . . . a true sense of one's time and identity" (1999, 93).

The monotopic account of identity is not only unrealistic but assumes no normative or ethical obligations to the Other who is outside of one's own cultural base. A phenomenological hermeneutics grounded in such a conception *is* in conflict with an anti-essentialist project, and cannot claim descriptive adequacy over the multiplicities and incoherences of interpellations in postmodern, postcolonial life, where "too many Others and Elsewheres disturb the placid surface" (1999, xii). The idea of a pluritopic hermeneutics is to situate identity within multiple traditions that are at play in the political contestation over meanings in a postcolonial world. As Mignolo puts it, "Pluritopic understanding implies that while the understanding subject has to assume the truth of what is known and understood, he or she also has to assume the existence of alternative politics of location with equal rights to claim the truth" (1995, 15). This becomes obvious when one's very own horizon, constitutive of one's identity, is itself pluritopic and multicultural, constituted by sometimes contradictory background meanings or value assumptions.

This leads Mignolo to observe:

> Colonial semiosis brings the following dilemma to the fore: what is the locus of enunciation from which the understanding subject comprehends colonial situations? In other words, in which of the cultural traditions to be understood does the understanding subject place him or herself by constructing his or her locus of enunciation? How can the act of reading and the concept of interpretation be rethought within a pluritopically oriented hermeneutics and the sphere of colonial semiosis? (1995, 16)

We need a critique of Western assumptions about knowing the colonized Other, in order to uncover their orientalist self-aggrandizing structure, but without relying on an unproblematic "authentic" alternative from the colonized, whose interpretive horizon is similarly historically dynamic and is undoubtedly distorted by colonialism as well. And we cannot assume that any hermeneutic horizon or background of understanding is in fact coherent or closed to other horizons. Thus, it is not simply that the other makes up the self, but that multiple others are constitutive aspects of our interpretive horizon, offering alternative and in some cases competing background assumptions and perceptual practices, fracturing the meanings of visible appearance and complicating embodied knowledge.

Answers to the questions that Mignolo and others are posing will require that we take seriously the existence of social identities as places from which knowing and perceptive analysis occurs, which operate as interpretive horizons, but whose knowledge is sometimes to be found in embodied practices and not just stated beliefs.

Identities of Race and Gender

> It all depends on the skin you're living in.
>
> Sekou Sundiata

Perhaps it doesn't *all* depend on the skin you're living in, but Sundiata's phrase is evocative of the way in which one's specific social identity is where one lives, or where one does one's living.

A summary of the argument can be put as follows. Rationality operates necessarily through the determination of qualitative distinctions; such distinctions are not algorithmic but are made on the basis of a form of practical reasoning that is grounded in our interpretive horizons as well as embodied knowledges; these horizons and knowledges, which are located at the very center of the self, in its embodiment, have a social rather than individual foundation. Rationality does not, then, require the individual to minimize his or her embeddedness within a social group. The fact that we are constituted by the Other, most clearly perhaps in our social identities, is no cause for automatic alarm until we have specific reasons for distrust.

Racial and gendered identities are socially produced, and yet they are funda-mental to our selves as knowing, feeling, and acting subjects. Raced and gendered identities operate as epistemological perspectives or horizons from which certain aspects or layers of reality are made visible. In stratified societies, differently iden-tified individuals do not have the same access to points of view or perceptual planes of observation or the same embodied knowledge. The queen may freely walk in the servants quarters, but she will not view them in the same way as the servants do. Two individuals may participate in the same event, but different aspects of that event will be perceptible to different people. Social identity operates, then, as a rough and fallible but useful indicator of differences in perceptual access. This argument does not rely on a uniformity of opinion within an identity group but on a claim about what aspects of reality are more or less easily accessible to an identity group.

If raced and gendered identities, among others, help to structure our con-temporary perception, then they help constitute the necessary background from which I know the world. Racial and sexual difference is manifest precisely in bodily comportment, in habit, feeling, and perceptual orientation. These make up a part of what appears to me as the natural setting of all my thoughts. Perceptual practices are tacit, almost hidden from view, and thus almost immune from critical reflection. As Merleau-Ponty says, "perception is, not presumed true, but defined as access to truth" (1962, xvi). And because they are nondiscursive, perceptual backgrounds are incapable of easy discernment or description.

Although perception is embodied, it is also learned and capable of variation. The realm of the visible, or what is taken as self-evidently visible (which is how the ideology of social identities naturalizes their specific designations), is argued by Foucault to be the product of a specific form of perceptual practice, rather than the natural result of human sight. Thus he claimed that "the object [of discourse] does not await in limbo the order that will free it and enable it to become embodied in a visible and prolix objectivity; it does not preexist itself, held back by some obstacle at the first edges of light. It exists under the positive conditions of a complex group of relations" (1972, 45). His central thesis in *The Birth of the Clinic* is that the gaze, though hailed as pure and preconceptual, can only function successfully as a source of cognition when it is connected to a system of understanding that dictates its use and interprets its results. On this account, which is hardly unique to Foucault, visibility itself cannot serve as the explanatory cause of perceptual outcomes. Thus Foucault shares the view now commonly held by philosophers of science that a "pure" observation is not an observation at all, in the sense that to count as an observation it must be able to serve as a support for a theory or diagnosis. It will not become an observation until and unless it can be deployed within a relevant theoretical context. Social identities such as race and gender are a part of the context in which observations occur and gain their significance.

What Merleau-Ponty's and Foucault's work, as well as that of Gadamer, Mead, and others, suggests is that perception is not the mere reportage of objects and their features, but serves as an orientation to the world, a background of experience that constitutes one's capacities of discernment and observation. Moreover, it is itself historically situated within particular discursive formations—as Foucault would have it—that structure the possibilities for delimiting objects, concepts, and subject positions or legitimate viewpoints to be taken up by knowing subjects. Foucault famously makes knowing practices—that is, justificatory practices—internal to a discourse, or discursive formation, rather than essentially unchanged across historical and cultural difference.

The interpretive process itself is both individual and social: the effort to establish meaning is performed by the individual and is subject to modification upon her critical reflection, but it is always conditioned by the concepts, narratives, values, and meanings that are available in her social and discursive context. Race and gender are sometimes relevant variables in these contexts. This is not of course to say that differently identified individuals live in different worlds, or experience globally different perceptions, but that prevalent narratives and concepts are often correlated to changes in social identity.

Charles Mills argues in his essay "Non-Cartesian Sums: Philosophy and the African-American Experience" that the concept of subpersonhood, or *Untermensch*, is a central way to understand "the defining feature of the African-American experience under conditions of white supremacy (both slavery and its aftermath)." By this concept, which Mills develops through a contrast drawn between the Cartesian sum and Ralph Ellison's invisible man, Mills elucidates the comprehensive ramifications that white racism had on "every sphere of black life—juridical standing, moral status, personal/racial identity, epistemic reliability, existential plight, political inclusion, social metaphysics, sexual relations, aesthetic worth" (1994, 228).

Mills suggests that the racial identity of philosophers affects the "array of concepts found useful, the set of paradigmatic dilemmas, the range of concerns" with which they each must grapple. He also suggests that the perspective one takes on specific theories and positions will be affected by one's identity: "The impatience, or indifference, that I have sometimes detected in black students [taking an ethics course] derives in part, I suggest, from their sense that there is something strange, for example, in spending a whole course describing the logic of different moral ideals without ever talking about how *all of them* were systematically violated for blacks" (226).

This results from an understanding that black lived experience "is not subsumed under these philosophical abstractions, despite their putative generality" (Mills 1994, 225). Such an understanding has generally not been available to others, who do not perceive the modernist debates over moral systems as unintelligibly silent about their systematic patterns of hypocrisy. Mills develops this argument further in *The Racial Contract*, in which he claims that racist social systems must develop corresponding moral epistemologies and norms of epistemic judgment. "There is agreement about what counts as a correct, objective interpretation of the world, and for agreeing to this view, one is . . . granted full cognitive standing in the polity, the official epistemic community" (1997, 18). This merely describes normal science, or any discursive community, but Mills further argues that

> on matters related to race, the Racial Contract prescribed for its signatories an inverted epistemology, an epistemology of ignorance, a particular pattern of localized and global cognitive dysfunctions (which are psychologically and socially functional), producing the ironic outcome that whites will in general be unable to understand the world they themselves have made. . . . One could say then, as a general rule, that white misunderstanding, misrepresentation, evasion, and self-deception on matters related to race are among the most pervasive mental phenomena of the past few hundred years, a cognitive and moral economy psychically required for conquest, colonization, and enslavement. (17–19)

These are strong claims. Mills neither naturalizes nor universalizes them; that is, he neither sees these cognitive dysfunctions as natural to whites nor universal among whites, and he sees whiteness itself with its concomitant perspective as socially constructed. Nonetheless, if his description of cognition at least with respect to racial matters holds true, then there is indeed a strong correlation between one's race (and I would add gender) and epistemic disposition at least in regard to certain kinds of issues.

My argument, then, is that basic level perception of events and of people, perception that surmises identity, credibility, salient evidence, probable causal relations, plausible explanations, relevant concepts and similarities, and other important epistemic judgments, can be affected by race and gender. Thus like Lorraine Code, I would argue that we need to reevaluate the status of ad hominem arguments. Code writes: "Prohibitions against appeals to ad hominem evidence derive their persuasiveness from a tacit endorsement of the interchangeability model of epistemic agency. . . . These prohibitions assume that the truth merely passes . . . through the cognitive (= observational) processes of the knowing subject" (1995, 70). But social identities are differentiated by perceptual orientations, which involves bodily comportments that serve as the background for knowledge, learned practices of perception, and narratives of meaning within which new observations become incorporated.

As John Christman has argued, theories of the self are always indexed to some project; there are so many possible aspects by which one can approach subjectivity that the route one chooses will be determined by what one wants the theory to be able to do. This doesn't imply that one can get any theory of the self one wants so that it aligns with one's aims, because any theory will still have to face the test of adequacy to experience and to the relevant facts. My project has been to explain how race and sex are related to the self. I have not sought to explain how things got to be this way, or to chart the future transformations, but to describe how we might conceptualize what it means to have a racialized and sexed self. In this chapter, I offered a conceptualization in broad and general terms, and in subsequent chapters I will look more specifically at particular aspects of these forms of identity and some of their associated problems. Finally, let me underscore that nothing I have argued here counsels for a *naturalist* explanation for the particular meanings we have attached to social identities, or for the *unchangeable stability* of current identity formations. In the summary of their "new view of the person," Lakoff and Johnson argue that the very characterization of human nature being developed now in the cognitive sciences, neurosciences, and biology (that is, the aspects of research from these fields that *they* draw from), is a human nature "without essence": "Human nature is conceptualized rather in terms of variation, change, and evolution, not in terms of a fixed list of central features. It is part of our nature to vary and change" (1999, 557).

TWO

GENDER IDENTITY AND GENDER DIFFERENCES

The Identity Crisis in Feminist Theory

What follows is a revised and shortened version of an essay I published in 1988 on the debate between cultural, or radical, feminists and poststructuralist feminists over the question of essentialism. Though this essay is now dated, it has the virtue of clearly setting out the two principal positions in the debate and their underlying philosophical commitments and political motivations. In order to explain the debate, I made recourse to a common practice of oversimplifying two large and diverse theoretical trends, in this case, poststructuralism and cultural feminism. Such oversimplifications are justified, however, when they help to present some major theoretical or methodological dividing line or principled disagreement. This was my goal. In this essay I also elaborated a concept of gender as positionality and argued that this way of approaching women's identity could be a solution to the identity crisis. For those less familiar with feminist theory, including this essay here will provide some helpful background and history to the way in which identity issues have figured in feminist debates. In a postscript at the end of the essay, I discuss some of the criticisms my argument received. In the following chapter, I offer an updated account of how this debate has evolved.

For many contemporary feminist theorists, the concept of woman is a problem. It is a problem of primary significance because the concept of woman is the central concept of feminist theory, and yet it is a concept that is impossible to formulate precisely for feminists. It is the central concept for feminists because the concept and category of woman is the necessary point of departure for any feminist theory and feminist politics, predicated as these are on the transformation of women's lived experience in contemporary culture and the reevaluation of social theory and practice from a woman's point of view. But as a concept it is radically problematic precisely because it is crowded with the overdeterminations of male supremacy, invoking in every formulation the limit, contrasting Other, or mediated self-reflection of a culture built on the control of females. In attempting to speak for women, feminism often seems to presuppose that it knows what women truly are, but such an assumption is foolhardy given that every source of knowledge about women has been contaminated with misogyny and sexism. No matter where we turn—to historical documentation, philosophical constructions, social scientific statistics, introspection, or daily practices—the mediation of female bodies into constructions of woman is dominated by misogynist discourse. For feminists, who seek to overcome this discourse, it appears we have nowhere to turn.[1]

Thus the dilemma facing feminist theorists is that our very self-definition is grounded in a concept that must be deconstructed and de-essentialized in all of its aspects. Man has said that woman can be defined, delineated, captured—understood, explained, and diagnosed—to a level of determination never accorded to man himself, who is conceived as a rational animal with free will. Where man's behavior is underdetermined, free to construct its own future along the course of its rational choice, woman's nature has overdetermined her behavior, the limits of her intellectual endeavors, and the inevitabilities of her emotional journey through life. Whether she is construed as essentially immoral and irrational (à la Schopenhauer) or essentially kind and benevolent (à la Kant), she is always construed as an essential *something* inevitably accessible to direct intuited apprehension by males.[2] Despite the variety of ways in which man has construed her essential characteristics, she is always the Object, a conglomeration of attributes to be predicted and controlled along with other natural phenomena. The place of the free-willed subject who can transcend nature's mandates is reserved exclusively for men.[3]

Feminist thinkers have articulated two main responses to this situation over the last ten years. The first response is to claim that feminists have the exclusive right to describe and evaluate woman. Thus cultural feminists argue that the problem of male supremacist culture is the problem of a process in which women are defined by men, that is, by a group who has a set of experiences and interests very different from that of women, as well as an evident fear and hatred of women. Their description has distorted and devalued feminine characteristics, which need now to be given a more accurate feminist description and appraisal. Thus the cultural feminist reappraisal construes woman's passivity as her peacefulness, her sentimentality as her proclivity to nurture, her subjectiveness as her advanced self-awareness, and so forth. Cultural feminists have not challenged the defining of woman but only that definition given by men.

The second major response has been to reject the possibility of defining woman as such at all. Feminists who take this tactic go about the business of deconstructing all concepts of woman and argue that both feminist and misogynist attempts to define woman are politically reactionary and ontologically mistaken. Replacing woman-as-housewife with woman-as-earth mother is no advance. Using poststructuralism theory, these feminists argue that such errors occur because we are in fundamental ways duplicating misogynist strategies when we try to define women, characterize women, or speak for women, even while allowing for a range of differences within the gender. The politics of gender or sexual difference must be replaced with a plurality of difference where gender loses its position of significance.

Briefly put, then, the cultural feminists response to Simone de Beauvoir's question, "Are there women?" is to answer yes and to define women by their activities and attributes in the present culture. The poststructuralism response is to answer no and to attack the category and the concept of woman by problematizing subjectivity. Each response has serious limitations, and it is becoming increasingly obvious that transcending these limitations while retaining the theoretical framework from which they emerge is impossible. In this chapter, I will first spell out more clearly the inadequacies of these responses and why I believe these inadequacies are inherent, and then develop an alternative response.

Cultural Feminism

Cultural feminism is the ideology of a female nature or female essence reappropriated by feminists themselves in an effort to revalidate undervalued female attributes. For cultural feminists, the enemy of women is not merely a social system or economic institution or set of backward beliefs but masculinity itself and in some cases male biology. Cultural feminist politics revolve around creating and maintaining a healthy environment—free of masculinist values and all their offshoots such as pornography—for the female principle. Feminist theory, the explanation of sexism, and the justification of feminist demands can all be grounded securely and unambiguously on the concept of the essential female.

Mary Daly and Adrienne Rich have been influential proponents of this position.[4] Breaking from the trend toward androgyny and the minimizing of gender differences that was popular among feminists in the early 1970s, both Daly and Rich argue for a returned focus on femaleness.

For Daly, male barrenness leads to parasitism on female energy, which flows from our life-affirming, life-creating biological condition: "Since female energy is essentially biophilic, the female spirit/body is the primary target in this perpetual war of aggression against life. Gyn/Ecology is the re-claiming of life-loving female energy"(Daly 1978, 355). Despite Daly's warnings against biological reductionism (see, e.g., 60), her own analysis of sexism uses gender-specific biological traits to explain male hatred of women. The childless state of "all males" leads to a dependency on women, which in turn leads men to "deeply identify with 'unwanted fetal tissue'" (59). Given their state of fear and insecurity it becomes almost understandable, then, that men would desire to dominate and control that which is so vitally necessary to them: the life-energy of women. Female energy, conceived by Daly as a natural essence, needs to be freed from its male parasites, released for creative expression and recharged through bonding with other women. In this free space women's "natural" attributes of love, creativity, and the ability to nurture can thrive.

Women's identification as female is their defining essence for Daly, their *haecceity*, overriding any other way in which they may be defined or may define themselves. Thus Daly states: "Women who accept false inclusion among the fathers and sons are easily polarized against other women on the basis of ethnic, national, class, religious, and other *male-defined differences*, applauding the defeat of 'enemy' women" (365; my emphasis). These differences are apparent rather than real, inessential rather than essential. The only real difference, the only difference that can change a person's ontological placement on Daly's dichotomous map, is sex difference. Our essence is defined here, in our sex, from which flow all the facts about us: who are our potential allies, who is our enemy, what are our objective interests, what is our true nature. Thus, Daly defines women again, and her definition is strongly linked to female biology.

Many of Rich's writings have exhibited similarities to Daly's position, surprising given their difference in style and temperament. Rich defines a "female consciousness" (1979, 18) that has a great deal to do with the female body.

> I have come to believe . . . that female biology—the diffuse, intense sensuality radiating out from clitoris, breasts, uterus, vagina; the lunar cycles of menstruation; the gestation and fruition of life which can take place in the female body—has far more radical implications than we have yet come to appreciate. Patriarchal thought has limited female biology to its own narrow specifications. The feminist vision has recoiled from female biology for these reasons; it will, I believe, come to view our physicality as a resource, rather than a destiny. . . . We must touch the unity and resonance of our physicality, our bond with the natural order, the corporeal ground of our intelligence. (1977, 21)

Thus Rich argues that we should not reject the importance of female biology simply because patriarchy has used it to subjugate us. Rich believes that "our biological grounding, the miracle and paradox of the female body and its spiritual and political meanings" holds the key to our rejuvenation and our reconnection with our specific female attributes, which she lists as "our great mental capacities . . . ; our highly developed tactile sense; our genius for close observation; our complicated, pain-enduring, multi-pleasured physicality" (1977, 290).

Rich further echoes Daly in her explanation of misogyny: "The ancient, continuing envy, awe and dread of the male for the female capacity to create life has repeatedly taken the form of hatred for every other female aspect of creativity" (1977, 21). Thus Rich, like Daly, identifies a female essence, defines patriarchy as the subjugation and colonization of this essence out of male envy and need, and then promotes a solution that revolves around rediscovering our essence and bonding with other women. Neither Rich nor Daly espouse biological reductionism, but this is because they reject the oppositional dichotomy of mind and body that such a reductionism presupposes. The female essence for Daly and Rich is not simply spiritual or simply biological—it is both. Yet the key point remains that it is our specifically female anatomy that is the primary constituent of our identity and the source of our female essence. Rich prophesies that "the repossession by women of our bodies will bring far more essential change to human society than the seizing of the means of production by workers. . . . In such a world women will truly create new life, bringing forth not only children (if and as we choose) but the visions, and the thinking, necessary to sustain, console and alter human existence—a new relationship to the universe. Sexuality, politics, intelligence, power, motherhood, work, community, intimacy will develop new meanings; thinking itself will be transformed" (Rich 1977, 292).[5]

The characterization of Rich's and Daly's views as part of an influential trend toward essentialism within feminism has been developed most extensively by Alice Echols. (Echols 1983, 1984, 1989; see also Eisenstein 1983, xvii–xix and 105–45; and

Donovan 1985, chap. 2). Echols prefers the name "cultural feminism" for this trend because it equates "women's liberation with the development and preservation of a female counter culture" (1983, 441). Echols identifies cultural feminist writings by their denigration of masculinity rather than male roles or practices, by their valorization of female traits, and by their commitment to preserve rather than diminish gender differences. Besides Daly and Rich, Echols names Susan Griffin, Kathleen Barry, Janice Raymond, Florence Rush, Susan Brownmiller, and Robin Morgan as important cultural feminist writers, and she documents her claim persuasively by highlighting key passages of their work. Although Echols finds a prototype of this trend in early radical feminist writings by Valerie Solanis and Joreen, she is careful to distinguish cultural feminism from radical feminism as a whole. The distinguishing marks between the two include their position on the mutability of sexism among men, the connection between biology and misogyny, and the degree of focus on valorized female attributes. As Hester Eisenstein pointed out, there is a tendency within many radical feminist works toward setting up an ahistorical and essentialist conception of female nature, but this tendency is developed and consolidated by cultural feminists, thus rendering their work significantly different from radical feminism.

However, although cultural feminist views sharply separate female from male traits, they certainly do not all give explicitly essentialist formulations of what it means to be a woman. So it may seem that Echols's characterization of cultural feminism makes it appear too homogeneous and that the charge of essentialism is on shaky ground. On the issue of essentialism Echols states:

> This preoccupation with defining the female sensibility not only leads these feminists to indulge in dangerously erroneous generalizations about women, but to imply that this identity is innate rather than socially constructed. At best, there has been a curiously cavalier disregard for whether these differences are biological or cultural in origin. Thus Janice Raymond argues: "Yet there are differences, and some feminists have come to realize that those differences are important whether they spring from socialization, from biology, or from the total history of existing as a woman in a patriarchal society." (1983, 440)

Against Raymond, Echols argues that the importance of the differences varies tremendously according to their source. If the differences are innate, it would be a waste of time to agitate in the public male-dominated realm for change, or to form open institutions so that women could express any variety of dispositions. The cultural feminist focus on building an alternative feminist culture for the expression of the female principle would then make political sense. If the differences are not innate, the focus of our activism should shift considerably.

In the absence of a clearly stated position on the ultimate source of gender difference, Echols infers from their emphasis on building a feminist free-space and women-centered culture that cultural feminists hold some version of essentialism. This may be an overstatement about the theoretical uniformity within cultural feminism. As Echols herself points out, the biological accounts of sexism given by Daly and Brownmiller, for example, are not embraced by Rush or Dworkin. But what is universally shared among these feminists is their tendency toward invoking universalizing conceptions of womanly and motherly attributes. And without exploring the historical context or cultural variability of the attributes they describe, cultural feminists offer an overly simplistic, undertheorized account.

It may not be a coincidence that cultural feminism developed and flourished best among white women. Radical feminists of color consistently rejected essentialist conceptions of gender. Consider the following passage from Cherríe Moraga: "When you start to talk about sexism, the world becomes increasingly complex. The power no longer breaks down into neat little hierarchical categories, but becomes a series of starts and detours. Since the categories are not so easy to arrive at, the enemy is not easy to name. It is all so difficult to unravel" (1986, 180). Moraga goes on to assert that "some men oppress the very women they love," implying that we need new categories and new concepts to describe such complex and contradictory relationships. Such an approach to sexism is far removed from Daly's Manichaean ontology or Rich's romanticized conception of the female. The simultaneity of oppressions experienced by women such as Moraga resists essentialist conclusions. Universalist conceptions of female or male experiences and attributes are not plausible in the context of such a complex network of relations, and without an ability to universalize, the essentialist argument is difficult if not impossible to make. White women cannot be all good or all bad; neither can men from oppressed groups be so. Reflected in such complex understandings of masculinity is then a richer and similarly more complex understanding of woman. The feminist theory written by women of color tends to resist the universalizing tendency of cultural feminism and highlights the differences between women, and between men, in a way that undercuts arguments for the existence of an overarching gendered essence. (See also, e.g., Moraga 1983; Smith 1983; Combahee River Collective 1979; Lorde 1984; and hooks 1984. An exception to this generalization may be in the writings by some indigenous women.)

One does not have to be influenced by poststructuralism to disagree with essentialism. Claims about the innateness of gender differences in personality and character are at this point at least empirically indefensible (see, e.g., Fausto-Sterling 1986; Ortner and Whitehead 1981). There are a host of divergent ways gender divisions occur in different societies, and the differences that appear to be universal can be explained in non-essentialist ways. However, the belief in women's innate peacefulness and ability to nurture has been common among feminists since the nineteenth century and enjoyed a resurgence in the 1970s and 1980s, most notably among feminist peace activists. I have met scores of young feminists drawn to actions like the Women's Peace Encampment and to groups like Women for a Non-Nuclear Future by their belief that the maternal love women have for their children is a vital force against violence and war. But Echols may well be right that their effect is to "reflect and reproduce dominant cultural assumptions about women," which not only fail to represent the variety in women's lives but promote unrealistic expectations about "normal" female behavior that most of us cannot satisfy (1983, 440). Our gender categories are positively constitutive and not mere hindsight descriptions of previous activities. There is a self-perpetuating circularity between defining woman as essentially peaceful and nurturing and the observations and judgment we shall make of women and the practices we shall engage in as women in the future. Do feminists want to buy another ticket for women of the world on the merry-go-round of feminine constructions? Don't we want rather to get off the merry-go-round and run away?

This should not imply that the political effects of cultural feminism have all been negative. Hester Eisenstein's treatment of cultural feminism, though critical, is certainly more two-sided than Echols's. While Echols apparently sees only the reactionary results of cultural feminism, Eisenstein sees in it a therapeutic self-affirmation necessary to offset the impact of misogynist culture. The insistence on viewing traditional feminine characteristics from a different point of view as a means of engendering a gestalt switch on our valuation of these traits has had a positive effect, and was certainly absent from de Beauvoir's and other early feminist views. Liberal feminists, existentialist feminists, and even some Marxist feminists maintained a higher status for male activities, and thus cultural feminism's message about the creditable virtues and values of a female realm was an important corrective. And surely much of their point was well taken: that it was our mothers who ensured our families' survival, that women's handiwork is truly artistic, that women's caregiving and empathy are superior in value to male competitiveness and individualism.

Unfortunately, however, the cultural feminist championing of a redefined "womanhood" cannot provide an adequate long-range program for a feminist movement and, in fact, places obstacles in the way of developing one. Under conditions of oppression and restrictions on freedom of movement, women, like other oppressed groups, sometimes develop strengths and attributes that should be correctly credited, valued, and promoted. What we clearly cannot promote, however, are the restrictive conditions that gave rise to those attributes: forced parenting, lack of physical autonomy, dependency for survival on mediation skills, for instance. What conditions for women do we want to promote? A freedom of movement such that we can compete in the capitalist world as well as fight imperialist wars alongside men? A continued restriction to child-centered activities? To the extent cultural feminism merely valorized genuinely positive attributes developed under oppression, it cannot map our long-range course. To the extent that it reinforces essentialist explanations of these attributes, it is in danger of solidifying an important bulwark for sexist oppression: the belief in an innate "womanhood" to which we must all adhere lest we be deemed either inferior or not "true" women.

Poststructuralism Feminism

For many feminists, the problem with the cultural feminist response to sexism is that it does not criticize the fundamental mechanism of sexism and in fact reinvokes that mechanism in its supposed solution. The mechanism of power referred to here is the construction of the subject by a discourse that weaves knowledge and power into a coercive structure that "forces the individual back on himself and ties him to his own identity in a constraining way" (Foucault 1983, 212). On this view, essentialist formulations of womanhood, even when made by feminists, "tie" the individual to her identity as a woman and thus cannot represent a solution to sexism.

This articulation of the problem has been borrowed by feminists from a number of recently influential French theorists who are sometimes called poststructuralist but who might also be called posthumanist, including most prominently Lacan, Derrida, and Foucault. Disparate as these theorists are, they share the view that the self-contained, authentic subject conceived by humanism as discoverable below a veneer of cultural and ideological overlay is in reality a construct of that very humanist discourse. The subject is not a locus of authorial intentions or natural attributes or even a privileged, separate consciousness. Lacan uses psychoanalysis, Derrida uses grammar, and Foucault uses the history of discourses all to attack and deconstruct our idea of the subject as having an essential, authentic core that has been repressed by society. Since there is no such authentic core, there is no repression in the humanist sense. Instead of criticizing the way in which society represses us, we should focus on the production of the human.

There is an interesting neodeterminism in this view. The subject is not determined by biology, nor is human history open to prediction or even explanation, and there is no naturalist grounding for human experience. On the other hand, the rejection of these varieties of determinism is not based on a belief that human subjects are underdetermined (or existentially free) but, rather, in a belief that we are overdetermined, or constructed, by a set of social discourses and cultural practices. Individual motivations and intentions count for nil or almost nil in the scheme of social reality, since the individual is a construct mediated by a social discourse well beyond individual control or intervention. As Foucault put it, we are bodies "totally imprinted by history" (1984, 83). What we think of as private, interior, subjective experiences are determined in some sense by macro-forces.

However, these macro forces, including some social discourses and social practices, are apparently not overdetermined, resulting as they do from such a complex and heterogeneous network of overlapping and crisscrossing elements that no unilinear directionality is perceivable and no final or efficient cause exists. Neither the form nor the content of discourse has a fixed or unified structure. What is interesting is that, to some extent, this view is similar to contemporary methodological individualism, whose advocates will usually concede that the complex of human intentions results in a social reality bearing no resemblance to the summarized categories of intentions but looking altogether different from any one party or sum of parties ever envisioned or desired. The difference, however, is that while methodological individualists admit that human intentions are ineffectual, poststructuralists deny not only the efficacy but also the ontological autonomy and even the existence of intentionality.

Poststructuralists unite with Marx in asserting the social dimension of individual traits and intentions. Thus, they say we cannot understand society as the conglomerate of individual intentions but, rather, must understand individual intentions as constructed within a social reality. Like many others, I find the emphasis on social explanations for individual practices and experiences illuminating and persuasive. Also like many others, I find less persuasive a total erasure of individual agency within a social discourse or set of institutions, that is, the totalization of history's imprint.

Applied to the concept of woman, poststructuralism's view results in what I shall call nominalism: the idea that the category "woman" is a fiction without objective basis and that feminist efforts must be directed toward dismantling this fiction. "Perhaps ... 'woman' is not a determinable identity. Perhaps woman is not some thing which announces itself from a distance, at a distance from some other thing. ... Perhaps woman—a non-identity, non-figure, simulacrum—is distance's very chasm, the out-distancing of distance, the interval's cadence, distance itself" (Derrida 1978, 49). Derrida's interest in feminism seems to stem from his belief, expressed above, that woman may represent a potential rupture in the discourses of hierarchy and the metaphysical violence of Kantian ontology. Because woman has in a sense been excluded from this discourse, it is possible to hope that she might provide a real source of resistance. But her resistance will not be at all effective if she continues to use the mechanism of logocentrism to redefine woman: her resistance will be effective only if she drifts and dodges all attempts to capture her. Derrida hopes that the following futuristic picture will come true: "Out of the depths, endless and unfathomable, she engulfs and distorts all vestige of essentiality, of identity, of property. And the philosophical discourse, blinded, founders on these shoals and is hurled down these depths to its ruin" (1978, 51). For Derrida, women have always been defined as a subjugated difference within a binary opposition: man/woman, culture/nature, positive/negative, analytical/intuitive. To assert an essential gender difference as cultural feminists do is to reinvoke this oppositional structure. The only way to break out of this structure, and in fact to subvert the structure itself, is to assert total difference, to be that which cannot be pinned down, compared, defined, and thus subjugated within a dichotomous hierarchy. Paradoxically, it is to be what is not. Thus feminists cannot demarcate a definitive category of "woman" without eliminating all possibility for the defeat of logocentrism and its oppressive power.

Foucault similarly rejects all constructions of oppositional subjects—whether the "criminal," "homosexual," or "proletariat"—as mirror images that merely reenforce and sustain the discursive influence of the contrasting term, the term by which they are defined and gain their meaning (e.g., the "normal citizen," or "heterosexual"). As Biddy Martin points out, "The point from which Foucault deconstructs is off-center, out of line, apparently unaligned. It is not the point of an imagined absolute otherness, but an 'alterity' which understands itself as an internal exclusion" (1982, 11).

Following Foucault and Derrida, an effective feminism could only be a wholly negative feminism, deconstructing everything and refusing to construct anything. This is the position Julia Kristeva adopts, herself an influential poststructuralist. She says, "A woman cannot be; it is something which does not even belong in the order of being. *It follows that a feminist practice can only be negative*, at odds with what already exists so that we may say 'that's not it' and 'that's still not it'" (1981b, 137; my italics). The problematic character of subjectivity does not mean, then, that there can be no political struggle, but that the struggle can have only a "negative function," rejecting "everything finite, definite, structured, loaded with meaning, in the existing state of society" (166).

The fact that any kind of political practice is argued for indicates a belief in the possibility of agency, and thus it might seem that the concern about poststructuralism's elimination of agency is unfounded. But consider how the arguments change if agency is assumed not only as a possibility of the future, but also as an ongoing feature of the past. In that case, we might understand the current construction of "woman" as the product in part of women's struggles and assertions, in parallel fashion to the way in which Michael Omi and Howard Winant have argued that the contemporary construction of racial identities needs to be understood not simply as that which has been imposed from above but also as that which takes the shape that they currently do in light of the forms of resistance taken by racialized subjects (Omi and Winant 1986). This is not to deny the reality of oppression, and of what Jorge Valadez has usefully named "epistemological oppression," but to deny that oppression can ever operate in a vacuum, uncontested, with total efficacy (Valadez 2001). Therefore, the concepts and categories we struggle against now have been formed in our negotiations and struggles as well as by our submission.

If we acknowledge agency, then, it is difficult to see why we must have a totalizing repudiation of the present. The power of an essential idea of "women" does not become totally efficacious and triumphant over individual agency just as a result of its metaphysical or linguistic form, for concepts gain their meanings in contexts of practice, to add a Wittgensteinian, as opposed to Kantian, ontology into the mix.

Despite this plausibility problem, the poststructuralist critique of "woman" has three prime attractions for feminists. First, it seems to hold out the promise of an increased freedom for women, the "free play" of a plurality of differences unhampered by any predetermined gender identity as formulated either by patriarchy or cultural feminism. Second, it moves decisively beyond cultural feminism and liberal feminism in further theorizing what they leave untouched: the construction of female (and not just feminine) subjectivity. We can learn a great deal here about the mechanisms of sexist oppression and the construction of specific gender categories by relating these to social discourse and by conceiving of the subject as a cultural product. Third, poststructuralism also gives us an enhanced capacity to explain women who embrace patriarchy, and to understand in general how ideology is reproduced and social progress blocked. However, adopting nominalism also creates serious problems for feminism. How can we seriously adopt Kristeva's plan to engage only in negative struggle? Movements are never mobilized only as negations or rejections; there must also be a vision of the future that can motivate people to sacrifice their time and energy and risk their resources toward its realization. Moreover, a feminist adoption of nominalism will be confronted with the same problem that theories of ideology generally have, that is, the difficulty of explaining why a right-wing women's consciousness has been constructed via social discourse but a feminist's consciousness is not. Poststructuralist characterizations of the construction of the subject must pertain to all subjects, or they will pertain to none. Poststructuralism thus threatens to deconstruct the feminist subject as well as the female subject, and thus threatens to wipe out feminism itself.

Some feminist poststructuralists are aware of this danger. Biddy Martin, among others, points out that "we cannot afford to refuse to take a political stance 'which pins us to our sex' for the sake of an abstract theoretical correctness. . . . There is the danger that Foucault's challenges to traditional categories, if taken to a logical conclusion . . . could make the question of women's oppression obsolete" (1982, 16–17). Based on her articulation of the problem with Foucault, we are left hopeful that Martin will provide a solution that transcends nominalism. Unfortunately, in her reading of Lou Andreas-Salome, Martin valorizes undecidability, ambiguity, and elusiveness, and intimates that by maintaining the undecidability of identity the life of Andreas-Salome provides a text from which feminists can usefully learn (Martin 1982, esp. 21, 24, and 29).

However, the claim that meaning is always undecidable cannot be a useful one for feminism, even if it were plausible. In support of his contention that the meaning of all texts is ultimately undecidable, Derrida offers us in *Spurs* three conflicting but purportedly equally warranted interpretations of how Nietzsche's writings construct and position the female. In one of these interpretations, Derrida argues, we can find feminist propositions (1978, esp. 57 and 97). Thus, Derrida seeks to demonstrate that even the seemingly incontrovertible interpretation of Nietzsche's works as misogynist can be challenged by an equally convincing argument that they are not. Note that this is not an argument that Nietzsche contradicts himself in different passages, but that in the identical passage the meaning is indeterminate. But how can this be helpful to feminists, who need to have their accusations of misogyny validated rather than rendered "undecidable"? The point is not that Derrida himself is antifeminist, nor that he offers nothing useful for feminists in any of his critiques of Western logocentrism. But the thesis of undecidability threatens to undermine every diagnosis of misogyny, and to view feminists, once again, as intellectually limited and perhaps "unimaginative," two common tropes of sexism. Moreover, the thesis of undecidability must inevitably return us to Kristeva's position, that we are left with a feminism that can be only deconstructive.[6]

A nominalist position on subjectivity has the deleterious effect of degendering our analysis, of in effect making gender invisible once again. If gender identity is simply a social construct, the need and even the possibility of a feminist politics becomes immediately problematic. What can we demand in the name of women if "women" do not exist and demands in their name simply reenforce the myth that they do? How can we speak out against sexism as detrimental to the interests of women if the category is a fiction? How can we demand legal abortions, adequate child care, or wages based on comparable worth without invoking the concept of "women"?

Poststructuralism undercuts our ability to oppose the dominant trend, and dominant danger, in mainstream Western intellectual inquiry, that is, the assumption of a universal, neutral, perspectiveless epistemology, metaphysics, and ethics. Too much of Anglo-American philosophy and European philosophy is still wedded to the idea (and ideal) of a universalizable, apolitical methodology and set of transhistorical basic truths unfettered by associations with particular genders, races, classes, or cultures. The rejection of subjectivity unintentionally colludes with this "generic human" thesis that particularities of individuals are irrelevant and improper influences on knowledge. Poststructuralism's negation of the authority of the subject thus colludes with classical liberalism's view that human particularities are irrelevant. For liberalism, particularities are irrelevant because "underneath we are all the same"; for the poststructuralist, race, class, and gender are all constructs and therefore incapable of decisively validating conceptions of justice and truth because underneath there is nothing—hence once again underneath we are all the same. Much of the cultural feminist glorification of femininity as a valid specificity legitimately grounding feminist theory is motivated by the desire to undermine the false universalism of the Western tradition.

In characterizing cultural feminism and poststructuralism in the broad ways that I have, there is an obvious problem of overhomogenization. However, I believe the tendencies I have outlined toward essentialism and toward nominalism represent the main current responses [as of 1988] by feminist theory to the task of reconceptualizing "woman." Both responses have advantages and disadvantages. Cultural feminism has provided a useful corrective to the generic human ideal of classical liberalism and has promoted community and self-affirmation, but it cannot provide a long-range future course of action for feminist theory or practice, and it is founded on an implausible claim of essentialism. The feminist appropriation of poststructuralism has provided suggestive insights on the construction of female and male subjectivity and has issued a crucial warning against creating a feminism that reinvokes mechanisms of oppression. Nonetheless, it limits feminism to the negative tactics of reaction and deconstruction and endangers the attack against classical liberalism by discrediting the notion of an epistemologically significant, specific subjectivity. What's a feminist to do?

We cannot simply embrace the paradox. In order to avoid the problems with cultural feminism and poststructuralism, feminism needs to develop a third course, an alternative theory of the subject that is neither essentialist nor nominalist.

Positionality

The problem of conceptualizing "woman" as a form of subjectivity and an associated category of identity can best be approached through combining three elements: the idea of experience as a reflective practice, the intuition behind identity politics, and the concept of positionality.

Teresa de Lauretis's influential book *Alice Doesn't* develops an account of experience through an eclectic weaving together of psychoanalytic and semiotic theories. The underlying motivation for developing this account is her concern to understand the link between gender, a social construct, and subjectivity, which involves human agency. The book is really a collection of essays organized around the difficulty of conceptualizing *woman* as subject, not the generic human as subject but a particularly gendered subjectivity. But immediately a problem arises as to the relation between "woman" as "fictional construct" and "women" as "real historical beings" (1984, 5). The idea of gender raises the specter of "woman," so how does one correct the gender-neutral errors of modern notions of subjectivity without getting embroiled in these hegemonic gender discourses? De Lauretis explains the problem:

> The feminist efforts have been more often than not caught in the logical trap set up by [a] paradox. Either they have assumed that "the subject," like "man," is a generic term, and as such can designate equally and at once the female and male subjects, with the result of erasing sexuality and sexual difference from subjectivity. Or else they have been obliged to resort to an oppositional notion of "feminine" subject defined by silence, negativity, a natural sexuality, or a closeness to nature not compromised by patriarchal culture. (161)

Here again is spelled out the dilemma between a poststructuralist genderless subject and a cultural feminist essentialized subject.

As de Lauretis points out, the poststructuralist alternative is constrained in its conceptualization of the female subject by the very act of distinguishing female from male subjectivity. The dilemma is that if we degender subjectivity, we are committed to a generic subject, and if we define the subject in terms of gender, articulating female subjectivity in a space clearly distinct from male subjectivity, then we become caught up in an oppositional dichotomy controlled by a misogynist discourse. A gender-bound subjectivity seems to force us to revert "women to the body and to sexuality as an immediacy of the biological, as nature" (161).

De Lauretis takes a large dose of social construction for granted, especially in its psychoanalytic variant. If the subject is constructed via discourse, then the feminist project cannot be simply to reveal "how to make visible the invisible." Yet de Lauretis does not give up on the possibility of producing "the condition of visibility for a different social subject" (8–9). In her view, a nominalist position on subjectivity can be avoided by linking subjectivity to a Peircean notion of practices and a further theorized notion of experience (11).

De Lauretis's main thesis is that subjectivity, that is, what one "perceives and comprehends as subjective," is constructed through a continuous process and ongoing constant renewal based on an interaction with the world, or, in a word, experience: "And thus [subjectivity] is produced not by external ideas, values, or material causes, but by one's personal, subjective engagement in the practices, discourses, and institutions that lend significance (value, meaning, and affect) to the events of the world" (159). This is the process through which one's subjectivity becomes engendered.

In reality, subjectivity is neither overdetermined by biology *nor* by "free, rational, intentionality" but, rather, by experience, which she defines (via Lacan, Eco, and Peirce) as "a complex of habits resulting from the semiotic interaction of our 'outer world' and 'inner world,' the continuous engagement of a self or subject in social reality" (182).[7] Given this definition, can we ascertain a "female experience?" Can we discern "that complex of habits, dispositions, associations, and perceptions, which engenders one as female?" (182). In a later work, de Lauretis claims that identity is constituted through a process in which one's history "is interpreted or reconstructed by each of us within the horizon of meanings and knowledges available in the culture at given historical moments, a horizon that also includes modes of political commitment and struggle. . . . Consciousness is, therefore, never fixed, never attained once and for all, because discursive boundaries change with historical conditions" (1986, 8). Agency consists in this process of interpretation, such that identities are not simply "prefigured . . . in an unchangeable symbolic order," or produced by external structures of meaning, or construed as merely "fragmented or intermittent," that is, undecidable or always indeterminate. The individual has agency on this account but is also placed within "particular discursive configurations" (de Lauretis 1986, 9).

Such an account accords with the hermeneutic account of identity I developed in chapter 4, but it lacks the materiality I tried to combine with the hermeneutic account. De Lauretis emphasizes meanings, discourses, and cultural knowledges, but not embodiment or material location. De Lauretis moves so far away from the traditional ideological associations of women with nature and the body that she formulates experience only in relation to meanings and discourses, not in relation to the embodied experiences unique to women or to the material and embodied social location women inhabit. She does argue that language is not the sole source and locus of meaning, and that habits and practices are crucial in the construction of meanings, but habits and practices are what the body does, not what it is, what it experiences, what it must live through, or how it is treated. Bringing back materiality will fill out an account of female subjectivity such as de Lauretis's and will correct the tendency to *overplay* agency. I will focus on the material basis of gender in the next chapter.

Despite this shortcoming, de Lauretis helps us to imagine a way to think about identity without fixity. Human subjectivity in all its forms emerges within historicized experience. Her account thus suggests that gender is not a point to start from in the sense of being a given thing but is, instead, a posit or construct, formalizable in a nonarbitrary way through a matrix of habits, practices, and discourses. The fluid historical context in which we negotiate our identities is a context in which we are both subjects of and subjected to social construction. The advantage of such an analysis is its ability to articulate a concept of gendered subjectivity without pinning it down for all time.

It seems to me equally important to add to this approach an identity politics, a concept that developed from the Combahee River Collective's "A Black Feminist Statement" and that I summarized in chapter 1. Their idea was precisely that one's identity is taken (and defined) as a political point of departure, as a motivation for action, and as a basis for one's politics. Elly Bulkin, Minnie Bruce Pratt, and Barbara Smith discuss and apply the idea of identity politics further in their book *Yours in Struggle: Three Feminist Perspectives on Anti-Semitism and Racism* (1988), in which each author takes her own identity as a political point of departure and as a focus for critical self-reflection. Identity politics as the three authors apply it is an acknowledgment of the relevance of one's identity and of the shifting and relational political effects of identity. Minnie Bruce Pratt recounts in her essay that her identity as white southern middle-class woman positions her in a superordinate position to African Americans in her town, but that as a lesbian she is positioned as so marginal and vilified that she cannot even retain custody of her children. Pratt offers a phenomenological description for this unsettling fluidity of identity as well as a testimony to the critical and undeniable power of identity to predetermine social intercourse and one's possibilities for making a meaningful life.[8] Thus, identity politics does not entail a denial of the complex and even contradictory nature of identity. One can recognize the contextual, relational, and fluid nature of identity while acknowledging that it is always the point of departure.

Such an account is surely intuitive to those of us with mixed race backgrounds or who have significantly distinct cultures in their background. That is, on the one hand, one's identity is set by genealogy, social recognition, the objective social location that one inhabits in a stratified society, but on the other hand, one has to make choices about how to understand, negotiate, and live one's identity. Mixed race and bicultural persons may intuit this better because we sometimes must consciously choose how to identify ourselves on various forms and how to deal with a host of other small and large issues. Identity politics means choosing one's identity as a member of one or more groups as a political point of departure. This is also, in fact, what happens when women who are not feminists downplay their identity as women, believing that just acting "as individuals" in social or work relations will ensure their fair treatment. After they perceive gender discrimination, or that the rules of the workplace favor men in certain important respects, they may become feminists and make an issue of their female identity, arguing for something not on the grounds of individual need but as a political right of a disadvantaged group. In recognizing the salience of their identity as women—whether that salience is chosen or not—and taking this more consciously as their point of departure they often become aware of, for example, gender-biased language that before they did not even notice.

This does not mean that their gender identity was not affecting their views or perceptions or orientation to the world earlier, but that with a heightened political consciousness they will now become more reflective about the relation between their identity and their life. In our libertarian cultural moment, this is now denigrated as playing the "race card" or the "gender card," and although mistaken evaluations of sexism or racism can certainly occur, sometimes such evaluations, or accusations, are simply true descriptions. Neither racism nor sexism is a card game.

Antifeminist women, of course, will often identify strongly as women and with women as a group, an identification they explain by reference to an essentialist account of femininity. Claiming that one's politics are grounded in one's essential identity avoids problematizing both identity and the connection between identity and politics and thus avoids the need to formulate beliefs and make choices and to take responsibility for those decisions. The difference between feminists and antifeminists strikes me as precisely this: the affirmation or denial of our right and our ability to construct, and take responsibility for, our gendered identity, our politics, and our choices.[9]

Identity politics rejects the generic human thesis and the mainstream methodology of Western political theory, which tries to approach theory through a "veil of ignorance" that sets aside the theorist's own social identity. If the theorist's particularity is transcended, then one can produce a theory of universal scope to which all ideally rational agents would be persuaded. Identity politics provides a materialist response to this, and in so doing it sides with Marx, who argued that when "free and rational agents" come together in a public forum for rational debate, they come *as* shopkeepers, landowners, proletarians, and so on—that is, as living individuals with commitments, ties, and interests. Political theory must come to terms with the fact that everyone has a fleshy, material existence that will influence the judgment of all political claims. The concept of identity politics does not presuppose a prepackaged set of objective needs or political implications but introduces identity as a factor in any political analysis and argues for a reflexive analysis of how any given identity may affect one's action, beliefs, and politics.

If we combine the concept of identity politics with a conception of the subject as positionality, we can conceive of the subject as non-essentialized and emergent from historical experience and yet objectively located in describably social structures and relations. Gender identity is not exhaustively determined by biology; it is not ahistorical or universally the same. Thus there is no gender essence all women share. But gender is, among other things, a position one occupies and from which one can act politically. What does position mean here?

When the concept "woman" is defined not by a particular set of attributes but by a particular position, the internal characteristics of the person thus identified are not denoted so much as the external context within which that person is situated. The external situation determines the person's relative position, just as the position of a pawn on a chessboard is safe or dangerous, powerful or weak, according to its relation to the other chess pieces. The essentialist definition of woman makes her identity independent of her external situation: because her nurturing or peaceful traits are innate, they are ontologically autonomous of her position with respect to others or to the external historical and social conditions generally. The positional definition, on the other hand, makes her identity relative to a constantly shifting context, to a situation that includes a network of elements involving others, the objective economic conditions, cultural and political institutions and ideologies, and so on. If it is possible to identify women by their position within this network of relations, then it becomes possible to ground a feminist argument for women not on a claim that their innate capacities are being stunted, but that their position within the network lacks power and mobility and requires radical change. The position of women is relative and not innate, and yet it is not "undecidable." Through social critique and analysis we can identify women via their position relative to an existing cultural and social network.

It may sound all too familiar to say that the oppression of women stems from their relative position within a society; but my claim goes further than this. The very subjectivity (or subjective experience of being a woman) and the very identity of women are constituted by women's position. However, this view should not imply that the woman herself is merely a passive recipient of an identity constructed by external forces. Rather, she herself is part of the historicized, fluid movement, and she therefore actively contributes to the context within which her position can be delineated. De Lauretis's point is that the identity of a woman is the product of her own interpretation and reconstruction of her history, as mediated through the cultural discursive context to which she has access (1986, 8–9). Therefore, the concept of positionality includes two points: first, as already stated, that the concept of woman is a relational term identifiable only within a (constantly moving) context; but second, that the position that women find themselves in can be actively utilized (rather than transcended) as a location for the construction of meaning, a place from where meaning can be *discovered* (the meaning of being female). The concept of woman as positionality shows how women use their positional perspective as a place from which values are interpreted and constructed rather than as a locus of an already determined set of values. When women become feminists the crucial thing that has occurred is not that they have learned any new facts about the world but that they have come to view those facts from a different position, from their own position as subjects. When colonized subjects begin to be critical of the formerly imitative attitude they had toward colonists, what is happening is that they begin to identify with the colonized rather than the colonizers (see Bhabha 1984; Rahman 1983). This difference in positional perspective does not necessitate a change in what are taken to be the facts, although new facts may come into view from the new position, but it does necessitate a political change in perspective because the point of departure, the point from which all things are measured, has changed.

In this analysis, then, the concept of positionality allows for a determinate though fluid identity of woman that does not fall into essentialism: woman is a position from which a feminist politics can emerge. Seen in this way, being a "woman" is to take up a position within a moving historical context and to be able to choose what we make of this position and how we alter this context. From the perspective of that fairly determinate though fluid and mutable position, women can themselves articulate a set of interests and ground a feminist politics.

The concept and the position of women is not ultimately undecidable or arbitrary. The concept I have outlined limits the construction of woman we can offer by defining subjectivity as positionality within a context. It thus avoids nominalism but also provides us with the means to argue against views like "oppression is all in your head."

At the same time, by highlighting historical movement and the subject's ability to alter her context, the concept of positionality avoids tying ourselves to any unending structure of gendered politics. Can we conceive of a future in which oppositional gender categories are not fundamental to one's self-concept or to the organization of social relations? Even if we cannot, our theory of subjectivity should not preclude or, moreover, prevent that eventual possibility. Our concept of woman as a category, then, needs to remain open to future radical alteration; else we will preempt the possible forms that eventual stages of the feminist transformation can take.

A Postscript

Ann Snitow and Teresa de Lauretis, two feminist authors that I have admired for many years, voiced concerns about not so much the final or general argument of the preceding essay, but about some of its framing assumptions. Snitow makes two main points. The first is that my shortened history of feminist theory makes it appear as if poststructuralism offers a measure of advance over cultural feminism, whereas if I had taken a longer point of view, so as to include the radical feminist work prior to cultural feminism, one would see a persistent oscillation rather than a developmental teleology. This is certainly true as a claim about the history of Western feminism. But I didn't intend to characterize that history: I looked at what I thought to be the two main dominant trends in Western feminist thought at the time I was writing the essay, concurrently influential. I did not mean to suggest that poststructuralism was an "advance," just that it avoided some of the problems of cultural feminism even while creating some of its own. But I take it that Snitow's more general concern is with the way in which the history of feminist thought has been getting parceled up, and particularly the way in which the variety of political positions *within* every made-up category is constantly elided. I see this as not just a concern with oversimplification per se in favor of more detailed accuracy, but a concern that the radical potential of a diverse variety of theoretical traditions is being obscured in the pursuit of a coherent narrative.

Snitow's second point is against my idea that we must transcend the paradox. She sees the history of oscillations between, as she puts it, the pressure women experience *to be* a woman and the pressure *not* to be one as endemic to our historical and cultural moment, not a mere theoretical impasse. What I have called cultural feminism and poststructuralist feminism are playing out this oscillation. But the oscillation itself, she persuasively argues, "will change only through historical process; it cannot be dissolved through thought alone" (1990, 19). This argument raises the large issue of how to understand feminist theory's problematics: are we feminist theorists really working on our own in conceptualizing women's liberation, sometimes constructing fly-bottle problems, but in any case generally autonomous from the pull of our culture's current ideological mystifications? Or can our work be read symptomatically as the epiphenomena of various cultural pathologies, for example, idealism, individualism, competitiveness, Eurocentrism, and so on?

De Lauretis is also concerned with the way in which my essay categorizes feminism into opposing camps, but her overall concern is with the de-legitimation of feminist theory, rather than its overestimation as a political resource. Why, she asks, "keep in the foreground an image of 'dominant' feminism that is at least reductive, at best tautological or superseded, and at worst not in our interests? Doesn't it feed the pernicious opposition of low versus high theory, a low-grade type of critical thinking (feminism) that is contrasted with the high-test theoretical grade of poststructuralism from which some feminists would have been smart enough to learn?" (1990, 263). I take it that de Lauretis is concerned here with a narrativizing of feminist theory that would limit its options as well as imply that *outside* of feminist theory there is *real* theory from which feminism must learn. In this essay, de Lauretis's aim is to privilege feminism as a space of thinking that is embodied and situated, and thus itself the backdrop or grounding of critique rather than the lesser cousin of real (objective, male, nonpolitical, etc.) theory. The essentialism debate, I believe she is suggesting, had the pernicious effect of implying that the criteria of adequacy for feminist theory resides outside of it. I agree with this, although I also believe there was a powerful *internal* stimulus for the debate which had nothing to do with whether it measured up to external standards, and I will explain this stimulus in the next chapter. Moreover, a further problem that de Lauretis has with my characterization is its attitude toward opposition: I take it for granted that opposition must be overcome rather than accepted as the creative fuel for feminism and for the erotic, conflictual energy of lesbian feminism in particular. In place of my dialectics that would seek resolutions, de Lauretis proposes we understand feminist theory through triangularity: the shifting negotiations and contestations between three poles and their relations—specific properties (sexed bodies), qualities or dispositions, and necessary attributes (living as a female). There are multiple ways that this triangle is manifested, which thus explains historical and cultural change and the existence of politically diverse options. But these do not need to be organized into a metanarrative of progress or essential preferences about how to be or to define femaleness: all that is essential is the triangle itself.

De Lauretis is right that *all* oppositions or political differences need not be resolved.

The Metaphysics of Gender and Sexual Difference

It is certainly true, as nominalists have been concerned to acknowledge, that judgments about kinds are determined in part by human interests, projects, and practices. But the possibility that human interests, projects, and practices sometimes develop as they do because the real (physical or social) world is as it is suggests that this sort of dependence is not by itself an argument against essentialism.

Susan Babbitt, *Impossible Dreams*

In the previous chapter, I argued for a concept of subjectivity as positionality to emphasize the role of variable social contexts in defining what it means to be a woman. What both the poststructuralists and cultural feminists seemed to me to underemphasize was the very concrete and historical social situation in which "one is made a woman." The cultural feminists had an essentialist conception of female identity that was based on an attachment to positive feminine attributes, attributes that they dehistoricized and decontextualized to such a degree that they could offer no account of how these attributes came into existence or under what conditions they might pass out of existence. On the other hand, the poststructuralists had an anti-essentialist conception that was motivated at least in part by an ahistorical approach to resistance, as if an antirealism about sexed identity would finally avoid the age-old problem of co-optation in which every construction of woman eventually gets turned against us. But they tried to achieve this impervious form of resistance through flying above material particularity into the netherworld of undifferentiated flux or negativity. Thus, I felt that the cultural feminists had dehistoricized feminine attributes while the poststructuralists dehistoricized resistance. Neither the essentialist nor the anti-essentialist position gave the temporal dimension, or the changeable nature of human characteristics and political contexts, enough significance in the development of their theories of women's identity.

My idea was that a concept of identity as positionality offered the means to give a content to women's identity without solidifying that content for all time, since positionality is a content that emerges in relational circumstances that are in constant change as we, and those around us, are engaged in a world that is itself in movement. Like the poststructuralists, I agreed we should avoid essentialist defini-tions that define women in terms of intrinsic internal characteristics, such as the disposition to nurture or an attentiveness to the corporeal and mundane details of life, as if these proclivities exist prior to our socialization. But like the cultural feminists, I did not want to be left with a mere politics of negation out of the fear of being essentialist, deterministic, or prescriptive. I believed we could do better than to say, "I will make demands in the name of women even though I don't accept the category of 'women.'"

I believed then and I believe today that we can make many accurate claims about women, as women exist here and now in particular locations, and thus we can make demands that reflect women's needs. The problem is not an absence of content for the category "women" but an overabundance and inconsistency of content, given the multiple situations in which women find themselves in various cultures. The fact that what it means to be a woman varies does not entail that one can say nothing about women, only that one must refrain from universal pronouncements about the nature of women's oppression or the content of their political goals. Feminist theory needs to locate and limit the scope of its presumed applicability. But women exist with many common problems across the globe and with widely shared needs for freedom from physical violation, for education, for meaningful work, for their rightful share in their societies' political self-determination, and for fair remuneration for all the kinds of work, whether or not it produces surplus value or shows up in a GDP. I stand by these arguments, and continue to believe that positionality is a helpful way to explain the contextual variability of women's identity. But positionality is a concept with general relevance to social identity and agency, without special relevance to gender or sexual difference. In this chapter, my focus will be on women's specifically gendered identity and its basis in sexual difference.

Fifteen years after that chapter was first published as a journal essay, the debate over essentialism has now become, thankfully, passé. There are two main reasons for this change. First, almost everyone agrees that the anti-essentialists won the debate, which does not mean that all have altered their views but that they must now show that their views are not, and were never, truly essentialist. Second, the conventional terms of the debate over essentialism are thought by many to have been mistaken in their ahistorical, falsely homogenized account of what essentialism as a concept or a doctrine entails. If the essentialists were guilty of overly homogenizing the category of women, the anti-essentialists were guilty of overly homogenizing the category or idea of essentialism. In fact, essentialism can coexist with nominalism and even historicism, since it is a doctrine about essences but not a doctrine about the metaphysical grounds or stability of those essences (at least it has not historically been; see, e.g., Babbitt 1996; Battersby 1998; de Lauretis 1990). This does not mean that the anti-essentialists are considered wrong in the substance of their claims, but only in their attribution of these claims to questions of essentialism.

There is also a third reason for the end of the debate, a reason that is given mainly by those drawing from a phenomenological tradition. This reason charges that the debate presented a false dilemma between attentiveness to embodi-ment and anti-essentialism. These feminists argue that attending to the body does not entail essentialism if we conceptualize it as, to use de Beauvoir's term, a "body-in-situation"—that is, as a lived body whose meanings are dynamic and contingent (see Bauer 2001; Moi 1999; Kruks 2001). Approaching the body in this way is highly plausible, but in some respects it can be categorized under the first group I mentioned above, that is, with those who are still trying to show that their position is not essentialist. Thus, however we deconstruct the terms of the debate, it seems as if the specter of essentialism continues to haunt feminist theory and continues to dictate the baseline conditions of theoretical acceptability.

Though there are several ways in which the debate over essentialism was conceptually problematic, for example, in projecting the Aristotelian version of essentialism as the only possible way to define an essence, I would argue against those such as Toril Moi (1999) who think that the debate was generated purely out of these kinds of conceptual confusions. In reality, the debate over essentialism crystallized and synthesized the two principal concerns of feminist theory over the last thirty years, which, despite a wide variety of topics, has ultimately focused on two things: first, how to address the significant differences among women that are mediated by race, ethnicity, class, nationality, religion, sexuality, age, and able-bodiedness without emptying out the category altogether; and second, how to resist the deterministic and naturalistic arguments that have been used to conceal both the coercive conditions under which many women must live highly circumscribed lives and to conceal women's labor as labor (and thus justify its exploitation). We are still exploring how the heterogeneity of women affects both feminist theory and feminist practice, but even while we pursue this question feminists are united in opposing the narrow determinisms that are used the world over to reject individual women's aspirations, even the aspiration for a life free of coercive sex or compulsory motherhood. Thus, feminist engagement with the question of essentialism was primarily motivated by these concerns over difference and determinism. Since essentialism, as it was defined, conflicted with difference and invited determinism, everyone agreed it had to be rejected (and those who wanted to retain it had to show how it could accept difference and thwart determinism).

However, I want to argue here that the *philosophical* core of the debate over essentialism was a debate over the metaphysics of gender, although this was not always made clear (certainly not by me), and despite the fact that the philosophical history of the concept of essences post-Aristotle indicates that essentialism entails no given metaphysics. The danger of homogeneity that feminists were concerned about does not in reality come from essentialism as a concept but rather from a metaphysical account of sexual difference or, in other words, from the claim that the category of sexual difference has a metaphysical basis. It is out of their concerns about difference and determinism that most feminists have fled the very idea of a metaphysics of gender or a politics based on metaphysical claims of sexual difference. Even the term "metaphysics" has become a pejorative, as when Kristeva famously claimed that "the very dichotomy man/woman as an opposition between two rival entities may be understood as belonging to *metaphysics*" (1986, 209; emphasis in original). That is, as wrong.

In fleeing from determinism, feminists have fled not only from essentialism and metaphysics but also from realism, naturalism, objectivism, and even the capacity to make truth claims (which I would define as evaluative distinctions based on epistemic and not merely strategic considerations). In this chapter I want to follow Susan Babbitt, Sally Haslanger, and others to ask whether giving metaphysical content to sexed identity is necessarily determinist, and whether in fact an objectivist (*post*positivist) account of sexed identity is philosophically sound. An objectivist account would be one that takes the categorization of human beings by sex as having good metaphysical grounds, irreducible to ideological grounds. I will explain this further in what follows. Existential phenomenological descriptions of women's embodied situation, which start from the inner world of subjective experience rather than an objective category that is transcendent of the subject, are not inconsistent with an objectivist account of sexed identity, and would in fact be the best approach in my view toward developing a *substantively* descriptive account of women's lives as sexed beings. But before we can produce such phenomenological ethnographies of women's embodiment, we must delimit the category of "women."

Haslanger has recently defended an objectivist account of gender and critiqued the antiobjectivist feminist position, particularly Judith Butler's work, and so it will be useful to begin by reviewing Haslanger's arguments. Though I agree with Haslanger in large measure, there is an important weakness in her analysis of the arguments against objectivism that has to do with her interpretation of some of the social constructionist arguments that draw from Foucault. I will consider how detrimental this weakness is to her objectivist conclusion about sexual difference. It is important to consider carefully the strongest antiobjectivist and antimetaphysical arguments, so before I discuss Haslanger's critique of antiobjectivism I will give an overview of her strongest opponents, which would include not only Butler but also Monique Wittig and Collette Guillamin.

The antiobjectivist position draws from four main claims: (1) a claim about the fluid variability of all categorizations, which means that categories are subject to (even reducible to) ideological manipulation; (2) a claim about the mediated nature of all descriptions, including the descriptions implicit in categorizations; (3) a claim about the inevitably prescriptive effects of description; and (4) a claim that objectivism about sexual difference will serve to reenforce compulsory heterosexuality. Against these four points, I will argue that there are persuasive grounds for an objective rather than totally fluid account of sex categories, that objectivity does not require an escape from mediation in human knowledge or the ability to have "out of theory experiences" (1996, 142), and that the tendency for descriptive accounts to become prescriptive is a variable rather than uniform or absolute tendency and can be offset. I will argue that the objective basis of sex categories is in the differential relationship to reproductive capacity between men and women, but that a sexual categorization based on the biological division of reproductive labor does not establish a necessary link between reproduction beyond conception and heterosexuality.

The Case against Sex

Before poststructuralism the most influential antideterministic strategy in feminist theory had been developed by Gayle Rubin in 1975, when she argued, based on some extensive empirical cross-cultural research, in favor of making a distinction between sex and gender. Rubin used the term "sex" to refer only to body type and the term "gender" to refer to masculinity and femininity or the substantive aspects of our identity as men, women, and others. Thus Rubin claimed, with some definite echoes of de Beauvoir, that "we are not only oppressed *as* women, we are oppressed by having to *be* women, or men as the case may be" (1975, 204). Rubin conceded the naturalism of sex in order to denaturalize gender, thus allowing for the common-sense idea that males and females have different bodies, but that these bodily differences are not sufficient to explain the elaborate cultural practices and beliefs surrounding gendered identities, which vary considerably across cultures but share economic motivations centering on, she argued, the ability to exchange women. Thus, Rubin's distinction actually worked both to resist determinism and to ac-knowledge significant differences among women. Sex is about biological repro-duction and it is not entirely under our control, but gender is about power and the cultural formations that solidify it, and these vary widely. Contra Shulamith Fire-stone, who had argued in 1970 that our liberation would require a technological dismembering of sexual differences in reproduction, Rubin argued that gender had to go, or at least be radically transformed, but sex could stay. Rubin thus brilliantly solved our problem without sacrificing theoretical plausibility or committing us to a technologically based form of liberation that many women distrust. We were made free and allowed to be different.

However, Rubin's view soon came under criticism for its too easy concession to a natural sexual division. Where does this idea of sex come from? Is sexed identity itself—male/female—so free from culture? All women do not have wombs, all men are not fertile, and thus an individual's actual reproductive *capacity* does not de-termine their position within the division of sex. Moreover, Moira Gatens (1991), among others, argued that the sex/gender divide replicated too closely the andro-centric oppositional binaries of mind/body and nature/culture, which are strongly associated with the conceptual justifications given for women's oppression. The problem with these binary distinctions is not just their hierarchical character, the fact that one term is always superior to the other, or even their nefarious political uses. The main problem is the assumption that one can neatly distinguish the two terms, to be able to say "this is nature over here, that is culture over there," as philosophers had once said, "this is mind, that is body." Surely Hegel was correct to portray these distinctions as useful heuristic devices in certain circumstances but not as representations of reality strictly speaking, since in reality everything is quite mixed up together. The nature/culture distinction, which Rubin's sex/gender dis-tinction did seem to imply, has come under increasing criticism as incoherent, because, in an important sense, everything is natural, including what human beings do and make, and everything natural is actually dynamic and changing, including what human beings can do and can make.[1]

In the 1980s, on the strength of the alignment that Gatens noted between sex/gender and nature/culture, the sex/gender distinction was replaced with a monistic account in favor of, not sex for once, but gender. Gatens stated that she wanted to avoid entrenching "the historical construction of dualistically conceived sexual difference" (1991, 139). But she, like other feminists, also wanted to avoid the mo-nistic alternative that favored the masculine as the center or paradigm of universal subjectivity. Thus, if dualism were to be replaced by monism, it would have to be a contingency: that is, what all human beings, both those designated males and those designated females, share is that all that we are, all the way down, is contingent. As a result, the most influential position on the metaphysics of sexual difference and gender became a great refusal not only of the metaphysical basis for gender but also of a metaphysical basis of sexed identity itself. This was the position developed in Judith Butler's *Gender Trouble*, first published in 1989, in Monique Wittig's 1979 essay "One Is Not Born a Woman," and in several essays by Collette Guillamin from the late '70s and throughout the '80s. Each claimed against Rubin that, rather than gender being the product of sex, sex, or sexually differentiated classification, is produced by gender, which Wittig and Guillamin theorized mostly in relation to labor and political economy and Butler theorized primarily as the effect of a "hegemonic cultural discourse."

For Wittig, "the category of sex is the product of heterosexual society that turns half the population into sexual beings, for sex is a category which women cannot be outside of" (1992, 7). Wittig's aim was to contest the idea put forward by previous feminist theorists such as de Beauvoir and Firestone that "the basis of women's oppression is biological as well as historical" (1992, 10). Other feminists, such as Adrienne Rich, had also contested de Beauvoir's and Firestone's view that female physiological experiences, such as menstruation and pregnancy, are necessarily constraining and oppressive, but Wittig's point was different. Her aim was not to contest the negative valuation or characterization of female biology but to challenge the very categorization of human beings into groups based on biology. Thus she held that it is "dominance" that

> teaches us from all directions: —that there are before all thinking, all society, "sexes" (two categories of individuals born) with a constitutive difference that has ontological consequences (the metaphysical approach), that there are before all thinking, all social order, "sexes" with a "natural" or "biological" or "hormonal" or "genetic" difference that has sociological consequences (the scientific approach),
> —that there is before all thinking, all social order, a "natural division of labor in the family," a "division of labor [that] was originally nothing *but* the division of labor in the sexual act" (the Marxist approach). . . . Belonging to the natural order, these relationships cannot be spoken of as social relationships. (4–5; emphasis in original)

Wittig's materialist feminism held that it is this fundamental ideological lie that works to justify the creation of women as a special class for exploitation. She claimed that "the making of women is like the making of eunuchs, the breeding of slaves, of animals" (1992, 6). And the categorization by sex, presented as objective and thus prior to "all thinking," is the necessary starting point for this process.

Collette Guillamin, in writings that in some cases predate both Wittig and Butler, made a similar antinaturalistic argument against both race and sex categories, developing early arguments about the social construction of race that are today widely accepted. Her aim was to overturn "the basic postulate of all the present forms of thinking" about race and sex, which "is the idea that a human group may be physically (or as common sense would put it, 'objectively') specific *in itself*, independently of its relationships or practices" (1995, 85). She argued instead that these categories are founded on social relations and produced through arbitrary marks and enforced practices, marks that confer symbolic meanings on parts of the body, and practices that constitute race and sex identity as their *effect*, just as Pascal had argued that prayers produce faith and Butler argues that performances produce gender.

Guillamin's version of a materialist feminism focuses on the materiality of power relations rather than the materiality of embodiment. It is power relations and the *"ideological effect*: the idea of 'nature'" that together "reduc[e] women to the state of material objects" (179). Guillamin thus analogizes gender to class, as the product of a form of political economy, and invokes the ideas of fetishism and reification to explain the naturalization of gender relations. In this she follows Firestone, but where Firestone accepted Engel's idea that the biological division of reproduction actually *predated* women's oppression, and thus that sexed identity is a natural division rather than merely the ideological effect of private property, Guillamin's relentless antinaturalism leads her to hold that what she calls "sexage" is always and only a social category. Guillamin's main concern, however, was not identity but the appropriation of labor, and, in my view, her best analyses are those that develop insightful characterizations of the way in which women's unpaid labor is collectively appropriated, for example the ways that not only wives and mothers but unmarried and celibate women are roped into care work. Her opposition to naturalism was primarily based on her view that it concealed and provided an alibi for this manmade appropriation of female labor.

Thus, the shared view of Guillamin, Wittig, and Butler is that sex and gender are fully socially real but not objective or independent of human belief systems and thus not natural. It was Butler who developed the metaphysical implications of this view most fully. In her account, concepts of identity act as forced and enforceable constraints on what is at bottom fluid and inherently unstable, including desire and sexuality. "The challenge for rethinking gender categories outside of the metaphysics of substance," she said, will be to overcome being by becoming and thus to conceptualize "gender as a doing" (1990, 25). And she famously conceptualized this "doing" in performative terms, building from Erving Goffman: "There is no gender identity behind the expressions of gender; that identity is performatively constituted by the very 'expressions' that are said to be its results" (1990, 25). The trope of performance was meant to eradicate metaphysics from the question of women's identity once and for all. "That the gendered body is performative," she says, "suggests that it has no ontological status apart from the various acts which constitute its reality" (136).

In reality, the idea that gender is a doing rather than a being would preclude a metaphysics of *substance* but not necessarily a *process* metaphysics à la Whitehead, Spinoza, or Bergson, wherein reality is described as a primordially dynamic, ever-changing present. The metaphysical basis of gender would then not be in a being or substance ontology but in a process, and such a process could be enacted via performance. However, although processes are dynamic, they still have describable form and characteristics, with the fundamental categories changing from "things" to patterns or organizations of movement such as a dialectic. Given the fact that processes are not random flux but organized patterns, processes can then invite

comparison with those same regulatory practices that Butler views as the techniques of oppression.[2] Since Butler's main target is not substances but regulative
norms, her move away from being and toward becoming and process has created
new dilemmas of determinism in Butler's more recent work. In *Bodies That
Matter*, her 1993 book with the subtitle *On the Discursive Limits of "Sex,"* she
replaces "matter as being" with matter as "a process of materialization that stabi-
lizes over time to produce the effect of boundary, fixity, and surface" (9). In this
way she seeks to explain the repetitive and recalcitrant features of current society:
how certain bodies are made abject, certain identities are reified, and certain
relations are stabilized. And the processes of subjectification she describes in *The
Psychic Life of Power* are, as I discussed in chapter 3, inescapably oppressive: it is
our very entanglement with the process of interpellation that inscribes us within
power and dooms us to desiring our own domination.[3]

In a sense, Butler's version of process metaphysics continues to operate with a
kind of nature/culture distinction, as many have noted, in that she makes matter
the *effect* of power and always postsignification. The real player in the field is then
ultimately discourse conceptualized as without material constraint, which is a
Derridean as opposed to Foucauldian account of discourse (see, e.g., Schrift 2001;
Weir 1996, 112–34).[4] This means that, in a sense, all is culture, in that there are no
objective or human-independent forms, categories, or limits. Butler's tendency to
focus on texts and linguistic terms and her avoidance of directly addressing materiality largely follows from her view that any account of materiality that does not
make discourse causally efficacious "in the final instance" would presume an
escape from mediation. She asks, "How are we to find the body that preexists its
cultural interpellation?" (1987, 129). Why theorize bodies, she seems to be saying,
if, when we refer to something in the world, we are operating on the basis of
discursive boundaries that delimit objects? If there is no possibility of reference
without relying on discursively constituted boundaries, then, she argues, there is no
possibility of attributing objective status to any entity or type. It is our discourse,
rather than the world, that constitutes objects and types.[5]

Another reason that Butler, Wittig, and Guillamin were concerned to free us
from a metaphysically grounded sex was because they saw this as a major player in
the ideology of heterosexism, that human beings are naturally or properly exclusively heterosexual. A dualistic binary or oppositional system of categorization that
divides us into male and female would seem to privilege heterosexual sex as the
foundation of sexed identity. Butler rhetorically asks, "To what extent does the
category of women achieve stability and coherence only in the context of the heterosexual matrix?"(1990, 5). Wittig argues that "the body's sexual responsiveness is
restricted through the institutionalization of binary sexual difference" (1992, 135).
Thus, the normative weight of heterosexist categories collapses the distinction
between description and prescription. Butler worried also that the descriptive binary categories imply a determinism. She says, "The presumption of a binary
gender system implicitly retains the belief in a mimetic relation of gender to sex
whereby gender mirrors sex or is otherwise restricted by it"(1990, 6). But ultimately
the concern with prescriptive effects and with determinism was based on a prior
claim that the description given of categories based on sex is simply wrong insofar

as it is presented as objective: privileging reproductive organs over other differences is arbitrary and explainable only in terms of ideological reasons. Butler argued that the heterogeneity within each sexed category cannot justify the homogeneity that the categories imply. And she shares Foucault's view that "it is the way that anatomy is socially invested that defines gender identity and not the body itself" (Benhabib and Cornell 1987, 14).

Butler, Wittig, and Guillamin pointed to the absence of correlation between actual sexed characteristics and sexed identities, to the variable way in which physical attributes can be grouped and signified, and in Butler's case to the necessity of linguistic mediation, and so concluded that sex is no less a product of culture than gender is. The bottom line was that sexual categories are not based on objective features in the world. Variable discursive formations and variable cultural systems for organizing and exploiting labor can pick out, name, conceptualize, and define the boundaries of the features that are used to demarcate sexual, and not just gendered, identities, and thus sex identity is no more natural or objective than gender. It is the contingent practices of gender that create sex, and not vice versa.

This view gained further plausibility from (as well as having a major influence on) the power of a new transgendered movement that has swept the United States and some other parts of the global North. There are two elements here, first, a new critique of surgery on transgendered babies and, second, a liberation movement of transgendered adults who have altered their assigned gender in surgical or nonsurgical ways. Up to an estimated 10 percent of all babies born have ambiguous, indeterminate, or multiple primary and secondary sexual characteristics, and it has recently become more widely known that U.S. physicians routinely perform surgery on these "naturally" transgendered children in order to force them into our culture's ideal of anatomical polarity. Such surgery is not always motivated by either a concern for ensuring reproductive capacity or sexual pleasure. Sometimes the children are surgically altered in such a way that they will conform to anatomical norms of appearance but have lost, because of the surgery, their capacity for orgasm or for other sexual pleasures. Critics argue against such surgery, at least until the children are old enough to decide for themselves what they would like to have done, if anything. Moreover, both surgical and nonsurgical practices have been developed as voluntary procedures for those individuals who wish to transcend the physical dualisms of male/female or who wish to cross over the divide. Not only is it increasingly common to encounter male-to-females and female-to-males, whose sexed identity must be located somewhere beyond the dualism whether or not they can publicly pass as unambiguous, but also to encounter those who have opted for secondary sexual characteristics of both male and female (at least in major cities). Sexed identity has undergone major cultural transformation, and there is no sign that this process will soon stop.

A second support for the denaturalizing of sex has come about through the new reproductive technologies. Artificial insemination, in vitro fertilization, embryo transfer, fertility enhancements, and surrogacy are creating new options in the biological process of reproduction, challenging the belief that there is a necessary connection between reproduction and heterosexuality and producing a proliferation of legally recognized reproductive roles, from surrogate, to birth mother, to egg donor, sperm donor, and so on.[6] This development seems capable of soon altering the biological division of reproduction in ways that Shulamith Fire-stone called for in 1970 as a necessity for women's liberation. The biological rev-olution is not merely expanding the opportunities for sexed individuals to reproduce in new ways; it is transforming the ways in which we conceptualize and define the boundaries of biological reproduction — boundaries that have long served as the basis for sexed identities, at least the discursive basis if not the metaphysical basis. As these boundaries are reorganized, so too must our categorization of identities based on reproductive function.

Thus, spurred by both the transgendered movement and the development of reproductive technologies, the naturalism of sex appears to be withering away. Certainly, the categories of reproductive roles, and the categories of sexed identity are subject to variation by cultural practices and forms of political economy.

Antinaturalism as Mastery over Nature

However, some feminists have opposed the antinaturalist tendencies of these recent cultural developments, which they see as an indication of the attempt to escape the realm of the immanent or the material (see, e.g., Schott 2002). The peculiar di-lemma feminism has which complicates its antideterministic project is that it has equal reason to pursue nature's transcendence and nature's acceptance. Can we be thoroughly antinaturalist and antideterminist in regard to gender without finding ourselves in collusion with the Enlightenment narrative of "mastery over nature"? Isn't the antinaturalism of some feminist theory in danger of imitating the project of mastery? Diana Fuss, for example, says that anti-essentialist feminists such as herself want a category of women that is a "*linguistic* rather than a natural kind" so that we can "hold onto the notion of women as a group without *submitting* to the idea that it is 'nature' which categorizes" us as such (Fuss 1989, 5; second emphasis mine. See also Babbitt 1996, 141).[7] Although she expresses this as submission to an idea, it implies a submission to nature or to any natural system that would limit the scope of our categorization. I believe this represents an aspect of much contemporary Western feminist theory. Despite the extensive critiques of reified conceptions of "nature," there persists a resistance to naturalized sex categories and an embrace of linguistic nominalism out of a general desire to avoid submitting to the dictates of nature.

It is without doubt that Butler, Wittig, and Guillamin are right to point out that a naturalistic-based determinism (as opposed to the earlier theistic-based forms of determinism) has been the trump card used since the early modern period to secure women in our pumpkins, but patriarchal ideologies have appealed to nature in this way at the same time that they have maintained a barely concealed contempt and disgust for all things designated natural, which men alone could leave behind in a trail of mathematical formulae. Thus, in the West, women have been oppressed by a two-prong attack: by being associated with nature (more closely than men) and by a simultaneous denigration of nature, putting it and us down with the animals and far away from the grace of God. Thinking purely strategically here, if women could manage to achieve transcendence from the realm of nature it wouldn't matter how nature is regarded. This was the strategy taken by Shulamith Firestone and, arguably, Simone de Beauvoir. But of course, no matter how we come to define the sphere of "nature," this strategy is unintelligible. Nature cannot be transcended in this way. Everything we make, transform, and build continues to change and decay, as we do ourselves, despite the dreams of genetic regeneration. The floor now under your feet, the metal and plastics that make up your computer or your car, and certainly the soft tissue surrounding your own skeleton, as well as the skeleton itself, are in constant, unstoppable processes of physical transformation, colloquially known as rot. Transcendence—insofar as this means a complete departure from natural processes—exists only in our heads. Given this, we should reconsider the devaluation of the natural from which the desire for transcendence (and mastery) gets its motivation.

Thus, some feminists are concerned that the currently dominant view of both sex and gender as the product of discursive construction is noncoincidentally aligned with the Enlightenment project of overcoming the materiality of our physical selves. Eco-feminists call for rejecting the project of transcendence even while we resist the deterministic justifications of patriarchal ideologies. As Chris Cuomo argues, eco-feminism offers "critiques of the ways in which the social and ecological worlds are gendered," and articulate "alternative perspectives on the world" (1998, 19). The project of mastery is an ethical relation to the non-human world, but it is built on a particular metaphysical account of that world and its relation to the human.

Feminist theory that has an antipathy to naturalism needs to develop a reflexive awareness of it's motivations and fears. It may be assuming that all forms of naturalism imply a clear nature/culture division. But the very opposition between a naturalistic and a linguistic basis of sex categories presupposes such a clear division or separation. In contrast, Moi supports Terry Eagleton's formulation that "we are not 'cultural' rather than 'natural' creatures, but cultural beings by virtue of our nature" (quoted in Moi 1999, 79). I interpret this as implying that our cultural practices and productions occur within a material world, which would eschew both a neat nature/culture divide and the commitment to transcend and master nature. I will return to this idea later in the chapter.

In sum, while I believe that the desire for a transcendent mastery is still manifest in some feminist treatments of sex categories, I also believe that at least some forms of naturalism continue to operate effectively as justificatory alibis for the oppression of women. But neither of these concerns can settle the matter of the metaphysics of sex and gender. We must ask whether this refusal of a metaphysics of sexual difference is persuasive on descriptive grounds and not merely as a political strategy. To what extent are the political concerns about determinism and difference, and the debate over whether we should refuse or embrace naturalism, acting as non-negotiable criteria for a feminist position on the metaphysics of sexual difference, and if so, does this make theoretical sense? If it is implausible to believe that materiality is *always*, or even, *only*, the effect of power, what are our real metaphysical options? In other words, what is the metaphysics of sexual difference?

Metaphysics, Objectivity, and Sex

The idea that there is a metaphysics of sex is associated mainly with the trend some call "difference feminism," which is based on a post-Freudian approach to the psychic figuration of woman, such as developed most interestingly and comprehensively by Irigaray. Difference feminists postulate that male/female anatomical differences produce, or at least are correlated with, differences in philosophical, psychological, erotic, and linguistic orientations and effects. Their emphasis is on the uncovering and valuation of these differences rather than on the denaturalization of sexed categories. However, the relationship between "difference feminism" and metaphysics is contested: Irigaray, for example, may be drawing on the body and insisting on the real significance of morphological difference, but she has also forcefully critiqued the traditions, methods, and presuppositions of Western metaphysics in Plato, Aristotle, Descartes, Locke, and Hegel. Even Nietzsche's own antimetaphysics has come under her critical analysis for its gendered symbolic organization and articulation of concepts. The implication of her critique is that metaphysics cannot be an objective description of what exists if it operates through a conceptual imagery that is variegated according to body type but presented as neutral. So, on the one hand, difference feminists are charged with naturalizing sexual difference as a metaphysical category, but, on the other hand, they are associated with the critique of metaphysics as a philosophical pursuit of objective description.

One way to resolve this paradox is to view the differences that difference feminists posit as other than objective or natural: that is, sexual difference may also be an *imagined* representation of the (physically) real, but a representation that is produced under given social conditions, such as the oppression of women, from which in turn alternative experiences and modes of conceptualization are developed. On this reading, to the extent that Irigaray is doing metaphysics, she is exploring the possible features of an alternative female symbolic and its ramifications for ethics and politics, rather than addressing the question of how to characterize the metaphysical basis for the categories of sexual difference. In other words, she is experimenting with alternative symbolic and conceptual imagery as a way to free us from the stranglehold of masculinist concepts that parade as universal. As interesting as this project is, it does not shed light on the question of whether there is a metaphysical basis for sexual difference, except perhaps as a negative warning against certain kinds of gendered concepts or metaphors that we might use in articulating a metaphysics.

Work in the 1990s and beyond by Sally Haslanger, Susan Babbitt, and others has reintroduced a different discussion about the metaphysics of sexual difference, not focused on the substance of the difference as much as on the possibility of an objective or natural basis for sexed difference. I want now to consider and assess some of the strongest of these arguments. For Haslanger and Babbitt, working more within an analytic tradition of philosophy, the key idea here is that gender is an objective type, while Continental feminist philosophers like Moi and Bauer use existential phenomenology to reassert a category of women that can be rendered with descriptive accuracy as well as positive political effect.

I see these two trends as united in a commitment to a kind of materialist analysis, which I would broadly define as an analysis that maintains the central importance of the material reality of the sexed body. Moi offers the most general explanation for why she believes it is time for a renewed insistence on the body.

The principal thesis of Moi's book, *What Is a Woman?*, is that the feminist error, starting as far back as Rubin's work, of separating sex from gender produced a kind of idealist trend in feminist theory, or a neglect of female embodiment. The idealist tendency and overemphasis on discourse results from two mistaken assumptions: first, that sex *exhausts* the facticity of the body, and second, that sex has no *determinate* effect on the practices of gender. The body, then, is reified in a certain sense as well as eliminated from any analysis of gender, a result that is counterintuitive given gender's consistent manifestation *through* the body. The resultant theoretical problem of relating sex to gender is analogous to Descartes's problem of explaining how the mind, which he thought of as a thing without extension, could affect the body, a thing with extension, once he had separated the mind and body in a qualitatively absolute way. The sex/gender division, Moi claims, tends similarly to effect an artificial separation and to reify sex outside of history and social situation, leaving "a gap where the historical and socialized body should be" (1999, 30). Even with the ongoing danger of determinism, we do not need to build an impenetrable wall between embodied sex and cultural practices of gender, she argues. Like Bauer, she argues for combining gender and the sexed body by using existential categories.

Thus, Moi suggests that the argument that gender constructs sex is unnecessary to thwart determinism once we understand the body as historical and social, that it therefore solves only a specious problem, and that it implausibly holds matter accountable to discourse without reciprocity. Moi argues that we can maintain *both* that the body is not reducible to sexual difference *and* that the body is subject to natural law as well as human-made meaning systems which are combined in such a way that they cannot be neatly disentangled (1999, 68–69). There are other interesting arguments against some current feminist doxa in Moi's book, contesting the claim that all concepts involve exclusion, for example, and to thwart determinism we need only show that biology does not determine social norms, rather than trying to make biology irrelevant to sexed embodiment. Moi claims that to avoid biological determinism without leaving the body behind all we need is to return to Beauvoir's concept of the body-in-situation, because the latter approach starts with a dialectical account of facticity and transcendence.

But before we can articulate such a dialectical account, I believe we must construe the nature of our facticity itself. What can we say about the body's relationship to, implication in, and even causality of the categories of sexual difference? Moi's account of the body-in-situation leaves these questions aside, perhaps because she thinks such questions imply the ability to make a neat divide between what is natural and what is interpreted or mediated, a divide that existential phenomenology rejects. Haslanger, however, offers an argument about why the repudiation of metaphysics does not require positing an escape from mediation, which I will turn to in a moment. But to begin to theorize sex/gender metaphysically, it will be useful to contrast it with race.

Is Sex Like Race?

Considering for a moment the comparison between sexual difference and race can shed some light here. Both are visible identities that are thought to be marked on the body. The ideologies of sexism and racism are predicated on a claim of causality between physical features and intellectual, moral, and emotional attributes. But there is an important difference between the two. Racism must convince us that biologically insignificant physical attributes such as skin color, the shape of the nose or eyes, or hair type are actually very significant and the signs of fundamental differences in human capacity. Thus Kant can claim with perfect certainty that "this fellow was quite black from head to foot, a clear proof that what he said was stupid" (Eze 1997, 57). One might speculate that the recent search for racial genomic differences was motivated by the need to find something more plausible than surface features on which to hang racist claims. But this search has turned out to prove the opposite: that there is no nontrivial genomic difference between socially recognized racial groups.

Thus racism has now turned increasingly to cultural differences to justify its hierarchies, holding that the fundamental differences are located in cultural traditions and practices—the culture of poverty, for example, or the irrationalism of strong religious commitment—rather than what are relatively insignificant human features. On this view, physical features become the sign not of *biological* difference, but of *cultural* difference. However, this change in referent changes the ability of the signs to "work" in reliably racist ways, that is, to circumscribe the potential of individuals. For racism to make use of culture in this way it must impute a stable bounded essence to an entity (culture) that is unstable, unbounded, and without essence. Cultures are simply not immutable. Linking racial identity not to biology but to culture, then, cannot justify differential treatment, the withholding of educational resources, or apartheid. Cultural difference can support racism only if it is seen as the effect of a more intractable biological difference, and thus it can only work on the basis of an assumption that is empirically insupportable. Nonetheless, culturalism is operating effectively under the current regime of "official" antiracism to conceal the racism that motivates the claim of cultural intractability.

Sexism has more to work with, one might say. The role one plays in the biological division of reproduction, the capacity to sustain an infant entirely on the production of one's own body, to give birth, to nurse, are much more significant attributes. There is thus a qualitative difference in the significance of these two sets of differences: skin color, hair type, and so on, versus role in biological reproduction. Of course, sexism would make female-specific attributes exhaustively and implausibly significant in determining women's lives, a claim that is losing credibility. Given that female children inherit fully half of their genes from their fathers, as do male children from their mothers, we cannot be that different. There is just a single chromosomal variable by which one's role in reproduction is determined, which is an implausible determinant over the whole range of human functional capacities as claimed by sexist ideology. Even Plato saw as much; he says, "If it appears that [the male and the female sex] differ only in just this respect that the female bears and the male begets, we shall say that no proof has yet been produced that the woman differs from the man for our purposes, but we shall continue to think that our guardians and their wives ought to follow the same pursuits" (*Republic*, bk. 5, 454d–e).

Yet, despite the outlandishness of the claims that have been made for its significance, it remains true that the variable of reproductive role provides a material infrastructure for sexual difference that is qualitatively different from the surface differences of racial categories.[8] It would be ridiculous to pursue a research project to study the significance of hair texture on the development of cultural systems; in regard to race it makes much more sense to look at the global political economy and the history of colonialism for an understanding of why and how skin shades gained such ontological significance in recent centuries. Furthermore, empirical evidence suggests that fear and distrust do not automatically arise from perceptual visible difference; something else must instill hostility because looks alone are not sufficient. As I will argue in chapter 7, this does not mitigate against the reality of race, or suggest that racial identity is a chimera, but it is to say that the *origin* of racialized differences and racial categories is less a metaphysical than a political story.

The physical foundation of sexual difference is another matter altogether. Gender identities in some variation seem to be, unlike race, historically ubiquitous, hardly recent, and based in a set of biological features with more morphological substance. Context and history are necessary to explain the political significance of racialized features; they are not necessary to explain the significance of differential roles in reproduction. The foolhardiness of formulating legal protections based on a presumed sameness between men and women has been well established by now, as pregnancy must be labeled disability and maternity-leave reforms are stymied by the insistence that they be absolutely equal to paternity leave. And there is no place for a provision for breast-feeding in a legal discourse predicated on individuals undifferentiated by sex. Whether women want to "overcome" such differences by technological means is a question that is altogether different in kind from the question of whether we want to overcome the historical and social conditions that make affirmative action necessary to redress racial inequality. One could make an overall point here about the lack of analogy between racial/ethnic/cultural identities, on the one hand, and identities such as age, disability, and sex on the other. All are generally visible identities, naturalized as marked on the body without mediation. But the markings that signify age, disability, and sex are qualitatively different in significance from those signifying race, ethnicity, and culture.[9] This is not an argument about the virulence or priority of various forms or targets of oppression. It is simply an argument about the quality of the physical basis for sex categories vis-à-vis race categories.

Denise Riley has become famous for her book *Am I that Name? Feminism and the Category of "Women" in History*, which argues that "women" is an indeterminate, unstable category for semantic and historical as well as political reasons. On her view, indeterminacy does not mean that we can say nothing about women or in their name, but that we must acknowledge that the only anchor for the concept of women is in "discursive historical formation" (1988, 5). Yet in earlier work, Riley was one of the first to articulate the mistake of repudiating any and all biological aspects of sexual difference. She argued that the problem is not biology but biological determinism, that is, the attempt to reduce "everything to the workings of a changeless biology" (1983, 2). And she pointed out that the "usual corrective to biologism" invoked by feminists is a cultural construction thesis so strong that it "ignores the fact that there really is a biology, which must be conceived more clearly" (1983, 6, 2). Thus, the cultural construction thesis implausibly "substitutes an unbounded sphere of social determination for that of biological determination" (1983, 3).

Again in this earlier work, Riley articulates the feminist project as follows: "The tactical problem is in naming and specifying sexual difference where it has been ignored or misread; but without doing so in a way which guarantees it an eternal life of its own ... as if the chance of one's gendered conception mercilessly guaranteed every subsequent facet of one's existence at all moments" (4). Perhaps twenty years later it is easier to see that biological facts are neither eternal nor all-determining, and thus to avoid the preemptive conclusion that Riley became influential for later that we must base sexual difference only on history, not on materiality, if we seek an escape from biological determinism. It should not be so difficult, after all, to develop an account of sexual difference that incorporates biology without having biology guarantee "every subsequent facet of one's existence at all moments." The question we must ask is whether this biological or material infrastructure for sexual difference yields a metaphysics of sexed identity.

Haslanger's Objectivism

Sally Haslanger has recently attempted to clarify the issues of debate over the metaphysics of gender, or sexed, identity, and has raised the specter of objectivism in relation to sexual categories, though her defense of objectivism is given abstractly, that is, without specifying what precisely is objective about sexual difference. Haslanger is a rare bridge figure, capable of drawing out the full implications of contemporary analytic approaches and relating these to current feminist and anti-racist discussions occurring at the margins of philosophy. In her essay "Feminism and Metaphysics: Negotiating the Natural," Haslanger begins with a consideration of the tension between feminism and metaphysics, given that most feminists reject metaphysics and most metaphysicians ignore feminist philosophy. She is critical of both. She argues that feminists who reject metaphysics are operating with an outdated notion of the field, in which metaphysics is still trying to access an unmediated Real and produce irrefutable truths. This characterization is not true of contemporary post-Quinean metaphysics, she holds, which understands itself as operating within a theory-laden field and with a preexisting set of doxastic commitments that are organized as more of a web than a foundationalist pyramid. But she also argues that post-Quinean metaphysics has been inattentive to the political influences affecting its priorities, its framing questions, and, consequently, its determination of what is central versus peripheral in the organization of the web. Thus, she tries to develop a metaphysical approach to feminist questions that will include a political reflexivity.

Haslanger's main thesis is to argue that the feminist tendency toward skeptical and nominalist views about the objective basis of gender distinctions is unwarranted both philosophically and politically. That is, feminists have not made sufficient arguments to show that there is no objective basis for gender distinctions, and they have incorrectly assumed that if there were such an objective basis, this could only provide support for patriarchy. Thus, her main argument is in the form of a negative: that the antirealism about gender is unwarranted. I find most of her reasoning compelling, but in one crucial part of her critique of the skeptical and nominalist position she ignores an important argument. Thus, my concern here will be to see what difference this makes to her realist conclusions.

Haslanger begins by reviewing the feminist critique of metaphysics as androcentric on the grounds that it tends "to draw uncritically on experiences and patterns of thought that are characteristically male or masculine." Such arguments, and demonstrations of androcentrism, have been made by Iris Young and Merrill Hintikka and Jaakko Hintikka, among others. But this raises the immediate question of what a better alternative to androcentrism might be, and it turns out that this is not so apparent. Obviously, to theorize from a gynocentric perspective is no improvement over androcentrism if one is trying to make general claims. But the even more difficult issue is to decide what would count as a gynocentric point of view. The basis for most claims about gender has been empirical research on sex differences, research that is now widely recognized as notoriously biased (see Fausto-Sterling 1986). Nor can we simply wait for better research to answer our questions about gender, because, as the critics of sex difference research have pointed out, the problem with the research is in the questions it poses as well as in the answers it gives. Why focus on measuring the variations between genders when the variations within each gender is often far larger, and other differentials, such as culture or age, are more relevant? Moreover, in defining gender through the measurement of gender differences we may in fact be setting up a new regulatory norm or stereotype for "how women (and men) should be" that will exclude or marginalize some or many or even most women. Thus, how can a concept of gynocentrism address the heterogeneity among women and avoid exaggerating the differences with men?

Haslanger argues that this set of problems does not mean, however, that gynocentric approaches are irretrievable. What one must do is retreat from either temporal or spatial universalizations about gender difference and instead make context-based claims. Thus we can make reasonable characterizations of gynocentric experiences within given contexts, as long as we acknowledge that there will still be variety even within a delimited context. This strikes me as an entirely reasonable conclusion. And because the claims are contextual, there is no claim being made about the absolute nature of a gynocentric point of view, and thus no regulatory norm exerting a command into the unending future.

Haslanger points out that even such a modified approach—one that would presume nothing more than the ability to make contextually limited generalizations about women—is still problematic for many feminist theorists, despite the fact that many feminist social scientists pursue just such generalizations. But for many theorists the contextual approach is not really telling us anything about gender, even in context, but only about the *discourse* of gender in that context.

It is on this point that Haslanger begins her real case against the critics of metaphysics, and to develop her case she first provides an updated characterization of post-Quinean metaphysics. Quine portrayed the empirical claims of the sciences as having a weblike structure rather than a foundationalist pyramidal structure, and argued that any part of the web—even basic empirical observation reports—will be revisable if we are prepared to alter the other parts of the web that are structurally dependent on the part we want to eliminate. And we may well be willing to make those structural adjustments given a particular anomaly we wish to resolve or a particular theoretical project we wish to complete, but these motivations are entirely contingent and variable. Thus, Quine's approach assumes neither absolute starting points nor access to an unmediated Real; it is non-foundationalist, with a holistic approach to justification, and adopts a fallibilist view of its best claims. Theorizing aims not at purity but at increasing the consistency of our beliefs. Haslanger calls this approach an "aporematic" metaphysics, and explains that it "might reasonably be considered immanent metaphysics: the questions, the puzzles, and the proposed answers arise within our thinking in response to current theoretical and practical demands" (2000, 114). Again, Haslanger is still critical of much of the work in metaphysics that uses this approach for its lack of reflexivity about its priorities and assumptions, but the point is that its antifoundationalism provides a greater *potential* openness to seeing the ways in which political realities can affect the discursive context in which questions are formulated and posed as well as the ways in which possible answers are developed and compared.[10]

According to Haslanger, then, the metaphysical question of gender is whether gender is a natural kind, which is a group that shares a common essence, or whether it is an objective type, which is a unity without an underlying essence, or whether it is neither of these. (I think Haslanger means to be referring to sexed identity here, not to gender in Rubin's sense, but I will use Haslanger's terminology while discussing her argument.) One could hold a realist view about gender being either a kind or a type, or one could be a skeptic, holding that we simply cannot know, or a nominalist, holding that the basis of either kinds or types is entirely nonobjective.

To say that a type is objective is to say that there is some nonrandom or nonarbitrary basis for its unity. The basis for some unities is weak, such as the unity of things on my desk which at the moment include paper, pens, matches, stones, garbage, tiles, plants, pictures, tissues, keys, candy, cough drops, chewing gum, buttons, and a cat. There is no way to incorporate this assemblage into one category except insofar as all these things share a temporary location. But some unities clearly have a stronger basis than this, such as the unity of red things, or mammals, or things that are carbon based. What makes a type objective is that the unifying factor is independent of us. I will address the issue of what "independence" can mean more thoroughly later on, but Haslanger is not putting forward a chimerical language of pure access to the noumena in claiming that the basis of some unities is independent of human practices. She is making a comparative judgment between what are obviously all linguistically conceptualized entities. One needn't be a positivist, who believes in pure uninterpreted bits of data, to be committed to a theory which holds that the basis for some categories are independent of human beings, such as whether something is carbon based, while other categories are not independent of human beings, such as social structures or literary conventions or even the degree of gender dimorphism in a given time and place.

Gender is, of course, very much a social kind of unity. It has been imbued with cultural values and meanings, and it is usually presented as a category of two after which exceptions are forcibly, even surgically, altered to fit. But Haslanger does not think these obvious facts are sufficient to dismiss the possibility that gender is an objective type. What I assume she is thinking here is that the objective type that is gender may be mistakenly characterized, made overly inclusive, and have longstanding crazy cultural associations, and yet the basis of the unity itself may be objective.

To show that this hypothesis—that gender is an objective type—should not be ruled out, Haslanger considers some of the arguments against the objectivity of gender from Wittig and Butler. She discusses their arguments that the fundamental importance attached to whether one has a penis or vagina comes after, not before, social conventions, in this case, compulsory heterosexuality. Butler's variant of this argument relies heavily, and Haslanger thinks too heavily, on the idea that all of our access to reality is mediated. From the latter claim Haslanger argues that Butler fallaciously comes to the conclusion that gender is not objective. Here is how the argument goes.

Butler argues that when we refer to something in the world we are operating on the basis of discursive boundaries that delimit objects. Thus there is no possibility of reference without relying on discursively constituted boundaries, and no possibility of attributing objective status to any entity or type. Haslanger is prepared to agree with Butler's claim that it is our discourse, rather than the world, that constitutes objects and types, if this is understood to be a claim about our language and about our knowledge, but she thinks Butler believes it is also a metaphysical claim about the absence of an independent basis for categories used in language.

To say that it is a claim about language and knowledge is to say that it is a claim about things *qua* things we refer to. But to say that it is a metaphysical claim is to say that it is a claim about *things*. Here's another way to put the distinction: in the first case, Butler is arguing that gender *as a concept* is discursively constructed, and in the second case she is arguing that *gender* is discursively constructed. Haslanger thinks Butler has no grounds for the latter claim simply on the basis of the idea that all of our relations with the world are discursively mediated. The ubiquity of mediation itself does not entail that *nothing* is independent of human beings, or that our knowledge is blocked by mediation, and here she uses the example of the phone system—an intermediary that improves rather than blocks access to things beyond our reach. Of course, what the phone brings us into contact with is not, under *any* circumstances, beyond our reach; we could conceivably travel to the person we are trying to communicate with and then communicate directly. So one might argue that, for this reason, the phone system is not analogous to discourse. But all Haslanger is trying to show here is that mediation in and of itself is not sufficient to justify skepticism. Even if we were *not* able to travel to the person we are speaking to, we might yet be able to communicate very effectively using the phone. In this case, mediation does not block knowledge, but in fact *aids* it.

Moreover, the dismissal of the possibility of knowledge about the world on the grounds that we are bounded by language presupposes very modernist pre-Hegelian bifurcations between phenomenal knowing and a noumenal world. According to Haslanger's portrayal of much of contemporary analytic metaphysics, a pure transparency between belief and world is no longer considered necessary to claim knowledge: we can settle with oblique relations of veridicality, but why deny our ability to reliably claim that the set of things on my desk has a weaker unity than the set of mammals, and that this is a fact independent of human categorical systems? Haslanger says:

> There is a temptation to think that if we cannot "get outside" of ourselves to test our beliefs against reality, then there's nothing further we can do epistemically to regulate belief; we're left with only political negotiation. But there are other epistemic considerations that can be brought to bear on belief, and provide grounds for claims to truth, e.g., coherence, evidential support, fruitfulness, etc. Oddly, many feminists feel pressed to skepticism about an independent reality because they implicitly endorse a traditional conception that requires certainty or direct access to reality in order to have knowledge of it, while at the same time they often find the traditional conception of knowledge problematic. (2000, 122)

This mistake about the limits of knowledge is related to the mistake some feminists make about analytic metaphysics: assuming that the failure of positivism leads to epistemological skepticism.

Haslanger's arguments in regard to the implications that follow from the ubiquity of mediation seem to me to be right. This is an important point that, although it has been repeatedly made over the past ten or more years, seems not to have been absorbed into poststructuralist feminist philosophy. Yes, we use concepts to know the world; no, that does not mean that we cannot say anything about the world but only about other concepts.

But where I differ with Haslanger is as follows. She assumes that once she has shown the problem with the argument about mediation, she can then show that categories of gender are not just about the discourse of gender but about gender itself. However, the ubiquity of mediation is not the sole reason Butler gives for the discursive constitution of sex. Butler's argument also invokes the Foucauldian idea that discourses have identity-altering, materialistic effects. That is, discourses do not merely categorize and rearrange what is in the world but, in some cases at least, create things that didn't exist previously. I am sure Haslanger would agree that discourse does create some things, like, for example, heterosexuality as a category of social identity, but the question is whether gender is also one of these things. From Butler's point of view, gender is performatively enacted on the basis of discursively constituted regulatory norms, but this means that it literally comes into existence as a lived experience and visible phenomenon through discourse. That is, gender *identity* comes into existence, which is not reducible to the possession of a type of genitals. As Pascal said, one kneels and prays, and belief comes after. For Butler there is no objective basis of gender, then, in the sense of a basis that is completely independent of human practices.

Are Butler and Haslanger perhaps talking about different things here? One might think that Butler is talking about a much more robust sense of gender whereas Haslanger is talking about a much more minimal sense. And Haslanger allows that the importance of the objective basis of gender is contestable: we can allow that there are prediscursive, objective bases for some of the properties used to demarcate gender, even while contesting whether it is *these* properties that are truly fundamental to gender in the robust sense, and whether it is political rather than metaphysical criteria in operation here. She says:

> The realist can agree with the non-realist that our classification schemes are often motivated by interest-laden concerns, and that we need to look beyond questions of what's ontologically fundamental to determine how to structure our political lives; these issues are not ones that divide the two sides of the debate. The realists begin to diverge from the non-realists, however, when they claim that in some cases it is important to know what sets are fundamental, e.g., what properties are causally significant, in order to effectively interact with or understand the world. (2000, 123)

I agree with Haslanger on this point, which causes me to part company with Butler, who cannot allow such "objective" criteria of significance in regard to *any* category. But what Haslanger does not consider, at least in this essay, is the possibility that genuinely causally significant properties can be discursively produced: that things, and not just things qua things referred to, can be discursively produced. Discourse is not simply about the way in which we interpret and organize the world: it can also produce new things in the world, and not just things like "football" or "money," but things with more of a material presence, such as inner subjective experiences of inferiority or a significant gender dimorphism or racial purity or the existence of two and only two sexes. Here I agree with Butler that, as Foucault taught us, we need to develop a hermeneutics of suspicion in regard to what looks natural.

If my argument is right, then Haslanger is wrong to say that Butler reaches her conclusions solely through the ubiquity of the mediation argument. If one wants to hold onto the idea that gender is an objective type, then, one needs more than a negative argument against the ubiquity of the mediation thesis—one needs to address the claim that discourse creates gender which creates sex, and address the issues of practices and not just the issue of naming. One needs to show what objective, fundamental, human independent basis there is for the category of gender or sex, and to show that this basis is not the product of discursive effect. This requires arguments that will go beyond Haslanger. I think we have a good candidate for such a fundamental, human independent basis in the division of labor in biological reproduction.

Sexed Identity

Simone de Beauvoir, often credited with inaugurating the idea that "woman" is a social construct, was herself clear about the grounds of the sex distinction itself. She said: "Woman cannot dream of exterminating the males. The bond that unites her to her oppressors is not comparable to any other. The division of the sexes is a biological fact, not an event in human history" (1989, xxxi). The meanings we confer on and the implications we draw from that "biological fact" are, of course, subject to free human interpretation, according to de Beauvoir, but the division itself is not. But how should we delimit the fact itself?

Consider the following as a possible objective basis for the category of sexed identity:

Women and men are differentiated by virtue of their different relationship of possibility to biological reproduction, with biological reproduction referring to conceiving, giving birth, and breast-feeding, involving one's own body.

By "possibility" here I mean something more than mere logical possibility, something closer to Aristotle's idea of concrete potentiality, in order to capture the idea that females are expected to have, or have had, the ability to give birth and lactate, whereas males are not. I want to capture the reality that this differential relationship of possibility to biological reproduction remains in place even for women who have had hysterectomies, women who have no desire or intention to reproduce, and women who are not fertile. Those classified as women will have a different set of practices, expectations, and feelings in regard to reproduction, no matter how actual their relationship of possibility is to it. That is, even infertile, prepubescent girls or postmenopausal women, and women who have no intention to reproduce *still* have a relationship to biological reproduction that is different from what males have. This differential relationship can be the basis of a variety of social segregations, it can engender the development of differential forms of embodiment experienced throughout life, and it can generate a wide variety of affective responses, from pride, delight, shame, guilt, regret, or great relief from having successfully avoided reproduction. But these various accompaniments to a relation of possibility with biological reproduction are themselves culture bound and not simply objective.

It is implausible to suggest a one-way linear, causal story from the objective fact of a differential relationship to biological reproduction to the richness of cultural genders; rather I would develop a holistic analysis in which this differential relation of possibility is *one* objective factor always at play, but one that can be moved about the web, from the center to the periphery, made more or less determinate over the construction of gender depending on cultural context.

An immediate question such a definition raises is its relationship to heterosexism and compulsory heterosexuality. This issue is connected with both the problem of determinism and the problem of difference that were raised at the start of this chapter as key motivating concerns behind the essentialism debate.

However, descriptive claims are not disproved by their pernicious prescriptive effects. I might correctly say to a child, "You have been getting consistently bad reports from your teachers," a descriptive claim, which may then have the effect of making the child think that he or she is simply "bad" even if I never say such a thing and don't intend to communicate that idea to the child. Yet current child therapeutic advice persuasively counsels adults to avoid such negative statements, even when they are descriptively accurate about past behavior and not stated as essential truths about the child, because the descriptive claims can have prescriptive effects. Even if I take such advice, however, I may still want to know the accuracy of the descriptive claim, and may want to look into the prejudices of the teachers, whether the reports were really consistently negative or only occasionally negative, and so on. In order to learn how to avoid prescribing the very behavior I want to sanction, I may well need to know as much as I can about the actual events. Prescriptive effects thus do not in all cases obviate the necessity of ascertaining the best descriptions.

Moreover, to assume that a descriptive claim will have a prescriptive effect is to already assume that what is being described is dynamic and changeable. It must be susceptible to suggestion, in other words, and not have a fixed character in regard to the features being described. Another assumption that might be operating here is the assumption that the description's *sole purpose* is to prescribe a norm. But it is implausible to claim that any and every descriptive claim is simply a means to enforce norms, so one must look with more care at the kind of claim being made. One might then explore how to avoid pernicious prescriptive effects, and what degree of actual instability or susceptibility to suggestion there is in what is being described.

The claim that sexed identities are objective types based on a biological division of labor in human reproduction does not prescribe compulsory heterosexuality in the sense of mandating heterosexual coupling as the necessary means for the reproduction of children. It may be used to make such claims, but these would not follow logically or empirically. Conception does require heterosexual coupling to the extent that biological material from both a male and a female are necessary, a fact that is potentially changeable. Yet it is a significant point that biological material is necessary from both male and female, and thus such a division and the anatomical differences necessary for this process are objective and objectively significant.

However, their significance justifies a type categorization consonant with the biological division; that is, it justifies us in categorizing human beings into males and females, but it does not justify the claim that heterosexual relationships are the necessary cornerstone to the reproduction of the species.

Human reproduction, in any full and meaningful sense, must include a plan for care beyond birth given the feebleness of human infants and the comparatively long period of full maturation, and thus is not reducible to conception or even parturition. Putting biological reproduction as the basis of sexual difference is not the same as putting heterosexuality at the basis or linking heterosexuality with reproduction in a broad sense. Under some contextual social conditions compulsory heterosexuality is demonstrably hurtful for reproduction, providing neither support nor nurturance necessary for a successful pregnancy, sufficient infant care and child care, and all that is necessary for the development of mature and reasonably functional human beings. Compulsory heterosexuality can contribute to the extreme vulnerability of mothers to violence and abuse. What is vital for reproduction is a child's access to a somewhat stable group of caring adults. Many of us (including me) owe our very survival to the care and support we received from one or more adults that we had no biological relation with, who made it possible to overcome neglect or abuse from our biological parents or simply their absence. Moreover, Firestone's most obvious error was to argue that biology contributed to patriarchy by creating a period where pregnant and nursing women are dependent on men, but there is no reason that such support must come from a male rather than a female. Reproduction thus does not *require sustained heterosexual coupling*. Sex may well be important in establishing stable, caring relationships; thus lesbian sex may be necessary to establish such relationships as are needed for some reproductive women.

Compulsory, exclusive heterosexuality, then, is not necessary for reproduction even without the use of adoption, surrogacy, or artificial insemination. Arguably, compulsory, exclusive heterosexuality is not the *optimal* condition for successful reproduction; many societies with compulsory, exclusive heterosexuality have epidemic proportions of child abuse and neglect. Adult care, some measure of stability, adults who have supportive loving relationships among themselves, and conception are needed for successful reproduction in the full sense.

The effort to avoid prescriptive effects does not require an avoidance of any and all description. More generally, the effort to overcome deterministic theories about women's innate limitations and orientations is not advanced by rejecting the idea that sex categories represent real and objective human differences. I strongly agree with Susan Babbitt, who says the following: "To the extent that feminist theorists have emphasized the significance of processes of investigation and development—for instance, the retelling of social myths and fantasies *in a more appropriate way*—a commitment to a plausible version of realism is the best expression of both theoretical and political concerns" (1996, 145).

There remains, then, the following question: What, if anything, follows from the material infrastructure of sexual difference in relation to the symbolic and cultural system of differentiating by gender? Feminist resistance to articulating a content to sexed identity is that any amount of content at all is seen as deterministic. But there is plenty of room between the sort of determinism that restricts women to domestic duties and a complete absence of material content.

Marx developed an approach to normative argument that made it anterior to empirical exploration. We determine as best we can the realistic possibilities that might emerge from a given historical starting point, and then we can engage in ethical debate over which of those possibilities is most desirable and just. In this way one avoids an empty utopianism and can better inspire action and thus enact change. So we must start by ascertaining the facts, but in regard to sexed identity, beyond conception this is not so easy. If we set aside practices and simply look at bodies, currently existing sexual differences cannot be used as proof of much of anything. Large muscle development (promoted by ball sports) continues to be discouraged in girls, encouraged in boys, while the opposite is true of small muscle, or hand, dexterity. Gender dimorphism, or the degree of difference between the average male and female in regard to height, weight, ration of muscle to fat, and so on, is selected for, so that in some societies the average height difference can be as much as six inches whereas in others it can be an inch or even less. Cultural practices and social environments affect everything from testosterone and sperm production, average age of menarch, and life expectancy. The thesis that women are and will always be naturally physically disadvantaged to men is an unproven hypothesis, with some reason to believe it can be eliminated. Though we may never be equal in upper body strength, the potential of lower body strength is already clearly equal, and women generally have balance advantages over men. The question of what our permanent physical differences are should be changed, so that rather than asking what we are, we need to ask what we want to be. Despite all this, the significance of the division of labor in the process of biological reproduction is not unstable or undecidable all the way down. There is much that is variable about it, and social conditions can make pregnancy a true disability, but it will never have the range of variable significance that eye color, skin color, or height can have. Its objective significance is transformable only by technology.

To categorize human beings on the basis of a biological division of reproductive roles is thus to recognize an objective type. In a sense, this could return us to Gayle Rubin's original position from thirty years ago, in which a distinction is made between sex as a biological category and gender as a cultural practice. Let me revisit again why this was rejected. First, it was rejected out of a concern that it replicated the nature/culture distinction, which presumes that we can clearly tell the effects of one from the other. Second, it was rejected because of the concern that filling anything into the category of sex will become viewed as the determining basis for gender.

With the benefit of hindsight, we can now see that maintaining a distinction between the objective category of sexed identity and the varied and culturally contingent practices of gender does not presume an absolute distinction of the old-fashioned sort between culture and a reified nature. By "old-fashioned" I mean the idea that nature is immutable and culture, alone, is mutable. In reality, what we put in the category of nature is mutable in several senses: (1) we can alter with technology many "natural" processes, such as the production of breast milk or various inhibitors to conception; (2) human ineptitude is altering the natural environment in catastrophic ways as we speak; and (3) even in regard to the immutability of scientific laws, the one absolutely predictable fact about science is that what we believe today about the universe to be justified by the best methods of science will be superceded in ways we cannot predict, and therefore our very ideas about the immutablity of the most confirmed laws must be held with a grain of salt. Thus, what we set aside as "nature" is in dialectical relation with "culture" insofar as it is altered by human practice, and what we know about it is constantly altered as practices evolve or devolve. Moreover, "culture" is not simply the flexible clay of human will, but is something that transforms within a "natural" context. We cannot, today at least, give a definitive answer to the question of determinism or the limits of sexual transformation. It would be exceeding hubris, either from sociogeneticists or feminist social constructionists (and both seem to have plenty) to claim to know the limits, or absence thereof, of human biological transformation. Thus we need to set our sites closer to the present. What might we become tomorrow? What do we want to become?

Sexed Identity as Embodied Horizon

Beyond this, the phenomenological and hermeneutic approaches are the best means of exploring how sexed identity is manifest in the lives of particular women in specific social contexts. Phenomenologically one needs to account for the ways in which the body is lived, perceived in the world, presented, and experienced.

Hermeneutics is just as important, however. The body is lived as it is lived in part because of the horizon with which it confronts the future. For girls, this horizon will generally include the future possibility of reproduction, even if this turns out never to come to pass and to have been physiologically impossible all along. Knowing that one may become pregnant and give birth to children in the future affects how one feels and thinks about pregnancy and childbirth, sexual relations, familial relations, and various possibilities for paid work or careers. Knowing that one's mother experienced pregnancy and childbirth under certain conditions has an effect on how one imagines oneself in such situations. These provide the constraints on undecidability and total fluidity for the development of female and male sexed identities. All of these possible experiences are open to vast differences of interpretation, but the point of the hermeneutic account is that they must be dealt with in a way that those who grow up male do not have to deal with, at least not in the same way. The possibility of pregnancy, childbirth, nursing, and in many societies, rape, are parts of females' horizons that we carry with us throughout childhood and much or all of our adult lives. The way these are figured, imagined, experienced, accepted, and so on, is as variable as culture. But these elements exist in the female horizon, and they exist there because of the ways in which we are embodied.

Substantive accounts of sexual difference beyond these bare sketches should be, I would suggest, existential descriptions of very particular situations within which groups of women, perhaps large groups, live. Even Irigaray's imaginative descriptions of female lived experience might be put in this category, as descriptions of the phenomenology of a female anatomy under specified contextual conditions. Also included here would be the work of Emily Martin, Elizabeth Grosz, de Beauvoir, and many others.

Elizabeth Grosz puts brakes on Derrida's deconstruction of sex in precisely this way, it seems to me. "It is not so easy to see," she remarks, "how sexuality—in the sense of sexed subjectivity, male and female—can be understood as indeterminate" (1995, 77). The possibilities of interpretation abound, but they occur within given conditions that, she hints, are "somehow ontological but entirely without qualities and attributes" (77). She explains:

> This is what I presume that the framework of sexual difference implies: that there is an irreducible specificity of each sex relative to the other, that there must be at least, but not necessarily only two sexes. In short, one lives one's sexual indeterminacy, one's possibilities for being sexed otherwise differently depending on whether one is male or female. This is not, however, to predetermine how one 'is' male or female, but simply to suggest that there is an ineradicable rift between the two, in whatever forms they are lived. Unless such a presumption is made, sexual difference remains in danger of collapsing into a sexual neutrality of precisely the kind Derrida problematizes in Heidegger and Levinas. Derrida's dream of a multiplicity of "sexually marked voices" seems to me worthy of careful consideration, as long as the question of the limits of possibility of each (sexed) body is recognized. Each sex has the capacity to (and frequently does) play with, become, a number of different sexualities; but not to take on the body and sex of the other. (77)

I cannot say it better than this.

THREE

RACIALIZED IDENTITIES
AND RACIST SUBJECTS

The Phenomenology of Racial Embodiment

When one realizes the indeterminacy of racial categories, their fluid borders, arbitrary criteria and cultural variety, it may be tempting to adopt a nominalism about race, that race is no more real than phlogiston or witchcraft. In this chapter I resist this conclusion primarily on phenomenological grounds. Race is real, certainly more real than phlogiston, though like witchcraft its "reality" is internal to certain schemas of social ontology that are themselves dependent on social practice. As an element of social ontology, the reality of race is certainly capable of radical transformation and perhaps eradication. My focus, however, will not be on the possible future permutations of racializing practices but on the intense present reality of race. I will explore reasons for the current confusion about race, consider various approaches to knowledge about race, and venture a preliminary phenomenological account of racial identity as it is lived in the body of various racialized subjects at a given cultural moment. Only when we come to be very clear about how race is lived, in its multiple manifestations, and only when we can come to appreciate its often hidden epistemic effects and its power over collective imaginations can we entertain even the remote possibility of its eventual transformation.

Modern Racism

Contemporary confusions about race can be directly traced to the historical genealogy of the present concept. Recently, the West (meaning Anglo-European cultures) has been credited with originating the idea of race as we use it today, during the era of early modernism or what Foucault called the classical episteme.[1] In this era, Foucault suggests, the newly emerging sciences understood knowledge primarily as a practice of ordering and classifying on the basis of essential differences (1970, 1994). Classification of human beings by race also had a strong conceptual relationship with mapmaking, in which the expanding geographical areas of the globe "discovered" by Europeans were given order and intelligibility in part through their association with racial types. Thus, the labeling and mapping of conquered terrain, the naturalist classifications of life forms of all types, and the typologies of "natural races" were all practices that enjoyed an analogical similarity and emerged in the first period of European conquest, no doubt motivated by Europeans' need to comprehend and manage their suddenly enlarged world. The increased diversity of the world would be less daunting if neutralized through the formulation of an ordering system. There is a wonderful moment in the 1993 film about mixed race identities, *Map of the Human Heart*, in which an Inuit man asks a white engineer who has come to northern Canada to map the region, "Why are you making maps?" Without hesitation, the white man responds, "They will be very accurate." To question the very project of mapmaking was unintelligible to this bureaucrat of empire. Similarly unintelligible to European elites was the question of whether human diversity should be ranked.

Arguing via Foucault, both Cornel West and David Theo Goldberg have attempted genealogies of modern racism that link the Western fetishistic practices of classification, the forming of tables and ordering schemas, and the consequent naturalistic primacy of the visible with the creation of metaphysical and moral hierarchies between racialized categories of human beings (Goldberg 1993; West 1982). West argues that the application of natural history techniques to the study of the human species produced a comparative analysis "*based on visible, especially physical, characteristics* [which] permit one to discern identity and difference, equality and inequality, beauty and ugliness among animals and human bodies" (1982, 55). Given this genesis, the concept of race and of racial difference emerged as that which is visible, classifiable, and morally salient.

However, in this same early modern period, the juxtaposition of these human classification practices with an emerging liberal ideology that espoused universalism produced a confused and contradictory account of race from which, I believe, Western discourses as well as Western "commonsense knowledge," in a Gramscian sense, are still suffering today. Visible differences are still relied upon for the classification of human types, and yet visible difference threatens the liberal universalistic concepts of justice based on sameness by invoking the specter of difference. Classification systems contain this threat by enclosing the entirety of difference within a taxonomy organized by a single logic, such as a table of IQ test scores grouped by race. Differences of kind become transformed into differences of degree. Ranking differences thus works to nullify relativism and protect universalism. But the resultant juxtaposition between universalist legitimation narratives that deny or trivialize difference (political science and the law) and the detailed taxonomies of physical, moral, and intellectual human difference (anthropology and genetics) is one of the greatest antinomies of modernism.[2]

The new development of critical race studies has begun to erode most of the theoretical props for racial hierarchies in academic discourses. Today the naturalistic classification systems which would reify human variability into moral categories and the Eurocentric teleologies that would excuse, if not justify, colonialism have been largely exposed as specious. And the realm of the visible, or what is taken as self-evidently visible (which is how the ideology of racism naturalizes racial designation), is recognized as the product of a specific form of perceptual practice, rather than the natural result of human sight. Anti-essentialisms have corroded the sense of visible difference as the "sign" of a deeper, more fundamental difference, a difference in behavioral disposition, in moral and rational capacity, or in cultural achievement. Moreover, there is a newly emerging biological consensus that race is a myth, that the term corresponds to no significant biological category, and that no existing racial classifications correlate in useful ways to gene frequencies, clinal variations, or any significant human biological difference.[3]

However, at the same time, and in a striking parallel to the earlier modernist contradictions regarding the significance of race, in the very midst of our contemporary skepticism toward race as a natural kind stands the compelling social reality that race, or racialized identities, have as much political, sociological, and economic salience as they ever had. As Goldberg puts it, liberal Western societies today maintain a paradoxical position whereby "Race is irrelevant, but all is race" (1993, 6). The legitimacy and moral relevance of racial concepts is officially denied even while race continues to determine job prospects, career possibilities, available places to live, potential friends and lovers, reactions from police, credence from jurors, and the amount of credibility one is given by one's students. Race may not correlate with clinal variations, but it persistently correlates with a statistically overwhelming significance in wage levels, unemployment levels, poverty levels, and the likelihood of incarceration. As of 1992, black and Latino men working full time in the United States earned an average of 68 percent of what white men earned, while black and Latina women earned 59 percent. As of 1995, Latino and black unemployment rates were more than double that of whites.[4]

But for those still working within a liberal framework, the devastating sociological reality of race is but an artificial overlay on more fundamental constituents of the self. The specificity of culturally embedded and marked bodies is routinely set aside in projects that aim toward a general analysis. Even for some poststructuralists, because race is a contingent construction, or the epiphenomenon of essentialist discourses, it is ultimately without any more explanatory power or epistemological relevance than on the liberal view. Thus, for all our critical innovations in understanding the vagaries of racist domination and the conceptual apparatus that yields racism, too many today remain stuck in the modernist paradox that race is determinant of a great deal of social reality, even while our scientists, policy makers and philosophers would have us deny its existence.

No wonder, then, that we are confused about what to do with the category of race. Naturalistic approaches to the "real"—in which conceptual frameworks are thought to be determined by nature itself—cannot make sense of the cultural variety, recent history, and biological invalidity of race, though there are some positions that endeavor to define race in this way nonetheless. Universalistic political systems in which justice is predicated on sameness cannot help but view racial consciousness with consternation and dismay. Thus, within the modern episteme, the continued use of racial categories leads inevitably to political paradox.

Contextualism about Race

Contemporary race theory has endeavored to transcend the paradoxes of classical liberalism and to make explicit the implicit ideologies of race. On the questions of the status of the category race and whether racial identity should be continued, this recent body of work falls roughly into three positions:

(1) *Nominalism* (or eliminativism). Race is not real, meaning that racial terms do not refer to anything "really real," principally because recent science has invalidated race as a salient or even meaningful biological category. It is the biological meaning of racial concepts that have led to racism, but racial concepts are *necessarily* biological claims (as opposed to ethnic or cultural concepts, for example). Therefore, the use of racial concepts should be avoided in order to be metaphysically accurate as well as to further an antiracist agenda.

(2) *Essentialism.* Race is an elemental category of identity with explanatory power. Members of racial groups share a set of characteristics, a set of political interests, and a historical destiny. The problem of racism has affected the content given to racial description rather than the method of racial description itself.

(3) *Contextualism.* Race is socially constructed, historically malleable, culturally contextual, and reproduced through learned perceptual practices. Whether or not it is valid to use racial concepts and whether or not their use will have positive or negative political effects depends on the context.

The first position—which I call nominalism—fails to capture the multiple meanings of race and assumes incorrectly that race can refer only to biology. It also falsely assumes on the basis of a commitment to semantic realism and an over-inflation of the importance of science that racial concepts can have no nonbiological referent and thus no valid meaning. It naively assumes that an end to the use of racial concepts will solve (or contribute toward solving) the current enormous sociological and economic determinism of racialized identities, and that this positive result can occur before we try to understand the ways in which beliefs and practices of racialization have informed every political theory, every conceptual framework, and every metanarrative, at least in the West.

The second position—which I call essentialism—fails to capture the fluidity and open-endedness of racial meanings. It wrongly assumes that racial identities are obvious and easily demarcated, that racialized groupings are homogeneous, and that ancestry is all-determining. It operates on a mistaken notion of what cultures are, as if they are merely the developing expression of an originary logic rather than the effect of negotiations from multiple sources. And it promotes the futile mission of opposing the tide of global hybridization and identity metamorphosis.

The third position—which I call contextualism—is clearly the best option both politically and as a metaphysical description.[5] It can acknowledge the current devastating reality of race while holding open the possibility that present-day racial formations may change significantly or perhaps wither away. It provides a better explanation for the variety of racial beliefs and practices across cultures, and thus acknowledges the contingency and uncertainty of racial identities and boundaries. One can hold without contradiction that racialized identities are produced, sustained, and sometimes transformed through social beliefs and practices and yet that race is real, as real as anything else in lived experience, with operative effects in the social world.

Contextualist approaches come in two forms: objectivist and subjectivist. Objectivist approaches attempt a definition of race general enough to be applicable across a variety of contexts even while recognizing that context will determine the specific content and political valence given to a racial concept. These approaches start with sociological facts, Census categories and their transformations, and the history of racializations to develop an account of how race organizes social relations. Sanjek, for example, defines race as "the framework of ranked categories segmenting the human population that was developed by western Europeans following their global expansion in the 1400's" (1994, 1). Most of the current debates over race concern only objective definitions of race and racial identity.

However, objectivist approaches to race that chart its effects in the public domain sometimes hinder an appreciation for the everydayness of racial experience. Objectivist approaches that define race by invoking metanarratives of historical experience, cultural traditions, or processes of colonization and that take a third-person perspective can be inattentive to the microinteractions in which racialization operates, is reproduced, and is sometimes resignified. In contrast, subjectivist approaches that begin from the lived experience of racialization can reveal how race is constitutive of bodily experience, subjectivity, judgment, and epistemic relationships. Such subjective descriptions, as Fanon gives, show how one's designated race is a constitutive element of fundamental, everyday embodied existence, psychic life, and social interaction.

During the building of the Panama Canal, workers were divided and identified by the U.S.-owned and run Panama Canal Commission as "gold" (whites) and "silver" (West Indian blacks), denoting the form of currency in which they were paid. "Gold" and "silver" workers were given separate and differently constructed living quarters, different currency for wages, different commissaries, and different tasks, and they were attributed different characteristics. In Canal Commission documents, gold workers were described as loyal, earnest, responsible, self-sacrificing, and enthusiastic. Silver workers were described as shiftless, inconstant, exasperating, irresponsible, carefree, "yet as reliable a workman as our own American cottonfield hand" (Haskin 1913, 162). Here race explicitly determined economic and social status, but it also was understood by the dominant white authorities to be the *determinate constitutive factor of subjectivity*, indicating personal character traits and internal constitution (for example, blacks were thought to be more resistant to yellow fever). Such publicly instituted and circulated associations between race and subjectivity must naturally have an effect on the self-perceptions of those persons so described. Thus, racialized identities affect not only one's public status but one's experienced selfhood as well.

Omi and Winant offer an account of race that attempts to include both the macrolevel and the microlevel, or objective and subjective levels, of social relations. The macrolevel consists of economic, political, and cultural structures, or "sites," in which the formation and management of racial collectivities occur, and thus is what I am calling an objectivist account. The microlevel consists of the microprocesses by which individual identities are formed (Omi and Winant 1986, 66–67). In regard to the microlevel, they claim that "one of the first things we notice about people when we meet them (along with their sex) is their race" (62). They also develop a description of "racial etiquette" as "a set of interpretive codes and racial meanings which operate in the interactions of daily life. Rules shaped by our perception of race in a comprehensively racial society determine the "presentation of self," distinction of status, and appropriate modes of conduct" (62). Although Omi and Winant don't pursue this idea of a racial etiquette much further, it is a productive way to explore how race operates preconsciously on spoken and unspoken interaction, gesture, affect, and stance, and in this way producing what I call a subjectivist account. Greetings, handshakes, proximity, tone of voice, all reveal the effects of racial awareness, the presumption of superiority vis-à-vis the other, or the protective defenses against the possibility of racism and misrecognition.[6] I will make use here once again of Merleau-Ponty's concept of the habitual body I introduced in chapter 4, which is the concept of a default position the body assumes in various commonly experienced circumstances that integrates and unifies our movements through a kind of unconscious physical shorthand. This idea could be useful here to understand how individuals fall into race-conscious habitual postures in cross-racial encounters.[7] Merleau-Ponty is mainly discussing motor habits of perception and movement used in performing various operations such as driving or typing, but the concept can easily be applied to postural attitudes and modes of perception taken in interactions with others whose identities are marked by gender, race, age, and so on. Following Fanon, Gordon, and Weiss, I will also argue that racialization structures the visual sphere and the imaginary self, and can block the development of coherent body images (Fanon 1967; Gordon 1995; Weiss 1998, esp. 26–33).[8]

Subjectivist and objectivist approaches to understanding race are not mutually exclusive; Fanon's account has elements of both. I agree with Omi and Winant that any adequate account of race would need to encompass both. But it seems to me that although subjectivist approaches have important advantages in accounting for how race works, they have been underdeveloped in the recent theoretical literature, even while there are many first-person memoirs and rich descriptions of racial experience that might be tapped for theoretical analysis.

A possible reason for the hesitancy one might have in going in this direction is a fear that phenomenological description will naturalize or fetishize racial experiences. This can happen when descriptions of felt experience begin to operate as *explanations* of felt experience, as if the experience itself is fully self-presenting and explanatory. In other words, the claim here would be that one need go no further than accessible experience to explain the experience. For example, if one believes that human beings group perceptual objects under concepts as the natural result of our need to cope with the blooming, buzzing variety of perceptual experience, then one might be led to think that racial categories are the understandable result of the need to group and categorize. In other words, racism is the unfortunate but inevitable result of human cognitive processes. Phenomenological descriptions that detail the overwhelming salience of racializations for given individuals might then be used as support for such a belief.

Against this, I will argue that although racial classification does operate on the basis of perceptual difference, it is also the case that, as Merleau-Ponty argues, perception represents sedimented contextual knowledges. So the process by which human bodies are differentiated and categorized by type is a process *preceded* by group oppression, rather than one that causes and thus "explains" racism as a natural result. Such an account is compatible with Hegel's view that conflict arises from our *parallel* desires rather than our "innate" differences, a view that has many advantages.

However, I would not want to say, as some nominalists seem almost to say, that racialization has only an arbitrary connection to the realm of the visible. Visual differences are "real" differences, and by that very fact they are especially valuable for the naturalizing ideologies of racism. But there is no perception of the visible that is not already imbued with value. And the body itself is a dynamic material domain, not just because it can be "seen" differently, but because the materiality of the body itself is, as Grosz puts it, volatile: "It is not simply that the body is re-presented in a variety of ways according to historical, social, and cultural exigencies while it remains basically the same; these factors actively produce the body of a determinate type" (1994, x).

In what follows, then, I will pursue a subjectivist approach that makes use of Merleau-Ponty's nonfoundationalist account of lived experience. A phenomeno-logical approach can render our tacit knowledge about racial embodiment explicit. Despite the fact that, at least until recently and at least for those whites not living in the South, it appears generally to be the case that most whites did not consciously "feel white," there were gestural and perceptual practices correlated to racial identity and a tacit but substantive racialized subjectivity. Other groups in the United States have often been very conscious of the ways in which racial categories affected experience and presentations of self, but some of their knowledge about race is also tacit and carried in the body.

By drawing from tacit knowledge about racial identity, subjectivist approaches also, I would argue, operate from a different epistemology or justificatory strategy, and one that can make productive use of Gramsci's account of "common sense" or everyday consciousness discernible in practices, rather than a self-consciousness achieved through reflection. Common sense is made up of that which seems ob-viously true and enjoys consensus or near consensus. Despite its felt naturalness, however, common sense is "culturally constituted—not as false consciousness is, by imposition from above, but by the sediment" of past historical beliefs and practices of a given society or culture (Gramsci 1971). If we apply this account to a racial common sense, we would understand it not as the imposition of ideology but as part of the backdrop of practical consciousness, circulating, as Foucault would say, from the bottom up as well as from the top down. Racial knowledges exist at the site of common sense. Effectively in agreement with this Foucauldian approach, Omi and Winant also argue that racialization should not be understood simply as something imposed; for example, they suggest that racial "etiquette is not mere universal adherence to the dominant group's rules, but a more dynamic combination of these rules with the values and beliefs of subordinated groups" (62). They emphasize that a subordinate group can play a role in shaping racial formations through the par-ticular patterns of resistance taken up.

The epistemically relevant point here is that the *source* of racializations, or at least one important source, is in the microprocesses of subjective existence. I would add to this, however, the obvious point that racial common sense varies both across and within racial groups, and the differences we find are likely to be significant. In any case, it has largely been an uninterrogated white common sense, albeit in all its internal variety, that has dominated the public discourse and theoretical analysis about race in the United States.

White Antiwhiteness

Here is Jack Kerouac, the iconized white Beat prophet, writing in his journal in 1949, describing a late-evening walk through the black and Mexican neighborhoods of Denver: "I stopped at a little shack where a man sold hot, red chili in paper containers. I bought some and ate it strolling in the dark, mysterious streets. I wished I was a Negro, a Denver Mexican, or even a Jap, anything but a white man disillusioned by the best in his own 'white' world. (And all my life I had white ambitions!)" (1998, 56). Kerouac in this passage is characteristically ahead of his time. Kerouac was aware of the racialized others, whom he recognizes in their unified nonwhiteness, but unlike many other whites (at least, Northern whites), he was also aware of his own whiteness and able to articulate the contours of its segregated subjective life in his comment that even ambitions have a racial identity. He is disillusioned with the pretensions of white culture, and out of this disillusionment he senses the arbitrariness of his dominant status, which makes it impossible for him to rest easy with it or relax in it. And thus he longs to escape it.

This felt disjuncture for Kerouac between his white body (or his non-nonwhiteness) and his sense of having a nonwhite sensibility operates in the very postural model of the body, a concept introduced by Sir Henry Head to name that nonlinguistic imaginary position of the body in the world and its imagined relation to its environment and to other bodies (see Grosz 1994, 64–69; Weiss 1998, 7–9). Kerouac pictured himself as outside "white society" or positioned on its margins. He thought of himself as having the aesthetic sensibility and temporal orientation of the other-than-white, in his irreverent cynicism toward the white world's self-presentations and declared intentions. In a different diary entry, he said that "the best the 'white world' has to offer [is] not enough ecstasy for me, not enough life, joy, kicks, music; not enough night" (56). Who is this "me" whose ability to appreciate and to desire joy, kicks, music, and life exceeds the white world? Who is it indeed whose virility and capacity for feeling is larger than the sallow, impotent blandness the white world (in his portrayal) can afford? It can only be a nonwhite, though Kerouac here relies precisely on the white world's own projection of ecstatic emotions outside of itself, outside of white identity. In other words, even in his "nonwhite" sensibility, he operates from within a white schema of signification (a paradox that can also beset nonwhite bodies).

Kerouac's nonwhite postural body image, though, is pierced by the experience of walking through these "dark" streets, encountering the "real" other in the flesh, which then prompts him to recognize the incoherence between his own felt body image—the one he surely felt in upper-class white society—and the body image now induced by the alienation he felt in what for him were foreign neighborhoods. Returning to the entry where he described his Denver walk, we find him say: "I was so sad—in the violet dark, strolling—wishing I could exchange worlds with the happy, true-minded, ecstatic Negroes of America.... How I yearned to be transformed into an Eddy, a Neal, a jazz musician, a nigger, a construction worker, a softball pitcher, anything in these wild, dark humming streets of Denver night—anything but myself so pale and unhappy, so dim" (56). Fanon suggested that for black people in the colonial world, it was Sartre's third ontological dimension of bodily experience—the consciousness of one's body as a body-for-others—that dominates (1967, chaps. 5 and 7). Kerouac experiences this in the nonwhite Denver neighborhoods, where the third dimension comes to dominate his own preferred body image, to render his postural model incoherent, leading him to a melancholic resignation of his "paleness."

Notice also that in these passages Kerouac juxtaposes, perhaps unconsciously, reiterations of the darkness and mystery of his surroundings with a characterization of "Negroes" as open, fully readable, transparent. What is "dark" to him is not their nature or state of mind, which he presumes to fully know, but their *ability* to be happy and true-minded. This capacity has escaped him; it is what he envies and longs for. He is not satisfied with the level of ecstasy available in the white world; and yet he cannot discover how to access the affect he perceives outside of it. He yearns to be "anything but myself so pale and unhappy, so dim." Just as ambitions are racialized, so too are *his* melancholia and *their* happiness.

Fanon also suggested that racism and colonialism create significant challenges for maintaining the equilibrium in one's body image, an equilibrium achieved, as Weiss helpfully explains, through reconciling one's own "'tactile, vestibular, kinesthetic, and visual' experiences with the structure imposed by this historico-racial schema, a structure that provides the 'racial parameters' within which the corporeal schema is supposed to fit" (1998, 27). The near incommensurability between first-person experience and historico-racial schema disenables equilibrium and creates what Fanon calls a "corporeal malediction." Kerouac, coming from the other side of the colonial equation, must have experienced this corporeal malediction as well. His desire to be transformed into an "Eddy" and so on is a desire to resolve the disequilibrium induced by conflicting first- and third-person dimensions of the body in favor of the first. I would suggest that today, more and more whites are experiencing a similar disequilibrium, as they come to perceive the racial parameters that structure whiteness differently in different communities—white and nonwhite—and may find that none of these can be made coherent with their own preferred body or postural image.

Perception

Because race works through the domain of the visible, the experience of race is predicated first and foremost on the perception of race, a perception whose specific mode is a learned ability. Merleau-Ponty says of perception:

> Perception is not a science of the world, it is not even an act, a deliberate taking up of a position; it is the background from which all acts stand out, and is presupposed by them. The world is not an object such that I have in my possession the law of its making; it is the natural setting of, and field for, all my thoughts and all my explicit perceptions. . . . [M]an is in the world, and only in the world does he know himself. (1962, x–xi)

If race is a structure of contemporary perception, then it helps constitute the necessary background from which I know myself. It makes up a part of what appears to me as the natural setting of all my thoughts. It is the field, rather than that which stands out. The perceptual practices involved in racializations are then tacit, almost hidden from view, and thus almost immune from critical reflection. Merleau-Ponty goes on: "Perception is, not presumed true, but defined as access to truth" (xvi). Inside such a system, perception cannot itself be the object of analysis. Thus, Kerouac could "see" with immediacy the character of nonwhite lives and nonwhite emotional subjectivity. And yet the mechanism of that act of perceiving itself could not be seen, and thus could not be seen by him as also racialized.

Perceptual practices can be organized, like bodily movements used to perform various operations, into integrated units that become habitual. In the following passage Merleau-Ponty explains his idea of perceptual habits through the example of a blind man's use of a stick to find objects: "It would appear in this case that perception is always a reading off from the same sensory data, but constantly accelerated, and operating with ever more attenuated signals. But habit does not *consist* in interpreting the pressures of the stick on the hand as indications of certain positions of the stick, and these as signs of an external object, since it *relieves us of the necessity* of doing so" (1962, 152; emphasis in original). In other words, the overt act of interpreting is skipped in an attenuated process of perceptual knowing. He goes on to contrast this account with a more positivist approach:

> Intellectualism cannot conceive any passage from the perspective to the thing itself, or from sign to significance otherwise than as an interpretation, an apperception, a cognitive intention.... But this analysis distorts both the sign and the meaning: it separates out, by a process of objectification of both, the sense-content, which is already "pregnant" with a meaning, and the invariant core.... [I]t conceals the organic relationship between subject and world, the active transcendence of consciousness, the momentum which carries it into a thing and into a world by means of its organs and instruments. The analysis of motor habit as an extension of existence leads on, then, to an analysis of perceptual habit as the coming into possession of a world.... In the gaze we have at our disposal a natural instrument analogous to the blind man's stick. (1962, 152–53)

This account would explain both why racializing attributions are nearly impossible to discern and why they are resistant to alteration or erasure. Our experience of habitual perceptions is so attenuated as to skip the stage of conscious interpretation and intent. Indeed, interpretation is the wrong word here: we are simply perceiving. And the traditional pre-Hegelian modernist account of perception, what I called above "positivism," blocks our appreciation of this. It is just such a modernist account that would explain why it is commonly believed that for one to be a racist one must be able to access in consciousness some racist belief, and that if introspection fails to produce such a belief then one is simply not racist. A fear of African Americans or a condescension toward Latinos is seen as simple perception of the real, justified by the nature of things in themselves without need of an interpretive intermediary of historico-cultural schemas of meaning.

If interpretation by this account operates as simple perception, at least in certain cases, are we not led to pessimism about the possibility of altering the perceptual habits of racializations? Here I would think that the multiple schemas operating in many if not most social spaces today would mitigate against an absolute determinism and thus pessimism. Perceptual practices are dynamic even when congealed into habit, and that dynamism can be activated by the existence of multiple forms of the gaze in various cultural productions and by the challenge of contradictory perceptions. To put it simply, people are capable of change. Merleau-Ponty's analysis helps to provide a more accurate understanding of where—that is, at what level of experience—change needs to occur.

White Ambitions

Phenomenological descriptions of racial identity can reveal a differentiation or distribution of felt connectedness to others. Kerouac's sadness is prompted by his lack of felt connection, a connection he may have anticipated when initiating his walk through the black and Mexican Denver neighborhoods, but one that does not present itself. However, felt connection is a complex issue, undetermined solely by phenotype. The felt connectedness to visibly similar others may produce either flight or empathic identification or other possible dispositions.

Compare Kerouac's perceptions with the autobiographical confession that dramatically opens Richard Rodriguez's book, *Days of Obligation*: "I used to stare at the Indian in the mirror. The wide nostrils, the thick lips. Starring Paul Muni as Benito Juarez. Such a long face—such a long nose—sculpted by indifferent, blunt thumbs, and of such common clay. No one in my family had a face as dark or as Indian as mine. My face could not portray the ambition I brought to it" (1992, 1). Here there is actually little contrast with Kerouac's account: Rodriguez echoes his white racialization of ambition, in which the desire to be a writer and a public intellectual in the United States cannot be associated with an "Indian" face. In an earlier memoir, he recounts how as an adolescent he tried to shave the darkness off his skin in a fit of agonized frustration (1983, 5). Like Kerouac again, Rodriguez wants to escape, and he experiences racial identity as a cage constraining his future, his aspirations; also like Kerouac he experiences it as somehow at odds with his felt subjectivity. His postural body image is internally incoherent, and Rodriguez struggles persistently against the racial parameters that Fanon says characterizes colonized consciousness. Where Kerouac forgoes white ambition and yet resigns himself to whiteness, Rodriguez pursues white ambitions and in this way seeks to escape his visible identity and to repudiate his felt connection with visibly similar others.

Rodriguez recounts a conversation he had with an American Indian student when he was teaching at Berkeley.

> "You're not Indian, you're Mexican," he said. "You wouldn't understand."
> He meant I was cut. Diluted.
> Understand what?
> He meant I was not an Indian in America. He meant he was an enemy of the history that had otherwise created me. . . . I saw his face—his refusal to consort with the living—as the face of a dead man. (1992, 5)

Rodriguez experiences Mexican identity as necessarily hybridized, "cut," "diluted." He projects onto his interlocutor the belief that Mexican identity is a deformed identity, when in reality the man simply said, "You are Mexican and not Indian," counterposing two identities rather than an identity and a dilution of identity. Yet Rodriguez's projection is of course overdetermined by the general denigration of mixed identities, particularly mixed racial identities, that is a painful feature of many contemporary societies. The mixed person, unless she or he declares in her self-representation as well as her everyday practices to be identified with one group or another, feels rejection from every group, and is ready to be slighted on an everyday basis for presuming an unjustified association. She is constantly on trial, and unable to claim epistemic authority to speak as or to represent. Rodriguez experiences a double hybridity: the hybridity of a Mexican American educated and enculturated in an Anglo environment, and the hybridity of *Latinidad* itself, between *indigenismo* and *conquistador*.

Rodriguez deflects this denigration by demarcating his hybrid world into neatly mapped spaces and urging their segregation. He argues that Spanish, the mother tongue, the female tongue, is proper to the private sphere, and should be spoken only at home for bilingual Latinos in the United States. He characterizes English as the public language, the language of social intercourse, the language for intervening in politics, and thus a language clearly coded masculine. English is justifiably normative because its universality is simply inevitable, Rodriguez argues. Thus he has been an important public critic of bilingual education programs and any policy that might have the effect of incorrectly merging what should be carefully sequestered realms of discourse.

In the above passage, Rodriguez also construes his own white ambitions—to master English and assimilate in a public Anglo world—as representing life. Life moves forward, it adapts, it transforms, and in this way it survives. Assimilation to an Anglo world is life; the resistance to assimilation is an embrace of death. Thus he sees the man's face in the cafeteria as the face of a dead man. Unlike Kerouac on this point, Rodriguez does not romanticize the nonwhite racial Other, which is a form of love Lewis Gordon aptly likens to pet loving.[9] By incorporating aspects of an Anglo identity, and pursuing an identity based on the metanarrative of "American" progress and cultural development, Rodriguez perceives himself as choosing life. He further describes his interlocutor in the conversation already quoted as a "moody brave," and "a near-somnambulist, beautiful in an off-putting way, but interesting, too, because I never saw him without the current issue of *The New York Review of Books* under his arm, which I took as an advertisement of ambition" (1992, 4–5). For Rodriguez, ambition can *only* be white; there is no conception of an ambition beyond or apart from intercourse in a dominant Anglo world. In the description just given, Rodriguez associates the man's physical appearance with distance: it is off-putting despite its beauty. Racial difference is often experienced as a distancing without regard to spatial proximity. Yet Rodriguez has hopes for the possibility of a relationship—of the man being included in Rodriguez's own wider frame of reference—by his possession of a journal that signifies for him a transcendence of the physical mark. Anglo identity is again associated with the public, the realm of ambition, the sphere of action in a social world, while Indian identity remains on the body, pulling against ambition, social intercourse, even, Rodriguez says, life itself. Thus, he sees the man as a near somnambulist, a man poised between the life embodied in the *New York Review of Books* and the death of a historical dreamworld.

The Visual Registry

No less than Kerouac, Rodriguez reads others and himself through visible signs on the body, reading his "long nose sculpted by indifferent, blunt thumbs" as "incapable of portraying" his ambition. I would argue that this mediation through the visible, working on both the inside and the outside, both on the way we read ourselves and the way others read us, is what is unique to racialized identities as opposed to ethnic and cultural identities. The criteria thought to determine racial identity have ranged from ancestry, experience, self-understanding, to habits and practices, yet these sources are coded through visible inscriptions on the body. The processes by which racial identities are produced work through the shapes and shades of human morphology, the size and shape of the nose, the design of the eye, the breadth of the cheekbones, the texture of hair, and the intensity of pigment, and these subordinate other markers such as dress, customs, and practices. And the visual registry thus produced has been correlated with rational capacity, epistemic reliability, moral condition, and, of course, aesthetic value. Rodriguez has learned this visual registry in its dominant white form, and thus he moves back and forth between exploring its racism[10] and adopting it as his own perspective, letting it dominate his body image almost as a perceptual habit-body, or habit of perception.

"Visibility is a trap," says Foucault (1979, 200). He explains: "Hence the major effect of the Panopticon: to induce in the inmate a state of conscious and permanent visibility that assures the automatic functioning of power" (201). What could be more permanently visible than that which is inscribed on the body itself?

As I have already argued, racial identities that are not readily visible create fear, consternation, and the sometimes hysterical determination to find their visible trace. The case of Alice Rhinelander that I discussed in the introduction, forced to bare her breasts in a court of law, exhibits this determination, as does the Nazi effort to find physical signs of Jewish identity that could be measured with calipers. English attitudes toward the Irish provide still another example. Similar to the Jews, the Irish were a racialized group internal to Europe until the twentieth century. L. Gibbons quotes the following passage in which a first-time English visitor to Ireland records his observations: "I am haunted by the human chimpanzees I saw along that hundred miles of horrible country. . . . But to see white chimpanzees was dreadful; if they were black, one would not feel it so much, but their skins, except where tanned by exposure, are as white as ours" (Gibbons 1991, 96; quoted in Loomba 1998, 109). The observer in this passage experienced a disequilibrium in his corporeal self-image prompted by finding his own features in the degraded Other.

Clearly, one source of the importance of visibility for racialized identities is the need to manage and segregate populations and to catch individuals who trespass beyond their rightful bounds. But there is another reason for the importance of visibility, a reason I would argue is as significant as the first: visible difference naturalizes racial meanings. Merleau-Ponty claims that "when we speak of the flesh of the visible, we do not mean to do anthropology, to describe a world covered over with our own projections" (1962, 136; emphasis added). In other words, the visible is not merely an epiphenomenon of culture, and thus precisely lies its value for racialization. We may need to be trained to pick out some features over others as the most salient to identity, but those features nonetheless have a material reality. This is why both Kerouac and Rodriguez experience racial identity as impossible to alter: Kerouac cannot "become Negro" no matter how much he would like to, and Rodriguez can only fail to shave the darkness off his skin. Locating race in the visible thus produces the experience that racial identity is immutable.

This is why race *must* work through the visible markers on the body, even if those markers are *made* more visible through learned processes. Visible difference, which is materially present even if its meanings are not, can be used to signify or provide purported access to a subjectivity through observable, "natural" attributes, to provide a window on the interiority of the self—thus making it possible for a Kerouac to confidently assume an ability to perceive directly ecstasy and true-mindedness even though he knows nothing more about the individuals that surround him than the color of their skin.

In some cases, the perceptual habits are so strong and so unnoticed that visible difference is deployed in every encounter. In other situations, the deployment of visible difference can be dependent on the presence of other elements to become salient or all-determining. For an example of such a situation, I will relate a case I discussed with a philosophy graduate student with whom I regularly converse about issues in the classroom. White undergraduates walking into an introductory philosophy course in upstate New York might not expect an Asian American instructor, but after an initial surprise the students appeared to feel at ease in the class as he (I'll call him "John") discussed Descartes and Leibniz and patiently explained to struggling undergraduates how to follow an argument in early modern texts. John himself then began to relax in the classroom, interacting without self-consciousness with a largely white class. His postural body image was at those moments normative, familiar, trustworthy. Despite the hierarchy between students and teacher, there seemed to be little or no racial distancing in their interactions.

However, at a certain point in the semester, John introduced the subject of race into the course through an assigned reading on the cognitive dimensions of racism. This topic had a visceral effect on classroom dynamics. Previously open-faced students lowered their eyes and declined to participate in discussion. John felt a different texture of perception, as if he were being watched or observed from a distance. His previously felt normativity eroded, and with it his teaching confidence. It was not that before he had thought of himself as white, but that he had imagined *and experienced* himself as normative, accepted, recognized as an instructor capable of leading students toward greater understanding. Now he was reminded, forcibly, that his body image self was unstable and contingent, and that his racialized identity was uppermost in the minds of white students who suddenly developed a skeptical attitude toward his analysis and imparted it in a manner they had not been confident enough to develop before.

I have experienced this scenario many times myself, if I raise the issue of race, cultural imperialism, the U.S. invasion of Panama, or sometimes issues of sexism

ents interested in these topics, and colleagues of
or Latino have described similar classroom ex-
hifted away from a professor of color when he or
from women addressing issues of gender. Sud-
nalytical docility and become vigilant critics of
dentity of the teacher counteracts all claims of
nower. Such an experience, as Eduardo Men-
nds oneself in the world ahead of oneself, the
upied. One's lived self is effectively dislodged
ifferent self appears to be operating in the same

because of his body, impedes the closing of the
" (1967, 160). But this disturbance of the nor-
s to occur only when something that seems to
apparent. Before a nonwhite professor assigns
postural body image can remain intact, un-
challenged. The teachers otherness at this stage can be subsumed under a number
of nonthreatening categories, from the compliant servant to the assimilated other
who demonstrably accepts a white worldview as the truth, and so on. The students
do not perceive the teachers' recognition of them as challenging in any way. When
race enters the classroom as a theme, and especially as a theme introduced by a
nonwhite, their confidence and ease about how the teacher is perceiving them
begins to erode, creating a break between first- and third-person perspectives. Only
then is their postural schema disrupted. Disequilibrium for whites is not an inevitable result of the mere presence of racial others, then, even in a historico-racial
schema of white supremacy, though it may be experienced as a potential disruption that the body appreciates and which puts it in the mode of watchfulness.

For a nonwhite called back from a normative postural image to a racialized
"epidermal schema" as Fanon put it, the habit body one falls into at such moments,
I would suggest, is protective, defensive. A hyperactive self-awareness must inter-
rogate the likely meanings that will be attributed to every utterance, gesture, or
action one takes. The available options of interaction across the visible difference
seem closed down to two: combative resistance without hope of persuasion, or an
attempt to return to the category of nonthreatening other, perhaps through attaining
the place of the not-really-other. Neither can yield a true relationship or dialogue;
both are options already given within the white dominant racial structure. No
original move can be recognized.

When I was much younger, I remember finding out with a shock that a white
lover, my first serious relationship, had pursued me because I was Latina, which no
doubt stimulated his vision of exoticism. We had grown up in the same neighborhood, attended the same schools, listened to the same music, and shared similar
ambitions toward college and escape from our shared class. Yet our first encounters,
our first dates, which I had naively believed were dominated by a powerful emotional and intellectual connection, were experienced by him as a fascinating
crossing over to the forbidden, to the Other in that reified, racializing sense.[11] I felt
incredulity, and then humiliation, trying to imagine myself as he saw me, replaying

my gestures and actions, reflecting back even on the clothes I wore, all in an attempt to discern the signs he may have picked up, to see myself as he must have seen me. I felt caught in that moment, finding myself occupying a position already occupied and fashioned elsewhere, incapable of mutual interaction.

There is a visual registry operating in social relations that is socially constructed, historically evolving, and culturally variegated but nonetheless powerfully determinant over individual experience. And for that reason, it also powerfully mediates body image and the postural model of the body. Racial self-awareness has its own habit-body, created by individual responses to racism, to challenges from racial others, and so on. The existence of multiple historico-racial schemas produces a disequilibrium that cannot easily be solved in multiracial democratic spaces—that is, spaces where no side is completely silenced. Racial identity, then, permeates our being in the world, our being-with-others, and our consciousness of our self as a being-for-others.

Phenomenological descriptions such as the ones I have discussed here operate uncomfortably to reactivate racist perception and experience. One might worry that such descriptions will have consolidating effects by repeating, even explaining, the process of racist attribution, suggesting its depth and impermeability. But the reactivations produced by critical phenomenological description don't simply repeat the racializing perception but can reorient the positionality of consciousness. Unveiling the steps that are now attenuated and habitual will force a recognition of one's agency in reconfiguring a postural body image or a habitual perception. Noticing the way in which meanings are located on the body has at least the potential to disrupt the current racializing processes.

If racism is manifest at the level of perception itself and in the very domain of visibility, then an amelioration of racism would be apparent in the world we perceive as visible. A reduction of racism will affect perception itself, as well as comportment, body image, and so on. Toward this, our first task, it seems to me, is to make visible the practices of visibility itself, to outline the background from which our knowledge of others and of ourselves appears in relief. From there we may be able to alter the associated meanings ascribed to visible difference.

Racism and Visible Race

When the critical legal theorist Gary Peller was growing up during the period of school desegregation in Atlanta, he was chosen among a select group of high school students to participate in a citywide project of "unlearning racism." The students were brought together in a large room, the lights were turned off, and they were then invited to touch each other's faces in the dark. The administrators hoped that, in the dark, the students would realize that race makes no difference. Peller persuasively critiques this exercise as a sham because, when the lights were turned back on, the economic and political disparities between the black and white communities in Atlanta were still in place, and a serious attempt to address racism would have had to address those disparities. But in one sense, the school administrators understood correctly the importance of racialized visible differences in student interaction. By eliminating visibility, they hoped the usual distrust, discomfort, and hostility would be absent and new forms of interaction might surface. Unfortunately, the lights had to be turned back on, and things were then indeed, as Peller says, just the same.

In this chapter I want to think through the relationship between racism and the visibility of racialized identity. If one believes that the very existence of racialized identity entails racism, this question will be a nonstarter, but this issue turns on the way in which we understand what racialized identities are. I have argued in earlier chapters that social identities are hermeneutic locations attached to historical experiences that are also concrete sites of interpretation and understanding. On this account, racial identity is not a product of "race"—as if this were a natural phenomena or meaningful biological category—but is historically evolving and culturally contextual, and thus it is not clear to me that racist hierarchies are necessarily entailed. The historical legacy of racial identities will always carry as a central feature the history of racism, and in this way there is an association of race with racism, but *future* meanings of racial identity itself are open-ended. Nonetheless, to identify social groups through their visible racialized features (that is, features in which race is thought to inhere) seems arbitrary and, at the very least, inherently dangerous. If the viability of race as a nonracist category of identity depends on its cultural horizon rather than physical manifestations, shouldn't the whole process of *seeing* race come to an end? This is the topic that I want to focus on in this chapter: the visibility of race. Peller is surely right that eliminating the visible practices of racialization is not *sufficient* for the elimination of racism, but we might still ask: is it perhaps *necessary*?

It is easy to imagine a situation, such as Danzy Senna describes in her auto-biographical novel, *Caucasia*, in which two sisters share the same two parents, grow up in the same house, but are assigned different racial identities (Senna 1998). If their parents differ in racial background, or if even just one parent comes from a "mixed" background, this scenario is all too common in social contexts, such as North America, where gradations of skin color or alterations in hair texture signify differences of type. In other words, though siblings are genetically closer than any other human relationship, racial identity can be assigned differentially without regard to ancestry, background experiences, or biology.

It is easy for me to imagine such a scenario because it is close to the one I experienced in childhood. As very young girls, my older sister and I came from Panama to the Jim Crow South, lived with our white mother's family in their home, and attended white schools. Through the accidents of birth, I could generally pass, but my sister was not so "lucky," and some of our white relatives had Klan-like sensibilities. The fact that she spoke only Spanish at first compounded the problem. She was consequently shunned at home, and she failed in school. As siblings, my sister and I shared close genetic ties, but our visible difference ensured a social disparity. I raise this to underscore the complete idiocy of practices of racial seeing that ground identity in such a way that family, experience, and background are trumped by trivial physical features. But one might then wonder the following: would I prefer that the two sisters Senna writes about share a racial identity, on one side or the other? Am I suggesting that though their "visible" race is thought to differ, their "real" race, based on genetic inheritance, is the same? This is equally absurd. It would seem then that neither biological nor morphological features should have the power of designating race.

However, it is an indisputable fact about the social reality of mainstream North America that racial consciousness works through learned practices and habits of visual discrimination and visible marks on the body. In this way, race operates differently from ethnic or cultural identities, which can be transcended, with enough effort. Inherent to the concept of race is the idea that it exists there on the body itself, not simply on its ornaments or in its behaviors. Races may have indeterminate borders, and some individuals may appear ambiguous, but many people believe that (a) there exists a fact of the matter about one's racial identity, usually determined by ancestry, and (b) that identity is discernible if one peers long enough at, or observes carefully enough, the person's physical features and practiced mannerisms. Though the commonly accepted definition of race explains it by ancestry, the ideology of race asserts its impervious visibility, despite the fact that the two are not always in sync.

Knowing how to pin down those of ambiguous lineage is crucial in this society because racializing perceptual practices are used to produce a visual registry of any given social field, as was argued in the last chapter. This field is organized differentially to distribute the likelihood of intersubjective trust, the extension of epistemic credence, and empathy. A look that is racialized, then, is overdetermined through racial classification and their associated attributions. This was what Fanon

was getting at when he wrote that he was a "slave not of the 'idea' others have of me but of my own appearance" (1967, 116).

Should We Unlearn Racial Seeing?

There are several reasons, one might argue, that we must unlearn racial seeing. Most simply, we could argue that without racial seeing, there could be no races, and thus no racism. Even if we want to hold onto the cultural or ethnic identities that race is sometimes used to signify, we could hold that it is the visible feature of *race*, as opposed to culture and ethnicity, that is inherently pernicious and that this is because the visualization of raced attributes works to naturalize the constructions of racial types. There is no doubt that visual differences are "real" differences, in the sense that the visual markers of race are manifest in real features even if those features are made to stand out in relief and are treated as type distinctions rather than gradations. Still, it is the very fact of visibility itself that makes such markers especially valuable for the naturalizing ideologies of race. All the more reason to disentangle social identity from visible bodily attributes.

Moreover, perception has the added attribute of being, as Merleau-Ponty said, "not presumed true, but defined as access to truth" (1962, xvi). As we saw in the previous chapter, this means that perception cannot readily or easily become the object of analysis itself. Recall Merleau-Ponty's description of how perceptual processes involved in cognition can become organized, like bodily movements used to perform various everyday operations, into integrated units that become attenuated to such a degree that they are experienced as simple, uninterpreted perception. This is surely how racial profiling is experienced most of the time: the profiler does not understand him or herself to be using judgment at all but simply perceiving danger. The development of the concept of racial profiling is an attempt to make such perceptual practices manifest and thus open to critique.

A vision-centric approach to cognition would seem to lend itself especially easily to a positivist ideology, as if the act of seeing were not an act of interpretation, and as if what is visible and thus what is seen were thus indubitable. In a series of recent studies on the effect of ocularcentrism in the history of philosophy, collected by David Michael Levin, a number of other problems with vision as a source of knowledge are explored (Levin 1993, 1997). According to Nietzsche, the will wants everything to be totally visible and totally clear, since unclarity produces anxiety. Thus we desire a form of knowing that is analogous to the certain reliability of clear sight, which explains the human tendency toward a metaphysics of presence. As Gary Shapiro points out, however, this indicates that for Nietzsche it is not that the organ of sight itself tends toward transcendental metaphysics, since here it is merely doing the bidding of the will (Shapiro 1993). But Nietzsche's observations do suggest that vision is especially useful in perpetrating the illusion of transparent cognition. Ocularcentric epistemologies also have the reverse effect, of not only characterizing the nature of the known but also defining with absolute finality the unknowable. What cannot be "made totally visible and clear" may disappear altogether from consciousness, as Herman Rapaport argues in regard to atrocities beyond our field of immediate vision or comprehension (1993). If knowing is seeing, then what cannot be seen cannot be known or considered.

A further danger of an ocularcentric epistemology follows from the fact that vision itself is all too often thought to operate as a *solitary* means to knowledge. Against claims from another, one demands to "see for oneself," as if sight is an individual operation that passes judgment on the claims that others make without also always relying on them. By contrast, knowledge based on the auditory sense, some have argued, is inherently dialogic, and encourages us to listen to what the other says, rather than merely confirming their claims or judging how they appear. And from Foucault we have developed a sensibility to the disciplining potential of visibility. Ours is an era where surveillance is the preferred route of power; where power expands itself through an expansion of visibility in work places, public spaces, and even private ones. On this point Foucault is in agreement with his nemesis, Sartre, for whom the look of the other is a source of domination.

Racism makes productive use of this look, using learned visual cues to demarcate and organize human kinds. Recall the suggestion from Goldberg and West that the genealogy of race itself emerged simultaneous to the ocularcentric tendencies of the Western episteme, in which the criterion for knowledge was classifiability, which in turn required visible difference. Without the operation through sight, then, perhaps race would truly wither away, or mutate into less oppressive forms of social identity such as ethnicity and culture, which make reference to the histories, experiences, and productions of a people, to their subjective lives, in other words, and not merely to objective and arbitrary bodily features.

Without too much effort, one can imagine a distant future in which human differences are not organized in terms of race; as I argued earlier, one can imagine this much more easily than, by contrast, one might imagine a future without gender. Unless we abolish the biological division of labor in the reproduction of the human species, there will continue to be a profound difference between the males and females of our species, even if the meanings, the implications, the boundaries, and the intensity of that difference continue to transform. Still, the bodily and visible differences that exist between most males and females is supervenient on the biological division of labor. Alternatively, the visible markers of race have no biological correlates, as Gould, Marshall, Washburn, Livingstone, and others have shown (see Harding 1993). Conventional race categories have no correspondence to genotype, genetic variability, or clinal variations. And the phenotypical features used to differentiate the races are underdetermined by genetic inheritance in any case. The claim that there is a behavioral or intellectual correlation to current race categories would require (a) a genetic frequency that conforms to race categories, but that in fact does not obtain, and (b) proof that genes determine phenotype, morphology, and behavior, but that also does not obtain (and could not given everything we know about genes). Thus, using racial categories to direct biological research has been described as focusing the microscope on the box the slides came in (see, esp., Livingstone 1993; Marshall 1993).

The physical features conventionally used to differentiate the races are almost laughably insignificant: skin tone, hair texture, shape of facial features. These markers do have *some* practical effects, in the effects of sun exposure on the skin, for example. But such facts are much less significant than one's role in reproduction. Thus, it is easier to imagine a future without race than without gender: if the complete elimination of gender would require a radical rehaul of biological reproduction, the elimination of race would seem to require only a retooling of our perceptual apparatuses. But here, I want to insert a worry: some white folks have declared, no doubt prematurely, that they have already reached utopia. While the rest of us continue to see in color, they declare themselves to be color-blind, to not notice whether people are "black, white, green or purple."

Color Blindness

Bernita Berry and Patricia Williams have both noted and analyzed the phenomenon of racial color blindness (Berry 1995; P. Williams 1997). Williams recounts that in her son's nursery school, color blindness had been pressed upon the children by well-meaning teachers, with the result of leaving "those in my son's position pulled between the clarity of their own experience and the often alienating terms in which they must seek social acceptance" (4). Despite the teachers' attempts to deny the relevance of color, racism was still active on the playground as the children fought over whether "black people could play 'good guys'" (3). Williams argues that although she embraces "color-blindness as a legitimate hope for the future," in our contemporary context "the very notion of blindness about color constitutes an ideological confusion at best, and denial at its very worst" (4). Berry similarly argues that such statements as "I just see people; I don't see color" reflect "a deeply hidden effect of racism. This statement reduces socially significant human differences to invisibleness and meaningless hype whereby one does not have to acknowledge what one does not see" (46). Ultimately, she explains, the statement is meant to impart that racism "may be a reality for those other people — 'those minorities' — but they do not exist for the speaker" (46). I found growing up in the post–civil rights South that color blindness was regularly claimed by white folks and regularly repudiated by folks of color. There seemed to be an anxiety about the perception of race on the part of some whites, a fear of acknowledging that one sees it.

The interesting independent and avant garde film *Suture* has been talked about as the best visual representation of postmodernism in the past decade, but I think it also evidences a revealing anxiety about seeing race. The film offers an intriguing narrative about a case of fratricide in which a white man (Vincent) attempts to murder his black brother (Clay) and stage it as his own suicide. The attempted murder fails, but Clay is severely burned and injured, and only after much surgery does Clay regain his body intact. The twist is that, although Vincent's attempt to murder Clay fails, his identity switch succeeds. As Clay recuperates, with his dark skin quite visible, we expect the hospital staff and Vincent's friend who visits him in the hospital to notice that the survivor of the accident is a different man, not the white Vincent as the identification papers on his body at the time of the accident led people to believe. But they all mistake him as Vincent.

And Clay's amnesia eventually results in his own belief that he is his white brother, despite the fact that he looks at pictures and even a videotape of the "original" Vincent.

Suture thus provides an effective dramatization of the way in which the self is constituted by the other: Clay becomes Vincent because everyone around him treats him as Vincent. And because Vincent is white and Clay is black, when Clay becomes Vincent his life takes a 180-degree turn, which is played to comic effect in, for example, his sudden development of a taste in classical music. Clay becomes Vincent in social position, sensibilities, and even memory. He assumes ownership of all of Vincent's possessions, and Vincent's friends and the police impose memories of Vincent's past on Clay. Thus, it is not simply that Clay has been mistaken for Vincent, but that Clay is transformed into Vincent when he is interpellated as white; his subjectivity and characteristics change so radically that, by the end, it is clear that Clay is, indeed, dead.

The term "suture" itself is, of course, a key concept from Lacan. Kalpana Seshadri-Crooks, who has developed a very interesting Lacanian reading of the film, explains Lacan's concept of suture as "the process by which the subject comes to find a place for itself in a signifying chain by inserting itself in what is perceived as a gap, a place-holder for it" (2000, 105). Clay becomes Vincent by such a process in which he, or his body, is inserted into the place-holder for Vincent. Seshadri-Crooks's reading of the film develops several different themes, but she shares my view that it foregrounds for the audience our own racial seeing, that is, the importance we attach to racial identity. The new Vincent's skin tone is not explained in reference to skin grafting or surgery; his friends and family all look at the old Vincent's photographs, then back to the new Vincent, and exclaim that there is an exact match. The movie ends with none of the characters noticing that the man who survived the car bombing has dark skin while the man they think him to be had light skin. As Seshadri-Crooks puts it, "By requiring us to suspend our *belief* [that is, that no one in the film recognizes the visible difference between Clay and Vincent], the film . . . puts pressure on our suturing into the narration and forces a purchase of our visual pleasure at the price of our own raced subjectivities" (104). The suturing we are made to be aware of, the filmmakers must have hoped, is ultimately not Clay's into his brother's life but our own suturing into racist society.

While I can appreciate the efficacy of the film toward this end, I also believe it manifests a (white) anxiety about seeing race. The coherence of the narrative depends on all the characters being, in effect, color blind, in the colloquial sense of the phrase that Williams and Berry critique. Yet if the audience is made to feel that their own racial seeing is racist, they must then aspire to become like the whites in the movie who apparently cannot see skin color. It is true that by the end of the movie, Clay no longer exists in any significant sense, and thus Clay *is* Vincent. But the audience is also privy to the knowledge that even if Clay no longer exists, the man who has assumed Vincent's life is not Vincent. By the logic of the film, however, anyone, of any body type, could be sutured into anyone else's life. On this view, the "true" self that exists below the surface can cast aside its racialized identity as an animal might shed its skin. Even if we can imagine a distant future without race, I would argue that today racial identity cannot be shed this easily and is not fully reducible to its visible markers such that without them, an individual would simply drop his racial identity.

In order to consider the viability and desirability of the view that *Suture* seems to endorse, let me start by raising again the question of whether the hope for an eradication of visible racial identity is in collusion with the color-blind declaration that Williams and Berry critique. Williams and Berry leave open the possibility of a future beyond race, but their critique of the color-blind position is, as I said, based not simply on skepticism of its likely reality but also on their insistence that race needs to be seen. As Berry puts it, the refusal to see race has the effect of reducing "socially significant human difference to invisibleness and meaningless hype." This argument could be interpreted in two possible ways: (1) race needs to be seen because only then will racism and the ways in which race has distorted human identity be seen, or (2) race needs to be seen in order to see racism and the ways in which race has distorted human identity, but also in order to acknowledge the positive sense of racial identity that has been carved from histories of oppression. Racial identity may have begun in oppression, but the experience of even these sorts of collective identities (i.e., racialized identities) is not always expressed as trauma or manifested as an antagonistic tribalism.

In *Black Orpheus* Sartre perceptively addressed some aspects of racism in Western literature but assumed that the future we all want would be not re-formulation and redemption of racial identity, but its disappearance. He seemed incapable of imagining social identities generally as anything but constraints on individual freedom. But social identities can take numerous forms, and collective differences can be articulated through historical experience, religion, cultural coherence, even geographical location, any of which is surely better than the arbitrary and insignificant phenotypic differences by which race is assigned. What is unique about race is this necessary marking of the body itself. Gender also operates in this way socially, but as I've said it bears a deeper relation to truly significant human difference than race has or can, and thus its visible markers have less of an air of arbitrary unfairness. Isn't it the visibility itself that gives race what Toni Morrison called its "lethal cling"?

If this is so, we might then want to ask: what are the real possibilities of reducing race visibility?

What's Possible?

Despite the fact that, since Locke, philosophers have characterized color as a secondary rather than primary quality, color perception is the result of external stimulation just as with all other forms of perception. In particular, as C. L. Hardin, a philosopher of color, explains, color perception is "the detection of electromagnetic radiation in the wavelength band extending from 380 to 760 nm (one nanometer = one millimicron = one billionth of a meter)" (1984, 125). The immediate source of visual stimulation is "light which has been reflected from the surface of physical objects. Such surfaces normally reflect incident light selectively; the pattern of wavelength selectivity determines the color which we see the object as having" (125). Variations in color perception are explained generally by "the state of adaptation of the eye, the character of the illuminant, and the color and brightness of surrounding objects" (125). There is disagreement among scientists who study color perception about why our vision is restricted to the color spectrum that runs from red to blue, and why the mix of hues is limited, but the facts about our perceptual limits are indisputable. For human beings, as the old example goes, "nothing can be red all over and green all over."

Such naturalized accounts of color perception may well create anxiety when linked to practices of racial identification, given that naturalized accounts of race and racism have been such an important part of racial ideology. And in fact, naturalized explanations of the creation of racial categories are still popular. Psychologist Lawrence Hirschfeld reports that "the prevalent point of view in psychology is that racialized thought is a by-product of the way information is organized and processed" (1996, 8). Here's how the argument goes: The propensity to classify facilitates thought by "reducing the sheer amount of information to which people need to attend" (8). Moreover, classifications can "extend our knowledge by capturing nonobvious similarities between their members" (8). We need only see that a given creature is a cat to be able to infer its food preferences, sleeping habits, and likely aversion to dogs without having to learn these facts from an extended observation of the individual animal. Psychologists then surmise that (a) because of the human propensity to classify on the basis of "conspicuous physical similarities" and (b) because gender and race have "prominent physical correlates," it follows that the categorization of humans by gender and race is natural to human cognition.

But would such a process be functional in the way that, say, the classification "cat" is functional? In regard to gender, the physical capacities for reproduction of males and females is certainly a fact that will at times be useful to know, but what do we learn when we classify people by race? What hair salon they might go to? What is pernicious about race classifications, which of course has also been pernicious about the history of gender classifications, is the host of attributes purportedly correlating to physical racial features. Here is where we clearly need more explanatory resources than the basic wiring of the human eye and the functional orientation of human cognition.

There is good evidence that the practice of othering those who are different in skin tone is historically and culturally particular rather than universal. In *The Black Notebooks*, Toi Derricotte describes what her life has been like as a black woman who is light enough to often pass as white. She recounts the following experience:

> A black boy in the fourth grade says to me, "I'd like to be your son."
> A white boy sitting near him responds, "You could *never* be her son."
> "Why not?" I ask.
> "Because he's black."
> [And then Toi says,] "But I'm black, too."
> He looks at me, his eyes swimming with confusion and pain.

Derricotte offers an explanation of this incident as follows:

> White children might have a more difficult time forming a concept of kinship with people of different colors. Black children grow up in families where there is

every conceivable color, texture of hair, thickness of feature. In white families there is much less difference. I decide to test this.

"How many in the room have people in their families that are all different colors, some people as light as I am, some people as dark as Sheldon?"

All the black kids raise their hands.

"How many have people in their family that are all just about the same color?"

All the white kids raise their hands. (1995, 105)

The propensity to identify those of different colors as potential family members is commonplace in Caribbean cultures as well, where families often include people who are of different "races," at least races by North American standards, and these are not just in-laws. This does not make racism or the preference for whiteness disappear, but it does shift the locus of othering such that skin tone is not sufficient for classification.

Lawrence Hirschfeld's work on children's construction of human kinds provides evidence that children come to know which visible features are relevant to human classifications only after they "integrate their perceptual knowledge with ontological knowledge" (1996, 137). This is not to say that the perceptual competences are irrelevant or secondary, but that they become operable in cognition only when children adapt to what Hirschfeld calls domain-specific competence, or the ability to gain, organize, and use "knowledge about a particular content area" (12). In other words, the mind is not, as previous psychologists typically imagined, like a general all-purpose problem solver but more like a "collection of . . . special-purpose tools, each targeting a specific problem or content."[1] Domain-specific competences direct attention "to certain sorts of data" and posit ontological organizations of perceptible phenomena. Hirschfeld's experiments provide an empirical confirmation of the claims of philosophers from Mead to Heidegger to Merleau-Ponty that the results of perception represent sedimented contextual knowledges, that "our individual sensibilities and perceptions are never purely individual, but are the result of our upbringing, heritage and identity" (137).

Previous researchers on race classification have generally hypothesized the construction of racial categories as building from perception in a linear causal sequence. In contrast, Hirschfeld hypothesized two types of cognitive competence: perceptual and domain-specific, which can work in tandem or sequentially in either order. For example, a child may learn the relevant conceptual domain of color in her culture, by which color is used to organize human kinds, and only then "begin to attend in earnest to the physical correlates that adults believe are important in racial classification" (137). To show this he devised a set of experiments to test the following prediction: that the ability to recall the racial identity of a person should be higher on "verbal rather than visual tasks," given his hypothesis that social ontologies are initially derived from discursive information rather than visual information alone. "The standard view," that is, the view that he put to empirical test, "predicts that racial cognition should be better evoked by visual than by verbal stimuli" (140). Hirschfeld's method was as follows: "Sixty-four 3- and 4-year-old French pre-schoolers" were read a series of simple stories in which the characters were each described in terms of race, occupation, gender, behavior, and a nonracial physical feature (such as body type or age).[2] The children's recall was then tested. In every case, occupation was remembered far better than any other attribute. However, four-year-olds showed a marked improvement over three-year-olds in their ability to remember race. These results were then compared to a similar study in which visual narratives rather than spoken narratives were used with a different group of children. Here, gender outranked occupation in the number of times it was recalled, and race dropped significantly down. In a further visual narrative experiment adding in more variables, children remembered clothing, gender, and behavior about equally, with race dropping to less than half and even to a quarter of the other markers. The fact that race was less well remembered when the narrative was visual rather than verbal strongly suggests that the visual cues of race become operable only after a child has developed a cognitive competence specific to the domain of race in his or her cultural context.

These results do not suggest that human beings might be led to confuse light with dark skin tone, as in the *Suture* example, or that we would become color-blind, but that color could certainly become less salient, less memorable, and that we could come to perceive skin tone in the way it more exactly is presented to consciousness: as a continuously varying attribute rather than a set of discrete categories.

The attempts to explain racial classifications by natural facts of human cognition are surely inadequate. Sight does not lead in a direct line to race. However, we still have the arguments of the philosophers that relying on vision for knowledge is itself a dangerous practice: it obscures its interpretive operations through a veneer of pure perception, and thus can lend itself to a metaphysics of presence where the perception of "sexual licentiousness" or "dull wittedness" appears as a fact in the world. But is sight really worse than other avenues in this regard? Differences of diction and accent can get as easily marked as the sign of innate inferiority as differences of appearance. The olfactory senses have also been used to legitimize discrimination. Racism is an equal-opportunity interpreter across the five senses.

One might well think that we should turn away from the senses altogether as too unreliable. But sometimes sight is our best chance for human communication, if we can only learn to be attentive enough. Adorno reminds us, against Levinas, that "the mechanism of 'pathic projection' determines that those in power perceive as human only their own reflected image" (Adorno 1988, 105; quoted in Levin 1993, 19). We are not always moved to ethical responsiveness by the face of the Other. Nonetheless, if our visual faculty did not by itself lead us to this depravity, then eliminating its role in cognition cannot be either necessary or sufficient if we wish to unlearn racism. Rather, we need new domain-specific competences within which to practice our sight. In the movie *My Dinner with Andre*, the egotistical Andre recounts to his dull-witted friend Wallace that he has suddenly seen anew the picture of his wife that he has carried in his wallet for twenty years. Before, he had always seen his wife in the picture as sensuous and beautiful; only much later did he look hard at the photograph and notice how sad she looked, how profoundly unhappy. It took maturity perhaps for Andre to see the truth that the picture held for him, to learn the competences by which he could notice what was right before his eyes all along. I suspect that we, like Andre, simply need to learn to see better.

The Whiteness Question

White identity poses almost unique problems for an account of social identity. Given its simultaneous invisibility and universality, whiteness has until recently enjoyed the unchallenged hegemony that any invisible contender in a ring full of visible bodies would experience. But is bringing whiteness into visibility the solution to this problem? Hasn't the racist right done just that, whether it is the White Aryan Councils or theorists like Samuel Huntington who credit Anglo-Protestantism with the creation of universal values like freedom and democracy? In this chapter, I give evidence of the increasing visibility of whiteness to whites themselves, and explore a variety of responses by white people as they struggle to understand the full political and historical meaning of white identity today.

One of the clearest representations of this changing white consciousness occurs in the movie *Dances with Wolves* (1991), in which Kevin Costner plays a white Union soldier stationed on the Indian frontier who undergoes a political transformation. He comes to realize that the native peoples his militia intends to kill are not the uncivilized heathens they were portrayed to be and in fact have a rich civilization in many ways superior to his own. Thus, he realizes that he is fighting on the wrong side, and the remainder of the movie chronicles his struggle to figure out what this realization means *for him.*

I believe that this narrative represents a collective, semiconscious undercurrent of psychic and political struggle occurring now in the United States among significant numbers of white Anglos. It is certainly true that throughout U.S. history, some white people have joined in common cause with people of color to fight slavery, racism, and imperialism, from the New York Conspiracy of 1741 to the John Brown uprising to white supporters of civil rights and white protesters against the racism of the Vietnam War (Ignatiev and Garvey 1996, 131). Since the civil rights movement and the Vietnam War, many whites have begun to doubt not only specific racist institutions or aggressions but also the racialized legitimation narratives of "Western civilization" and the purported superiority of all things European.

Dances with Wolves, though politically flawed, nonetheless revealed the significance of this awakened white consciousness by winning the Academy Award for Best Picture of 1991.[1] White support for antiracism is often similarly flawed: riven with supremacist pretensions and an extension at times of the colonizer's privilege to decide the true, the just, and the culturally valuable. However, it is unwarranted to argue that these deep layers of persistent racism represent the core of all apparent white antiracism. Although it is important—and often easy—to expose the persistent racism that can mar avowedly antiracist efforts, we need also to affirm that *some* of the time, *in some* respects, whites empathize and identify with nonwhites, abhor the social injustice of white supremacy, and are willing to make significant sacrifices toward the eradication of white privilege.

For white North Americans, nevertheless, coming to terms with white privilege exacts a price. For Costner's Captain Dunbar, the effort costs him a good beating and nearly his life, and some whites during the civil rights movement were firebombed, beaten, and even killed (see, e.g., Fosl 2002). But for most contemporary whites, the price that has to be paid is more often psychological. When one realizes how one's own hermeneutic horizon of shared meanings has been infected by white supremacy, one's own sense of identity becomes invalidated. As James Baldwin said years ago, "It is not really a 'negro revolution' that is upsetting the country. What is upsetting the country is a sense of its own identity" (1988, 8). And as one white student put it in a recent study, "I mean now I really have to think about it. Like now I feel white. I feel white" (Gallagher 1994, 165). This "feeling white," when coupled with a repudiation of white privilege, can disable a positive self-image as well as a felt connection to community and history, and generally can disorient identity formation.

Chauvinist legitimation narratives that portrayed European-based societies as the progressive vanguard of the human race produced an almost invisible support structure for the collective self-esteem of all those who could claim such a European identity. In the first half of the twentieth century, the plausibility of these narratives was undermined by the profit-motivated violence of World War I and the technologically orchestrated genocides of World War II. As a response to that disillusionment, new narratives were developed, based on a thorough repudiation of "old world" ethnic hatreds and blind political obedience. The "new" or "modern world" legitimation narratives proclaimed that European-based societies were superior not because Europeans were closer to God than all others in the Great Chain of Being but because they had developed concrete political values and institutions that maximized individualism, civil liberties, and economic prosperity, which were assumed to be the highest human goods. Of course, many nonwhites are able to participate in these narratives and to see themselves to some extent as a part of the global liberatory vanguard. But because it was the cultural traditions and economic methods of Europe and the United States that inspired and guided this progress, naturally whites were at the center and the forefront, with nonwhite allies alongside but to the back.

In the second half of the twentieth century, internal disillusionment with these white-vanguard narratives grew strong once again, primarily because of the civil rights movement and the Vietnam War, but also in light of events in South Africa,

Ireland, and Central Europe, as well as U.S.-led aggressions and abuses in Iraq, which have engendered doubt about whether the white race is less violent, less "uncivilized," or more democratic than any other. As a result, the cultural mechanisms supporting white self-esteem are breaking down, and a growing white backlash has developed in response to this psychic threat. Twenty-seven states have proposed English-only statutes of various sorts, and white support for affirmative action is well below a majority.

Backlash, however, is not the only contemporary white response to the declining plausibility of white supremacist narratives. This chapter explores other kinds of white responses, all of which, in one way or another, seek to transcend white vanguardism and move toward a proactive position against racism that will amount to more than mere self-criticism.

One of the most difficult aspects of these white anti-racist projects is what I have called "the whiteness question," meaning the question of white identity. Many race theorists have argued that antiracist struggles require whites' acknowledgment that they are *white*; that is, that their experience, perceptions, and economic position have been profoundly affected by being constituted as white (Frankenberg 1993). Race may be a social construction without biological validity, yet it is real and powerful enough to alter the fundamental shape of all our lives (Gooding-Williams 1995; Taylor 2003). Part of white privilege has been precisely whites' ability to ignore the ways white racial identity has benefited them.

But what is it to acknowledge one's whiteness? Is it to acknowledge that one is inherently tied to structures of domination and oppression, that one is irrevocably on the wrong side? In other words, can the acknowledgment of whiteness produce only self-criticism, even shame and self-loathing? Is it possible to feel okay about being white?

Every individual, I would argue, needs to feel a connection to community, to a history, and to a human project larger than his or her own life. Without this connection, we are bereft of a concern for the future or an investment in the fate of our community. Nihilism is the result; and we see abundant signs of it all around, from the unchecked frenzy of consumption that ignores its likely long-term effects to the anarcho-libertarianism that is rife in the corporate United States at all levels and that values only immediate individual desires. This tendency to disconnect from community and history may well be a symptom of the whiteness problem, or the desire of whites to escape their identity.

If this analysis is correct, and everyone does need some felt connection to a community with both past and future, what are North American whites to do? Should they assimilate, like Captain John Dunbar in *Dances with Wolves*, as far as possible into non-European cultures, as some New Age advocates argue? Should they become, as Noel Ignatiev and John Garvey argue, race traitors who disavow all claims or ties to whiteness? Can a liberal repudiation of racial identity and an avowal of "color blindness" produce the consciousness of white privilege that antiracism requires? Can a deracialized individualism provide the sense of historical continuity that moral action seems to require?

Feminism has usefully problematized the notion of a monolithic white identity by raising issues of gender and class in relation to whiteness. In the next section I will analyze some of the leading feminists' pathbreaking analyses of the relationship between whiteness and power in light of the fragmentation of whiteness itself. Then, in the following three sections, I will explore three further "answers" to the whiteness question: the early, influential antiracist "white awareness training" methods as developed by Judith Katz and others and still practiced in institutional settings today, the "race traitor" politics developed by Ignatiev and Garvey, and, finally, the progressive white revisionism being attempted at the University of Mississippi, of which I'll offer a case study. Each of these is an example of a response to the whiteness question developed by whites for whites.

I have experienced some white chauvinism in the form of supremacist attitudes toward Latinos, but I'm sure I have also benefited from white skin privilege given that I am closer to my mother's skin color than my father's. Thus, I know something about white privilege from the inside, despite my mixed genealogy. I once heard the legal theorist Gerald Torres joke that Latinos have a tendency toward arrogance about racial matters: he said that because Latinos are usually racially mixed, they often assume that they know what it is to be Indian, to be white, *and* to be black! Latinos also sometimes assume ourselves incapable of antiblack or anti-Indian racism because most of us have some black and indigenous forebears. (For an excellent antidote to this, see Ramos 1995.) I do not want to make these assumptions, but I have tried to use my intersectional location as a resource for considering the multiple "lived experiences" of racialized identity in the United States.

White Women and Identity

Whiteness is both homogeneous and fractured. Unlike Latino identity, which is understood to be mixed, and unlike African American identity under the strictures of the one-drop rule, whiteness is accorded only to those who are (supposedly) "pure" white. In the recent historical past this was not so clear-cut, as Jews, Irish, Italians, and other southern Europeans were sometimes excluded from whiteness and at other times enjoyed a halfway status as almost white, but not quite (unlike those with partial African heritage, no matter how light). But today, in mainstream white-bread America, southern Europeans have been assimilated, and the borders around whiteness are assumed to be clear.

In another sense, whiteness has always been fractured by class, gender, sexuality, ethnicity, age, and able-bodiedness. The privileges whiteness bestowed were differentially distributed and were also simply different (for example, the privilege to get the job for a man, the privilege not to have to get a job for women, and so on). In much feminist literature the normative, dominant subject position is described in detail as a white, heterosexual, middle-class, able-bodied male. This normative figure carries the weight as well in the cultural narrative of reconfiguring black-white relations; there have been far more "buddy" movies about white men and black men than films exploring women's relationships.[2] In *Dances with Wolves*, the revision of the Manifest Destiny narrative requires a white, normative male to carry the story; this seems to assume that if "whiteness" is to be recast, it must be recast from the center out. Anything else—any revision that centered on a woman, for example—would not have the cultural force, the felt *significance*, of a white man relearning his place. Thus the question arises, what are white women's relation to whiteness?

Feminist theory has given various answers to this question, and much of the debate has centered on the question of whether white women benefit on the whole from whiteness, or whether whiteness is a ruse to divide women and to keep white women from understanding their true interests. Some feminists have argued that sexism is more fundamental than racism, in the sense that sexual identity is more important than racial identity in determining social status. For example, Shulamith Firestone (1970) argues that the racism that exists among white women is a form of inauthenticity or false consciousness that does not represent their true interests. Mary Daly (1978) similarly argued in her middle period work that charges of racism against feminists serve patriarchal ends by promoting divisiveness among women. According to Daly, feminists should disengage from male-created identifications with race, nation, or ethnicity.

Other feminists have criticized this view. In an early article, Margaret A. Simons (1979) argues against making sexism primary on the grounds that this trivializes racist oppression and implausibly assumes that sexism alone can provide an adequate explanation for genocide and war (by holding, for example, that white men "feminized" nonwhite or Jewish men). The existence of some form of sexist oppression in every society does not justify a conception of patriarchy that generalizes across the relations between all men and all women in one undifferentiated analysis. According to Simons, white women's identity must be understood *both* as white *and* as female. Gloria Joseph (1981) also argued that white women are both tools and benefactors of racism, and that feminists must recognize and address white women's social position as both oppressors and oppressed. In fact, Joseph contends that given the extensive privileges of whiteness, white women's immediate self-interest is to maintain racism. She suggests that we need to explore the concept of "white female supremacy" as well as white male supremacy. The involvement of white women in the abuses at the Abu Graib prison in Iraq lends support for Joseph's position. It is interesting to note that in that situation, it was two male soldiers of color and a Jewish journalist who played the most instrumental roles in breaking the story to stop the abuse, while white women were directly involved in abusing prisoners and the CEO of the prison was a white woman.

Adrienne Rich's "Disloyal to Civilization: Feminism, Racism, Gynephobia" (1979), a paper that has been very widely used in women's studies courses, takes up these issues of white women's complicity in a way that mainly addresses a white feminist audience. In this paper, Rich develops the concept of "white solipsism" to describe a perceptual practice that implicitly takes a white perspective as universal. She argues that "color blindness," or the ideal of ignoring racial identities, is actually a form of white solipsism because a racist society has no truly accessible color-blind perspective. The claim to a color-blind perspective by whites works to conceal the partiality of their perceptions, which will make it less likely they will be able to foreground their perceptual practices, as I argued in chapter 7.

Rich provides a very perceptive critique of color blindness and, unlike some other radical feminists, she acknowledges the significance of white women's racism. However, Rich continues to put sexism at the center of all women's lives and to portray white women as primarily victims of racism rather than agents who help to sustain it. Rich claims that white women did not create racism but have been forced to serve racist institutions, and that those who think they benefit from racism are deluded. In her view, white women's racism is actually a misdirected outlet for their rage over their own powerlessness, a view that only slightly revises Firestone's. In Rich's account, slavery is more accurately described as an institution of patriarchy than one of white supremacy, presumably because white women were disenfranchised during that period; to blame white women for crimes committed by powerful white men is to impede the process of forging political and emotional connections between white and nonwhite women. Rich believes that the apparent protection some white women receive from patriarchy degrades them by enforcing childishness and helplessness. Therefore, white women do not benefit in the long run from white men's protection and their true interests lie in making alliances with other women, not with men. This analysis suggests that the "whiteness" of white women is not in any sense the same as the "whiteness" of white men. Rich seems to see white women as experiencing a specific form of oppression insofar as they are white women, and not just in so far as they are women.

In contrast, Marilyn Frye (1983, 1992) argues that despite the severity of sexism, white women do not escape race privilege. It is a feature of this race privilege that white women have an option to hear or not to hear—and to respond to or not to respond to—the demands and criticisms of women of color. She points out that racism differentially distributes general epistemic authority to make judgments and determinations, such that, for example, whites often assume the right to decide the true or accurate racial identity of everyone. When white feminists proclaim that white women are primarily *women*, this is an extension of an essentially white privilege.

In Frye's view, white feminists should be disloyal to whiteness. Because white women understandably want to be treated as human beings, their feminism often takes the form of pursuing the full entitlements of what Frye calls "whiteliness," which she defines as a socially constructed racial status that confers entitlements and authority. For example, the liberal feminist demand for equality has implicitly and practically meant the demand for equality with white men (a demand for equality with, say, *puertorriqueños* would hardly mean liberation). But the demand to be equal to white men is necessarily a demand to achieve whiteliness, a status that depends on racist structures of social relations for its power and autonomy. Like Rich and Firestone, Frye argues that solidarity with white men is not in white women's ultimate interest. Frye suggests further that racism has motivated white men to oppress and constrain white women's sexuality and reproductive powers in order to secure the regeneration of a "pure" white population.

My own view is that many white women have divided interests, just as many men of color have divided interests in both maintaining patriarchy for the privileges it affords them but also in overcoming patriarchy so that they can build solidarity with women of color and the antiracist movement can take advantage of its full potential. Similarly, some, perhaps many, white women attain real advantages from whiteness, to use Frye's term—economic, political, legal, physical, and psychological. At the same time, many white women experience a comparative disadvantage vis-à-vis white men. The question for any given individual white woman is, Is she more interested in attaining as much as possible of what white men now have, or would she prefer to live in and contribute toward a just society?

Despite differences over the question of white women's "objective" interests, white feminists (other than some of the liberals) are generally united in calling for white women to become disloyal, that is, to disrupt white solidarity. But what would "becoming disloyal" mean in practice? For Frye and Rich, it clearly cannot mean color blindness or the pursuit of individual gain, which would only conceal white privilege and implicit white perspectives. So how can whites be disloyal to whiteness while acknowledging their responsibility for their own racial identity?

Antiracism Training

A liberal approach to answering this question is developed in Judith Katz's now-classic *White Awareness: Handbook for Anti-racism Training* (1978). This book is representative of the popularized psychological approach to antiracism, an approach often generated in, and aiming to be suited for, the kinds of in-house workshops and encounter groups that have developed from corporate America since the 1960s, though Katz's own context was closer to universities. Many corporations have discovered that racism (sometimes) impedes productivity, and therefore they have hired consultants to retrain and "sensitize" white management personnel. This is, of course, only part of the audience for antiracism training; some universities and movement organizations have also tried approaches such as Katz's. But the specific social location and source of funding needs to be kept in mind when analyzing the reeducation approaches used in antiracism workshops.

White Awareness attributes widespread responsibility for racism to whites. However, Katz is highly critical of white guilt fixations on the grounds that these are self-indulgent. She explains that such criticisms led her to move from black-white group encounters to all-white groups. She also avoided using people of color to reeducate whites, she says, because she found that this led whites to focus on getting acceptance and forgiveness from their nonwhite trainers.

Katz describes facing the enormity and depth of racism as painful and demoralizing, since one loses one's sense of self-trust and even self-love; but she nonetheless holds out the hope that whites can become antiracist and that "we may ultimately find comfort in our move to liberation" (vii). She holds that racism causes whites to suffer; it cripples their intellectual and psychological development and locks them "in a psychological prison that victimizes and oppresses them every day of their lives" (14). Such claims do not, of course, entail that whites' victimization by racism is worse than or equal to that of other groups, but Katz's wording is striking. Throughout the book, racism is portrayed as a kind of macro-agent with its own agenda, operating separately from white people.

This problem takes on added significance given that antiracism and "sensitivity" training occur within the context of a corporate culture that continues to use racism and cultural chauvinism as an excuse to pay people of color far lower wages by undervaluing comparably challenging or even more difficult work. Katz makes no reference to exploitation or the need for a redistribution of resources, and instead treats racism as a psychological pathology that can be solved through behavior modification. Although racism no doubt is debilitating for whites in a number of ways, unless we analyze who benefits from and promotes racism, both objectively and subjectively, we cannot see clearly what needs to be done to counter it.

Despite these weaknesses, *White Awareness* offers procedures that can permit collective exploration of and critical reflection on white racial consciousness. It builds on whites' own tacit knowledge of racism to promote reflection, thereby enhancing whites' confidence in their own agency and counteracting fatalism. And it helpfully acknowledges the likelihood of white emotional responses like anger, guilt, and resistance without seeing these as indicative of an insurmountable racism. Stage 3 of the process involves asking participants to reflect on what they fear might happen if they "work on their racism" as she asks them to. She thus develops group processes and supportive environments in which such emotional responses can be aired, worked through, and transcended. Katz argues that "it is not enough to deal with racism solely on a cognitive level. If participants are not touched personally—if their emotional base does not change at this point—they are unlikely to change their attitudes and behaviors" (93). I have at least anecdotal reports that the book has been used productively in contexts of political organizing to initiate an exploration and reflection by whites about the many subtle layers of racism and supremacist assumptions embedded in their interactions.

A notable weakness of *White Awareness* is that it does not offer a transformative, substantive white identity. Katz argues persuasively against replacing generic whiteness with white ethnic identities on the grounds that this obscures the racialized organization of white supremacy, and thus she maintains the need to self-identify as white. But whiteness figures in *White Awareness* only as an identity of unfair privilege based on white supremacy; unlike ethnic identities, it has no other substantive cultural content. Stage 5 of the training process is called "Individual Racism: The Meaning of Whiteness," and the first goal listed is to help participants "explore their White culture and develop a sense of positive identification with their whiteness" (135). However, the workshops in this stage discuss only the luxuries and privileges associated with whiteness. Among the directions to the facilitator is the following: "You should also help the group identify positive aspects of being White. It is important for them to feel good about themselves as White people. All too often Whites deny their whiteness because they feel that being White is negative" (145). However, the book provides no help in determining what these positive aspects might be, and, given its context, readers must find it difficult to guess how Katz would substantively define whiteness except in terms of racism and unfair privilege.

Let me end this section with another story that reveals the way in which identity issues are important here. In 1992, on the quincentenary of Columbus's invasion, I participated in a public debate in Syracuse, New York, with the local Italian American booster club over the political meanings of Columbus Day. They argued that Italian Americans suffered intense and ongoing discrimination in this country and that the celebration of Columbus Day was very important for raising community pride and instilling recognition of the important contributions Italians have made. I agreed with their depiction of the situation and the need for positive cultural symbols but asked why Leonardo da Vinci, Michelangelo, and even Mario Cuomo could not be used instead of a man who encouraged the enslavement of Native Americans. The Italians of all groups have a particular wealth of admirable cultural leaders, and this club's continued insistence on Columbus suggested to me that more than achieving group equality was at stake.

If white identity is to be transformed, it does need more of a substantive reconstruction, including a revision of historical narratives and cultural focuses. The following two sections explore more recent attempts to transform whiteness, both of which take some issue with the liberal approach.

Traitors to Whiteness

One of the most radical positions on white antiracism that has emerged in recent years can be found in the journal *Race Traitor: A Journal of the New Abolitionism*. The journal has created a space where radical whites can share and spread ideas, get feedback and criticism from people of color, and help to educate themselves and their readers on the "true" history of the Civil War and the neglected legacy of white resistance to racism. They can also develop their critical analyses of current social phenomena, such as the increasing incidence of cultural crossover by white youths.

Journal editors Noel Ignatiev and John Garvey are anticapitalist, and they believe that we must be willing to take up arms. Their politics are probably best classified as libertarian anarchist, and it is other anarchist journals and "zines" that seem most often to reprint or refer to *Race Traitor*. The editors strive for a strong working-class political perspective, and they have managed to develop class inclusiveness among the journal's writers, a characteristic too rarely found in leftist journals of any type. In an interesting way, they have put less effort into making allies among feminists or gay activists, perhaps because they do not view the struggles against sexism and homophobia as centrally connected to white supremacy. This follows from an analysis found regularly in the journal that "white supremacy" has largely been an ideology used by the wealthy and powerful to fool the white poor into being more race-loyal than class-loyal, blinding them to their own interests. In other words, the journal tends toward class reductionism that sidelines other kinds of struggles and homogenizes class interests.

The most interesting aspect of *Race Traitor* is its declared focus on whites. Unlike other leftist publications that have tried to develop multiracial groups, *Race Traitor* seems to believe that a political network of white traitors is needed to focus on retrieving white antiracist history, deepening the analysis of whiteness and racism, and encouraging the small but growing tendency among white youth to rebel against racist cultural hierarchies and enforced segregation. Consider the editors' report of the following news item:

> According to press reports and our own correspondents, the white race is showing signs of fracture in the rural midwest. Several female students at North Newton Junior-Senior High School near Morocco, Indiana, who call themselves the "Free to Be Me" group, recently started braiding their hair in dreadlocks and wearing baggy jeans and combat boots, a style identified with Hip-Hop culture. Morocco is a small farming community seventy miles south of Chicago; of the 850 students at

the school, two are black. Whites in the town accuse the group of "acting black," and male students have reacted by calling them names, spitting at them, punching and pushing them into lockers, and threatening them with further violence. Since mid-November there have been death threats, a bomb scare, and a Ku Klux Klan rally at the school. "This is a white community," said one sixteen-year-old male student. "If they don't want to be white, they should leave." (Ignatiev and Garvey 1996, flyleaf)

Not only have the students encountered violent opposition, but school officials have suspended them with the excuse of dress-code violations. This example, which received wide publicity on the *Montel Williams Show*, is clearly the kind of spontaneous, in-your-face rebellion that *Race Traitor* hopes to encourage. The editors comment, "This incident reveals ... the tremendous power of crossover culture to undermine both white solidarity and male authority."

It is important to understand why *this* sort of event is what *Race Traitor* finds so hopeful, rather than the more common and certainly more tame occurrences of white antiracist organizing on college campuses and white support for such political efforts as the Free Mumia Abu-Jamal campaign, union campaigns, and Martin Luther King Day rallies. What happened in Morocco, Indiana, differs from those events in that it was a rebellion that involved a *repudiation of white identity*.

The cornerstone of the *Race Traitor* position is that "nothing less than the abolition of the white race will lay the foundation for a new departure" (1996, 2). The journal's main slogan is "treason to whiteness is loyalty to humanity" (10). Whites need to challenge the "normal operation" of "the institutions that reproduce race as a social category" (3). Sounding like Foucault at times, the editors argue that whiteness is made real through social practices that occur in a multitude of daily social interactions, and that this process works only because it assumes that people designated white will play by the rules. "But if enough of those who looked white broke the rules of the club" such that, for example, the police would "come to doubt their ability to recognize a white person," this could disrupt the whole mechanism, and whiteness might be abolished (13). How many such white dissidents would it take? "One John Brown—against the background of slave resistance—was enough for Virginia" (13). His deeds "were part of a chain of events that involved mutual actions and reactions on a scale beyond anything they could have anticipated—until a war began" (13). Thus, given the persistence of rebellions by people of color, white acts of treason might be just what is needed to ignite a civil war, one that perhaps this time could truly be a revolutionary war as well.

Such strategic thinking obviously resonates with the postmodern sensibilities of radical youth today, which accounts in part, I believe, for the increased interest in anarchist theories of social change. That is, both postmodernism and anarchism offer a theoretical justification for the current belief that barricade-style "wars of position" are hopeless in a shifting terrain of decentralized, geographically unstable capitalist power. In a situation in which political power cannot be mapped, economic power exists on no fixed grid, and the causal relations between politics, economics, and culture have no stability, it is possible to hope that enough incidents like the Morocco case might be just the catalyst needed.

But what other sorts of white treason can one engage in today? In the civil rights movement, white individuals refused white solidarity over Jim Crow and sat in at lunch counters with African Americans, rode in the backs of buses, and marched in open opposition to their communities. These were public acts of social treason without a doubt, and they incited violent reactions sometimes as brutal as those that black people themselves suffered. In the absence of such a political movement, there are other actions whites can take that are less dramatic but that can send similar messages, such as the clothing styles chosen by the "Free To Be Me" group in Morocco, or the choice of schools and neighborhoods, real estate brokers and other services or businesses. However, outside the context of a widely publicized political movement, the meanings of such acts are less predictable, and they may even have harmful unintended effects, as when the choice of a minority neighborhood by whites actually aids gentrification. In the Morocco case, one of the two black students also was threatened and harassed, and his mother was attacked and beaten by two white men while she was shopping in town. Thus the most violence was suffered by the black families in the school, families that were not consulted and probably unprepared for the attack. Given that we lack total control over the meanings and the effects of our actions, and given the absence of a widely publicized political movement of "white treason" that could clarify the intended meaning, the real effects of individual actions are uncertain.

The most obvious problem with *Race Traitor's* proposal, however, is that whites cannot completely disavow whiteness or distance themselves from their white identity. One's appearance of being white will still operate to confer privilege in numerous and significant ways, and to avow treason does not render whites ineligible for these privileges, even if they work hard to avoid them. In one essay for the journal, Edward H. Peeples recounts something that happened to him at a Richmond newsstand in 1976. When he went to purchase an African American newspaper, the white cashier looked at him and explained, "You don't want this newspaper; it's the colored newspaper." Peeples responded, loudly enough for others in the shop to hear, "You must think I'm white." He explains what happened next. "[The cashier] was startled. But within seconds she came to realize that these simple words represented a profound act of racial sedition. I had betrayed her precious 'white race.' . . . The cashier became furious. But she was clearly at a loss of what to do with this Judas" (quoted in Ignatiev and Garvey 1996, 82).

I do not doubt that such an act in some parts of the South *is* a profound sedition. But such acts cannot completely eliminate the operation of white privilege, and the subsequent treatment of the "white Judas" will be affected by both his whiteness and his treason.[3] And some "treasonous" whites, with white privilege still largely in place, might then feel entitled to disengage with whiteness without feeling any link of responsibility for white racist atrocities of the past; or they might consider a declaration that they are "not white" as a sufficient solution to racism without the trouble of organizing or collective action. This position would then end up uncomfortably similar to the color-blindness attitude that pretends ignorance about one's own white identity and refuses responsibility.

These worries relate to another feature I found in *Race Traitor*, the tendency to emphasize that most whites have not committed racist violence (see, for example,

16–17). The authors have developed a rhetorical strategy intended to promote a disassociation or disidentification between whites (especially the working class) and racist institutions; to say, in effect, "This is not really *your* history, so why defend it?" On the one hand, this strategy is based on a more accurate telling of southern history than I myself received in grade school: I was never told that there were a significant number of white deserters and dissenters during the Civil War. Among whites in the South, it was commonly said during the civil rights movement that the only whites who crossed lines of racial solidarity and supported the "rabble-rousers" like Dr. Martin Luther King Jr. were Northerners (Yankees!), and Jewish to boot. An accurate revision of white history would be enlightening and encouraging to whites with antiracist tendencies.

Yet there is a danger in the strategy of disassociating white workers from past racist violence: some white workers *did* participate in such violence. It is notoriously difficult to tell how many, given the secretive nature of Ku Klux Klan activity.[5] Judging from the documented public announcements and celebrations of lynching, as when W. E. B. Du Bois sorrowfully describes passing a severed black finger displayed for the public while he was on his way to work in Atlanta, we have to conclude that, like the German population during the Nazi regime, white working-class people in the South and elsewhere largely knew about the atrocities and largely approved of them.

Shortly before he died, I discovered that my own grandfather had participated in Klan violence in his youth. He was a semiliterate working-class Irish American who lived poor and died poor, sneered at by the rich folks he worked for; but I also believe that his sense of white superiority must have helped to produce the self-confidence it took for him to go back to school as an adult and learn to read, write, and do enough arithmetic to improve his job skills. Therefore, although I believe, like Ignatiev and Garvey, that an argument can be constructed that it is actually not in poor whites' overall economic interest to maintain racism (certainly, taking more than one generation into account), I think these authors sidestep the issue of moral culpability and its relation to social identity. Ignatiev writes, "It is our faith . . . that the majority of so-called whites in this country are neither deeply nor consciously committed to white supremacy; like most human beings in most times and places, they would do the right thing if it were convenient" (12). But white supremacy may be deeply held *because* it is not conscious. If the collective structures of identity formation that are necessary to create a positive and confident sense of self—a self that is capable of being loved—require racism, then only the creation of new structures of identity formation can redress this balance. Racism appears to be deeply sedimented into white psyches in a process that is newly reenforced each day.

Thus, the issue of convenience unfortunately misses the point. In regard to clearly identified racist acts of commission that require conscious intent, Ignatiev may be right. But this notion can coexist with the idea that white people's sense of who they are in the world, especially in this country, depends deeply on white supremacy. And this dependence may often operate precisely because they are themselves oppressed; that is, because their immigrant relations were a humble lot without other cultural resources from which to draw a sense of entitlement. White supremacy may be all that poor whites have to hold onto to maintain a sense of the most basic entitlement to human rights, such as the right of political enfranchisement.

The very genealogy of whiteness was entwined from the beginning with a racial hierarchy, which can be found in every major cultural narrative from Christopher Columbus to manifest destiny to the space race and the computer revolution. Staying in the vanguard is quite often inconvenient; it requires war and great sacrifice to remain "ahead." But it is pursued nevertheless, precisely because it is necessary for the possibility of self-esteem. So here is the predicament: we *must* tell the full story of white racism in all its complexity, and this complexity cannot be fully resolved through a class analysis that sequesters the guilty as only among the rich. Yet facing the reality of whites' moral culpability threatens their very ability to be moral today, because it threatens their ability to imagine themselves as having a socially coherent relation to a past toward which anyone could feel a positive attachment.

Race Traitor's attention to crossover culture may be motivated by this concern, in the hope that a "mixed" cultural identity could replace whiteness and thereby avoid its moral legacy. Paradoxically, although its contributors criticize all variants of multiculturalism because, among other reasons, it tends to talk about oppression without naming any oppressors, *Race Traitor* is very optimistic about white crossover. The editors recognize that "the willingness to borrow from black culture does not equal race treason" (3). Yet they interpret the increase in white crossover as signaling the fracturing of white supremacy. Phil Rubio even claims that "white cultural assimilation . . . is already a form of political awareness" (161).

This position has elicited skepticism from some readers of color, whose critiques the journal has printed. Salim Washington and Paul Garon both have expressed concern that examples of race traitors are being romanticized. Washington points out that black artists continue to "suffer through diminished access to and control of the means of cultural production" (166). Merely to appreciate and acknowledge black influences in dominant culture does nothing to remedy this. Garon similarly stresses that the usual economic effects of crossover are that white performers are enriched and black performers have even less chance to make a living. Garon also challenges the view (not necessarily held by Rubio) that no essential musical integrity is lost when white performers play the blues. Context affects the meaning imparted, and in Garon's view, race is a salient feature of musical context.

This issue illuminates the difficulties of white transformation. When does the transcendence of cultural chauvinism merge into cultural appropriation? Especially in a consumer society, the core of white privilege is the ability to consume anything, anyone, anywhere. The desire to cross over is itself coterminous with a colonizing desire of appropriation, even to the trappings of social identity through a hip hop clothing style.

Contemporary music does model, at times, an exemplary globalism, in which borrowings are so rapid and multidirectional that the concepts of "origin" and "identity," as well as "private property," are quickly losing their intelligibility. This does not mean that the culture industry transcends the racial hierarchies of existing political economies; hybridity in cultural forms does not entail a corresponding distribution of economic success. However, in trying to overcome unfair distributions of financial resources or access to cultural production, it is unrealistic to propose a voluntary self-segregation or, for example, that whites stick to white music. Hybridity, and therefore crossover, is an unstoppable force. Racism has not, on the whole, slowed cultural hybridization. This means that cultural hybridization is not a sufficient cause or even a necessary indicator of antiracism.

To analyze the political implications of crossover culture, it might be helpful to use Sartre's analysis of the look and its role in social relations. According to Sartre, in the look of the Other we perceive the Other's subjective consciousness—that is, the Other's interior life similar to our own. We also perceive our being-for-others, or the value and meaning we have in the eyes of the Other. As Lewis Gordon argued in his interesting book *Bad Faith and Antiblack Racism*, white racism is generally predicated on the need and desire of whites to deflect the look of the black Other, a look that will reveal guilt, accusation, and moral deficiency (1995, esp. chap. 14). If racism is the attempt to deflect a black look, then what is crossover?

Sartre, who was famously pessimistic about the egalitarian potential of human relations, presented two options as to actions that can be taken toward the Other. The first involves an attempt to transcend the Other's transcendence, or negate the Other's own freedom, especially the freedom to judge and value. This mode is characteristic of hate and sadism. The other mode involves the attempt to incorporate the transcendence of the Other; that is, to have the Other's love, but freely of the Other's own choosing. This is the paradox of love: we want the Other to love us in a way that is absolute, unchanging, and reliable, but we want this love to be freely given without coercion. Thus we want the love to be simultaneously noncontingent and contingent. Sartre characterizes this as the desire to incorporate the Other's freedom *within me*, such that my needs and desires are still at the center and the Other exists only as a portion of my arranged world without real autonomy.

White attempts to appropriate black culture may fall into this category, as a strategy that does not seek to deflect the black look or repress it into blank submission but instead seeks to incorporate the black look within oneself. In other words, attempts by whites to assimilate wholly to blackness may be motivated by the desire to make the black look—or black subjectivity, which is what the look signifies—safely internal and thus nonthreatening to the self. The recognition of an irreducible difference, a difference that crossover tries to overcome, would maintain the Other's own point of departure, the Other's own space of autonomous judgment, and thus the possibility for a truly reciprocal recognition of full subjectivity.

Such an analysis does not require a wholesale rejection of crossover, but counsels a careful scrutiny of crossover postures that would seek to erase difference. An example of such a posture would be one that Garon criticizes, the view that the blues are a transracial, universally accessible cultural form. It may be that the denial of the black specificity of blues, with the argument that suffering is available across race, is motivated by unease about what expressions of *black* suffering especially signify for white listeners. Universal suffering is nonaccusatory; black suffering is implicitly accusatory, just by making reference to black history. Thus, to incorporate the blues as a cultural form that is proper to American experience without a racial specificity helpfully deflects the potential meaning for whites of a blues identified as black. This does not entail that white antiracists should never sing the blues, or that they cannot develop new forms of the blues, but that the blackness of the blues, or at least of its cultural genesis, should not be dismissed as irrelevant.

New Traditions in Mississippi

If the main problem with Katz's *White Awareness* is a lack of social and historical context or class analysis, *Race Traitor* provides class analysis without sufficient attention to cultural processes of identity formation. The final white antiracist example I will discuss is more consciously situated in a particular context and aimed at transforming white self-understanding.

The conclusions of Ruth Frankenberg's 1993 ethnographic study of white women suggest that whiteness is an invisible racial identity to whites. Katz similarly argues that the first task of antiracism is for whites to come to understand that they are white. But where I grew up, whiteness was a substantive racial identity whose political privileges were well known and mostly considered justified. The cultural substance of whiteness consisted in such elements as putting peanuts in your R.C. Cola and souping up your car engine. There was a recognizably white way to dance, get drunk, and sing in church. Ethnic differences among whites were subordinated to the all-important racial identification that secured one's place in a segregated society. Because southern whiteness has had a high degree of racial self-consciousness, then, it should be an instructive location at which to observe attempts at antiracist transformation.

About fifteen years ago, the University of Mississippi decided to go proactive against racism, as well as sexism, by instituting a mandatory course for all freshmen. Michael L. Harrington, chair of the philosophy department, was asked to design a suitable course. Harrington established a course, university studies 101, taught it himself for a number of years, and developed a textbook that continues to be used. Harrington is a white southerner who both knows the mind-set of white Mississippians very well and has fought racism in the South and at the University of Mississippi since the 1960s. Being asked to design this course was just the sort of chance he had been waiting for.

The University of Mississippi, or "Ole Miss," as it is affectionately called, is one of the most racist institutions in the South. It has played key roles in defending the Confederacy, fighting Reconstruction, and maintaining segregation. In 1963, it took more than 30,000 federal troops to enforce the admission of Ole Miss's first African American student, James Meredith. White residents of Oxford, the town that Bob Dylan memorialized, came to campus armed and organized when the court order was issued to admit Meredith, and several journalists and soldiers were killed before the rioting was over. Even after this, the university administration continued actively to oppose integration. Ten years passed before faculty could speak up in favor of integration without losing their jobs. To this day, Ole Miss keeps its reputation across the South as a school where whites can go and be openly racist, as I remember vividly from a conversation I had with the homecoming queen in my high school in Florida who decided to attend college there. At Ole Miss, rebel flags wave at sports events and hang from dormitory windows; the university band plays "Dixie" as a fight song.[4] For obvious reasons, then, in a state in which African Americans make up nearly half the population, the black student body at Ole Miss is still under 10 percent. In this environment, to teach against racism in a mandatory course was surely to engage the struggle in the belly of the beast.

Harrington's strategy was to envelop an antiracist and antisexist message in a course ostensibly organized around the topic of university life, what a university is, and what an intellectual community needs in order to flourish. In this way, the message could be framed as a series of do's rather than don'ts. For example, maintaining a university with high standards is in every student's interest; to protect and develop such a university, students need to value and respect cultural diversity and gender equality. The university traditions of intellectual diversity and academic freedom require sufficient tolerance of diversity so that critical debate can develop. The textbook for the course, *Traditions and Changes: The University of Mississippi in Principle and in Practice*, thus presents three full chapters before the subject of racism is broached. Both the textbook and the course, then, are as strategically thought out and organized as the workshops in *White Awareness* and as carefully directed in their goal of producing lasting changes in the thinking and behavior of whites.

Harrington did not shy away from providing an accurate history of racism at Ole Miss, although the text acknowledges the pain and shame these accounts invoke. He gives and assesses the entire history of the institution, so that students have the historical facts concerning the university's legacy of official support for white supremacy. Harrington provides a revised narrative of U.S. history and southern history as well, but here he adopts a two-sided approach. U.S. cultural and political traditions are argued to have a dual character, on the one hand institutionalizing inequality and on the other hand valuing and slowly extending equality. The overall argument is that there *is* something positive from the past to draw from, but it is a potential not yet fully realized. White Mississippians will benefit overall from developing a cooperative spirit with black Mississippians in order to advance common goals, but this can come about only through fully acknowledging and overcoming racism. Harrington hopefully declares that from the "disaster of the human spirit in Mississippi" arises "the opportunity for a phoenix redemption" (1996, 141). The significant diversity of the state can be a rich resource from which to build a stronger society that is a "shining symbol to a nation and to a world battling the same demons we can exorcize" (141).

Traditions and Changes has significant limitations. It offers no class analysis, nor does it explore any issues of reparations or redistribution of economic resources. The projection of a shared interest glosses over real class disparities that are likely to continue to be disproportionately distributed between whites and blacks, even though many whites are also poor in the state. This is, however, a course for freshmen at the University of Mississippi, and its task is to move students from an initial starting position that is comparatively low.

It is interesting to note the different strategies offered here and in *Race Traitor*. The latter makes its appeal to whites by arguing that racist practices really served only the interests of the rich, and thus that poor whites were used as dupes to support racism. Although this strategy supplies a needed class analysis of the history

of racism, it does not help whites think about how to overcome their own connection to a racist past. It simply says, "You are not really connected to that racist
past." But in the South, white culture has been more widely supportive of racist
practices like segregation and discrimination and racist symbols, such as the Rebel
flag and "Dixie." Whites gain benefits other than economic ones from racism, such
as a collective sense of superiority and entitlement. Reductive arguments that
portray these as merely bourgeois scams cannot make sense of the complicated
realities and psychological pull of white myths.

In relation to this issue, it is interesting that both *Race Traitor* and *Traditions
and Changes* reject multiculturalism. Harrington defines multiculturalism as the
premise that "all cultural differences are equal in value," contrasting it with cultural diversity, which promotes "tolerance for cultural differences, leaving open the
question of which are desirable or superior" (1996, 38). In Mississippi, an antiracist
cannot argue for the equal rights of diverse cultural traditions without undercutting
the ability to argue against continued veneration of the Rebel flag.

Thus, despite its limitations, I found *Traditions and Changes* to provide a
helpful model for acknowledging white complicity in racism and the need to repudiate key aspects of white identity within an overall project that seeks to develop a
collective transformation toward a nonracist white identity. Utilizing the positive
traditions of critical, open, and democratic reflection, university studies 101 and its
textbook aim to create a series of open-ended discussions that will get white students to contribute in transforming their university, their community, and in the
process, themselves.

White Double Consciousness

In this chapter I have wanted to suggest that there is an ongoing but rarely named
struggle among whites as a result of liberation movements and the declining
plausibility of white supremacist narratives. Antiracist theorists need to acknowledge
that the struggle occurs not only in relation to conscious choices and objectively
determinable economic interests but in relation to psychic processes of identity
formation, which means that rational arguments against racism will not be sufficient
to make a progressive move. As whites lose their psychic social status, and as processes of positive identity construction are derailed, intense anxiety, hysteria, shame,
and resulting forms of projection and displacement are occurring. The most likely
solution to this will be, of course, for new processes to develop that simply shift
targets to create new categories of the abject through which to inflate collective self-
esteem, and this is already happening in revivals of nativism, the vilification of illegal
immigrants, a state-sponsored homophobia, and so on. In other words, if it can no
longer be maintained that whites, collectively, are better than nonwhites, collectively, just by virtue of race, supremacy can be reorganized on the basis of citizenship, patriotism, family values, Christian practice, or other features that most
whites can believe they share.

Such developments may prompt the question: why maintain white identity
at all, given that any group identity will be based on exclusion and an implicit
superiority, and given that whiteness itself has been historically constituted as

supremacist since its inception? However, dissolving white identity is not something that critical theorists can do by fiat. We are simply participant observers of social forces who try to develop analyses and critiques, but we are not the makers of history. Moreover, I am doubtful that race categories will wither away anytime soon. The weight of too much history is sedimented in these marked bodies with inscriptions that are very deep, and the current global military conflicts are so racialized that the racial contract, as Charles Mills perceptively named it, seems fully alive and well.

Rather than attempting to transcend whiteness as a first step, it seems to me we are witnessing a period of reinscription in which what we see when we see race or conceptualize whiteness is being redescribed and reunderstood, of course under conditions of contestation. We might take a lesson here from Paul Gilroy's study *The Black Atlantic: Modernity and Double Consciousness* (1993), which traces outlines of an identity configuration of a multinational black culture that does not seem to rely on an objectification (or abjectification) process involving repudiation and denigration of some Other or even all Others. Gilroy's characterization of black Atlantic identity, at least in this work, portrays it as working more through an invocation of a shared history and shared present cultural expressive forms than through a shared discrete set of substantive or essential Afrocentric elements that require contrasting, excluded alternatives.[6] This approach allows for an open-ended future transformation while it acknowledges the significance and even a certain coherence of the present identity.

Daniel Boyarin and Jonathan Boyarin have done similar work in relation to Jewish identity, invoking an idealized Diaspora identity that is not based on an exclusivist claim to territoriality but on "a perpetual, creative, diasporic tension" (Boyarin and Boyarin 1995, 326). Their project of finding grounds for a Jewish identity that do not involve racism, ethnocentrism, or supremacist tenets is analogous to the project of rearticulating whiteness without racism. And using the example of sexism, they also raise another interesting point:

> If overcoming sexism involves the breaking up of the community of males, does it necessarily imply the breaking up of the community of females? And does this, then, not entail a breaking up of community, *tout court*? Putting it another way, are we not simply imposing a more coercive universal? On the other hand, if indeed the very existence of the dominant group is dependent on domination, if identity is always formed in a master-slave relationship, is the price not too high? What we wish to struggle for, theoretically, is a notion of identity in which there are only slaves but no masters. (323)

In order to conceptualize a nondominating and antisupremacist identity, both the Boyarins and Gilroy avoid essentialist constructions of identity by relying heavily on a shared history, but this is precisely what is problematic for whites. And there is no long history that whites can draw from as Jewish theorists can that is prior to domination: the history of white identity, just as is the case with black identity, is coterminous with European colonialism.

Perhaps white identity needs to develop its own version of "double consciousness," to name as such that two-sided sense of the past and the future that can be found in aspects of the works on whiteness discussed in this chapter. A white double consciousness would not involve the move between white and black subjectivities or black and American perspectives, as Du Bois and Fanon developed the notion. Instead, for whites, double consciousness requires an ever-present acknowledgment of the historical legacy of white identity constructions in the persistent structures of inequality and exploitation, as well as a newly awakened memory of the many white traitors to white privilege who have struggled to contribute to the building of an inclusive human community. The Michelangelos stand beside the Christopher Columbuses, and Michael Moores next to the Pat Buchanans. The legacy of European-based cultures is a complicated one. It is better approached through a two-sided analysis than through an argument that obscures either its positive or negative aspects. White representations within multiculturalism must then be similarly dialectical, retrieving from obscurity the history of white antiracism even while providing a detailed account of colonialism and its many cultural effects. This, then, is the challenge: to transform the basis of collective self-respect from global, racial vanguardism to a dedicated commitment to end racism.

FOUR

LATINO/A PARTICULARITY

Latinos and the Categories of Race

Apparently, Latinos are "taking over."[1] With news that Latinos have become the largest minority group in the United States, the public airwaves are filled with concerned voices about the impact that a non-English dominant, Catholic, non-white, largely poor population will have on "American" identity. But aside from the hysteria, Latino identity poses some authentically new questions for the standard way in which minority identities are conceptualized. Are Latinos a race, an ethnicity, or some combination? What does it mean to have hybridity as the foundation of an identity, as is the case for mestizos and most Latinos? The term "Latino" signifies people from an entire continent, subcontinent, and several large islands, with diverse racial, national, ethnic, religious, and linguistic aspects to their identity. Given all this internal diversity, is "Latino" a meaningful identity at all?

Latino identity is, with few exceptions, a visible identity, for all its variability, and I will argue that unless we pay close attention to the way in which Latino identity operates as a visible identity in public, social spaces, our analyses of its social meanings and political effects will be compromised. In the following three chapters, I will address three issues that Latino identity raises, issues that have political ramifications but that also require us to think about the philosophical assumptions at work behind common ideas about race and ethnicity. First, what is the relationship between Latino identity and racial categories? Second, how do Latinos fit into, and challenge, the black/white binary thinking about race that has long dominated public discourse in the United States? And third, what does it mean to have a mixed identity, for Latinos or for other mixed race groups? Throughout, we will have to pay close attention to the especially significant heterogeneity of this particular population. Does such diversity threaten identity or does it reveal that identity has never presumed uniformity?

Only recently has the concept of pan-Latino, or generic Hispanic, identity overtaken the older identity monikers of "Cuban," "Mexican," "Puerto Rican," and so on in significant national discourses across the United States. For Latinos themselves, Juan Flores argues that the decision whether to use the broad "Latino" or the more specific national terms is not an either/or but a both/and that can be determined by context.(2000). But what is it to be "Latino"? More than the national interpellations like Cuban or Mexican, Latino identity generally signifies one's situatedness outside of Latin America. This spatial referentiality brings the concept, the identity, and the experience under the domain of North American symbolic systems and conceptual schemas to a greater extent, which is one reason some give to reject the label entirely.

Like many others, I am doubtful we can hold our collective breath and make it go away. The discourse in the United States (as well as elsewhere in the global North) about encroaching majority minorities tends toward aggregation, and the sometimes hysterical concern about the Spanish language, national loyalty, and non-Anglo cultural traditions makes the differences among Mexican, Puerto Ricans, Dominicans, and Cubans less important than the similarities (see, e.g., Huntington 2004). But the concept of "Latino" identity is not coming solely from Anglos. It is no longer the case that Puerto Ricans dominate Latin New York, or that Cubans have total hegemony in Miami, or even that Mexicans totally dominate Los Angeles. Other immigrants from South America, Central America, and the Spanish-speaking Caribbean are now sizable enough in numbers to make their cultures and their accents widely apparent. Thus, as Juan Flores says, " 'Latinos in New York' no longer rhymes with Puerto Rican," which means that the more inclusive term "Latino" has more real relevance and a real or objective referent (1996, 171).

Despite the objective nature of Latino identity as just explained, there can be no decontextualized, final, or essential account of what the identity is, given the social basis and the dynamic, historical nature of racialized and ethnic identities. My question then can be formulated as a project of social ontology in the following way: what is the best, or most apt, account of Latino identity's relationship to race that makes the most sense of the current political and social realities within which we must negotiate our social environment?

Although I am interested here in the politics of identity, that is, the political effects of various accounts of identity in and on popular consciousness, both among Latinos and among Anglos, my principal concern is at the level of experience, ideology, and meaning rather than the attendant political rights and implications that may be associated with identity. As will be seen, much of the debate over Latinas/os and race weave both strategic considerations (a concern with political effects) and metaphysical considerations (a concern with the most apt description) together. There are two reasons for this. First is that strategic proposals for the way a community should represent itself or should be represented cannot work if there is no connection whatsoever to lived experience or to the common meanings that are prominent in the relevant discourses. Thus, the strategic efficacy of political proposals are dependent on correct assessments of social ontological realities. But, second, the question of what is the most apt description of those ontological realities is not as clear-cut as some philosophers might suppose. This is because the concepts of "race" and "Latino" admit of different meanings and are under heavy contestation. Any given descriptive account will presuppose some judgment calls about which meanings are most salient and plausible, and these judgment calls will be underdetermined by usage, history, science, or even phenomenological description of experience. And in making these judgment calls, we must look to the future and not just the past. In other words, given that we are participating in the *construction* of meanings, we must carefully consider their likely real-world effects.

Three Options

The question of Latino identity's relationship to the conventional categories of race that have been historically dominant in the United States is a particularly vexing one. To put it straightforwardly, we simply don't fit. Racialized identities in the North have long connoted homogeneity and easily visible identifying features, but this doesn't apply to Latinos in the United States, nor even to any one national subset, such as Cuban Americans or Puerto Ricans. We have no homogeneous culture, we come in every conceivable color, and identities such as "mestizo" signify the very absence of boundaries.

Moreover, the corresponding practices of racialization in the United States — such as racial border control, legal sanctions on cross-racial marriage, and the multitude of demands for racial self-identification on nearly every application form from day care to college admissions — are also relatively unfamiliar south of the border. Angel R. Oquendo recounts that before he could even take the SAT in Puerto Rico he was asked to identify himself racially. "I was caught off guard," he says. "I had never thought of myself in terms of race" (1998, 61). Fortunately, the SAT included "Puerto Rican" among the choices of "race," and Oquendo was spared what he called a "profound existential dilemma." Even while many Latinos consider color a relevant factor for marriage, and antiblack and anti-indigenous racism persists in Latin America, the institutional and ideological forms that racism has taken in the Latin South are generally not analogous to those in the Anglo North, focusing on shades of difference rather than sharply divided categories. This is why many of us find our identity as well as our social status changing as we step off the plane or cross the river: race suddenly becomes an all-important aspect of our identity, and sometimes our racial identity dramatically changes in ways over which it feels we have no control.

There are at least three general options possible in the face of this transcontinental experiential dissonance as a way of characterizing the relationship between Latino identity and race. The first option is to refuse a racialized designation and understand "Latino" to signify an ethnicity (or perhaps a related group of ethnicities). This would avoid the problem of racial diversity within Latino communities and yet recognize the cultural, social, and political links among Latinos in the North. Theorists such as Angelo Corlett defend this option on the grounds that the concept of ethnicity builds on cultural practices, customs, language, religion, and history, rather than the specious biological connotations of race (2003, 6–17). A second option would resist the ethnic paradigm on the grounds that, whatever the historical basis of Latino identity is, living in the context of North America we have become a racialized population, and we need a self-understanding that will accurately assess our portrayal here. A third option, adopted by neoconservatives and neoliberals, is to attempt to assimilate to the individualist ideology of the United States both in body and in mind, and reject the salience of group identities a priori.

In my view, none of these responses is fully adequate, though some have more problems than others. In regard to the second option, it is hard to see how the racial diversity among Latinos could be fairly represented in any unified concept of race. And in regard to the third option, the visible features of many Latinos makes it doubtful that they could succeed in transcending racialization or group stereotypes. On the face of it, the first option—understanding Latino identity as an ethnic identity—seems to make the most sense for a variety of reasons that I will explore in this chapter. This option could allow for more internal heterogeneity and resist the racializing that brings racism as well as often mischaracterizing our own sense of self. However, I will ultimately argue that the "ethnic option" is not fully adequate to the contemporary social realities we face, and may inhibit the development of useful political strategies for our diverse communities. Primarily my argument in this chapter will take the form of a negative: the ethnic option is not adequate. Developing a fully adequate alternative is beyond my ability, but the very failure of the ethnic option will establish some of the necessary criteria for such an alternative.

Before any of these options can be fairly assessed, we need to begin by understanding the specificity of Latino identity.

Latino Specificity

Irish, Italian, Polish, Ukrainian, and other so-called "white ethnic" communities have organized cultural events on the basis of their identities at least since the 1960s, with the cooperation of police and city councils across the country. Certainly for the Irish and the Italians, this movement of ethnic assertion has been precisely motivated by their discrimination and vilification throughout much of U.S. history, a vilification that has sometimes taken racialized forms. Thus, there are some clear parallels between Latinos and white ethnics: many have immigrant family histories, and many today share a cultural pride and desire to maintain some cultural traditions, perhaps motivated by an awareness of historical if not ongoing discrimination. So why does the growth of a visible, politically assertive Latino population so often elicit such strong negative reactions and a flurry of political analysis about its likely degenerative effects on the general society?

If I may be permitted a gross overgeneralization, many European Americans are afraid of strongly felt ethnic identities, but only certain ones. There is a different attitude among whites in general toward *nonwhite* public celebrations of ethnic identity and toward those of white ethnic celebrations. And this is, I suspect, because it is one thing to say to the dominant culture, "You have been unfairly prejudiced against me," as southern European ethnicities might say; and quite another to say, "You have stolen my lands and enslaved my people and through these means created the wealth of your country," as African Americans, Latinos, and Native Americans might say. The latter message is harder to hear; it challenges the basic legitimating narratives of the United States' formation and global status, and it understandably elicits the worry, "What will be the full extent of their demands?" Of course, all of the cultural programs that celebrate African, indigenous, or Latino heritage do not make these explicit claims. But in a sense, the claims do not need to *be* explicit: any reference to slavery or indigenous peoples or Chicano or Puerto Rican history implies challenges to the legitimating narrative of the United States, and any expression of solidarity among such groups elicits concern, consciously or unconsciously, about the political and economic demands such groups may eventually make, even if they are not made now.

This is surely part of what is going on when European Americans express puzzlement about the importance attached to identity by non–European Americans, when young whites complain about African Americans sitting together in their cafeterias or wanting to live together in college dormitories, or when both left and liberal political theorists, such as Gitlin, Schlesinger, and others, jump to the conclusion that a strong sense of group solidarity and its resultant "identity politics" among people of color in this country will fracture the body politic and disable our democracy (see Gitlin 1995; Schlesinger 1992; Elshtain 1997; Hochschild 1996).

As I discussed earlier, a prominent explanation given for these attachments to identity, attachments that are considered otherwise inexplicable, is that there is opportunism at work, among leaders if not among the rank and file, to secure government "handouts" or claim special rights. However, there are two problems with this assumption. Identities themselves require interpretation, and thus their political implications will be subject to contestation. Moreover, celebrations of Latino identity such as Puerto Rican Day parades or Caribbean festivals are venues for the possibility of cultural expression no different from any sports event or holiday that allows for the public expression of European American cultural identity: the ubiquitous playing of "We Will Rock You," the ending of each Yankees game with a recording of Sinatra singing "New York, New York," the holding of Easter egg hunts at public parks. But Latino-themed events are *marked* in a way that white cultural traditions are not—the latter are seen as simply "American" or "Christian" rather than white American or Anglo Christian. Whites who enjoy a surfeit of opportunities for their own cultural expression often do not realize this privilege, and then feel mystified and threatened by the cultural expressions of other groups. Given this mystification and feeling of amorphous threat, assumptions of opportunism become plausible.

Assumptions about the opportunism behind identity politics also operate on the basis of the following understanding of the recent historical past: in the 1960s, some groups clamored for recognition of their identities; they resisted and critiqued the cultural assimilationism of liberal politics, and they argued that state institutions should give these identities public recognition. According to this narrative, *first* we had identity politics asserting the political importance of these identities, *and then* we had (coerced) state recognition of them. But denigrated identity designations have *originated* with and been enforced by the state in U.S. history. Obviously, it is the U.S. state and U.S. courts that initially insisted on the overwhelming salience of some racial and ethnic identities, to the exclusion of rights to suffrage, education, property, marital and custody rights, immigration, and so on. Denigrated groups are trying to *reverse* this process; they are not the initiators of it. It seems to me that they have two aims: (1) to publicly valorize identities that are derided by the dominant culture, and (2) to have their own hand at re-presenting these identities and interpreting their political implications.

The U.S. pan-Latino identity is perhaps the newest and most important identity that has emerged in the recent period. The concept of a pan-Latino identity is not new in Latin America: Simon Bolivar called for it nearly 200 years ago as a strategy of anticolonialism but also because it provided a name for the "new peoples" that had emerged from the conquest. And influential leaders like José Martí and Che Guevara followed Bolivar in promoting a broad Latin American solidarity. It is important to note that populations "on the ground" have not often resonated with these grand visions, and that national political and economic leaders continue to obstruct regional accords and trade agreements that might enhance solidarity. But the point remains that the invocation of a pan-Latino identity does not actually originate in the North.

Only much more recently is it the case that some Latino political groups in the North have organized on a pan-Latino basis, although Latino politics here has usually been organized along national lines, for example as Puerto Ricans or Chicanos, and these only within specific communities or sectors (such as students). But what is especially new, and what is being largely foisted on us from the outside, is the representation of a pan-Latino identity in the dominant North American media, and it is this representation which we want to have a hand in shaping. Marketing agencies have discovered/created a marketing niche for the "generic" Latino. And Latino-owned marketing agencies and advertising agencies are working on the construction of this identity as much as anyone, though of course in ways dominated by strategic interests or what Habermas calls purposive rationality (see Dávila 2001). There are also more and more cultural representations of Latinos in the dominant media and in government productions such as the Census. Thus, the solicitous concern that U.S. Latinos have with our identity is not spontaneous or originating entirely or even mostly from within our communities; neither is the ongoing representation of our identity something we can easily ignore (see, e.g., Flores and Yudice 1990).

Contexts Spatial and Temporal

Social identities, whether racial or ethnic, are dynamic. In their study of what they call "racial formations," Michael Omi and Howard Winant argue that "racial categories and the meanings of race are given concrete expression by the specific social relations and historical context in which they are embedded" (1986, 60). Racial concepts and identity categories are constantly facing forms of resistance and contestation that transform both their effects and their effective meaning. Clearly, this is the case with ethnic as well as racial identities, as the transformations of "Latino" indicate. As social constructions imposed on variable experiential facts, they exist with no stable referent or essential core. This is not to say that they do not refer, but that what they refer to is dynamic. There is, moreover, a feedback loop between referential descriptions, personal experience, and political resistance. Because racial and ethnic identities in particular are also the site of conflict over political power and economic resources, they are especially volatile. Any analysis of Latino identity, then, must chart historical trends and contextual influences.

Since the immigration law was passed in 1965 that ended the quotas on immigration from South America, Central America, and the Caribbean, millions of Latinos have entered the United States from various countries, diversifying previously dominant Chicano, Puerto Rican, and Cuban communities. As the immigrant communities settle in, younger generations develop cultural practices, musical tastes, political orientations, and even religious beliefs that differ from those of their parents, and in some cases are no longer Spanish-dominant or practicing Catholics. So in one sense diversity has increased as new immigrations continue to diversify present communities and as new generations of younger Latinos develop new formations of cultural identity. But in another sense diversity has decreased as Latino immigrants experience common forms of discrimination and chauvinism in the United States and an increasingly generic cultural and racialized interpellation.

In the 1960s, U.S. state agencies began to disseminate the ethnic label "Hispanic" as the proper term for identifying all people of Latin American and even Spanish descent (Oboler 1995, xiii). So today we have a population of 30 million or so "Hispanics" in the United States. The mass media, entertainment, and advertising industries have increasingly addressed this large population as if it were a coherent community (Mato 1997, 2). Suzanne Oboler's study suggests that this generic identity category feels especially socially constructed to many of the people named by it, given that it is not how they self-identified previously (1995, chap. 1). Oboler asks, somewhat rhetorically: "Are marketers merely taking advantage of an existing 'group' as a potentially lucrative target population? Or are their advertising strategies in fact helping to 'design' the group, 'invent' its traditions, and hence 'create' this homogeneous ethnic group?" (13). One might well be concerned that adapting to any such pan-Latino identity as constructed by dominant institutions — whether economic or political ones — represents a capitulation, or is simply the inevitable effect of what Foucault called "governmentality."

However, much of the debate over this interpellation among those named by it does not so much critique the fact of its social construction or even the fact that its genesis lies in government and marketing agencies, but focuses instead on its political implications and its coherence with lived experience, for example, the way in which it disallows multiplicity or the way in which it erases national allegiance. In this way, the debate shifts to a more productive set of concerns, it seems to me. I witnessed an interesting exchange on some of these points at the "Hispanics: Cultural Locations" conference held at the University of San Francisco in 1997. Ofelia Schutte, a leading Latina philosopher, presented a paper which argued that a pan-U.S. Latino identity may be a means to disaffiliate us from our nations of birth or ancestry, nations that maybe invaded or otherwise harmed by the U.S. government. Thus, thinking of ourselves primarily as U.S. Latinos rather than, say, Panamanians or Salvadorans may work to dislodge or weaken feelings of loyalty to countries outside the U.S. borders. In the discussion period after her paper, one member of the audience, Professor of Spanish Susan Sanchez-Casal argued strongly that, as a half-Spanish, half–Puerto Rican woman who grew up among Chicanos in southern California, she had found the emergence of a pan-Latino identity a welcome relief. Although she recognized the dangers that Ofelia was describing, identifying herself simply as Latina allowed her to avoid having to make complicated choices between the various components of her identity, and it helpfully named her experience of connection with a multiplicity of Latino communities. I myself resonated with Ofelia's concerns, having met Latinos in the U.S. Army who participated in the 1989 invasion of Panama. But given that I have lived most of my life in the United States and grew up in Florida among mostly Cubans, I could also understand Susan's point: in some cases, "Latina" is not only the easiest identity to use—it also feels like an apt description.

Another important political consideration in regard to homogenizing Latino identities is that this can allow those members of the group who are themselves less disadvantaged to benefit from affirmative action and other forms of economic redress that have been created mainly for (and often mainly fought for by) Chicanos and Puerto Ricans, the more disadvantaged constituencies. This has been a clear effect of the generic label "Hispanic," and it is the reason that many institutions will use more specific designations, such as Mexican American and Puerto Rican, in their affirmative action policies. However, here the problem is that one cannot assume that no South Americans or other Central Americans in the United States have suffered racial and ethnic discrimination. Many are not able to pass as white, even if they were to try. Since the Mariel boat lift in the 1980s, even Miami Cubans are no longer almost all light skinned and middle or upper class. Given the class, ethnic, and racial heterogeneity of every Latin American and Caribbean country, one cannot exclude entire countries from measures aimed at redressing discrimination without excluding many who are marked as inferior north of the border. In my experience, some individuals who have not experienced much discrimination (for one reason or another, e.g., looks, class, lack of accent) will remove themselves from consideration for scholarships or other programs aimed at redressing anti-Latino injustices. I think more of this goes on than some imagine, but it is very difficult to tell how effective such self-policing measures can be on the whole.[2]

Although some programs do specify nationalities in an effort to avoid the overly homogenizing effects of a pan-Latino identity, both government and marketing agencies are increasingly relying on the latter. And, as both Dávila and Mato have argued in separate studies, the marketing and advertising agencies are not simply forcing us to use labels that have no real purchase on our lives. Rather, they are participating in a new subject construction that affects how Latinos think about and experience our identity and our interrelatedness to other groups of Latinos to whom we may have felt little kinship with before. Mato points out that the television corporation Univisión, which is jointly owned by U.S. and Latin American companies, is exposing its viewers to a wide array of programming from diverse countries and regions. In this way, "Univisión is participating in the social construction of an imagined community" (1997, 2). To say that an identity is socially constructed is not to say that it does not refer to anything in reality, but that what it refers to is a contingent product of social practices rather than a natural kind. And even beyond the experience of community produced by the media, the exchange I described above at the "Hispanics" conference indicates that because of migrations both intra- and international, and because of cross-nationality parenting relationships, the pan-Latino identity corresponds to at least some contemporary Latinos' lived experience.

Latin America itself is undoubtedly the most diverse continent in the world, which in turn creates extreme racial and ethnic diversity *within* Latino communities.

By U.S. categories, there are black, brown, white, East Asian, South Asian, Jewish, Arab, Native American Latinos, and more. (George Lopez jokes that this shows that Latinos will sleep with *anybody.*) There are many Latinos from the southern cone whose families are of recent European origin, a large number of Latinos from the western coastal areas of Latin America whose families came from Asia, and of course a large number of Latinos whose lineage is entirely indigenous to the Americas or entirely African. The majority of Latinos in North America and South America are no doubt the product of a mix of two or more of these groups. And being mixed is true, as Jorge Gracia reminds us, even of the so-called "Hispanics" who are direct descendants of Spain and Portugal, given those countries' multiethnic and multiracial past as part of the Ottoman Empire. And it is true as well of many or most of the people identified as black or *moreno,* as is the case in the United States.

Latin American Categories

Latin Americans are thus generally categorized "racially" in the following way: white (which often involves a double deceit: a claim to pure Spanish descent, very rare, and a claim that pure Spanish descent is purely white or European, also very rare); black (meaning wholly or mostly of African descent, usually sub-Saharan); Indian (meaning having some or mostly Amerindian descent); and mixed (which is sometimes divided into subcategories *mestizo, mulatto, cholito,* etc.) with the mixed category always enjoying a majority. Asians are often entirely left off the list, even though their numbers in several countries are significant.

Different countries vary these main racial designations, however. During a recent weekend festival for "Latino Heritage Month" in Syracuse, New York, Latinos of different nationalities provided information about their countries for passers-by, which included statistics culled from government sources on what in every case was called the country's "ethnic makeup." Racial categories of identity were given *within* this larger rubric of ethnic makeup, suggesting an equation between ethnicity and race. For example, in the Dominican Republic the ethnic makeup is reported to consist of 73 percent mixed, 16 percent white, 11 percent black. In Ecuador the categories are listed as mestizo, Indian, Spanish, and black. In Chile there is a single category called "European and mestizo" which makes up 95 percent of the population. In Cuba we get categories of mulatto, which is 51 percent of the population; and we also get categories of white, black, and Chinese. In Bolivia the breakdown is between Quechua (25 percent), Aymara (30 percent), mestizo (30 percent), and white (15 percent).

One is reminded by this list of the encyclopedia invented by Borges which divides dogs into such categories as "[a] belonging to the Emperor . . . [b] tame . . . [c] drawn with a very fine camel hair brush . . . and [d] having just broken the water pitcher" (quoted in Foucault 1970, xv). There is no internally consistent or coherent theory of ethnic or racial identity underlying the diversity of categorizations. Under the rubric of ethnicity are included a mix of cultural, national, and racial groups, from Spanish, to Quechua, to white. The only point that seems to be consistent throughout is that the category black is the only category that is invariably racialized—that is, it is presented as black or mulatto and never as "West

Indian" or "African." Interestingly, the category white is also often racialized, though it is sometimes replaced with "European" or "Spanish." I would suggest that there is a strong relationship between these two facts. That is, it becomes important to use the category white and to self-identify as white when the category black is present in order to establish one's clear demarcation, and out of concern that a category like "mestizo" might be allowed to include black people. The category white is also used to separate out so-called whites from "Indians," a category that bears racialized meanings in Latin America and negative associations similar to the associations with African Americans in the United States.

Blackness of course signifies differently in Latin America; thus it is not likely that a typical white American landing in Santo Domingo would look around himself and think that only 11 percent of the population is black. However, it seems clear that the striking use of the term "black" for all people of African descent, employed in a schema that uses cultural and national markers like Spanish and European for other groups, is an indication of antiblack racism. Black people so designated are reduced to skin color as if this were their primary characteristic rather than some self-created marker like nationality, language, culture, or (if slavery removed the salience of these first three), at least geographical genealogy. One may have been born into a culture and language not of one's own choosing, but these are still more indicative of human agency than is any classification by phenotype. From this, one might argue that replacing "black" with another ethnicity category, such as Caribbean or West African, might help equalize and dignify the identities.

The category Indian, however, even though it might initially seem more of an ethnicity than a race (since it is not merely the name of a color), has primarily a racial meaning, given that one cannot tell anything about language, mode of life, religion, or specific origin from the term "Indian." Also, the term often carries as many negative associations as does the term "black" in non-indigenous communities of discourse. Here, one might argue that disaggregating the category Indian would be helpful. If the primary meaning connoted by the word "Indian" is a kind of racial meaning, then the use of "Quechua" and "Aymara," "Mayan," and so on reduces the significance of the racialized connotations of the identity, subordinating those to the specificity of linguistic and cultural markers.

Despite all this variety and heterogeneity, when Latinos enter the United States, we are often homogenized into one overarching Latino or Hispanic identity. Latinas who don't look like "Maria" from Sesame Street or who don't eat spicy food often encounter Anglo skepticism about our identity (even though most Latin American foods are rather mild). This expected generic Hispanicity is not, as Jorge Gracia reminds me, actually homogeneous. That is, in European American eyes, "Hispanic" identity does not carry the same connotations in every part of the United States. Gracia explains: "In Miami it means Cuban; in New York City it means Puerto Rican; and in the southwest it means Mexican. So in California I am supposed to have as my native food tacos, in New York City, *arroz con gandules*, and in Miami, *arroz con frijoles negros!*"[3]

Still, there is one feature that persists across this variety of "generic" Latino or Hispanic identities, and that is that our identity in the United States, whether or not it is homogenized, is quite often presented as a racial identity. Anthropologist

Gloria A. Marshall reported in 1969 that appellations such as "Spanish," "Cuban," and "Puerto Rican," are used in many U.S. contexts "as if they were equivalent to the racial designations currently in use" (1993, 119). A recent report in the *Chronicle of Higher Education* illustrates how such equivalences continue to occur. Differences in average SAT scores were reported in the following way: "The average verbal scores *by race* were: white, 526; black, 434; Asian-American, 498; American Indian, 480; Mexican-American, 453; Puerto Rican, 452; and other Hispanic students, 461."[4] So again, like Angel Oquendo, we find that "Puerto Rican" is a racial identity, and a different one at that from the "race" of Mexican Americans. Whereas in the categorizations I just analyzed from Latin America, racial categories are subsumed within an overall account of "ethnic makeup," in this example from the United States, ethnic categories are subsumed within an overall account of racial difference. But in both cases, race and ethnicity are all but equated.

"The Ethnicity Paradigm"

Latinos in the United States have responded to their racialization in a variety of ways. One response, still ongoing, has been to claim either racial neutrality or whiteness, two claims that end up with the same implications. The scandal is that 80 percent of Puerto Ricans in the 2000 census self-identified as white, apparently thinking that, if they are going to have to be racialized, whiteness is the race they want. Other Latinos have literally campaigned to be called white. Anita Allen reported in 1994 that the largest petitioning group that had thus far requested changes for the 2000 U.S. Census was the Association of White Hispanics, who were agitating for that designation to be on the Census form. In the self-interested scramble for social status, many Latinos perceived correctly where the advantages lay (for further analysis of this phenomenon and its history, see Darity et al. 2003; Santiago-Valles 1996). But at best, such a strategy would have to be specified for a Latino subgroup, as the Association of White Hispanics understood, and would not be applicable to the majority of Latinos. Claiming whiteness for oneself does not work unless there is public acceptance of such a designation.

Another response has been to use the discourse of racialization as it exists in the United States to self-identify as brown but a in positive rather than derogatory way. Oquendo, after having overcome his existential dilemma, supports this strategy. He says: "Attacking racial exploitation and making amends for a long history of racial oppression requires taking the existing categories and turning them against their original purpose. The conceptual structure that singled out people in order to undermine them must now be used to empower them" (1998, 67). As examples of this approach, Chicanos in the August Twenty-ninth Movement and in the student group MECHA, as well as the primarily *puertorriqueño* Young Lords in Chicago and New York, at times adopted and adapted the concept of a *brown* racial identity to signify solidarity and resistance, as with the Brown Berets.

But neither the moniker "white" nor "brown" works across the board for a pan-Latino identity (or even for the specific nationalities they want to represent). Many argue that what better unites Latinos both across and even within our specific national cultures is not race or phenotype but precisely those features associated with culture: language, religious and familial traditions, cultural values, musical styles, and characteristics of comportment. The ethnicity paradigm denies that race applies to Latino identity because to be Latino is to belong to an ethnic group that encompasses different nationalities and races within it (see, e.g., Corlett 2003; Klor de Alva and West 1996). The U.S. Census supported this paradigm when it listed its Latino category as an ethnic category in 2000, with no Latino option listed under race.

Whether Latinos want to work with or reject racial categories depends not just on their visible features but also on their political orientation and history. Puerto Ricans have a long history of U.S. colonization, which imposed racialization even before they left the island, and this may account for their comparatively quick adaptation to the "race rules" in the United States. Latinos from countries without this experience of intensive colonization are more surprised by being racially designated when they come here and may be more resistant (see, e.g., Grosfoguel and Georas 1996). There is certainly a powerful sentiment among many Latinos toward resisting the imposition of U.S. racializations and U.S. categories of identity. Luis Angel Toro thus calls on us to *"abandon the outdated racial ideology embodied in* [the Office of Management and Budget's Statistical] *Directive no. 15 and replace it with questions designed to determine an individual's membership in a socially constructed, cultural subgroup"* (1998, 58). It is not as if the system of racial classification here has benefited anyone except the white majority. As Jorge Klor de Alva provocatively put it to Cornel West in a conversation in *Harper's*, "What advantage has it been, Cornel, for blacks to identify as blacks?" (Klor de Alva and West 1996, 56). Although Oquendo supports a political reformulation of racial categories, he rejects the imposition of the United States' black/white binary on Latinos and argues against the use of such racial terms as "black Hispanics" and "white Hispanics" on the grounds that these categories "project onto the Latino/a community a divisive racial dualism that, much as it may pervade U.S. society, is alien to that community" (1998, 60).

Just because we are located within the United States does not mean we must accept existing categories: we can challenge and change them. Moreover, our identity is about culture and nationality rather than race, according to many Latinos. The majority of Puerto Ricans may have chosen white over black on a racial list, but their first form of self-identification, as Clara Rodriguez has shown, is as Puerto Rican (1989). However, in the United States, cultural, national, ethnic, religious, and other forms of identification are constantly subordinated to race. So Afro-Cubans, English-speaking West Indians, and Afro-Brazilians are grouped as "black" in ways that often counter people's own felt sense of identity or primary group alliances. Race trumps culture, and culture is sometimes even seen as a simple outgrowth of race. Part of this is a descriptive argument to the effect that identity categories in the North are inappropriate to Latino experience. But there is also a political claim made here that we should oppose and strive to diminish the ridiculous biological essentialism implied in race and therefore the use of race as an identity. It is not just that the categories in the North are inappropriate; they are also specious on their own terms. Thus Corlett argues:

I reject primitive race theories that categorize peoples into different "races" based solely on certain genetic traits possessed by members of each putative racial group.... [E]thnicity...in no way supposes, however, any distinctions between ethnic groups on the basis of genetic or any other kind of innate ordering so that one group is classified as "superior" to another. If any such distinctions of quality do exist, it is because, on average, one group or another has outperformed others in certain ways, perhaps because it has had greater social advantages or opportunities than other groups, or it exists in an environment more congenial to its own flourishing than other groups in the same or different environments. (2003, 7)

For just these sorts of reasons many African Americans have been opting out of racial categories as well, since Jesse Jackson started pushing for the use of the term "African American" in the late 1980s. This was a self-conscious strategy to encourage analogies between African American identity and other hyphenated ethnic groups, to, in a sense, normalize African American identity by no longer having it set apart from everyone else. The strategy of using ethnic terms rather than racial ones is based on the hope that this will have the effect of reducing racism or prejudice generally, because, as Corlett explains, a representation by ethnic terms rather than racial confers agency on a people, it invokes historical experience, cultural and linguistic practices, all of which are associations with human subjectivity, not objectivity.

In contrast, race is often said to be something one has no control over, that is not shaped by collective practice. This surely perpetuates the association between denigrated racial categories and victimhood, animal-driven natures, inherent inferiority or superiority and so on. For whites, racial essentialism confers superiority whether they've done anything to deserve it or not; superior intelligence is just in their genes. These beliefs may be more unconscious than conscious, but given the historically sedimented and persistent layers of the ideology of race as the essential determinant, no matter what one intends by use of a word, its historical meanings will be brought into play when it is in use. Thus Corlett is far from alone in his view that any use of racial terms will be inevitably embedded with biological essentialism and historically persistent hierarchies of moral and cognitive competence (besides Klor de Alva and West 1886, see, e.g., Appiah 1992; Zack 1993). The goal here, of course, is not only to change whites' assumptions about racialized groups but also to help alter the self-image of people in those groups themselves toward a more affirming identity, an identity in which one can take justifiable pride.

Some point to the relative success of Jamaican immigrants in the United States as an example here. Grosfoguel and Georas write:

The Jamaican community's strategy was to emphasize ethnic over racial identity. The fact that Jamaicans were not subsumed under the categorization "African American" avoided offsetting the positive impact of their skilled background. Thus Jamaicans were successfully incorporated into the host labor market in well-paid public and private service jobs... [and] are currently portrayed by the white establishment in New York as a model minority. (1996, 197)

One should note here, however, the contrast between this kind of exceptionalism strategy (to emphasize one's positive differences from the devalued group) and the strategy of resisting racialization as a way to join with others who are victimized by racism. Also, Grosfoguel and Georas's claims are questionable if they are taken to be representations of self-conscious choices made by the majority of Jamaicans, many of whom have been strong supporters, participants, and even leaders of the African American civil and political rights struggle. But their claim is helpful in its representation of a common view about the superiority of an ethnic or cultural as opposed to racial form of self-identification.

To summarize the arguments in favor of the ethnicity paradigm, we can divide them into the political arguments and the metaphysical arguments. The political arguments are that the use of ethnicity will (a) reduce racism because it refers to self-created features rather than merely physiological ones, and (b) also resist the imposition of U.S. forms of identifying people, thus disabusing North Americans from their tendency to naturalize and universalize the predominant categories used in the United States. The metaphysical arguments are that ethnicity (c) more accurately identifies what really holds groups together and how they self-identify, and (d) is simply closer to the truth of Latino identity, given its racial heterogeneity. All of these arguments are, in my view, good ones. But unfortunately, there are other considerations that complicate the picture.

Racial Realities

Let us look, for example, at the case of Cuban Americans. By all measures, they have fared very well in this country in terms of both economic success and political power. They have largely run both politics and the press in Miami for some time, and presidential candidates neglect the Cuban American community at their peril. Of course, one cannot argue, as some do in the case of Jamaican Americans, that Cuban Americans' strong ethnic identification is the main reason for their success: most important is their ability to play an ideological (and at times military) role for the United States in the Cold War. The enormous government assistance provided to the Cubans who fled the Cuban revolution is simply unprecedented in U.S. immigration history. They received language training, educational and business loans, job placement assistance, and housing allocations, and their professional degrees from Cuban institutions were legally recognized to an extent that other Third World immigrants still envy. When President Johnson began his Great Society programs in 1965, the amount of assistance from the government to Cuban Americans was actually increased (Grosfoguel and Georas 1996, 198).

But one may legitimately wonder whether the Cubans' status as refugees of communism was all that was at work here, or even the overriding factor. The Cubans who came in the 1960s were overwhelmingly white or light skinned. They were generally from the top strata of Cuban society. One wonders whether Haitians would ever have been treated the same way. The Cubans who left Cuba after 1980, known as the Marielitos, were from a lower strata of Cuban society, and a large number were Afro-Cubans and mulattos (Grosfoguel and Georas 1996, 199). These Cubans found a decidedly colder welcoming. They were left penned in refugee camps for months on end, and those who were not sent back to Cuba were released into U.S. society with little or no assistance, joining the labor ranks at the level of

Puerto Ricans and Dominicans. There are no doubt many factors at work in these disparate experiences of Cuban immigration, having to do, for example, with the geopolitical climate. But surely one of these important factors is race or racialized identity. Perceived racial identity often *does* trump ethnic or cultural identity.

Clearly, racialization operates differently for diverse Latino identities. As the Cuban example illustrates, class as well as physical appearance will mediate ethnic and cultural labels to determine meanings. Some groups—notably Puerto Ricans and Mexicans—have "enjoyed" a long history with the United States in which their identities have been interpellated through dominant U.S. schemas. In terms of the pan-Latino identity, this means that when Mexican Americans or Puerto Ricans are called Latino, the latter term will connote racial meanings; whereas Argentineans who are called Latino in the North may escape these connotations. Identity terms, as Omi and Winant argue, gain their meaning from their context. Just as Gracia said "Latino" means tacos in California and *arroz con gandules* in New York, it may well mean race in California, Texas, New York, and Florida, and perhaps ethnicity only in a few specific locations and in regard only to certain subsets of the group.

The even broader problem for the attempt to escape racialization is that ethnicity itself signifies race even without further mediations. Look again at the passage about Jamaicans quoted earlier from Grosfoguel and Georas: "The Jamaican's community's strategy was to emphasize *ethnic* over *racial* identity. The fact that *Jamaicans* were not subsumed under the categorization 'African American' avoided offsetting the positive impact of their skilled background" (emphases added). Grosfoguel and Georas contrast the *ethnic* Jamaican identity with what they revealingly take to be a *racial* African American identity, even though the term "African American" was Jackson's attempt to replace race with ethnicity. This again suggests that the racialization of black Americans will overpower any ethnic or cultural marker, interpreting the latter to *mean* race. It may also be the case that the term "African" is overly inclusive, since under its umbrella huge cultural and linguistic differences would be subsumed, and thus it is incapable of signifying an intelligible ethnic identity. But that may be assuming more knowledge about Africa among white Americans or even among Latinos than one reasonably should. More likely is the fact that "African American" is still understood primarily as a racial designation, in a way that terms like German American or Irish American are never understood. Thus, it is questionable whether the strategy of using an ethnic term for a currently racialized group will have the effect of reducing racism if it continues to simply signify race.

And after all, the first meaning given for the word "ethnic" in *Webster's Unabridged Dictionary* is "heathen, pagan." The history of the concept of ethnicity has close ties to the concept of race, emerging in the same period of global history, European colonialism. For many people in the United States, "ethnic" connotes not only nonwhite but also the typical negative associations of nonwhite racial identity. Meanings given for the word "heathen" in the same dictionary include "rude, illiterate, barbarous, and irreligious." In this list, it is striking that "irreligious" comes last.

Like "African American," the category Latino generally operates as a racialized category in the United States. Grosfoguel and Georas themselves argue that "no matter how 'blonde or blue-eyed' a person may be, and no matter how successfully he can 'pass' as white, the moment a person self-identifies as Puerto Rican, he enters the labyrinth of racial Otherness" (1996, 195). Nina Glick Schiller makes a similar case in regard not only to ethnicity but to cultural identity, and not just in the United States. She explains that case studies from Canada to Brazil reveal that "people may speak culture but continue to think race. Whether in the form of cultural pluralism or of the current idiom of multiculturalism, the concept of culture is used in ways that naturalize and essentialize difference" (1995, iii). In the special issue "(Multi) Culturalism and the Baggage of 'Race'" of *Identities: Global Studies in Culture and Power*, from which Schiller's comments are taken, the editor Virginia R. Dominguez calls into question whether the employment of culture is an effective means to fight racism. Study after study shows that culturalism operates very similarly as racism to differentiate groups on the basis of essential characteristics that can be hierarchically organized. Phyllis Pease Chock's study of the *Harvard Encyclopedia of American Ethnic Groups* shows that even this putatively progressive compilation "reified ethnic groups with simplified cultures and uniform histories" (1995, 316). The differences between race, ethnicity, and culture pointed to by such antirace theorists as Corlett begin to recede once we look at how the terms are actually used.

Thus, moving from race to ethnicity is not necessarily moving away from race.

An optimist might want to interject here that the persistence of racial connotations evoked by ethnic categories is not insurmountable. After all, the Irish *did* transform in wide popular consciousness from a race to an ethnicity, and Jews are making the same transition. Is it truly the case that only light-skinned people can enjoy this transformation, and that darker-skinned people will *never* be able to? In order to answer this question, we need to ask another one: What *are* the obstacles to deracializing people of color in general?[5] Is it really the mere fact of skin tone?

I would make two suggestions. First, race, unlike ethnicity, has historically worked through visible markers on the body which trump dress, speech, and cultural practices. Certainly for antiblack racists, the differences in ethnicity and nationality between Africans, Caribbeans, and African Americans are not morally significant. Race demarcates groups visually, which is why racist institutions have been so upset about nonvisible members of "races" and is why they have taken such trouble in these cases to enforce racial identifications. What I am suggesting is that, in popular consciousness and in the implicit perceptual practices we use in everyday life to discern how to relate to each other, ethnicity does not "replace" race. When ethnic identities are used instead of racial ones, the perceptual practices of visual demarcation by which we slot people into racial categories continue to operate because ethnic categories offer no substituting perceptual practice. In other words, the fact that race and ethnicity do not map onto the same kinds of identifying practices will make race harder to dislodge. This was not the case for the Irish or for many if not most Jewish people, who could blend into the European American melting pot without noticeable distinctiveness (thus, those who are themselves Irish or Jewish are the best at "spotting" persons within their group). For them, ethnicity could replace race, because their racial identity as Irish and Jewish did not operate exclusively or primarily through visible markers on the body so much as through contextual factors like neighborhood and accent. So their identity could shift to "white" race and Jewish or Irish ethnicity without troubling the dominant perceptual practices of racial identification. However, for those who are visibly identified as nonwhite by these same dominant practices or who, in other words, are "raced," the shift to a primary ethnic identity would require no longer engaging in these racial perceptual practices. It is unlikely that the use of new terms alone will have that effect. At best, for people of color, ethnic identities will operate *alongside* racial ones in everyday interactions, without in any way dislodging the racial identities. At worst, ethnic identities, like perhaps "African American," will operate simply *as* a racial identity.

Although this is a fact about the visible features of the body, it is not an immutable fact: the meanings of the visible are of course subject to change. However, the phenomenology of perception is such that change will be neither quick nor easily susceptible to conscious manipulation, and that substituting the terms we use for identities will be nowhere near sufficient to make this change. The transformation of perceptual habits will require a more active and a more practical intervention.

The second obstacle to the deracialization of (at least most) people of color has nothing to with perception or bodily features. This obstacle refers back to a claim I made at the beginning, that assertions of group solidarity among African American, Native American, and Latinos in the United States provoke resistance among many whites because they invoke the history of colonialism, annexation of lands, slavery, and genocide. Thus, our acceptance as full players within U.S. society comes at much greater cost than the acceptance of previously vilified groups like the Irish and Jews, groups that suffered just as much discrimination and violence, without a doubt, but groups whose genealogy is not a thorn in the side of "Pilgrim's Progress," "Manifest Destiny," "Leader of the Free World," and other such mythic narratives that legitimate U.S. world dominance and provide white Americans with a strong sense of pride. The Irish and Jews were (the Irish arguably still are) colonized peoples in Europe, and *there* they are reminders of colonization and genocide. But they do not play this role in the legitimation narratives of the U.S. state. Thus, the line between European ethnicities and people of color is not merely or perhaps even primarily about skin tone but about history and power and the narratives by which currently existing power arrangements are justified.

So what are we to do? If the move from race to ethnicity is not as easy as some have thought, how can we be more realistic without becoming fatalistic about racialization? How can we avoid both defeatism and naivety? Are we to accept, then, that Latino identity is a racial identity, despite all the facts I have reviewed about our heterogeneity and different methods of self-identification, and all the pernicious effects of racialized identity?

Changing the Meaning of Race

Although racial ideology and practices of racialization seem always to carry within them some commitment to biological essentialism, perhaps the *meaning* of race is open to transformation. If race is going to be with us for some time to come as a

244 Latino/a Particularity

mode of identification based on visible markers on the body, it might still be the case that race itself can alter in meaning, even before we can eradicate the perceptual practices of racialization. Such an alteration is exactly what much of the new work in black studies, for example, by Paul Gilroy, Robert Gooding-Williams, bell hooks, Lewis Gordon, and Patricia Williams is aiming for. In these works there is an intentional use of the term "black" rather than African American, which seems to be a way of addressing with honesty and directness the social reality we live in, and also as a way to suggest a "linked fate" between all black people in the diaspora across nationalities and other cultural differences. But in their works, blackness has been decidedly de-essentialized and given a meaning that consists of historical experience, collective memory, chosen social practices and forms of cultural expression. Gilroy's early works invokes a "blackness" that transcends and survives the differences of the United Kingdom, Caribbean, and U.S. nationalities, a blackness that can be seen in cultural form and narrative focus. Blackness is formed out of social location, shared history, and a shared perception about the world. For Gooding-Williams, black identity requires a certain self-consciousness about creating the meaning of blackness. It requires, in other words, not only that one is treated as a black person, or that one is "objectively" black, but that one is "subjectively" black as well in the sense of actively interpreting the implications of this imposed category for one's sense of self and community life. Thus black identity requires agency, rather than imposing only obstacles or curtailments of agency.

Whether such an approach can be used for Latinos, I am not sure. There is probably even greater diversity among Latinos in relation to history, social location, and forms of cultural expression than among black people across the diaspora (because, for example, an experience such as slavery is not shared by Latinos). And the question of where black Latinos "fit" is still unresolved, even when we make racial identity a matter of self-creation. This is a serious weakness in Gilroy's broad conceptualization of a "black Atlantic": Brazil, as large a country as it is, is nowhere to be found on his conceptual map. Theories of "black identity" must address this critical Anglo/Latino divide, and theorists in the United States must recognize the way in which U.S. hemispheric imperialism, as well as cultural and linguistic differences, create real resistance against an assimilation to the predominantly Anglo-constructed cultural articulation of black identity.[6]

But I believe that we can take an important lesson from this body of work because it suggests that even though we must remember the persistent power of racialization and the inability of ethnicity easily to take its place, the meanings of race are subject to some movement. Only a semantic essentialist could argue that race can *only* mean biological essentialism; in reality, this is not the way meaning works. Let me be clear about my position here: I don't believe, à la *some* postmodernists, that signifiers are slippery items whose meanings and associations can be easily transformed. Just because we have seen the successful transformation of some such derogatory terms (e.g., "black," "Chicano") does not establish that *any* term can be. It is true that meaning works through iterability: that is, the invocation of prior meanings, but when those prior meanings are centuries old and globally influential, they will be difficult to dislodge. On the other hand, words do not simply pick out things that exist prior to their being picked out, and thus reference is mutable.

So the first point I am making is this. Despite our hopes that the influx of Latinos on the North American continent, in all of our beautiful diversity, would transform and annihilate the binaries and purist racial ideologies prevalent in the United States, this is not likely, at least not likely very soon. The racializing practices long dominant in the United States will not simply implode because of the pressure of Latino self-representation as nonraced or as racially mixed. Latinos in the United States have without a doubt been racialized. And I would argue that the history and even contemporary socioeconomic situation of Latinos in the United States simply cannot be understood using ethnicity categories alone; we have been shut out of the melting pot because we have been seen as racial and not merely cultural "Others." However, although we may be stuck with racial categories for longer than some of us would wish, it may be easier to help "race" slowly evolve by engaging with it in new ways rather than trying to evade it.

One might still argue at this point that various Latinos have different relationships to racial categories. Mexicans, Puerto Ricans, and Dominicans have been racialized, but not all others. And lumping us all together can dilute the political efforts to redress discrimination, allowing white or light Latinos to reap benefits we do not even need. So what are we to do in the face of this diversity of historical experience and social location? Is race perhaps a way to understand some of Latino identities but not all? For a pan-Latino moniker, shouldn't we refer to ethnicity?

Given the persistent racialization of many Latinos, and the ways in which ethnic and cultural categories can carry race within them, the adoption of the ethnic paradigm will leave most Latinos behind. That is, some of us will no doubt be assimilated to the nonracial paradigm of ethnicity that has been operative for European Americans in this century, while other Latinos will continue to be racialized. This will exacerbate the hierarchies and divisions among Latinos, and weaken the political power of the overall group. It will also mean that Latinos will be unable or at least unlikely to address the racial issue *from within* Latino identity: if "Latino" comes to mean merely ethnicity, race will come to be viewed as an issue that may affect many of us but is properly outside of our identity as Latinos. Light Latinos will do what too many white *estadounidenses* have done: believe that race has nothing to do with them.

This is surely both a political and a metaphysical mistake. Raced identities are mediated by cultural context: the racialization of various Latinos differs according to our specific national or cultural identity. Blackness signifies very differently in the Caribbean than in other parts of South America, in terms especially of its marginalization vis-à-vis the cultural "norm," that is, Puerto Rican versus Colombian. Thus, race cannot be understood except in its cultural, or ethnic, context. Racial essentialists would hope that this was not true, but racial essentialism is simply false: race is a system of meanings that varies by context, not an inherent quality that is manifest everywhere the same. Moreover, all Latinos are in almost all cases racially different than Anglos, certainly in the common usage of race categories in the United States. That is, even for Spaniards, as Jorge Gracia argues, we are not "purely European," claims of white Hispanicism notwithstanding. By pursuing the ethnic paradigm, Latinos may appear to be lacking in solidarity with other racialized people of color, seeking to better our social status by differentiating ourselves from African and Asian Americans who remain persistently racialized. Shouldn't we rather unite with the efforts of those like Gilroy and Gooding-Williams who seek to give race itself a cultural meaning? Moreover, because Latino identity—in its "impurity" and variability—challenges the shibboleths of U.S. race ideology, we have a better chance to affect that ideology by acknowledging our racialization than in trying to escape it.

Of course, it does not make sense to say simply that Latinos constitute *a* "race," either by the commonsense meaning or even by more nuanced references to historical narrative and cultural production. I do believe that if the concept of mestizo enters into U.S. culture it can have some good effects against the presumption of purity as having an intrinsic value. The problems caused by this presumption are both persistent and significant, as mixed race children are still asked to "choose," and integrity and autonomy are still thought to require homogeny.[7] Still, the concept of mestizo when applied to Latinos in general, as if all Latinos or the essence of being Latino is to be mestizo or mixed Spanish and Indian, has the effect of subordinating all Latinos both North and South whose descendants are entirely African, Indian, or Asian. Mestizos then become the cornerstone of the culture, with others pushed off to the side. This is clearly intolerable.

A concept that might be helpful here has been coined by David Theo Goldberg: ethnorace. Unlike the category race, ethnorace might have the advantage of bringing into play both the elements of human agency and subjectivity involved in ethnicity, that is, an identity that is the product of self-creation, at the same time that it acknowledges the uncontrolled racializing aspects associated with the visible body. And the term would remind us that there are at least two concepts, rather than one, that are vitally necessary to the understanding of Latino identity in the United States: ethnicity and race. Using only "ethnicity" belies the reality of most Latinos' everyday experiences, as well as obscures our own awareness about how ethnic identifications often do the work of race while seeming to be theoretically correct and politically advanced. Race dogs our steps; let us not run from it lest we cause it to increase its determination.

Latinos, Asian Americans, and the Black-White Binary

If W. E. B. Du Bois were alive today, he would probably tell us that the problem of the twenty-first century will prove to be the lines between communities of color, or the question of cross-ethnic relations. Coalitions across these communities are as critically important today as they are difficult to maintain. This chapter argues that even if we try to build coalition around what might seem to be our most obvious common concern—reducing racism—the black-white paradigm that dominates racial discourse in the United States inhibits our comprehension of the variety of racisms and racial identities and thus proves more of an obstacle to coalition building than an aid.

I will use the situation of Latinos and Asian Americans to explore the black-white binary, what it is, how it operates, and how it is limiting. There are some interesting similarities between the history of oppression specifically faced by Latinos and Asian Americans in the United States. Historically both groups were often brought to this country as cheap labor and then denied political and civil rights, thus making them a more vulnerable and exploitable labor force once on U.S. shores (a practice that of course continues to this day in sweatshops in many cities on the East and West coasts and on the Mexican border, and in the erosion of basic protections or emergency hospital services for "illegals" or undocumented workers) (Acuña 1988; Lowe 1996; Okihiro 1994; Shorris 1992; Suro 1999; Takaki 1990 and 1993; Tchen 1999). Both groups often come from countries of origin that have been the site of imperialist wars, invasions, and civil wars instigated by the Cold War, some of which involved the United States' imperialist aggressions, as in the Philippines, Puerto Rico, El Salvador, Vietnam, Laos, Cambodia, Nicaragua, Guatemala, Korea, the Dominican Republic, and most recently, Colombia (Barry et al. 1983; Burbach and Flynn 1984; Chomsky 1993; Galeano 1967 and 1973; Kim and Yu 1995; Okihiro 1995; Perea 1993; Uribe 1975). In this sense, many of these immigrants had experience with the U.S. government, direct or indirect, well before they became refugees or immigrants here. There are also similarities that Latinos and Asian Americans share with other people of color after they come here: they have to continually face vicious and demeaning stereotyping along with discrimination in language, education, health care, housing, and employment, and they are the target of random identity-based violence and murder (random in the sense that any Mexican farm laborer or Asian American or Arab American or African American or Jewish person will do).

Perhaps because of their similar genealogy as sources of cheap and vulnerable labor, there are some important commonalities between the ideological justifications and legal methods that have been used to persecute and discriminate against Latinos and Asian Americans (Bender and Braveman 1995). Both have been the main victims of "nativist" arguments that advocate limiting the rights of immigrants or foreign-born Americans, and both have often been portrayed as ineradicably "foreign" no matter how many generations they have lived here. Yet an account of these nativist-based forms of discrimination and persecution has not been adequately incorporated into the civil rights paradigm of progressive politics, and this has led to a misunderstanding about the interrelationships between racism and anti-immigrant attacks.

The Black/White Paradigm

The discourse of social justice in regard to issues involving race has been dominated in the United States by what many theorists call the "black/white paradigm," which operates to govern racial classifications and racial politics in the United States, most clearly in the formulation of civil rights law but also in more informal arenas of discussion. Juan Perea defines this paradigm as "the conception that race in America consists, either exclusively or primarily, of only two constituent racial groups, the Black and White. . . . In addition, the paradigm dictates that all other racial identities and groups in the United States are best understood through the Black/White binary paradigm" (1998, 361). Openly espousing this view, Mary Frances Berry, former chair of the U.S. Civil Rights Commission, has stated that the United States comprises "three nations, one Black, one White, and one in which people strive to be something other than Black to avoid the sting of White Supremacy" (quoted in Wu 2002, 34). To understand race in this way is to assume that white supremacy targets only black identity. Others can be affected by racism, on this view, but the dominance of the black/white paradigm works to interpret all other effects as "collateral damage" ultimately caused by the same phenomena, in both economic and psychological terms, in which the given other, whether Latino, Asian American, or something else, is placed in the category of "black" or "close to black." In other words, there is basically one form of racism, and one continuum of racial identity, along which all groups will be placed.[1]

The black/white paradigm can be understood either descriptively or prescriptively or both. As a descriptive claim, the black/white paradigm intends to describe the fundamental nature of racializations and racisms in the United States. As a prescriptive claim, it intends to enforce the applicability of the paradigm by controlling how race operates; some of the legal history can be read as having (or aiming for) such prescriptive effects.

A growing number of theorists of race and racism, such as Elaine Kim, Gary Okihiro, Elizabeth Martinez, Richard Delgado, and Juan Perea, have argued that the black/white paradigm is not adequate, and certainly not sufficient, to explain racial realities in the United States. They have thus contested its claim to *descriptive adequacy* and argued that the hegemony of the black/white paradigm in racial thinking has had many deleterious effects for Latinos and Asian Americans (see, esp., Delgado 1998; Kim 1993; E. Martinez 1998; Okihiro 1994; Perea 1998; and Takagi 1992). In this chapter, I will summarize and discuss what I consider the strongest of these arguments and then develop two further arguments. It is important to stress that the black/white paradigm does have some descriptive reach, as I shall discuss, even though it is inadequate when taken as the whole story of racism. It is true, for example, that Asian Americans and Latinos have been sometimes categorized and treated in ways that reflect the fact that we have been positioned as either "near black" or "near white," but this is not nearly adequate to understand our ideological representation or political treatment overall. One might also argue that, although the black/white paradigm is obviously not *descriptively* adequate to the complexity and plurality of racialized identities, it yet operates with *prescriptive* force to organize these complexities into its bipolar schema. But I will also argue that it does not operate with *effective* hegemony as a prescriptive force. I believe these arguments will show that continuing to theorize race in the United States as operating exclusively through the black/white paradigm is actually disadvantageous for all people of color, and in many respects for whites as well (or at least for white union households and the white poor, whose political disenfranchisement is linked to that of people of color).

Legal Puzzles

I want to start with a story that exemplifies the close association between Latinos and Asians in the ideological traditions embedded in the legal history of the United States. In 1854 the California Supreme Court defined Chinese Americans as Indians, that is, Native Americans. This ruling came about after a white man, George W. Hall, was convicted of murder based upon the eyewitness testimony of a Chinese American. Hall's defense lawyer appealed the conviction by invoking the law that said "no black or mulatto person, or Indian, shall be allowed to give evidence in favor of, or against a white man" (Okihiro 1994, 50; see also Lyman 1994). In support of his claim that this law was relevant to Hall's case, the defense lawyer cited the hypothesis that all native peoples of the Americas were originally from Asia and traveled to the Western hemisphere over the Bering Straights. Thus, he argued, the Chinese American man was actually the racial ancestor of Native Americans, and because the latter were lawfully excluded from giving testimony in court, this Chinese man should be excluded also. The California Supreme Court was delighted by this argument, upheld the appeal, freed Hall, and thus linked the legal status of Asian Americans and all those with indigenous American ancestry, a category that includes many or most Latinos.

The story does not end there. The California Supreme Court was concerned that as a scientific hypothesis the Bering Straights theory might one day be disproved, which would then destroy the basis for Chinese exclusion in the courts and allow them to give testimony. Wanting to avoid this outcome, however unlikely it might be, the court decided to embellish on the arguments made in appeal. Justice Charles J. Murray interpreted legal precedent to argue that the terms "black" and "white" are oppositional terms, from which he concluded that black must mean nonwhite and white must exclude all people of color. Thus, by the law of binary logic, Chinese Americans, after having become Native American, then also became black.

Of the many questions that one might like to go back and pose to Charles Murray, perhaps the most obvious is the following: if black and white are oppositional terms, then, instead of black meaning nonwhite, doesn't it just as logically follow that white could mean nonblack, in which case all people of color except African Americans would be white? This conclusion is no more or less fallacious or absurd than Murray's conclusion that black means nonwhite. That such an idea was, apparently, beyond the imagination of the court at that time begins to reveal the strategy at work here. Defining whites as only those without one drop of "other" blood has been a tool to maintain a clear and distinct border around white identity. On the other hand, the borders of other identities—their distinctiveness from each other—are not important for the law to define and maintain. The controlling term here is not race but whiteness. To be black is to be nonwhite, but this equation is not reversible if one is using the usual meaning of "black" today, since for Murray "black" includes virtually every Asian American, Latino, Native American, and mixed race person as well as all those of African origin. Although this case began with a strategy to link the Chinese to American Indians, it ends in a ruling that prescribes a black/white binary. The ruling essentially allowed the state to make one all-purpose argument against the civil and political rights of nonwhites, thus increasing the efficiency with which it could maintain discrimination.

Asian Americans and Latinos have been tossed back and forth across this black/white binary for 150 years (see Haney López 1996; Lee 1993; G. Martinez 1998; Okihiro 1994; Omi and Winant 1986; C. Rodríguez, 2000). To continue with the example of Chinese Americans, in 1860 Chinese Americans were classified as white in Louisiana. By 1870 they were classified as Chinese. But in 1900, the children of Chinese and non-Chinese parents were reclassified as *either white or black*. Other states had similarly convoluted histories of classification. In 1927 the U.S. Supreme Court ended this confusion and defined the Chinese as nonwhite, thus more firmly subjecting them to all the segregationist and Jim Crow legislation then in effect. Similar stories of variable racial classification can be told about Mexicans in Texas and in New Mexico, Japanese in California, and other groups. Needless to say, the variable classifications tell a story of strategic reasoning in which arguments for legal discriminations are deployed against people of color by whatever opportune classification presents itself in the context.

Contrary to what one might imagine, it has not always or even generally been to the advantage of Asian Americans and Latinos to be legally classified as white. An illustration of this is found in another important legal case decided by the U.S. Supreme Court in 1954, just two weeks before they issued the decision in *Brown vs. Board of Education*. The case of *Hernandez v. Texas* involved a Mexican American man convicted of murder by an all-white jury and sentenced to life imprisonment (G. Martinez 1998; Suro 1999). His lawyer appealed the conviction by arguing that the absence of Mexican Americans on the jury was discriminatory, making reference to the famous Scottsboro case in which the U.S. Supreme Court overturned (after many years) the conviction of nine African American men on the grounds of an absence of African Americans from the jury. But in the Hernandez case, the Texas Supreme Court ruled that Mexicans were white people of Spanish descent, and therefore that there was no discrimination in the all-white makeup of the jury. Forty years later, Hernandez's lawyer, James DeAnda, recounted how he made his argument appealing this ruling:

> Right there in the Jackson County Courthouse, where no Hispanic had served on any kind of a jury in living memory because Mexicans were white and so it was okay to bring them before all-white juries, they had two men's rooms. One had a nice sign that just said MEN on it. The other had a sign on it that said COL-ORED MEN and below that was a hand-scrawled sign that said HOMBRES AQUI [men here]. In that jury pool, Mexicans may have been white, but when it came to nature's functions, they were not. (Suro 1999, 85)

In fact, in Texas not only were Mexicans subject to Jim Crow in public facilities from restaurants to bathrooms, they were also excluded from business and community groups, and children of Mexican descent were required to attend a segregated school for the first four grades, whether they spoke fluent English or not. Thus, when they were classified as nonwhite, Latinos were overtly denied certain civil rights; when they were classified as white, the de facto denial of their civil rights could not be appealed.

Although the U.S. Supreme Court overturned the Texas court's decision in the Hernandez case, its final decision indicated a perplexity regarding Mexican American identity. The court did not want to classify Mexicans as black, and it didn't want to alter the legal classification of Mexicans as white; since these were the only racial terms the justices thought were available, they ended up explaining the discrimination Mexicans faced as based on "other differences," left undefined. Thus, oddly, the court upheld that there was racial discrimination against Mexicans, but it denied that Mexicans constituted a race (Haney López 1998, 182–83).

One clear lesson to be learned from this legal history is that race is a construction that is variable enough to be stretched opportunistically as the need arises in order to maintain and expand discrimination. Racism, in other words, molds racial categories to fit its design. And the legal history also shows that white supremacy has moved Latinos and Asian Americans around the classification schema for its own benefit. Nonetheless, one might take these legal cases to indicate that discrimination against African Americans was the paradigm case that U.S. courts stretched when they could to justify discrimination against other nonwhites, and thus to provide support for the black/white paradigm of race.

Modeling Arguments

The distinguished historian John Hope Franklin made such an argument at the first official meeting of the Race Relations Commission, which was convened by former U.S. President Bill Clinton to advance his initiative for a national dialogue on race.

Franklin maintained that "racism in the black/white sphere" developed first in North America when slavery was introduced in the Jamestown colony in 1619 and has served as a model for the treatment of race in the United States. Attorney Angela Oh, also serving on the commission, argued against Franklin on this point, using the example of the uprising of April 29, 1992, in Los Angeles to show that the specific history and racist treatment of Asian Americans needs to be accounted for in order to understand the complex varieties of racism that sparked that event. "I just want to make sure we go beyond the black-white paradigm . . . because the world is about much more than that," she said (see Wu 2002, 32–35). Frank Wu, commenting on this exchange, tries diplomatically to unite both Oh and Franklin's points. He affirms that "African Americans bear the greatest burden of racial discrimination" but adds that the Los Angeles uprising needs to be understood in relation both to African American history as well as Korean American history (and, I would add, Latino history, since Latinos were the largest number of persons arrested). Wu advocates the following commonsense approach:

> Whatever any of us concludes about race relations, we should start by including all of us. . . . Our leaders should speak to all individuals, about every group, and for the country as a whole. A unified theory of race, race relations, and racial tensions must have whites, African Americans, and all the rest, and even within groups must include Arab Americans, Jewish Americans, white ethnicities, and so forth. Our theory is an inadequate account otherwise. (Wu 2002, 36)

The question Wu does not address directly is whether the continued acceptance of the black/white paradigm, what Oh is contesting and Franklin is defending, will allow such a comprehensive account.

To say that racism has been modeled on slavery might or might not entail a black/white binary, depending on how much is presumed in the concept of "modeling." But the reality of race and racism in the North American continent has been more complicated than black/white since the initial conquest of native peoples by European Americans. Slavery was itself an idea put forward by Columbus when he suggested that the indigenous population could be enslaved in order to bring profits to the Spanish crown because the amount of gold and silver here was initially found wanting. The concept of race itself was inspired in large measure without a doubt by the "discovery" of native peoples and the subsequent debates among learned Europeans about their nature, their humanity, and their rights. Later on, emerging legal practice developed typologies of rights based on typologies of peoples, such as the exclusionary laws concerning testimony in court, as mentioned earlier, which grouped "blacks, mulattoes, and Native Americans." The Chinese laborers brought to the West in the 1800s were subjected to very specific rulings restricting their rights not only to vote or own property but even to marry other Chinese. This latter ruling outlasted slavery and was justified by invoking images of Asian overpopulation, another quite specific racist ideology. To control their reproduction, Chinese women were allowed to come as prostitutes but not as wives, a restriction no other group faced.

The Mexicans defeated in the Mexican-American War were portrayed as cruel and cowardly barbarians, and although the Treaty of Guadalupe-Hidalgo ratified in 1848 guaranteed for the Mexicans who stayed in the United States full rights of citizenship, like the treaties with Native Americans neither local governments nor the federal courts upheld the Mexicans' right to vote or respected the land deeds they held before the treaty (see Acuña 1988; Shorris 1992). By the time of the Spanish-American War of 1898 the image of barbarism used against Mexicans was consistently attributed to a Latin Catholic heritage and expanded for use throughout Latin America and the Caribbean, thus subsequently affecting the immigrant populations coming from these areas as well as justifying U.S. claims of hegemony in the region (Mignolo 2000). The so-called Zoot Suit riots in Los Angeles in 1943 targeted Mexican Americans and their ethnically specific style of dress. The attempts made to geographically sequester and also to forcibly assimilate Native American groups were not experienced by any other group, and had their own ideological justifications that combined contradictory images of the Great Chain of Being with the romanticized Noble Savage. Native peoples were represented as vanquished, disappearing, and thus of no account.

Thus, the paradigm of an antiblack racism intertwined with slavery does not help to illuminate these specific forms and experiences of oppression, where ideologies often relied on charges of innate evil, religious backwardness, horde mentalities, the inevitability of extinction, and other projections not used in regard to African Americans. I will argue that the hegemony of the black/white paradigm has stymied the development of an adequate account of the diverse racial realities in the United States and weakened the general accounts of racism that attempt to be truly inclusive. This has had a negative effect on our ability to develop effective solutions to the various forms that racism can take, to make common cause against ethnic- and race-based forms of oppression and to create lasting coalitions, and has recently played a significant role in the demise of affirmative action. I will support these claims further in what follows.

Criticisms

Critics of the black/white paradigm have argued that, although all communities of color have shared the experience of political and economic disenfranchisement in the United States, there are significant differences between the *causes* and the *forms* of this disenfranchisement. Bong Hwan Kim, a Korean American community leader who has worked both as the director of the Korean Community Center of East Bay in Oakland and as director of the Korean Youth and Community Center in Los Angeles, blames the black/white binary for disabling relationships among people of color and even for creating the conditions leading to the Los Angeles civil disaster of April 1992, in which 2300 small Korean-owned businesses were destroyed by mostly Latino and African American looters. Kim cites the xenophobia marshaled by African American leader Danny Bakewell before the looting occurred, and argues that the Korean American community had been and continues to be systematically rendered incapable of responding to such rhetoric because they are not recognized in the media as a player in racial politics.[2] Elaine Kim explains:

> It is difficult to describe how disempowered and frustrated many Korean Americans felt during and after the *sa-i-ku p'ok-dong* (the April 29 "riots"). Korean

Americans across the country shared the anguish and despair of the Los Angeles
tongp'o (community), which everyone seemed to have abandoned—the police
and fire departments, black and white political leaders, the Asian and Pacific
American advocates who tried to dissociate themselves from us because our
tragedy disputed their narrow and risk-free focus on white violence against
Asians.... [T]he Korean Americans at the center of the storm were mostly
voiceless and all but invisible (except when stereotyped as hysterically inarticulate,
and mostly female, ruined shopkeepers.) (Kim 1994, 71–72)

Similar to the Mexican Americans in Texas, the Korean Americans have been
denied the legal or socially recognized category of being a politicized group at the
same time that they are made subject to group-based scapegoating. Moreover, as
this event demonstrates, the black/white paradigm of race is incapable of theoretically or politically addressing racism *among* communities of color, or addressing
racism, in other words, that is not all about white people.

A response to this line of reasoning might be that it is white supremacy which
is at the root of the conflictual relations among communities of color and responsible for their acceptance of stereotypes manufactured by a white dominant
power structure. Thus, on this reading, what occurred in Los Angeles can be reductively explained as the result of white supremacy. Although I often find explanatory arguments that focus on political economy compelling, it is simplistic to
imagine cultural conflicts as the mere epiphenomena of economic forces with no
life or grounding of their own. To blame only white supremacy for what occurred
in Los Angeles would deny power and agency to any groups but the dominant,
which is increasingly untrue. However, one could hold a monocausal account of
the genealogy of racism and still acknowledge that racism has multiple targets and
a variety of forms.

Supporting the arguments of both Elaine Kim and Bong Hwan Kim, Juan
Perea argues that because of the wide acceptance of the black/white paradigm,
"other racialized groups like Latinos/as, Asian Americans, and Native Americans
are often marginalized or ignored altogether" (1998, 361). He points out that the
concerns of Asian Americans and Latinos cannot be addressed through immigration legislation because not all are immigrants. This is one reason to reject the
claim of some ethnic theorists that these groups will follow the path of European
immigrants in gradual assimilation and economic success (the other reason to
reject this claim is their racialization or status as nonwhites).[3]

Roberto Suro argues that the black/white binary forces Latinos and other
people of color who are not African Americans to adopt the strategies of civil rights
litigation even though these are "not particularly well-suited to Latinos" because
Latinos are a much more diverse group (1999, 87). For example, any meaningful
redress of economic discrimination affecting Latinos and Asian Americans will
need to disaggregate these groups, as some "target of opportunity" programs today
in fact do, since the gap between median incomes in Filipino and Japanese
households, or between Puerto Rican and Cuban households, makes averaging
these incomes useless as an indicator of economic success. Richard Delgado argues
that "if one's paradigm identifies only one group as deserving of protection, everyone else is likely to suffer" (Delgado 1998, 370). Current civil rights legislation,

in Delgado's view, has provided legal advantages for African Americans, unwittingly perhaps, over other people of color. I don't take Delgado to be implying that the legislation has necessarily been very effective in benefiting the African American population, but that the language of the law, however much it has yet to be applied, is based on the experience of only one group. Just as the protection of the right of property advantages the propertied, and the protection of free speech "increases the influence of those who are articulate and can afford microphones, TV air time, and so on . . . the Equal Protection Clause produces a social good, namely equality, for those falling under its coverage—blacks and whites. These it genuinely helps—at least on occasion. But it leaves everyone else unprotected (1998, 370–71).

Put in more general terms, these arguments can be summarized as follows:

1) The black/white paradigm has disempowered various racial and ethnic groups from being able to define their own identity, to mark their difference and specificity beyond what could be captured on this limited map. Instead of naming and describing our own identity and social circumstance, we have had descriptions foisted on us from outside.

2) Asian Americans and Latinos (among others) have historically been ignored or marginalized in the public discourse in the United States on race and racism. This is a problem for two reasons, first, because it is simply unfair to be excluded from what concerns one, and second, because it has considerably weakened the analysis of race and racism in the mainstream discussions. To explain the social situation of Asian Americans or Latinos simply in terms of their de jure and de facto treatment as nonwhites is to describe our condition only on the most shallow terms. We must be included in the discussions so that a more adequate account can be developed.

3) By eliminating specificities within the large "black" or nonwhite group, the black/white binary has undercut the possibility of developing appropriate and effective legal and political solutions for the variable forms that racial oppression can take. A broad united movement for civil rights does not require that we ignore the specific circumstances of different racial or ethnic identities, nor does it mandate that only the similarities can figure into the formulation of protective legislation. I will discuss an example of this problem, one that concerns the application of affirmative action in higher education, at the end of this chapter.

4) Eliminating specificities within the large "black" or nonwhite group also makes it difficult to understand or address the real conflicts and differences within this amalgam of peoples. The black/white paradigm proposes to understand all conflicts between communities of color through antiblack racism and white supremacy, when the reality is more complex.

5) For all these reasons, the black/white paradigm seriously undermines the possibility of achieving coalitions. It is obvious that keeping us in conflict with each other and not in coalition is in the interests of the current power structure.

I would add to these arguments the following two.

6) The black/white binary and the constant invocation of all race discourses and conflicts as between blacks and whites has produced an imaginary of race in this country in which a very large white majority confronts a relatively small black

minority. This imagery has the effect of reenforcing the sense of inevitability to white domination.

This is not the reality of racial percentages in almost any major urban center in the country today. Nonwhites outnumber whites in New York, Miami, Chicago, Atlanta, and Los Angeles, and come very close in San Francisco, Dallas, and Washington, D.C. There is thus a real potential for a major shift in political power, but there are two main challenges before this shift can take place. The first is the ability of nonwhites to unite and to also make common cause with progressive antiracist whites. The second is the Electoral College. The original intent of the Electoral College was to protect small states and also to create a buffer between the hoi polloi and the government, but the current effect of the Electoral College, given these changed demographics, has the added "advantage" of disenfranchising the occupants of cities generally and people of color specifically from influencing national electoral outcomes. The fact is that if the popular vote determined elections, the cities would have the determining numbers of votes, since this is where the majority of U.S. citizens now live and where the trend of movement is toward. *The numbers and concentrations of people of color in the United States means that we are quickly moving past the politics of recognition, in which people of color must clamor for recognition from the all-powerful majority, and reaching the politics of power negotiation, in which we can negotiate from a position of power rather than having to rely exclusively on moral appeals.* The white majority will not maintain its near hegemonic political control as new configurations of alliances develop.[4] Moreover, the white majority is far from monolithic, splintering most notably along gender and class lines: the gender gap has widened in electoral politics along with the gap between union and nonunion households, with droves of white women and white union members voting the same as the majority of people of color.

Thus, thinking of race only in terms of black and white produces a sense of inevitability to white domination and thus a sense of fatalism, even though the facts call for the opposite. I believe this issue of imagery is very significant: it affects people's choices, voting (or nonvoting) practices, and the level of energy they are willing to devote to political activism. By opening up the binary imagery to rainbow images and the like, as Jesse Jackson did with great effect in his presidential campaign, we can more accurately and thus helpfully present the growing and future conditions within which political action and contestations will occur. This is in everyone's interests (or at least, the majority's).

7) The next argument that I would make in regard to the black/white binary is that it mistakenly configures race imagistically as exclusively having to do with color, as if color alone determines racial identity and is the sole object of racism. Equating race with color makes it seem as if all the races other than black and white must be lined up between them since they clearly represent the polar extremes. There is certainly a racist continuum of color operating in this and in many countries, but my point is that this continuum is not the *only* axis by which racism operates.

Some have taken the horrific hierarchy of adoption preferences in the United States, that runs basically from white to Asian to Latino to black, as representative of a continuum of color. Related to this idea is the claim that Asian Americans and Latinos are closer to white and will eventually "become" white. Let me address this latter idea first. The claim that Asian Americans and Latinos will become white is first of all premised on the assumption that we have two choices of racialized identities: white and black. The assumption presupposed is then that if a group is not economically and politically located at or near the bottom of the society, which the black/white paradigm associates exclusively with "blackness," then such a group is assumed to have achieved "whiteness." But class does not perfectly map onto race: the poor come in all colors. Moreover, there is significant racial and class variety within each of these large amalgamated groups with highly variant median incomes. Moreover, the discrimination faced by Asian Americans and Latinos will not likely lose its focus on language and cultural issues; the more Latinos there are, the more virulent "English Only" campaigns become (see e.g., Huntington 2004). The claim also ignores the overwhelming evidence showing that most Latinos persist in their identities for multiple generations, against their own economic interests (Cruz 1998; Flores 2000; Jones Correa 1998; Rodriguez 1991). And it seems inapplicable entirely to Asian Americans, who may be represented as having some so-called white attributes, but who have never been legally or socially accepted here as white (Okihiro 1994; Prashad 2000; Wu 2002).

There are three major differences between the groups who have had "success" in becoming white and Latinos and Asian Americans. The groups I am referring to here, and about whom there is some very good historical research emerging, are the Irish Americans and (white Anglo) Jews. Whether Jews have wholly made it is debatable; they seem to move back and forth, as they did in Germany. For the Klan, still influential in many parts of the United States, Jews are not white. And even the U.S. mainstream, one might suggest, seems able to accept an Alan Greenspan as "finance czar" but not a Jewish president. The United States has already had presidents who were Irish American.

In regard, however, to the differences between Irish Americans and Jews on the one hand and Asian Americans and Latinos on the other, the first obvious significant difference is in color and physical appearance. The Irish and Jews can "blend in" to U.S. society in a way that Asian Americans and most Latinos cannot. The admission of the Irish and Jews into the category "white" did not require challenging the idea that superior characteristics come from European societies, and that superior characteristics are correlated to light skin color. On the other hand, if nonwhites or non-light-skinned people were to become white, whiteness would begin to deconstruct, perhaps mutating to a cultural and ethnic designation still marked by superiority. But it is not obvious that whiteness is on the threshold of deconstruction. Thus, to admit Asians and Latinos into the category would cause necessary changes that were not necessary for the Irish and Jews.

The second difference concerns historical memory. The Irish and Jews represent bad memories within Europe, memories of colonialism and genocide, and thus they operate as the symbolic representation of Europe's moral failings. The Irish and Jews do not have that symbolic meaning in the United States and in fact may carry the opposite symbolic meaning by representing the idea that "anyone" can make it and be accepted here, even those who were despised in Europe.

In contrast, African Americans and Mexican Americans and Native Americans, most notably, among others, represent a symbolic reminder of the hollowness of claims to white moral superiority. The Irish and Jews are not a psychic threat to the ideological supremacy of white identity in the same way that many Latinos, Asian Americans, and certainly African Americans are.

A third major difference concerns perceived assimilability, although here the Irish and Jews must separate. The Irish are perceived as entirely assimilable, Jews only partly so because of religion (which is another reason Jews tend to be moved back and forth). Latinos, to the extent they are European, come from a Spanish Catholic culture considered premodern and less civilized, and to the extent they are also indigenous, come from a culture perceived as totally different than Anglo-European. The symbolic opposition between "East" and "West," or the Orient and the Occident, is a major prop of the Anglo-European self-image fomenting a plethora of such dichotomies as between "individualism versus collectivism," "democracy versus despotism," and future-oriented versus static societies. These binary formulations rule out the possibility of synthesis and present assimilation as a doubtful project at best (which explains the FBI's ungrounded suspicions against Asian immigrants such as Wen Ho Lee). This issue of assimilability has become more rather than less important in recent years, with political theorists such as Peter Brimelow and Samuel Huntington openly defending the goal of maintaining hegemony for Anglo-European cultural traditions, against liberal immigration laws and cultural integration, and asserting that the very survival of Western civilization is at stake (Brimelow 1995; Huntington 1998 and 2004).

These three major differences present obstacles to Asian Americans and Latinos following the path of white ethnics to "become" white. It is still proving difficult enough to be seen as "American." The claim that Asian Americans and Latinos will become white ignores the issue of color and other racial differences, takes no notice of the varying symbolic meanings and historical challenges posed by these groups in regard to "American" metanarratives of moral and political superiority, and forgets the problem of "assimilability." It thus returns us to the problem of misidentification discussed earlier, refusing to recognize the specificity and complexity by which people are vilified. To give another example of this complexity, Asians and Jews have been similarly grouped together in the representations of their cultures as superior, threatening, and monolithic. In other words, unlike for African Americans and Latinos, Asians and Jews are not seen as having inferior intelligence or primitive cultures, but as groups with collective goals to take over the world and/or evil intent toward those outside their groups (the "yellow peril" and "Jewish world conspiracy"). This kind of ideology requires specific analysis, because it operates differently vis-à-vis, among other issues, affirmative action concerns in regard to higher education.

The complications of racism in the United States have further multiplied since the events of September 11, 2001. The most recent issue that has arisen since 9/11 involves the representations of Arab Americans, a group that is very much racialized and essentialized with group attributes considered similar to Asians and Jews. Yet again, their racialization works in specific ways mediated by ideological claims about their cultures and most notably the religion of Islam.

Racisms

What makes all of these diverse examples of vilification forms of racism is the fact that the threats each group poses flow from group attributes. In other words, it is not that each member of these groups *chooses* to exemplify or pursue the negative quality attributed to them. Racism denies that kind of individual agency. Rather, racism sees each member of the racialized and despised group as harboring tendencies and manifesting character traits as a result of their genealogical identity. To consider Christianity a higher religion than Islam would be a form of cultural chauvinism; to consider Muslims as all potential suicide bombers is a form of racism.

Racism can be defined, then, as a negative value or set of values projected as an essential attribute onto a group whose members are defined through genea-logical connection, as sharing some origin, and who are demarcated on the basis of some visible features. In order to take account of the variety of specific instances of racism, we need a typology for the variety of forms racism can take.

Racial oppression works on multiple axes, I would argue, with color being the most *dominant* and currently the most *pernicious*. But color is not *exhaustive* of all the forms racial oppression can take. The most pejorative terms used against Asian Americans often have a racial connotation but one without a color component—"Chinks," "slant-eyes," and, for the Vietnamese, "gooks." These terms denigrate a whole people, not a particular set of customs or a specific history, and thus parallel the essentializing move of racist discourse that universalizes negative value across a group. The two most pejorative terms widely used against Latinos in this country have been the terms "spic"—a word whose genealogy references people who were heard by Anglos as saying "no spic English"—and "wetback." The first invokes the denigration of language, the second denigrates both where people came from and how they got here: from Mexico across the Rio Grande. Mexican Americans were also called "greasers," which connoted the condition of their hair, not their skin color. Thus, these terms demonstrate the possibility of a racialization and racism that works by constructing and then denigrating racialized features and charac-teristics other than skin color. We might think of these as two independent axes of racialization that operate through physical features other than color, and through genealogies of cultural origin. There is, then, the color axis, the physical- char-acteristics-other-than-color axis, and the cultural-origin axis.

The discrimination against Asian Americans and Latinos has also operated very strongly on a fourth axis, "nativism." Nativism is a prejudice against immigrants; thus it is distinct, though often related to, xenophobia or the rejection of foreigners. Acuña explains that historical nativism is also distinct from anthropological nativ-ism, which refers to a "revival of indigenous culture," because historical nativism refers to the belief of some Anglo-Americans that they are "the true Americans, excluding even the Indian" because they represent in their cultural heritage the "idea" of "America" (1988, 158).[5] On this view, the problem with Asian Americans and Latinos is not just that they are seen as foreign; they are seen as ineluctably foreign. Their cultures of origin are seen as so inferior (morally and politically if not intellectually), they are incapable of and unmotivated toward assimilation to the superior mainstream white Anglo culture. They want to keep their languages, demand instruction in public schools in their primary languages, and they often maintain their own holidays, cuisines, religions, and living areas (the latter sometimes by choice). Despite the fact that Mexican Americans have been living within the current U.S. borders for longer than most Anglo-Americans, they are all too often seen as squatters on U.S. soil, interlopers who "belong" elsewhere. This "xenophobia directed within" has been especially virulent at specific times in our history, during and after both world wars, for example, and is enjoying a resurgence since 9/11 and the war against Iraq.

Another feature of nativism is its use to justify claims of differential rights for various minority groups. In my view, there is no question that African Americans together with American Indians have a moral claim on this country larger than any group, and that the redress made thus far is completely inadequate toward repairing the present inequities that persist as a legacy of past state-organized mass atrocities. Some may believe that a kind of nativist argument would provide further justification for these legitimate claims to redress, on the grounds that these groups' forebears were here longer and/or their labor and ingenuity contributed a great deal to the wealth of this country. More recent immigrants, it may be thought, "deserve" less by way of protected opportunities or government assistance. The issue of nativism is thus important to address in relation to the differences and potential conflicts among communities of color, since many Asian Americans and Latinos are post-1965 immigrants (when the restrictions on immigration based on geography were lifted). One might well ask, What is wrong with nativist arguments when they are used to differentiate groups' moral claims based on histories of oppression, and is the critique of nativism based ultimately on opportunistic self-interest?

There are both consequentialist and non-consequentialist arguments one can make against nativism. The principal consequentialist argument against using nativism to justify differential rights is that it will produce (or in reality, merely maintain) a hierarchy of first- and second-class citizens. Nativist arguments might well tend to encourage people to turn a blind eye to what happens to "non-native" peoples, especially those trying to cross borders (see, e.g., Marmon Silko 1994). Such enforced hierarchies of status within a society must surely share responsibility for creating the problems of crime and social insecurity that adversely affect everyone.

These provide consequentialist arguments against nativism based on its subsequent effects on the nation, but one might also make non-consequentialist arguments against nativism. The logic of nativism is based on the idea that those native to this country "deserve" more, not just because they have been here longer, but because they or their relatives contributed the labor and ingenuity that made this country wealthy. There are several arguments one could make against this view. One might first point out that there are numerous groups within the United States who contributed labor and ingenuity toward the nation's wealth and who have not received any approximation of fair compensation. In other words, nativists like Buchanan are hypocrites unless they are vigorously pursuing reparations. But one could also argue that the wealth of the United States has been the product in no small part of neocolonial and imperial global relations that ensured the extraction of natural resources at a price U.S. companies determined, as well as the super-exploitation of labor (i.e., a much larger extraction of surplus value) that produced the capital brought back here. The building of the Panama Canal gives just one small but clear example. The United States contributed capital and some of the engineers for the project, helped to plan a coup to separate the country off from Colombia, who would have been a much more powerful negotiating adversary, and manufactured a treaty which no Panamanian signed guaranteeing that all profits from the canal would go to the United States "in perpetuity." Not only did the treaty guarantee capital flight, it gave the United States complete political autonomy over the canal zone, cutting right through the heart of Panama and thus splitting it in half. The United States was also given the right to intervene with military force whenever it unilaterally determined that canal security was at stake, a proviso that had major negative effects on the political developments in the country and in particular in the development of social justice movements. The people who actually labored to build the canal, enticed from the West Indies and Asia as well as local people, were paid 10 cents a day and died from yellow fever in tens of thousands (see Coniff 1985; LeFeber 1990). Nonetheless, antitreaty rhetoric in the United States persists in calling it "our canal."

Such facts as these contest the true referent of the term "nativist." Peoples in foreign lands have been native if that means contributing the labor and resources that made the United States wealthy. The descendants of those who built the Panama Canal mostly live in Panama today, but some have immigrated here. And the so-called "illegals" working here today make a substantial economic contribution, to the general national wealth. Nativism thus obscures more than it clarifies various groups' relationships to the history and prosperity of the United States. It is important to note that many Asian American and Latino subgroups have been here for multiple centuries as well, in various forms of indentured servitude (especially Mexicans, Chinese, and Japanese). But the more recent immigrants, from places like El Salvador, Nicaragua, Guatemala, the Dominican Republic, the Philippines, Vietnam, Laos, and Cambodia, can also be directly tied to U.S. policies that made their countries literally unlivable for them. Surely these immigrants therefore have a moral claim on this nation's wealth that has no relation to their number of years here. Nativism has neither a moral or historical justification; it is just another divide-and-conquer tactic.

Thus, the color axis is only one of the axes that need to be understood as pivotal in racist ideologies. Racism can and has operated in ways in which color is not central but other physical features, cultural characteristics and origins, and status as "native" or "non-native" operate to the same effect. It is important to note that these other axes are forms of racism that produce other ways to classify and delimit subsets of people and then justify discrimination against them. All immigrant groups are not racialized in the sense of universalizing negative value across a group that is demarcated on the basis of visible features or essentializing their cultural characteristics as static. Russian and Eastern European immigrants, though often living in horribly poor conditions with little community help of any kind, are not singled out, as are recent Southeast Asian and Central American immigrants, as the targets of group-based violence and scapegoating. European immigrants are not tagged as cultural inferiors, and their difference is not racialized in the way that Latinos and

Asian Americans experience. The latter groups' categorization as "foreign" is marked on their body, as Wen Ho Lee was forcibly reminded when he was put in solitary confinement with chained legs for nine months as a result of being "racially profiled" and suspected of a loyalty to China unrelated to his citizenship or his political commitments.

My basic thesis, then, is simply that we need an expanded analysis of racism and an attentiveness to the specificities of various forms it can take in regard to different groups, rather than continuing to accept the idea that it operates in basically one way, with one axis, that is differentially distributed among various groups.

What's at Stake

I want to end with an example that links the false homogenization of people of color with the recent demise of affirmative action programs in higher education, which I think will show how much is at stake in our need to recognize the complexity of our differences. Dana Takagi argues persuasively that the recent disabling of affirmative action policies "grew out of fluid discourse(s) on racial minorities in higher education in which the main issues were pivotally constructed in, and encapsulated by, the debate over Asian admissions" and specifically the debate over claims that Asian Americans were overrepresented in American universities (1992, 7). In other words, the alleged overrepresentation of Asian Americans in colleges and universities was used to argue that the problem of minority underrepresentation in higher education is not caused by race, and therefore an affirmative action based on race is neither helpful nor justifiable.

What I would argue here is that the black/white binary is operating in this case to obscure the real problems. Conservatives argued that Asian Americans are non-white so that their case can be used to dismantle affirmative action for all: if they can get in, we all can get in. But this would follow only if the category "nonwhite" is undifferentiated in terms of how racism operates. Others wanted to argue that Asian Americans are being treated here as white, and thus have no interest in an antiracist coalition.

It is certainly true that it is a white power structure that privileges such things as test scores. But Asian Americans were still not actually being treated as whites. Takagi points out that the claims of overrepresentation conveniently ignored the large disparity between Asian American admission rates and white admission rates (the percentage of admissions in relation to the pool of applicants), a disparity that cannot be accounted for by SAT scores or grades. That is, holding scores and grades constant, white individuals were more likely to be admitted than Asian Americans, even if in real numbers on some campuses Asian American acceptances outnumbered whites. (To give one example of this, the Asian American Student Association at Brown University discovered that between 1979 and 1987 there was a 750 percent increase in Asian applications, even while there was a steadily declining admission rate—from 44 percent in 1979 to 14 percent in 1987) (1992, 28). So there has been a covert quota system operating against Asian American applicants in many university systems, which is covered over by their high numbers of admission and is no doubt motivated by the same fears of "yellow peril" that were used to justify discrimination in the 1800s. Asian Americans are not seen as white despite the fact that they have so-called "white" attributes because they are seen as unassimilable; they are suspected of retaining loyalty to Asian countries and thus of being a threat to "the nation." The concern about overrepresentation targeted Asian Americans exclusively; the only people similarly targeted in the past were Jews, and these cases are clearly attributable to anti-Semitism. This concern certainly has not been raised in regard to the poor, who are underrepresented, or to the children of alumni or to athletes, both of whom are overrepresented.

Takagi traces the empirical studies, public discourse, and policy changes prompted by this concern over overrepresentation to the argument that affirmative action should ignore race and address only class, even though the claim that racism can be addressed in this way can be easily empirically disproved given the disparity of SAT scores within classes across racial difference.[6]

What this case demonstrates is not that all nonwhites should be grouped together in all cases of attempts to redress social inequities, but precisely the opposite: they should not be lumped together. The problems of discrimination that Asian Americans face in higher education in the United States have had to do with overt policies that apply quotas based on specific forms of racism directed against them. The problem of discrimination that African Americans and Latinos have faced in higher education has to do with the use of SAT scores and the quality of their public education, which is vastly unequal to that received by whites. Racism is the culprit in each case, but the means and ideology vary, and thus the effective redress will have to vary.

Takagi recounts that some Asian American activists who wanted to end the unfair quotas on their admission rates called for a meritocracy of admissions based on SAT scores and grades. But this would block only one form of racism, leaving others not only intact but ideologically reenforced. Meritocracy is still an illusion highly disadvantageous to African Americans and Latinos. Thus, strategies that seek to eliminate discrimination, including argumentative strategies used to defend affirmative action, must either be made specific to certain historically disadvantaged groups or, if they are general, must consider their possible effects on other groups. Only a rich knowledge of the specific and variable forms of racism in the United States will make such considerations possible.

On Being Mixed

Latin Americans have never been able to take a racial or cultural identity for granted:

> Who are we? asks the Liberator [Venezuelan] Simon Bolivar. "...We are not Europeans, we are not Indians, but a species in between.... [W]e find ourselves in the difficult position of challenging the natives for title of possession, and of upholding the country that saw us born against the opposition of the invaders.... It is impossible to identify correctly to what human family we belong." (Zea 1988–89, 37)

Part European, part indigenous, culturally a mix between the legacy of colonial aggression and colonial oppression, neither Latin Americans nor U.S. Latinos have ever had an unproblematic relationship to the questions of culture, identity, race, ethnicity, or even liberation. Alicia Gaspar de Alba goes so far as to call this hybridity a "cultural schizophrenia" that afflicts all "New World" peoples as the psychological effect of the Conquest and subsequent split identity (1998, 227).

At the same time, Latin American thought has been in constant dialogue with European thought, and the latter has tended toward purist constructions of race, ethnicity, and culture. The subsequent contradiction between those ideas and Latin American reality has produced a rich tradition of philosophical work on the concept of cultural identity and its relation to the self (see esp. Schutte 1993). In countries where nationalist aspirations cannot attach themselves to purist constructions of identity (as is invoked by the phrase "as American as apple pie" in the United States), a different set of practices and concepts around identity has emerged, one not without its own racisms, but one that might evoke an alternative conceptualization for mixed race and ethnic identities.[1]

In the 1980s and 1990s, the movement of mixed racial identity first became widely public in the United States, as new political groups formed, magazines and journals were created, and major lobbying efforts were launched to open up the Census categories (see discussions in Root 1996; Root 1992; and Camper 1994). This movement raises a number of important, concrete political questions in regard to a state-recognized mixed race category, with implications for apportionment, representation, educational funding, and the statistical claims that can be made about the overall situation of racialized groups. Many, many more people in the United States are of mixed races than is often acknowledged—as much as 90 percent of African Americans, 30 percent of southern whites by some estimates, and almost all Latinos, Filipinos, and Native Americans—and marriages between people of different races are increasing in every category. If all of these people were removed from statistical calculations of group identity the assessments of many groups would be significantly altered.

There are essentially two sets of questions that the mixed race movement raises: the first set concerns policy issues of various sorts, and the second concerns philosophical issues. As Maria P. P. Root explains, "The existence of racially mixed persons challenges long-held notions about the biological, moral, and social meaning of race" (1992, 3). What is the identity of a mixed race person? Can we meaningfully adumbrate identities by percentages based on familial genealogy? Or do mixed persons transcend existing categories altogether? And besides the metaphysical question about the "real" identity of mixed race persons, there are also philosophical questions about the political and symbolic meanings of being mixed. Is mixing a form of identity degeneration, a politics of conquest, or a laudable goal within a liberatory politics? Do mixed race persons symbolize positive political values or problematic ones?

In this chapter, as in earlier ones, I will not attempt to formulate policy, and thus I will not pursue the first set of questions just described. Rather, my interest is again more philosophical, toward exploring the metaphysics and politics of being mixed, as well as the conditions (metaphysical, historical, etc.) under which being mixed creates an identity problem in the first place. I will also consider various proposed solutions to the problem, including assimilationism and nomadic subjectivity, and I will conclude with a description, assessment, and political analysis of the two main metaphysical options for conceptualizing mixed identity. The primary focus will remain on mixed racial identity, but race is mediated by ethnic and cultural identities in such a way that these cannot always be neatly disentangled. In certain respects the philosophical issue at stake is the same whether the object is mixed race, mixed ethnicity, or mixed culture: all have been devalued as incoherent, diluted, and thus weak.

Raced Purely or Purely Erased

Did I piss in their gene pool
If I did it wouldn't matter
they kept me in the deep end
'cause the slightest dilution
in their solution
was perceived as pollution
Sometimes I feel like a socio-genetic experiment
A petri-dish community's token of infection.

Disposable Heroes of Hiphoprisy

For a variety of reasons that I will explore in the next section, during the European conquest of the Americas, Spanish colonizers intermarried with indigenous people at a higher rate than did the English colonizers of the North. Moreover, Africans were involved in the conquest from the beginning, initially as participants alongside the Europeans. And the importation of slaves from Africa two centuries after the Conquest began had the same effect wherever it occurred throughout the Americas: a mixing of groups, both through massive coercion as well as some voluntary unions. The result is that the population of Hispanics today is a mix of Spanish, indigenous, and/or African heritages. Neocolonial relations between the United States and Latin America since 1898 (the date of the so-called Spanish-American War, which inaugurated the period of U.S. imperialism) have created the conditions to continue this practice of intermarrying (the joke in Panama is that the most lasting effect of the 1989 U.S. invasion of Panama will be found neither in politics nor in the drug trade but in the thousand marriages and births that resulted).

My own family is a typical case. My father's father was an immigrant from Spain, who came to Panama in the early part of the twentieth century and married a woman from the interior (my Grandmother Eugenia's precise racial ancestry is unknown, but her African ancestry was visibly apparent). The subsequent canal-based relations between Panama and the United States created conditions in which my father came to study in Florida and married a white Anglo-Irish woman, that is, my mother. And through my father's subsequent liaisons, I have a range of siblings from black to brown to tan to freckled, spanning five countries and three continents at last count (Panama, Costa Rica, Spain, Venezuela, and the United States). Ours is truly the postcolonial postmodernist family, an open-ended set of indeterminate national, cultural, racial, and even linguistic allegiances.

However, despite the normality of such mixing in Panama, in the United States it is a different story, and my own experience of my identity has been at times painful and confusing. In Panama, my older sister and I were prized for our light skin, and in fact, because I was exceptionally light, with auburn hair, my father named me "Linda," meaning pretty. There, the mix itself did not pose any difficulties; the issue of concern was the *nature* of the mix—lighter or darker—and we were of the appropriately valued lighter type. When my parents divorced, my sister and I moved with our mother to her white parents' home in central Florida, and here the social meanings of our racial identity were wholly transformed. We were always referred to as her "Latin daughters," and the fact that we were mixed made us objects of peculiarity and subject to a certain amount of familial alienation. My white extended family had not wholly embraced my mother's marriage to a nonwhite foreigner, and my sister and I instantiated the "mistake" they felt she had made. Moreover, in the central Florida of the 1950s, a biracial system and the "one-drop rule" still reigned, and our mixed race status meant that we had a complex relationship to white identity: if assimilated in language, dress, and behavior, we could be accepted as "almost white"; but if we maintained Spanish and other markings of "otherness," our situation was much more precarious.[2] My sister, who was darker and spoke only Spanish at first, had to make a dramatic transition, but she still suffered discrimination at school and second-class status at home. We eventually became highly assimilated, but for both of us this process created feelings of alienation and inferiority. Passing requires vigilance and self-censorship, and thus it causes one to dislike those aspects of self that reveal otherness. I believe these experiences also, however, helped us to critique the Jim Crow system, for through the experience of having racist whites sometimes unknowingly accept us we could see all too clearly the speciousness of the biracial illusion as well as the hurtfulness and irrationality of racial hierarchies and systems of exclusion. I remember hearing a popular white girl refer to people in racist ways one day while I was standing in the lunch line at school, and thinking "You could be talking about me." For those of us who could pass, our community acceptance was always at the price of mis-recognition and the troubling knowledge that our social self was grounded in a lie.[3]

In cultures defined by racialized identities, infected with the illusion of purity, and divided by racial hierarchies, mixed white/nonwhite persons face an irresolvable status ambiguity. They are rejected by the dominant race as impure and therefore inferior, but they are also sometimes disliked and distrusted by the oppressed race for their privileges of closer association with domination. Surprisingly consistent re-pudiations of mixing are found across differences of social status: both oppressed and dominant communities have often disapproved of open mixing, both sometimes fail to acknowledge and accept mixed offspring, and both often value a purity for racial identity.[4] The mixed race person cannot easily escape condemnation: if they are perceived to be trying to pass, they will be condemned by dominant groups for lying and by oppressed groups for individualist opportunism; but if they announce their nondominant status, they will be condemned for another kind of political oppor-tunism. These problems are particularly obvious for persons whose mix includes whiteness, but it can even beset those who have two nonwhite parents of different races, since the races are so often placed on a scale of oppression with one race seen as less oppressed or "almost dominant." Of course, there is some truth to the political valence accorded various kinds of mixed identities and certainly to that accorded various kinds of opportunistic behavior: I am not repudiating the very legitimacy of all political judgment here. But what is also true is that the judgment of mixed identities themselves, as opposed to the behavior of mixed race persons—for ex-ample, to see the mixed person as the manifestation of conquest, or as the result of one parent's attempt to assimilate—is based on historical events to which the mixed person herself did not in any way contribute.

Interestingly, this problem has not been restricted to a single political ideology: both left and right political discourses have placed a premium on racial purity. For the right, race mixing is a form of "pollution" that requires intermittent processes of ethnic cleansing, which can take the form of genocide, segregation, or simply rural terrorism (the kind practiced by the Ku Klux Klan, the Confederate Knights of America, and the White Aryan Resistance). The very concept of "rape as geno-cide"—the belief that a massive transcommunity-orchestrated series of rapes will result in the genocide of a culture—assumes purity as a necessary and prized cultural identity attribute. Right-wing nationalist movements have also been grounded, in some cases, on the claimed need for a separate political formation that is coextensive with a racial or ethnic identity; here the state becomes the representative of a race or ethnic group and the arbiter over questions of group inclusion.[5] The state must then make it its business to oversee the reproduction of this group, thus to engage in what

Foucault called "bio-power," in order to ensure a continuation of its constituency (Foucault 1980).

For the left, cultural autonomy and community integrity are held up as having an intrinsic value, resulting in mixed race persons treated as symbols of colonial aggression or cultural dilution. The very demand for self-determination too often presupposes an authentic self, with clear, unambiguous commitments and allegiances. Thus, as Richard Rodriguez suggests sarcastically, the "Indian [has] become the mascot of an international ecology movement," but not just any Indian. "The industrial countries of the world romanticize the Indian who no longer exists [i.e. the authentic, culturally autonomous Indian without any connection to capitalist economic formations], ignoring the Indian who does — the Indian who is poised to chop down his rain forest, for example. Or the Indian who reads *The New York Times*" (1992, 6). The mythic authentic voice of the oppressed, valorized by the left, is culturally *un*changed, racially *un*mixed, and, as a matter of fact, extinct. The veneration of authenticity leads the left to disregard (when they do not scorn) the survivors of colonialism.

Thus, in many cultures today, mixed race people are treated as the corporeal instantiation of a lack — the lack of an identity that can provide a public status. They (we) are turned away from as if from an unpleasant sight, the sight and mark of an unclean copulation, the product of a taboo, the sign of racial impurity, cultural dilution, colonial aggression, or even emasculation. Which particular attribution is chosen will reflect the particular community's cultural self-understanding and its position as dominant or subordinate. But the result is too often the same: children with impure racial identities are treated as an unwanted reminder of something shameful or painful, and are alienated (to a greater or lesser extent) from every community to which they have some claim of attachment.

Some theorists have suggested that when such a rigidity around racial identity manifests itself among oppressed people, it is the result of their internalization of oppression and acceptance of racist, self-denigrating cultural values (see, e.g., Root 1992). But I am not sure that this is the cause in every case, or the whole story — the problem may be deeper, in that foundational concepts of self and identity are founded on purity, wholeness, and coherence. A self that is internally heterogeneous beyond repair or resolution becomes a candidate for pathology in a society where the integration of self is taken to be necessary for mental health. We need to reflect upon this premium put on internal coherence and racial purity, and how this is manifested in Western concepts and practices of identity as a public persona as well as subjectivity as a foundational understanding of the self. We need to consider what role this preference for purity and racial separateness has had on dominant formulations of identity and subjectivity, and what the effects might be if this preference was no longer operative.

Behind my claim that an important relationship exists between purity and racial identity is of course the presupposition that an important relationship exists between race and identity, a relationship that may not always exist but isn't in danger of imminent deconstruction. Today, it is easily apparent that acceptance and status within a community is tied to one's racial identification and *identifiability*. In the U.S., Census forms as well as application forms of many types confer various sorts of benefits or resources according to racial identity, thus affecting one's social status. Less formally, one's ability to be accepted in various kinds of social circles, religious groups, and neighborhoods is tied to one's (apparent) race. And I would also argue that not only social status is affected here, but one's lived interiority as well. Such things as government benefits and employment opportunities have an effect on one's subjectivity, one's sense of oneself as a unique, individuated person, and as competent, acceptable, or inferior. In other words, without a coherent identity, an individual can feel an absence of agency. Dominant discourses, whether they are publicly regulated and institutionalized or more amorphous and decentralized, can affect the lived experience of subjectivity. Discourses and institutions implicitly invoke selves that have specific racial identities, which are correlated to those selves' specific legal status, discursive authority, epistemic credibility, and social standing.

Identity is not, of course, monopolized by race, and race does not operate on identity as an autonomous determinant. Mixed race persons probably notice more than others the extent to which "race" is a social construction, ontologically dependent on a host of contextual factors. The meanings of both race and such things as skin color or hair texture are mediated by language, religion, nationality, and culture, to produce a racialized identity. As a result, an individual's racial identity and identifiability can change across communities, and a family's race can change across history. In the Dominican Republic, "black" is defined as Haitian, and dark-skinned Dominicans do not self-identify as black but as dark Indians or mestizos. Coming to the United States, Dominicans "become" black by the dominant U.S. standards. Under apartheid in South Africa, numbers of people would petition the government every year to change their official racial classification, resulting in odd official announcements from the Home Affairs Minister that, for example, this year "nine whites became colored, 506 coloreds became white, two whites became Malay...40 coloreds became black, 666 blacks became colored, 87 coloreds became Indian..." (quoted in Minh-Ha 1991, 73).[6] The point here is not that racial identities are often misidentified, but that race does not stand alone: race identity is mediated by other factors, political and economic as well as national ones. And appearance is also socially mediated: the dominant perspective in the United States on a person's racial identity or whether they "look" Latino or black or even white is not based on natural perception. Appearances "appear" differently across cultural contexts.

To the extent that this public and private self involves a racial construction, this self, in the United States, has been constructed with a premium on purity and separation. The valorization of cultural integrity and autonomy found in diverse political orientations, from left to right, brings along with it the valorization of purity over dilution, of the authentic voice over the voice of collusion, and of autonomy over what might be called "biopolitical intercourse."

Racial Hierarchies and the Melting Pot

> What, then, is the American, this new man?...He is an American, who, leaving behind him all his ancient prejudices and manners, receives

new ones from the new mode of the life he has embraced, the new government he obeys, and the new rank he holds.

Hector St. Jean de Crèvecoeur, 1782

If it is generally true that selves are constituted in relationship to communities that have been racially constructed, what happens when there are multiple, conflicting communities through which a self is constituted? What would a concept of the self look like that did not valorize purity and coherence? If we reject the belief that retaining group integrity is an intrinsic good, how will this effect our political goals of resisting the oppression of racialized groups?

Within the United States, assimilationism has been the primary alternative to a racial purity and separateness, but it has notoriously been restricted to European ethnicities, and it has worked to assimilate them all to a northern European WASP norm—thus Jewish and Catholic Southern Europeans were more difficult to assimilate to this norm and never quite made it into the melting pot. And of course, the melting pot failed to diminish racial hierarchies because it was never really intended to include different races; no proponent of the melting pot ideology ever promoted miscegenation (see Franklin 1989).

Moreover, as Homi Bhabha remarks, "Fixity, as the sign of cultural/historical/racial difference in the discourse of colonialism, is a paradoxical mode of representation: it connotes rigidity and an unchanging order as well as disorder, degeneracy and daemonic repetition" (1994, 66). Thus, the fluidity of cultural identity promoted by the assimilationist discourse actually was used to bolster northern European-American's claims to cultural superiority: their (supposed) "fluidity" was contrasted with and presented as a higher cultural achievement than the (supposed) fixity and rigidity of colonized cultures. Here, fixity symbolized inferiority while flexibility symbolized superiority (although of course, in reality, the designation of "fixity" generally only meant the inability or unwillingness to conform to the northern European norm). This paradox of the meaning of fixity explains how it was possible that, simultaneous to the Panama Canal Commission's construction of rigid racial groups working on the canal, the ideology at home (i.e., the United States) was dominated by the melting-pot imagery. The WASPs could be fluid, tolerant, and evolving, but the natives could not be so. The very fluidity of identity that one might think would break down hierarchies was used to justify them as superior to rigidly traditional societies. Given this, there exists a prima facie danger in drawing on assimilationist rhetoric, as it was espoused in the United States, to reconfigure relations of domination.

The fact of the matter is that throughout Latin America and the Caribbean, a true melting pot of peoples, cultures, and races was created unlike anything north of the border. The liberal, modernist-based vision of assimilation succeeded best in the premodernist, Catholic, Iberian-influenced countries, while the proponents of secularism and modernism to the north were too busy to notice. Richard Rodriguez points out that, still today, "Mexico City is modern in ways that 'multiracial,' ethnically 'diverse' New York is not yet. Mexico City is centuries more modern than racially 'pure,' provincial Tokyo.... Mexico is the capital of modernity, for in the sixteenth century, ... Mexico initiated the task of the twenty-first century—the renewal of the old, the known world, through miscegenation. Mexico carries the idea of a round world to its biological conclusion" (1992, 24–25).

Today, the liberalism that spawned assimilationism has metamorphosed into an ethic of appreciation for the diversity of cultures. In the name of preserving cultural diversity, and in the secret hope of appropriating native wisdom and the stimulation that only exotica can provide to a consumption-weary middle class, indigenous cultures and peoples are commodified, fetishized, and fossilized as standing outside of history and social evolution (if they are not totally different than "us," then they will not be exotic enough to have commodity value). Thus, an image of the American Indian straddling a snowmobile (as appeared in the *New York Times*) evokes affected protestations from educated Anglos about the tragic demise of a cultural identity, as if American Indian identity can only exist where it is pure, unsullied, fixed in time and place (R. Rodriguez 1992, 6). The project of "protecting" the cultural "integrity" of indigenous peoples in the guise of cultural appreciation secures a sense of superiority for those who see their own cultures as dynamic and evolving. Anglo culture can grow and improve through what it learns from "native" cultures, and thus the natives are prized for an exchange value that is dependent on their stagnation.

Assimilation North and South

> Jose Vasconcelos, Mexican philosopher, envisaged *una raza mestiza, una mezcla de razas afines, una raza de color—la primera raza sintesis del globo*. He called it a cosmic race, *la raza cosmica*, a fifth race embracing the four major races of the world. Opposite to the theory of the pure Aryan ... his theory is one of inclusivity.
>
> Gloria Anzaldua, *Borderlands/La Frontera*

In North America, then, assimilationism and its heir apparent, cultural appreciation, have not led to a true mixing of races or cultures, or to an end to the relations of domination among cultures. However, interestingly, both the concept and the practice of assimilation resonate very differently in South America and Central America. As I will discuss later in this chapter, for Mexican philosophers such as Samuel Ramos and Leopoldo Zea, assimilation did not require conformity to a dominant norm; instead, assimilation was associated with an anti-xenophobic cosmopolitanism that sought to integrate diverse elements into a new formation. What can account for the different practices and theories of assimilation in North and South cultures? And what were the elements involved in U.S. assimilationism that allowed it to coexist with racism rather than come into conflict with it? Finding the answer to such questions can be instructive for the project of developing a better alternative to identity constructions than those based on racial purity. Toward this, I have already suggested that assimilationism in the North was organized around an implicit normative identity (WASP) to which others were expected to conform; hence its exclusive application to northern Europeans. And I have also suggested that the flexibility of identity claimed by assimilationists was used to bolster WASP claims to cultural superiority over the supposedly rigid peoples and cultures that could not be made to conform. I want to offer two further elements toward such an answer, one taken from cultural history and the other involving the Enlightenment concept of secular reason.

Latin American and North American countries have different cultural genealogies based on the different origins of their colonizing settlers: respectively, Roman Catholic Iberia and Germano-Protestant England. In North America, race mixing generally was perceived with abhorrence and made illegal. In the countries colonized by Spain, by contrast, "elaborate racial taxonomies gained official recognition from the outset . . . and these casta designations became distinct identities unto themselves, with legal rights as well as disabilities attaching to each" (Fernandez 1992, 135). After independence, the casta system was eliminated from official discourses, and racial discrimination was made illegal, since such practices of discrimination obviously could not work in countries where as few as 5 percent of the population were *not* mestizo of some varied racial combination.

According to Carlos Fernandez and the historian A. Castro, this contrast in practices regarding racial difference can be accounted for in the historical differences between Nordic and Latin cultures.

> Due primarily to its imperial character, the Roman world of which Spain (Hispania) was an integral part developed over time a multiethnically tolerant culture, a culture virtually devoid of xenophobia. The Romans typically absorbed the cultures as well as the territories of the peoples they conquered. Outstanding among their cultural acquisitions were the Greek tradition and, later, the Judaic tradition. It was the Roman co-optation of Judaic Christianity that the Spanish inherited as Catholicism. (Fernandez 1992, 135)

Thus, in the missionary zeal of the Spanish Christians can be found both the spirit of Roman imperialism as well as its cosmopolitanism.

By contrast, the Germanic peoples of northern Europe "emerged into history at the margins of the Roman empire, constantly at war with the legions, not fully conquered or assimilated into Roman life." Fernandez hypothesizes that this "condition of perpetual resistance against an alien power and culture" produced the generally negative attitude of the Germans toward foreigners, especially since the Roman legions with which they fought included numerous ethnic groups. This attitude had profound historical results: "The persistence of the German peoples, born of their struggles against the Romans, can also be seen later in history as an important element in the Protestant schism with Rome accomplished by the German Martin Luther. It is no coincidence that Protestantism is primarily a phenomenon of Northwestern Europe while Catholicism is mainly associated with Southern Europe" (136).

Leopoldo Zea's analysis supports Fernandez's account, although, as we will see, Zea portrays the difference as between Christianity and modernism rather than between kinds of Christianity.

Whether founded on Christianity, the history of Germanic tribes, or Spain's multicultural past, the different attitudes toward race-mixing is not the whole story as to why genecide was so widespread in America and not in the South: "The difference in the size and nature of the Native American populations in Anglo and

Latin America also helps account for the emergence of different attitudes about race" (136). In the North, the indigenous peoples were generally nomadic and seminomadic and comparatively less numerous; in the South, the indigenous peoples were very numerous and "lived a settled, advanced (even by European standards) agricultural life with large cities and developed class systems" (137). So the resultant integrations between race and cultural formations that developed differently in the North and the South were the product not just of different European traditions but also their interaction with the different cultures in the New World.

And certainly Roman imperialism was not less oppressive than Germanic forms of domination: both perpetrated a strategy of domination. But it is instructive to note the different forms domination can take, and the different legacies each form has yielded in the present. In the North, the melting pot set up a border patrol reminiscent of the strategy by which Germanic peoples resisted being incorporated into the Roman superpower, which was ethnically and racially diverse but centered always in Rome. Thus, for Nordic peoples, assimilation and cultural integrity were posed in conflict, and in order to maintain the distinctness of their borders they were willing to commit sweeping annihilations. Such a view was held by Louis Agassiz, an influential nineteenth-century Swiss naturalist, who stated: "The production of half-breeds is as much a sin against nature, as incest in a civilized community is a sin against purity of character.... No efforts should be spared to check that which is abhorrent to our better nature, and to the progress of a higher civilization and a purer morality" (quoted in Gould 1993, 98). For Rome and Hispania, however, assimilation meant expansion, development, growth. Cultural supremacy did not require isolationism or separation but precisely the constant absorption and blending of difference into an ever larger, more complex, heterogeneous whole. Border control was thus not the highest priority or even considered an intrinsic good. This is why the concept of assimilationism has never had the same meaning in the South as it has in the North, either conceptually or in practice; in the North assimilation has always meant in practice that "others" must conform to the dominant norm, whereas in the South it signifies what is always more the reality, that two or more identities are each altered as a result of juxtaposition and interrelationship.

This quick overview and history is no doubt simplistic, and it should be stressed again that racism of color shades continues to plague Latin America. But the story Fernandez provides remains useful if only for helping us to reconceptualize the relationship between purity and cultural flourishing.

The second part of the story about assimilation involves the Enlightenment concept of secular reason. The northern variant of assimilationism was strongly tied to the development of a liberal anti-feudal ideology that espoused humanism against the aristocracy and secularism against the fusion of church and civil society. The Enlightenment in northern Europe put forward a vision of universal humanism with equality and civil freedoms for all citizens of a secular state. Diverse ethnicities and religious allegiances could coexist and unite under the auspices of a larger community founded on natural law, and that natural law could be discerned through the use of secular reason, which was conceived as the common denominator across cultural differences. Thus, reason became the means through which the Nordic immigrants to North America could relax their borders enough to create a new ethnically mixed society.

But why was the banner of reason incapable of expanding beyond white WASP communities? To understand this it helps to recall that the European Enlightenment was flourishing at exactly the same time that European countries were most successfully colonizing the globe—exploiting, enslaving, and in some cases eliminating indigenous populations.[7] What can account for this juxtaposition between the invocations of liberty for all and the callous disregard of the liberty as well as well-being of non-Europeans? To answer this we need to look more critically at what grounded the claims to liberty.

Universalist humanism was based on a supposedly innate but unevenly developed capacity to reason. Both Leopoldo Zea and Enrique Dussel have written about the ways in which the western notion of reason is Eurocentric and was used from the beginning of the Conquest to judge the humanity of the Indians and then later the *criollos* and mestizos (See Zea 1988–1989; Dussel 1995). When the paradigm of reason is represented as culturally neutral but defined as the scientific practices of European-based countries, the result is a flattering contrast between Europe and its colonies. Reason is contrasted with ignorance, religion to superstition, and history to myth, producing a cultural hierarchy that vindicates colonialist arrogance. Dussel argues that the trick to produce such contrasts is to constitute "the other . . . as part of the Same": the practices of other cultures cannot be understood in their alterity so they are portrayed as inferior copies or less mature developments of European forms of rationality (Dussel 1995, 36). In this way, (purportedly) universal standards and articulations of rationality serve colonial and neocolonial policies by providing a uniform yardstick for measuring uneven development.

Following this, Zea has argued that identity is a central philosophical problematic within Latin America. The question of identity is not only relevant within cultural studies but also within the public sphere where the use of power is contested. (See Schutte 1993, 86). Recall from chapter 4 that the capacity for reasoning and science on the Western model requires an ability to detach oneself, to be objective, to subdue one's own passionate attachments and emotions. Such a personality type was associated with northern Europeans and contrasted with Latin temperaments, or any group mixed with Latins.

Thus a humanism based on secular reason, far from conflicting with racism and cultural chauvinism, supported their continuation. In its most benign form, reason could only support Europe's role as beneficent teacher for the backward Other, but could never sustain a relationship of equality. It is for this reason that Zea concludes:

> The racial mestizahe that did not bother the Iberian conquerors and colonizers was to disturb greatly the creators of the new empires of America, Asia, and Africa. Christianity blessed the unity of men and cultures regardless of race, more a function of their ability to be Christian. But modern civilization stressed racial purity, the having or lacking of particular habits and customs proper to a specific type of racial and cultural humanity. (Zea 1988–89, 37)

Thus, secularization actually promoted racial purity by replacing Christian values with culturally specific habits and customs. In challenging what is still a powerful orthodoxy—the claim that secularization has only progressive effects—Zea's critique of modernism strikes more deeply than even much of postmodernism. To today pretend that these existing concepts—of reason, of philosophy, and of religion—can be extracted from their cultural history and purged of their racial associations and racial content is a delusion. Reason, it turns out, is constitutively associated with whiteness, at least in its specific articulations in Western canonical discourses. Therefore, an account of the core of human nature which is based on a reasoning capacity is a racialized concept of the self *passing* for a universal one.

Given this history, then, it is no longer a surprise that the concept and practice of assimilationism that developed in this northern European context sought (a) to maintain its borders against the devouring capacities and polluting effects of other cultures, and (b) to unite its diverse ethnic groups on the basis of a criterion that simultaneously excluded others: the capacity for reason and science in the mode of northern Europe. Can the concept of assimilation be transformed and salvaged? This is doubtful, given that its legacy and connotations in the United States remain powerfully problematic. But the idea of *assimilao*—of two-way rather than one-way cultural influence—is surely on the right track.

Nomadic Identities

> Nomadic consciousness consists in not taking any kind of identity as permanent. The nomad is only passing through; s/he makes those necessarily situated connections that can help her/him to survive, but s/he never takes on fully the limits of one national, fixed identity. The nomad has no passport—or has too many of them.
>
> Rosi Braidotti, *Nomadic Subjects*

I want to look briefly at one other, more current alternative to conceptions of identity based on purity—the notion of nomad subjectivity introduced in the work of Deleuze and Guattari and developed as a political concept by feminist theorist Rosi Braidotti (see Deleuze and Guattari 1983, 1986, and 1987; for a critique, see Kaplan 1987). This concept is not analogous to assimilationism in being widely disseminated within dominant cultural discourses, but it is influential in certain academic, theoretical circles that take aim at essentialism and the outdated metaphysics of modernism. Proponents of nomad subjectivity announce that fluidity and indeterminateness will break up racial and cultural hierarchies that inflict oppression and subordination. Freed from state-imposed structures of identity by the indeterminate yet powerful flows of capital, which melts all traditions, belief systems, and institutions in its path just like a lava flow, nomad subjectivity deterritorializes the self toward becoming like "a nomad, an immigrant, and a gypsy" (Deleuze and Guattari 1986, 19). Within language, as within subjectivity,

> there is no longer any proper sense or figurative sense, but only a distribution of states that is part of the range of the word. The thing and other things are no longer anything

but intensities overrun by deterritorialized sound or words that are following their lines of escape.... Instead, it is now a question of a becoming that includes the maximum of difference as a difference of intensity, the crossing of a barrier. (22)

The flow of deterritorialization does not move between points but "has abandoned points, coordinates, and measure, like a drunken boat" (Deleuze and Guattari 1987, 296). Deterritorializations thus have the effect of deconstructing racial and morphological identity categories along with national, cultural, and ethnic ones, and so the result is not a multiply situated subject but a nomadic subject. The concept of the situated subject was developed by feminist theorists to counter an abstract, immaterial subject—the knower who is represented only by mind without body. The idea of being situated is that one is in a material place, a concrete or objectively describable context, that there is no knowing except knowing from a context, but Deleuze and Guattari's description of the nomad subject floats free of all fixed locations and is not bound by the limits or barriers of a concrete materiality.

This sort of view obviously connects more generally to the postmodernist notion of the indeterminate self, a self defined only by its negation of or resistance to categories of identity (see P. Smith 1988; Alcoff 1993). And as we have seen, there is a strand of this in academic feminism among theorists who repudiate identity-based politics in the name of anti-essentialism. Liberation is associated with the refusal to be characterized, described, or classified, and the only true strategy of resistance can be one of negation, a kind of permanent revolution on the metaphysical front.

In her book *Nomadic Subjects*, Rosi Braidotti argues that a feminist emphasis on the embodiment of the self leads directly to an anti-essentialist account of female identity. To "be" a woman is simply to be the "site of multiple complex, and potentially contradictory sets of experiences, defined by overlapping variables such as class, race, age, lifestyle, sexual preference, and others" (1994, 4). An attentiveness to embodiment works to undermine any monocausal characterization that would privilege one variable over another, on Braidotti's view. The best model for such a self is "the nomad," that is, "a situated, postmodern, culturally differentiated understanding of the subject in general.... In so far as axes of differentiation such as class, race, ethnicity, gender, age, and others intersect and interact with each other in the constitution of subjectivity, the notion of nomad refers to the simultaneous occurrence of many of these at once" (4).

Braidotti puts forward nomad subjectivity as a strategy designed to help feminist theory refigure the grounds of its own liberatory project, so that it will not be caught privileging gender over race or any of the other array of constitutive variables. She argues that "nomadic consciousness ... is a form of resisting assimilation or homologation into dominant ways of representing the self.... The nomadic tense is the imperfect; it is active, continuous; ... The nomad's relationship to the earth is one of transitory attachment and cyclical frequentation; the antithesis of the farmer, the nomad gathers, reaps, and exchanges but does not exploit" (25).

On the one hand, I can appreciate Braidotti's goal of incorporating difference and rejecting the certainties that tend toward dogmatism and stifle both theoretical and political creativity. On the other hand, this does not work for me at all. Multiply entangled relationships complicate life but do not uproot it. Gathering and reaping can be terribly exploitative when it is disrespectful of people's historical ties to a land. Braidotti's imagery evokes for me the figure of the person who resists commitment and obligation, one who tries to avoid responsibility by having only "transitory" attachments. Most ungenerously, I have images of white feminists trying to unload their attachment to whiteness. And as I argued in chapter 6, a real attentiveness to embodiment would privilege our differential relationship to reproduction as the basis of female identity. The fact that any given individual female or male is never reducible to her or his relationship to reproduction does not require us to cast our identities as nomadic.

Braidotti herself tries actually to combine her nomadic strategy together with political activism within communities. She says that being a nomad does not require one to sever all the ties that sustain identity, nor does it mean that one has no sense of identity (31, 33). And she rejects the gender eliminativism that would counsel feminists to simply refuse female identity in any and every articulation. However, this combinatory project is unsuccessful. Imagine having a transitory attachment to a child; no less troublesome is the idea of a transitory attachment to a community. Oppressed communities have long voiced anger at those activists who come and go, who have the class mobility to withdraw their energy and resources whenever they choose. Activism itself—Braidotti's overarching concern—requires more than transitory commitment. The model she supplies is full of good intentions but seems best suited to maintain the volitional freedom for middle-class activists who can pick and choose their battles.

Thus in my view nomadic subjectivity works no better than assimilationist doctrine to interpellate mixed identity: the nomad self is bounded to no community and in actuality represents an *absence* of identity rather than a multiply entangled and engaged identity. This is not the situation of mixed race peoples who have deep (even if complex and problematic) ties to specific communities: to be a free-floating unbound variable is not the same as being multiply categorized, or ostracized, by specific racial communities. It strikes me that the postmodern nomadic vision fits far better the multinational CEO with fax machine and cell phone in hand who is bound to, or by, no national agenda, tax structure, cultural boundary, or geographical border. And what this suggests is that a simplistic promotion of fluidity will not suffice.

I am concerned with the way in which a refusal of identity might be useful for the purposes of the current global market. The project of global capitalism is to transform the whole world into postcolonial consumers and producers of goods in an acultural world commodity market, a Benetton-like vision in which the only visible differences are those that can be commodified and sold. Somewhere between that vision and the vision of a purist identity construction that requires intermittent ethnic cleansing we must develop another option, an alternative that can offer a normative reconstruction of raced identity applicable to mixed race peoples.

A Mestizo Race

> The offspring of so-called interracial relationships have not been accorded a distinctive identity [in the United States], either socially or

officially, an identity in which the quality of being mixed is vested, embodied, or otherwise given real meaning.

Carlos Fernandez, "La Raza and the Melting Pot"

Oh, you're one of those "mixed-up" people.

My hairdresser

In this final section I want to consider how we might best understand and come to terms with mixed race identity both metaphysically and politically. One possible solution to the problem with identity that mixed race people have is to propound a racial eliminativism—on the assumption that doing away with race will do away with the problems of mixed race. Naomi Zack argues for this position. In fact, she argues that there are irresolvable problems with the belief in race, and that mixed race concepts, far from subverting racial purity, simply reenforce race (1993).

However, as I argued in chapter 7, it seems clear that, within the context of racially based and organized systems of oppression, race will continue to be a salient internal and external component of identity. Systems of oppression, segregated communities, and practices of discrimination create a collective experience and a shared history for a racialized grouping. More than any physiological or morphological features, it is that shared experience and history that cements the community and creates connections with others along racial lines, although morphological features that are given social significance produce a shared experience which is part of what builds identity. And that shared experience and history do not disappear when new scientific accounts dispute the characterization of race as a natural kind (see Zack 1994). Accounts of race as a social and historical identity, which bring in elements that are temporally contingent and mutable, will probably prove to have more persistence than accounts of race that tie it to biology; history will probably have more permanence than biology.

Moreover, I would argue that, given current social conditions, any materialist account of the self must take race into account. This is not to deny that generic and universalist concepts of human being are both possible and necessary. Despite my concern expressed in the last section against formulating a universal humanism based on reason, there do exist connections between persons that endure across differences of sexuality, race, culture, even class. Thus, articulating a new non-hierarchical universalist humanism is a politically valuable goal. However, if we restrict a philosophical analysis of identity and subjectivity to only those elements that can be universally applied, our resulting account will be too thin to do much philosophical work. In the concrete everydayness of "actually existing" human life, the variabilities of racial designation mediates experience in ways we are just beginning to recognize.

Racial eliminativism is not viable. Mixed race persons are racialized, but the particular form of their racialization has not been accorded a general social recognition, which I would suggest is likely to lead to problems of self-alienation. Many theorists of oppressed identity have described a pattern of self-alienation in which the oppressed person views himself or herself from an imaginary perspective of the dominant. Du Bois and Fanon were perhaps the first to describe how nonwhite peoples internalize the perspective of white identity. In *The Bluest Eye*, Toni Morrison dramatically captures this pathology for the young black child who wants blond hair and blue eyes, having internalized a white aesthetic in which only whiteness has value or beauty. Simone de Beauvoir and Sandra Bartky have written about a form of female alienation in which women see themselves and their bodies through a generalized male gaze that produces feelings of disgust at normal female embodied experiences and disciplines behavior to a degree worthy of Foucault's description of the Benthamite Panopticon. And Samuel Ramos argued that the Mexican peoples' shame in their poverty led to a problem of self-alienation with disastrous results: "As a consequence of living outside the reality of our being, we are lost in a chaotic world, in the midst of which we walk blindly and aimlessly, buffeted about by the four winds" (Ramos 2004, 282). Ramos and other philosophers-analysts of colonialism such as Zea and Dussel have suggested that Eurocentric versions of modernism effected a temporal displacement of the "now" as experienced in countries such as Mexico, so that the "now" is seen as what is happening in the United States or Europe, whereas the present tense of the Global South has not yet "caught up."

Such patterns of alienation from one's own perspectival experience have profound effects on the capacity for self-knowledge, a capacity that Western philosophers as diverse as Plato and Hegel have seen as critical for the possibility of any knowledge whatsoever. If knowledge represents a concrete vision correlated to a particular social location, then the alienation one suffers from one's own perspectival vision—or one's own denigration of that first-person perspective—will have ramifications throughout one's life. For mixed race persons in North America and many other places in the world, this problem can be particularly difficult to overcome. The mixed race person has been denied that social recognition of self which Hegel understood as necessarily constitutive of self-consciousness and full self-development.[8] For us, it is not a question of reorienting perspective from the alien to the familiar, since no ready-made, available, or socially acknowledged perspective captures our contradictory experience. Without a social recognition of mixed identity, the mixed race person is told to choose one or another perspective. This creates not only alienation, but the sensation of having a mode of being which is an incessant, unrecoverable lack, an unsurpassable inferiority, or simply an unintelligible mess. This blocks the possibility of self-knowledge: the epistemic authority and credibility that accrues to nearly everyone at least with respect to their "ownmost" perspective, is denied to the mixed race person. Vis-à-vis each community or social location to which s/he might claim a connection, s/he can never claim authority to speak unproblematically for or from that position. Ramos warns that without a connection to an ongoing history and community, human consciousness devolves to an animal existence that has no ability "to project the imagination toward the future" (Ramos 1986, 69; see also Schutte 1993, 77). Only communities have continuity beyond individual life; cast off from all communities, the individual has no historical identity and thus is unlikely to value the community's future.

Because nationality, culture, and language are so critical to identity, some propose that, for example, nationality could be taken as a more important distinguishing characteristic than race. For example, the opponents of multiculturalism such as Hollinger and Schlesinger promote national identifications to racial or ethnic identifications. Nationality could provide a strong connection across racialized communities, increasing their unity and sympathetic relationships. However, nationality does not provide an all-inclusive identity; it merely shifts the contradictions and criteria of inclusion from race to immigration status. U.S. nationalism in particular encourages minority communities to become anti-immigrant, even when the immigrants are of the same racial group or share a cultural background. Thus African American schoolchildren fight with West Indians in Brooklyn, and Cubans disdain the Central American immigrants flooding Miami. Such conflict is sometimes based on class, but it is also based on a claim to the so-called "American" identity. In this way, U.S. minorities can ally with the (still) powerful white majority against new immigrants and perhaps share in the feeling if not the reality of dominance. Politically, then, an identification that places nationality over race portends, at least for the present, an increase in anti-immigrant violence. Metaphysically, nationalism is too weak as a substantive form of subjective identification to completely replace other ethnic, cultural, and racial identifications, and because of its political problems, many in minority communities resist the imposition of nationalism as hegemonic over other ties (see, e.g., Albó 1995).

Eliminating racial identification or replacing it entirely with nationality are unrealistic options. Racialization remains a powerful determinant over identity, and the increase in cross-racial alliances will create an increasing constituency of mixed race persons. We need a positive (in the sense of substantive) reconstruction of mixed race identity. What can this mean? It must begin with facing squarely the phenomenological features of mixed identity.

In her celebrated book *Borderlands/La Frontera*, the late Gloria Anzaldua offered a powerful and lyrical vision of the difficulties that Chicanos can endure because of their position between cultures and races. Contrast the following description with Deleuze and Guattari's romantic portrait of the nomad and the schizophrenic as a paradigm of liberation. She writes: "The ambivalence from the clash of voices results in mental and emotional states of perplexity. Internal strife results in insecurity and indecisiveness. The mestiza's dual or multiple personality is plagued by psychic restlessness" (1987, 78). Anzaldua worried that the shame and rootlessness of the mestizo would lead to excessive compensation, especially in the form of machismo:

> In the Gringo world, the Chicano suffers from excessive humility and self-effacement, shame of self and self-deprecation. Around Latinos he suffers from a sense of language inadequacy and its accompanying discomfort; with Native Americans he suffers from a racial amnesia which ignores our common blood, and from guilt because the Spanish part of him took their land and oppressed them. He has an excessive compensatory hubris when around Mexicans from the other side. It overlays a deep sense of racial shame...which leads him to put down women and even to brutalize them. (83)

For Anzaldua, developing an alternative positive articulation of mestizo consciousness and identity is essential to provide some degree of coherence and to avoid the incessant cultural collisions or violent compensations that result from the shame and frustration of self-negation. And note that for her, any adequate artic-ulation must be accurate to the truth: it cannot pretend to an amnesia about a difficult aspect of the identity as a way to achieve comfort. Thus her aim is not simply a political solution at any cost, but a more accurate rendering. Her argu-ment is also, however, that some of the political discomfort comes from a value system that eschews hybridity as an inadequate basis for self-respect.

Anzaldua suggests that we can draw out a positive identity through seeing how the mixed race person is engaged in the valuable though often exhausting role of border crosser, negotiator, and mediator between races, and sometimes also be-tween cultures, nations, and linguistic communities. The mixed person is a trav-eler often within her own home or neighborhood, translating and negotiating the diversity of meanings, practices, and forms of life. This vision provides a positive alternative to the mixed race person's usual representation as lack or as the tragi-cally alienated figure. Being mixed means having resources for communication and understanding that are vital for political movements.

One should note here the significant difference between Anzaldua's positive formulation and Vasconcelos's, for whom the mestizo represented something like a biological and cultural vanguard with Hegelian world-historical powers (Vascon-celos 1979). Vasconcelos's view worked to counter the European denigration of mixed identities as infertile, cultural dead ends by representing hybridization as more culturally rich and advanced than the stale, unmixed idealized cultures aspired to in Europe. Thus, his view *promotes* the mixed identity through a *den-igration* of the unmixed. Although Anzaldua seems to share Vasconcelos's view that hybridity has important advantages, she does not make this a comparative claim. In fact, the advantages of being mixed that Anzaldua cites are advantages because they provide resources for the various cultural communities to which she has some connection.

My only worry with Anzaldua's strategy is based on the fact that such figures who can negotiate between cultures have been notoriously useful for the domi-nant, who can use them to better control their colonized subjects. Thus, such figures as la Malinche (Cortes' concubine) and Pocahontas are often reviled for their cooperation with dominant communities and their love for specific indi-viduals from those communities. There is no question that such border negotia-tions can exacerbate and not just ameliorate oppression. Today large numbers of bilingual and biracial individuals are recruited by the U.S. military and the FBI to infiltrate suspected gangs or communities and countries designated as U.S. enemies. To my dismay, many Latinos in the U.S. military were deployed in the invasion of Panama. Here again, an allegiance based on nationality is used to circumvent a racial or cultural tie. I suspect that for mixed race persons, especially those who have suffered some degree of rejection from the communities to which they have some attachment, such jobs hold a seductive attraction as a way to overcome feelings of inferiority and to find advantage for the first time in the situation of being mixed. Where I agree with Anzaldua is the positive spin she puts on the mixed race identity. But where I would place a note of caution is the idea that border crossing is in and of itself a political good; it is always a valuable ability, but it can be put to both positive and negative uses.

Another element worth exploring is Samuel Ramos's concept of an assimilation that does not demand conformity to the dominant or consist of imitation. Assimilation in Ramos's sense is an incorporation or absorption of different elements. This is similar to the Hegelian concept of sublation in the sense of a synthesis that does not simply unite differences but develops them into a higher and better formulation. In the context of Latin America, Ramos called for a new self-integration that would appropriate both its European and Indian elements. An imitative stance toward the other is based on cultural inequality, but an assimilative stance in this sense comes out of self-knowledge combined with a healthy self-regard. It is less a volitional act than a natural outcome of the metaphysics of hybrid experience. "When we reach some understanding of the idiosyncrasies of our national soul, we will have a standard to guide us through the complexities of European culture," and thus become capable of "selecting conscientiously and methodically the forms of European culture potentially adaptable to our own environment" (Ramos 2004, 284). Ramos believed that this process of active assimilation cannot occur without reflective self-knowledge. An imitative stance toward the other, and a conformity to dominant norms, will occur unless the empty self-image of the Mexican is replaced by a more substantive perspective indexed to the Mexican's own cultural, political, and racial location.

I believe that the concept of mestizo consciousness and identity can contribute toward the development of such a perspective by creating a linguistic, public, socially affirmed identity for mixed race persons. Mestizo consciousness is a kind of double vision, a conscious articulation of more than one heritage, allegiance, and tradition. Jose Vasconcelos called this new identity the cosmic race, *la raza cosmica*, to signal its inclusivity and dynamism.

There are three possible ways to name and characterize mixed race identity: (1) as a generic "mixed" identity; (2) as a mixed identity of a specific type, such as mestizo; (3) as a combinatory identity straddling two or more identities. The movement to create a new Census category for mixed race persons in the United States seems to follow this first option in conceptualizing the mixed race person as having a new identity with substantive attributes of its own. By not specifying anything other than the fact of being mixed itself, this option encompasses Asian/white, African American/Latino, Native American/African American, and so on without specification or differentiation. But because of the immense variety of possible combinations, and the variable way such persons will be publicly interpellated and treated, it seems to make little sense to create a social category based on simply being bi- or multiracial. There are probably some experiences such persons have in common, but the variability seems too great to warrant a single category for all. Imagine a group of people brought together because they are all mixed race of one sort or another. Each may potentially have experienced some challenges in life due to this feature of their identity, but the specific challenges that they faced would probably have much to do with the specific communities to which they were attached. And such a category would not be parallel to "mestizo," which does not really mean simply "mixed" but rather refers to a very specific mix. Thus, the first option would have allowed the Census to have persons pick a box marked simply "mixed," implying that more important than the kind of mix they are is the fact of being mixed itself. In providing such a box the Census would not have been able to count how many of such persons are part black, part Latino, part Native, part Arab, or part Asian American, thus skewing the statistical tabulations of these communities. Thus, the first option for characterizing mixed identity is too metaphysically and phenomenologically thin to provide much information and has political disadvantages for minority communities as a system of counting.

The second characterization follows the Latin American concept of mestizo more accurately, which is not simply a way to note mixing of any and every type but is an acknowledgment of a very specific mix: in this case Spanish and Indian. On this understanding, the mixed race person manifests an identity of a new type, with its own substantive features, its own phenomenological being in the world and hermeneutic horizon. For Vasconcelos, the mestizo combines elements of its diverse forebears but creates something new, a new identity with new and different political values and possibilities. The question here is whether mixed race persons in the United States *have* created something new, an identity, a political orientation, a way of thinking about themselves in the world, all of which have come out of being positioned in a certain way in the society. Mestizo peoples in much of Latin American have existed for several centuries, have held a unique political and social status, have been recognized by the state as mestizos, and thus arguably have developed an identity (or features that contribute toward their identity). This is not obviously the case in North America, where mixed race persons have generally been identified by only one of their multiple identities, where there has been almost no official or even social recognition, and where there is little community and historical experience from which a horizon might emerge.

The third option for understanding mixed race identity is the model of hyphenation, in which the person is understood as both or all of what they are, in combination. That is, rather than interpellated by an entirely new category, the person is interpellated by combining his or her actual genealogy, such as Latino/white, African American/Asian American, and so on. This method would actually follow the mestizo model more accurately because it would preserve a social recognition of the particular groups in the person's genealogy. Moreover, by preserving the particular identities that the mixed person has connections with, the capacity for moving between such groups might be acknowledged. It seems to me that this is the most accurate characterization for many mixed race persons in the North today: they are often capable of negotiating elements of more than one identity, perhaps experiencing the double consciousness Du Bois describes in a new way. So their social or public recognition needs to acknowledge not *simply* that they are mixed, but what the mix is in particular to understand that person.

Two arguments against such a hyphenated model come immediately to mind. First, some will argue, rightly, that for some mixed race persons their phenomenological experience of embodiment is tantamount to having a single racial identity. In the context of the United States, this is most often true of persons with a black parent, who are then simply assimilated to blackness by the dominant culture because of the one-drop rule. Phenomenologically, white people are much more used to accepting that black people come in a huge array of shades than they are to the idea that white people could come in just as many shades. This is a historical fact, and it is changing, but slowly. The rule of hypodescent continues to exert a powerful influence.

However, I would argue that the public interpellation cannot be the sole determinant of a person's identity in any true and meaningful sense. In the account I developed in chapter 4, identity includes lived experience, the horizon of meanings to which a person has access, in other words, their own subjectivity. We especially should not take white people's point of view as the determinant criterion here, such as would be the case if we were to argue that, because white people will tend to see person A as having X identity, then person A *has* X identity. If person A is viewed as an X by whites, that will be a significant aspect of their existence without doubt, but it is not all-determining over their life experience, what historical narratives they experience a connection with, what cultural resources they have access to, how various nonwhite groups will categorize them, and so on. Thus, I would argue that the hyphenated model might still make intelligible sense as an accurate description of an identity that is part black.

A second argument against the hyphenated model comes from those who are concerned that any mixed conception retains the essentialist and homogeneous understanding of the identities that the mixed race person combines. This is, for example, Zack's argument against use of a mixed race identity: that it works to preserve rather than subvert the idea of race itself. However, here again my argument would be that identities—even racial ones—do not need to be understood in these kinds of biologistic, ahistorical, nondynamic, and essentialist ways, nor is it necessarily the case that their everyday usage implies these elements. Thus, on this third option, a hyphenated identity simply marks a person as having a connection to more than one historically changeable, dynamic, and complex social identity.

My defense of this third option is very tentative. The three options as I described them are meant simply to help us begin a conversation about representing mixed race identities.

Only recently have I finally come to some acceptance of my ambiguous identity. I am not simply white nor simply Latina, and the gap that exists between my two identities (indeed, my two families)—a gap that is cultural, racial, linguistic, and national—feels too wide and deep for me to span. I cannot bridge the gap, so I negotiate it, standing at one point here, and then there, moving between locations as events or other people's responses propel me. I never reach shore: I never wholly occupy either the Anglo or the Latina identity. Paradoxically but predictably, in white society I feel my *latinidad*, and in Latin society I feel my whiteness, as that which is left out: an invisible present, sometimes as intrusive as an elephant in the room and sometimes more as a pulled thread that subtly alters the design of my fabricated self. Peace has come for me by no longer seeking some permanent home onshore. What I seek now is no longer a home, but perhaps a lighthouse that might illuminate this place in which I live, for myself as much as for others.

Conclusion

In the West, the principal social struggles of the modern era can be characterized as, first, struggles of social status, then, of social class, and only then of social identity. The struggle of social status was waged against landed aristocracies and their systems of permanent servitude that predetermined an individual's vocation and limited his geographic mobility; the struggle of social class was fought against the unbridled power of the "Mr. Moneybags" of the world to extract labor power with few protections for those suffering the extractions; and the struggles of social identity have been fought against the subtle social contracts by which whole identity groups are denied equality and basic human rights. Contra the story told by some critics of the 1960s, who lament that decade's focus on social identities such as race, gender, and sexuality, identity-based political movements did not *only then* become politically visible and significant. From the beginning of the Conquest, Europeans justified genocide and enslavement via claims about the cultural identity and inherent characteristics of indigenous groups, and their opponents, such as Bartolomé de Las Casas, developed counterarguments that claimed the Indians' right to *cultural* self-determination, a right Las Casas made strong enough to dismiss even the missionaries' rhetoric of eternal salvation. The abolitionist and women's suffrage struggles of the nineteenth century were also and necessarily identity-based movements, with identity-based organizations and newspapers. The great Mexican revolution at the start of the twentieth century itself articulated its demands in the name of not simply the abstractions workers and peasants, or *trabajadores y campesinos*, but in the name of *los Indios y mestizos*, that is, the founding categories of Mexican national identity itself. In all of these struggles, social identity was at the center. Social identities were understood to be both the crux of the oppression and the nodal point of the imperialist project. Thus, the focal point of the resistance was a contestation over the meanings, limitations, significance, and future possibilities of those very identities.

We have yet to formulate a theory that can incorporate with explanatory adequacy the struggles regarding social status, social class, and social identity into one overarching account. Liberalism, Marxism, and even feminism and critical race theories tend to focus on, or highlight, one type of struggle at a time. One of the most serious obstacles facing any attempt to formulate an overarching theory is, as I have argued, that the ontological basis of the focal point is very different if we are talking about status, about class, or about social identity. We cannot make simple analogies here. The Marxist critique of liberalism, for example, argued that the individualist ontology liberalism used to critique the aristocratic view did not work for class; it could only justify negative liberty, and more than this was needed to understand the ways in which people became constituted as workers and the ways in which the relations of production affected interests and choices. Liberalism could effectively liberate the bourgeois class against the strictures put on their capital accumulation by the aristocratic system of noble inheritance, but it could not effectively liberate the working class from being forced to engage in alienated labor. For that, one needed to understand the ontology of class identity in a different way, as a social and historical construction that required radical structural transformation in society from the ground up.

Similarly today, many of us are urging that the ontologies of liberalism and Marxism not be misapplied to social identity. The ontology of status and class calls for a dissolution of the constitutive conditions in which these categories are formed, but this does not follow in a simple analogy for social identities. Freedom from class and status forms of oppression can plausibly be articulated in terms of collective and individual freedom *from* one's imprisonment in the wage earners or landless peasant group. Liberation comes, in other words, when the very categories of class and status are deconstructed, when we dismantle the social structures that create a class whose only option is to sell its labor power. But the social ontology of *these* forms of oppression are not explanatory of social identities such as sex/gender or race/ethnicity. Race may be a modern phenomenon (this is still under debate), but racial eliminativists are generally concerned about group identity of any sort, which they see as scripts that compromise moral commitments and constrain individual choice. The discourse of antisexist and antiracist identity-based liberation movements has by and large not demanded a dissolution of the categories, but has demanded instead a radical transformation of the ways they are interpreted and valued, how their relation to other categories is understood, and how their relation to historical events and social systems is accounted for. It is quite clear that equality and human dignity cannot be maximized in societies organized through permanent hierarchies of status and class, but it is far from clear that equality and human dignity require the elimination of the rich differences of life interpretation that are developed via the social identities based on ethnicity, gender, sexuality, and other such group categories. Neither the ontology nor the social genealogy of all of these diverse kinds of categories are identical, nor are they even similar in some important respects.

In short, there are excellent reasons to eliminate class and status differences, but these reasons do not apply to all other identity groups *per se*. Some theorists have been too quick to assume that the theoretical analysis of one type of oppression can be applied to all.

The contribution of this book has been to provide a critique of that over-generalization of identity categories and also a multitude of arguments about the specific salience of race and gender to an account of the self. I have given an explanation and account of the epistemic and political salience of social identities, and addressed specific issues of debate regarding the grounds for these identities, for example, in embodiment and visible difference. My overall aim has been to strengthen the case for taking social identities into account as deep features of the self, even while I have argued against the idea that identities have ready-made political orientations or fixed meanings. Social identities are not simply foisted on people from the outside, as it were, but are more properly understood as sites from which we perceive, act, and engage with others. These sites are not *simply* social locations or positions, but also hermeneutic horizons comprised of experiences, basic beliefs, and communal values, all of which influence our orientation toward and responses to future experiences.

It should be clear, then, that identities are not analogous to scripts that we are consigned to play out. Nor are we boxed in by them, constrained, restricted, or held captive—unless, that is, one thinks it make sense to say that we are boxed in by the fact that we have bodies, as some transcendentalists have imagined; to justify such an idea, one would need a strenuous ontological distinction between "self" and "body." It may be precisely the hold of that kind of classical transcendentalism that leads some to view social identities as simply forms of restraint. I have argued that such a view is incoherent. To say that we have identities, histories, social locations, experiences, cultures, and so on is simply to say that we exist.

Identities are best understood as ways in which we and others around us represent our material ties to historical events and social structures. Those events may be traumatic and those structures may be oppressive, but this indicates that the events need to be carefully understood and analyzed and that the structures need to be transformed, not that the identities themselves need to be left behind. We will always have a material tie to historical events and structures, even under the best of circumstances.

The implication of this argument is that we need a different understanding of the relationship between identity and oppression. The view I have criticized holds that identities just *are* oppressive, under any conditions, although perhaps some are more oppressive than others. But all are basically forms of coercion and constraint. On my account of identities, they are not per se oppressive. Identities can be used as the alibis for oppressive treatment, to justify a group's unequal treatment, or as a mechanism for segregation, confinement, and exploitation. They can be inaccurately represented and mistakenly characterized. And they can in some cases be created as a strategy for oppression. But even in this latter case, to say that they have been created is to say that they truly exist; thus they are not simply mistakes in reference, or mistaken ways to characterize human experience. The question is not how to overcome identity, but how to transform our current interpretations and understandings of them. How might we imagine them differently within a less violent and stratified social context?

The more specific question of this book has been whether social identities of race and gender are necessary, or are necessarily problematic. That is, does that material tie to historical events and social structures need to be represented in the way that race and gender categories represents it, to categorize and group humans into these particular kinds? I have raised this question about race and gender in this book because of the commonality between raced and gendered identities. In these identities, that material tie operates through our very physical and visible embodiment: how we appear, how we are shaped, how we behave and comport ourselves, how we interact, and what range of sensations we have accessible to us (lest someone claim universality in regard to this last category, I'd remind you that a male cannot, for example, have the sensation of tingling breasts when his infant cries). I have wanted to emphasize the material, visible, and physical character of race and gender, but I have also argued that the meanings and implications of even these visible identities will be determined largely by how the historical events and social structures that demarcate identities are interpreted and understood. This is an ongoing, active process involving both individual and collective agency. Individuals cannot transform the public meanings, effects, and implications of their identities by a sheer act of will, but collective acts of creative expression and resistance constantly contest and transform the meanings, implications, and political effects of such identity markers as skin color, body shape, language use, and role in reproduction.

Identities are embodied horizons from which we each must confront and negotiate our shared world and specific life condition. They are largely unchosen (just as our bodies are unchosen), but just as in the case of bodies, our identities can be reshaped, and they absolutely require interpretation. As I argued in the last chapter, the situation of mixed race persons today most obviously requires interpretation and involves a range of choice; it is becoming increasingly clear to many people that the identity of a mixed race person is not simply one *thing*, but a combination that involves both their public interpellations depending on their appearance and their context, as well as their personal history, experience, political values, beliefs, and community commitments. Mixed race individuals cannot *individually* create meaningfully effective identity options for themselves; their interpretations will be misunderstood and misread if there are no available and accessible social meanings through which they can exert the new and different self-presentation that they may wish to put forward. Yet every individual presentation can influence the possibilities for new configurations of identity. This dialectic between the individual and the collective interpretation and self-formation is true for every type of social identity.

Gendered identity is both more fundamental than sometimes supposed and less determinate than it has historically been portrayed. I have argued that there is a material basis for gendered identity in terms of possibility for reproduction, a basis that is independent of social practice as long as human beings continue to engage in forms of biological reproduction that require biological material from two different sexes and/or involve wombs inside women's bodies. But this is only *one* feature within a constellation of elements that go to make up gender identity in any given culture and society, all of which involve interpretive practices. The cultural revolution that is called feminism is precisely a collective contestation over the formation of that identity in the large and meaningful sense, not restricted simply to the meaning and organization of reproductive capacities and activities. Feminism has contested both the meanings and the significance accorded to women's differential relationship to reproduction, and in this way has developed a range of new possibilities in understanding the meaning of gender identity.

In this book I have argued that gender is both positional and material; it is positionally relational and thus dependent for its status on other existing structures, but it also has an objective material basis that is stable across past and present cultural variability. The fact of this material basis does not yield any political consensus among women, but it provides a necessary knowledge base from which to engage in political debate. Democracy for women requires that those who share a material and positional gender must have control over the policies that assume knowledge about the experiences only women can have. Otherwise women will become chattel once again, or remain so.

Like gender, raced identity permeates multiple aspects of lived experience. It does not simply involve social status but also involves one's affective, genealogical, and familial relationship to historical events and traumas. Race operates, then, as a historical consciousness, and as such is not subject to deconstruction but always requires interpretation; it will be enacted differently in different generations and political communities. More than gender, race is essentially determined by history, but its historical legacy lives in our embodied selves at their deepest level of emotion, perception, imagination, and practiced movement. Race thus affects our mechanisms of perceptual attunement and the organization of our attentive senses, influencing our operations of discernment and judgment. Since this is based in history rather than biology, none of this is unalterable, obviously, and so the claims of closure for racialized communities—and the fear of an unceasing or inevitable hostility between groups—are without valid grounds. But given the embodied reality of racialization, its deep structure and only semiconscious presence to mind (for some), no democratic aspiration should pretend or presume that a blindness to race will dissolve its presence. In order to offset its power to impose expectations and limit relationships, we need to enhance and become more mature in the manner in which we are attentive to racial formations.

Any given individual is interpellated by multiple social identity categories and will be included in multiple social identity groups. This provides one important way to explain the inevitable political differences within identity groups. Intragroup political differences are not always random or attributable to highly personal individual biographies, but are sometimes correlated to grosser lines of demarcation such as, for example, class and gender differences among African Americans, nationality differences among Latinos and Asian Americans, and age and sexuality differences among women. Such differences need not lead to stalemate or separatism if they are explored, respected, and taken as an opportunity for a broader political understanding.

Thus, any aspiration toward democracy is enjoined to recognize the salience of social identities. But obviously, liberation requires more than just a recognition and exploration of the difference that identities make. The liberatory lexicon of the era of national liberation movements has come under a variety of critiques in the past thirty years, some justifiable and some not, but I have wanted to join with those such as Edward Said who, while accepting the validity of the critiques in part, would seek to rearticulate and renew the universalist language of progressive social movements. We have seen terms and concepts like progress, liberation, identity, morality, "the people," race, humanism, objectivity, truth, and universalism analyzed, criticized, and deconstructed for harboring unsustainable assumptions about a transcendental nature of human experience, or about an inevitable teleology to human history, or about an absolute and decontextualized character of knowledge. Much of the language of social justice developed in the colonial centers was found to harbor unsavory aspects of its own genealogical context, such as Eurocentrism, an implicit gender hierarchy, and other forms of elitism.

Most deconstructionists and poststructuralists have readily acknowledged the need to go beyond critique and toward reconstruction of this language of justice. But what terms or concepts have been put forward that can do the positive work of the above list, that can replace the ability of universal humanism to mobilize moral acts? Poststructuralists propose using aesthetic criteria to justify political direction and the notion of formless flux to replace categories of identity. Instead of seeking knowledge or morality, all politics and inquiry are reductively relegated to strategic operations. Such language is insufficient even to interpret our current social reality, much less change it.

I have argued that the concept of identity, as it is actually used in common practice, does not entail or even necessarily suggest the reifying effects that identity critics portend, and I have argued that what identities really are (as opposed to what they are sometimes said to be) is nothing to be politically afraid of. Besides identity, terms like realism, objectivity, and truth need to be resuscitated. This does not mean that we should reinstate their meanings prior to the period of antipositivist critique but rather that we must reconceptualize them from a position that acknowledges the ineliminable importance of culture and history and the context of power.

So what of universal humanism? Perhaps none of the terms anyone has attempted to rethink has been more dangerous or misused than this. The problem was put forth most succinctly by Fanon when he said that in Europe "they are never done talking of Man, yet murder men everywhere they find them" (1967, 311). Fanon's observation is perfectly manifested in the quote from Rudolf Giuliani that appears as an epigraph in this book's first chapter. When Giuliani was asked at a press conference whether his administration favored white racist police over their nonwhite victims, he replied, "There is too much group identification in our society and too little human identification."

The discourse of humanism is thus continually used as a smokescreen for oppression, to divert attention away from discriminatory practices and identity-based patterns of segregation and exclusion. Liberals and progressives who believe that identity politics has derailed the development and/or recognition of common interests are thus blaming the wrong source. They need to acknowledge the inadequacies of the social ontologies and theoretical paradigms that they are trying to apply to identity-based oppression. If we are to formulate a truly universal humanism, as Fanon, Said, and all of the other great theoreticians of colonialism held out hope for till the end of their lives, we must begin with a better understanding of the whole human.

Notes

Introduction

   1. See Earl Lewis and Heidi Ardizzone, *Love on Trial: An American Scandal in Black and White* (New York: W. W. Norton, 2002). I learned of this case from Anita Allen, who discusses it in *Why Privacy Isn't Everything: Feminist Reflections on Personal Accountability* (New York: Rowman and Littlefield, 2003).

Chapter 1

   1. Clyde Haberman, "NYC: Whose God Is It, Anyway?" New York Times, Sept. 6, 2000.
   2. The "scare tactic" of invoking balkanization has been used to effectively silence any discussion of secessionist claims no matter how morally justifiable a given case may be. For a cool-headed look at the conditions under which arguments for secession and separation may be morally justifiable, see Jorge Valadez 2001.
   3. Compare Nussbaum 1997 for a liberal defense of multiculturalism.

Chapter 2

   1. I elaborate this argument in *Real Knowing*. There, I argue that "we have to pay careful attention to the discursive arrangement in order to understand the full meaning of any given discursive event. For example, in a situation where a well-meaning First World person is speaking for a person or group in the Third World, the very discursive arrangement may reinscribe the 'hierarchy of civilizations' view where the U. S. lands squarely at the top. This effect occurs because the speaker is positioned as authoritative and empowered, as the knowledgeable subject, while the group in the Third World is reduced, merely because of the structure of the speaking practice, to an object and victim that must be championed from afar. Though the speaker may be trying to materially improve the situation of some lesser-privileged group, one of the effects of her discourse is to reenforce racist, imperialist conceptions and perhaps also to further silence the lesser-privileged group's own ability to speak and be heard."
   2. Such as the October League (ML), I Wor Kuen, August Twenty Ninth Movement, Dodge Revolutionary Union Movement, and others. The Revolutionary Community Party

took the opposite position, and saw race- or gender-based organizing as "splittist." See Elbaum 2002.

3. Of course, how these jobs become labeled "skilled" and "unskilled" is involved in a history of gendered and racialized work, which needs to be dismantled. And the goal of this union as well as any others worth their salt is to raise the wages of the unskilled workers to a living wage, in which case job choices might be based on work preference rather than money. But contract negotiations can advance toward these aims only one step at a time. Certainly, if in-house advancement results in diversifying the trades at that hospital, this will have the effect of beginning to eradicate the racialization of the professional crafts.

4. Sometimes one hears the view that recognition is a fight waged by middle-class minorities, women, or gays who underemphasize class issues. This is certainly true some of the time, but it is not true all of the time. It is not true, for example, of the Urban League, ACT-UP, or Planned Parenthood. The latter two organizations have in fact gone through a decade of self-criticism and rectification of earlier agendas that contained middle-class and/ or white bias.

5. And it is has generated a great deal of debate and critique. Among the best critiques of Fraser are Olsen 2001, Young 1998.

6. Fraser, in her characteristically pragmatic approach, does not express concern with the social ontological commitments that such a politics may imply, and in this regard her concerns are wholly different from the concerns of someone like Judith Butler, for whom the ontological issues involved in identity politics are primary (though this is at least in part because they are seen as determinant over the political effects). I share Butler's view that the metaphysical basis of identity needs and warrants analysis also, and I will address this in the following chapter, which addresses the philosophical critique of identity. Fraser, in contrast to Butler, is concerned only with the effects of various discursive and practical strategies on political mobilization and progressive agendas.

7. See, e.g., www.mediawatch.com.

8. Fraser could explain that her target is meant to be groups like Media Watch, but it seems surely inappropriate to target every group organized around a specific reform and extrapolate from these to claims about identity-based movements. I doubt Fraser would demand that Media Watch include an account of redistribution on its web page; this seems to me akin to the way that some Marxist Leninist groups used to demand that every labor struggle take a position on the Soviet Union. Moreover, I would argue, as I suspect the founders of Media Watch would, that issues of media representation have a direct impact on practices of social discrimination that affect hiring and promotion, and are in fact linked to redistribution.

9. I think he was right on this point, though his own account of Jewish identity was wholly inadequate. See Walzer's introduction.

10. Encarnacion tempers this with the observation that because of the country's lack of political institutionalization (effective political leadership, coherent state apparatus, and well-organized political parties), the flowering of civil society in Brazil has not had much of an impact on the actual consolidation of democracy.

11. The Labor Party is currently being reorganized and may have changed this structure since this book was published. See http://www.igc.org/lpa/.

Chapter 3

1. For a Wittgensteinian approach to identity that provides further arguments about why identities are not essentially essentialist, see Medina 2003.

2. I will draw from aspects of Taylor's unquestionably brilliant account of the development of concepts such as autonomy that bear in self/other relations, but I should note

here that I largely agree with the critics who have charged that Taylor's history of Western thought is, mistakenly, "largely celebratory," which then, for example, portrays the Nazis as a mere interruption of "a victorious ethic of reducing suffering." This claim is both wrong and dangerous, which is not to say that there haven't been genuinely progressive elements in Western thought. But the juxtaposition of a brutal global colonialism with the "flowering" of democracy in the Enlightenment throughout Europe must counsel a more wary assessment of even Europe's best ideas (see LaCapra 1994, 186; and Langer 1991). This oversight does not, however, affect most of Taylor's historical arguments.

3. I should note here Richard Bernstein's alternative interpretation of the account of the self in the Phenomenology, in which he takes the negation operative here to be determinate rather than indeterminate, or substantive and specific rather than analogous to a Pyrrhonic skepticism that leads nowhere because it denies without reason (see Bernstein 1971, 25-28 and 91-92). If the self's negation of the Other is a determinate negation, there would be a subsequent substantive effect on the self just by that very act of negation. This is an important difference because it gives the relationship to the Other a substantive effect on the way the self takes shape. But it seems to me that this would still deny agency to the Other over the self, since the effect on me is produced by my action, not the Other's, and would thus seem to be under my control. I am still looking for an intersubjective interdependent relation that does not make negation the cornerstone of individual integrity but can accept a positive contribution from the other without loss to the self.

4. And the ethical relation with the self Foucault explored—when he talks about the cultivation of the self, the care of the self, or techniques of the self—stop firmly short of creating collective categories of identity or ways of being in a public domain that might reconfigure the collective imaginary.

5. Here I will restrict myself to the aspects of Butler's theory that relate to the question of social identity, but readers who want more details of my views on Butler can see my "Philosophy Matters: A Review of Recent Work in Feminist Philosophy" (2000).

6. This claim that Butler is being ahistorically universalist will likely elicit protest, but my counterargument would be that although she apparently endeavors to historicize identity formation, she does not succeed. Consider the following contradictory passage: "If, then, we understand certain kinds of interpolations to confer identity, those injurious interpolations will constitute identity through injury. This is not the same as saying that such an identity will remain always and forever rooted in its injury as long as it remains an identity, but it does imply that the possibilities of resignification will rework and unsettle the passionate attachment to subjection without which subject formation-and re-formation-cannot succeed" (1997, 105). Here she allows that an identity that was originally constituted through injury may develop beyond this injurious constitution, but then she asserts that a "passionate attachment to subjection" is *necessary* to subject formation, including even subject re-formation. Thus, she is claiming that identity has an absolute dependence on injury. An identity may transcend its genesis in injury, which is a historical event such as enslavement or colonization, but it cannot transcend its imbrication in subjection, which is a psychic process theorized by psychoanalysis in typically universal fashion. I suggest this is the problem with Butler's project, however admirable it is to wed the highly historical Foucault with the ahistorical psychology of Freud/Lacan. As we will see, her ahistorical approach comes out especially forcefully in her criticisms of social naming (see also Benhabib et al. 1995, 42-43, 139, 143 n. 5).

7. Actually, I read Butler as allowing for recognition but one that recognizes a different concept of the self. Butler wants social recognition or acknowledgment of a nonsubstantive acting self-in-process, a self that resists, that exists beyond content. This demand for recognition undergirds her anti-essentialist politics and vision of progress. I believe this account is mistaken and unnecessary for progressive politics.

8. As I take leave of Butler at this point I want to clarify my differences with her work. Butler has been enormously influential but certainly controversial, and some of the tide of criticisms against her work have been off the mark. I want to distinguish my own disagreements with her from the attacks that have accused her of quietism, of willful obfuscation, and of patent liberalism. Although like some others I too find trace elements of a liberal ontology in her work (which is by itself insufficient reason to condemn a theory—liberalism is not wrong in every instance, just in most), I view her as a theorist with radical politics who aims at a radical articulation of the philosophical aspects of social theorizing. I understand both of us to be radicals, but of different sorts-her radicalism is much more sympathetic to anarchism while mine is a variant of communism. These old-fashioned terms may be outdated but they mark broad differences of orientation that continue to resonate in contemporary theory. Thus, my criticisms of Butler should be interpreted as, to use another quaint set of phrases, a contradiction among the people, not a contradiction with the enemy.

Chapter 4

1. The project here is not to offer an entirely original or comprehensive account of the self and social identity; that is far beyond my powers. Rather, I will draw from a variety of sources to construct an account that is sufficiently adequate to explain how we might understand raced and sexed identities as ascriptions without their being *innately* stifling to the self.

2. See Warnke 1999 for a helpful discussion of the debate over the effect of cultural difference among three leading Anglo-European theorists who start from a hermeneutic approach: Richard Rorty, Bernard Williams, and Jürgen Habermas. If forms of life are grounded in judgments that are themselves grounded in cultural difference, then there is no objective way to assess and compare divergences among them. Rorty acknowledges that the effect of cultural difference is to weaken the foundation of judgment even about our own values, but argues this is irrelevant: only philosophers think they need foundations. Williams also acknowledges the lack of foundation but argues that we can still say that by *our* lights our way of life is worth living. We cannot claim objective comparison this way but at least we avoid nihilism. Habermas argues that there is a meta-level of procedural rationality beyond cultural difference, on the basis of which we can negotiate differences and achieve agreement. Warnke herself weighs in, dismissing Rorty's nonchalance in the face of intransigent disagreements, but argues that Habermas's account is implausible since cultural difference enters in even at the level of procedure (a claim with which Charles Taylor concurs). But she hopes that, once we understand that values can have more than one valid interpretation and that there can thus be more than one valid form of life, we are more easily led toward tolerance of difference.

3. See Alcoff , 2004.

4. See, e.g., Steele and Aribsib, 1995.

5. See Frankenberg 1993. I don't think this analysis applies to the U.S. South.

Chapter 5

1. It may seem that we can solve this dilemma easily enough by simply defining women as those with female anatomies, but the question remains, What is the significance, if any, of those anatomies? What is the connection between female anatomy and the concept of woman? It should be remembered that the dominant discourse does not include in the category woman everyone with a female anatomy: it is often said that aggressive, self-serving, or powerful women are not "true" or "real" women. Moreover, the problem cannot be avoided by simply rejecting the concept of "woman" while retaining the category of

"women." If there are women, then there must exist a basis for the category and a criterion for inclusion within it. This criterion need not posit a universal, homogeneous essence, but there must be a criterion nonetheless.

2. For Schopenhauer's, Kant's, and nearly every other major Western philosopher's conception of women, and for an insight into just how contradictory and incoherent these are, see Bell 1983.

3. For an interesting discussion of whether feminists should even seek such transcendence, see Lloyd 1984, 86–102.

4. Both Rich and Daly departed from their early feminist analysis that I shall describe here, though both continued to emphasize the importance of gender in all women's lives over other aspects of their identity such as race and class, and both maintained an explanation of women through biological features. See Rich 1986; Daly 1984.

5. Three pages earlier Rich castigates the view that to solve the world's problems, we need only to release on the world women's ability to nurture, which may seem incongruous with the quoted passage. The two positions are consistent, however; Rich is trying to correct the patriarchal conception of women as essentially nurturers with a view that is more comprehensive and complicated than the patriarchal one.

6. Martin's more recent work departs from this in a positive direction. In an essay co-authored with Chandra Talpade Mohanty (1986, 191–212, esp. 194), Martin points out "the political limitations of an insistence on 'indeterminacy' which implicitly, when not explicitly, denies the critic's own situatedness in the social, and in effect refuses to acknowledge the critic's own institutional home." Martin and Mohanty seek to develop a more positive, though still problematized, conception of the subject as having a "multiple and shifting" perspective. In this, their work makes a significant contribution toward the development of an alternative account of subjectivity, a conception not unlike the one I will discuss in the rest of this essay.

7. The principal texts de Lauretis relies on in her exposition of Lacan, Eco and Peirce are Lacan 1966, Eco 1976 and 1979, and Peirce 1931–1958.

8. A wonderful reading of Pratt's essay that brings into full relief the way in which she articulates an identity politics can be found in Martin and Mohanty 1986.

9. I would never say that women, or anyone, have the freedom to choose their situation in life, but I do believe that of the multiple ways we are held in check, internalized oppressive mechanisms play a significant role, and we have more options for achieving control over these. On this point I must say I have learned from the work of Mary Daly, particularly *Gyn/Ecology*, which reveals and describes these mechanisms and challenges us to repudiate them. Other wonderful sources on this include de Beauvoir 1989 and Bartky 1991.

Chapter 6

1. The compatibilist position that has come to dominate the free-will debate argues that the belief in incompatibility between free will and determinism rested on the idea that the human decisions that we take to motivate our actions are special kinds of processes, unlike any other processes. But many today agree that decisions are processes like any other—decisions are based on what we know, what we have experienced, what we want, and so on. One can give causal stories about *decisions* as easily as any other sorts of processes. Thus a certain sort of Davidsonian-inspired monism has begun to gain influence in a variety of philosophical realms, and there is increasing interest in returning to previous formulations of monism in the history of Western philosophy, such as the writings of Spinoza, by feminists as well as others. Monism would suggest that, to the extent that it presumes a nature/culture divide in regard to sexual identity, Rubin's sex/gender distinction cannot be metaphysically sustained.

2. Another problem of process metaphysics for Butler would be their naturalism—even Nietzsche's dynamic flux is arguably a naturalistic account.

3. See Weir 1996 and Ferguson 2004 for more elaborated criticisms of the contradiction in Butler's work between the assertions of fluidity in *Gender Trouble* and the recalcitrance of organizing norms in *The Psychic Life of Power*.

4. To give the agency to discourse rather than intentional subjects can produce another form of determinism, it is true, but it always appears less absolute than laws of the universe or the plans of the gods.

5. To clarify my point here, I do think her account of performativity was misread as voluntaristic, but I don't think she was misread as holding that a sex/gender distinction or any objectivist account of sexual difference assumed unmediated access to the real, a point that Haslanger puts a lot of weight on, as I shall discuss.

6. As Angela Davis (1998) has noted, however, some of this variety in reproductive role is not in fact new but quite old, such as the wet nurses of slavery and feudalism, and surrogate mothers based class and station from biblical times. Davis urges us to consider *why* we think (and *who* thinks) that we have only now overcome the two-person system of reproduction. I would further suggest that the currently escalating globalizations of adoption follow a predictable path of political economy, in which poorer and largely nonwhite women give up their children to be raised by richer and largely white women. I strongly agree with Davis that reproductive technologies are neither good nor bad necessarily, but their development is structured by privilege and power, and they are not in fact subverting structures of privilege. The case is similar for adoption, which is neither good nor bad necessarily, but which is evolving through a global capitalist political economy and in no way challenging to it.

7. To be completely accurate, Fuss does not present herself as an anti-essentialist, and argues that the anti-essentialist mistakenly essentializes the effects and nature of essentialism, an argument with which I agree. The position that she herself argues for, however, is based on the idea that a more *consistent* anti-essentialist will not be consistently anti-essentialist. I would again agree, but this simply takes anti-essentialism to the meta-level and makes it non-negotiable as a theoretical constraint. This is a deconstructive position I reject.

8. Let me be clear: I am not suggesting that racial categories won't exist in the future or will naturally wither away. On that issue the jury is still out. Racial identity has two meanings: one is about biology and is based on specious science; the other meaning, just as common, is about culture. Because of history, racialized physical features have become correlated with cultural groups who have real identities. Thus, race is significant because of the cultural or ethnic groups that have emerged out of, in part, racial experiences. Reproduction, on the other hand, is not solely significant because cultures have attached various meanings to it.

9. In regard to disability, this is an ongoing debate. I have been very persuaded by the work of Tobin Siebers.

10. As an aside, this has become an interesting pattern in the postpositivist, antifoundationalist developments of twentieth century analytic epistemology and metaphysics, which has taken various forms through the later Carnap's pragmatic approach, Neurath's coherentism, Wittgenstein's emphasis on games and forms of life, Quine's holism, Davidson's Principle of Charity, Putnam's internal realism, Brandom's pragmatic semantics, even Bayesian decision theory. The pattern is this: analytic philosophers develop more sophisticated and nuanced understandings of how philosophical reasoning actually proceeds, jettisoning the modernist attachment to substance, essence, pure datum, the thing in itself, and so on, and recognizing indeterminacy, holism, the ultimate grounds of justification in practices and forms of life, and the pluralities of forms of life. But what continually

surprises many of us is that analytic philosophers remain singularly uninterested in pursuing the social and political implications of their new models; if they have destabilized the starting point from which philosophical reasoning occurs, they continue to be solely interested in producing rational reconstructions of the later steps of the process rather than becoming reflective about the cultural embeddedness of its initial assumptions. By contrast, Continental philosophers have tended to pay sole attention to the less rational and less conscious, more socially situated foundations of philosophical questions, without pursuing the reasoning that occurs after a question has been posed. One might imagine the two traditions could someday be patched together. But the analytic philosopher's inattention to the social aspects of the philosophical process means that they have often stopped short of facing up to the real implications of their own theses. Lynn Nelson's book on Quine (1990) shows this most brilliantly. I have tried to show some similar results with Putnam (Alcoff 1995). Naomi Scheman (1993) has developed Wittgenstein in these directions, and there are other examples. The point is not that our feminist readings of these figures are creative adaptations, but that they are simply following the original theory through to its logical conclusions. One could do an interesting piece of sociology of knowledge to diagnose the causes for this pattern of "theoria interruptus." A generous reading would be that analytic philosophy has simply not yet realized the full implications of the death of positivism, a death that they, more than anyone, brought about. A perhaps less generous reading would be that the unconscious of analytic philosophy cannot face or acknowledge its own maturation, and continues to hold onto a dream world or infantile fantasy life of a parthenogenetic pure reason. They suffer, as John McCumber puts it, from postpositivist depression.

Chapter 7

1. On the origin of race as an idea, see Omi and Winant 1985, 58–59; Gregory and Sanjek 1994, 2; and Eze 1997, in which are collected the original sources.

2. The widespread popularity of *The Bell Curve* thesis, which classifies and ranks intellectual ability by racial identity, and assumes a single standard of intelligence, is proof that vestiges of the classical episteme remain in place today. See Herrnstein and Murray 1994.

3. On these points, see the essays in Harding 1993. Harding explains that a cline is "a continuous gradation over space in the form of a frequency of a trait" (133). Frank B. Livingstone's essay in this collection argues that the differences in gene frequency among populations can be adequately explained without any reference to race.

4. For more statistics on racial disparities, see Hacker 1995.

5. I prefer contextualism to social constructionism because of the wide misuse and misunderstandings too often prevalent with the use of the second term. Social constructionism is sometimes interpreted along the lines of an idealism in which total agency is given to individual actors, as if we can construct new identities out of whole cloth. I hope that contextualism will convey the idea that what race *is* is dependent on context.

6. Mixed race people who are not easily categorizable by visible markers create unease precisely because one doesn't know how to act or talk with them. All of these practices change enormously across cultures; for example, in Latin America, mixed race persons do not create a cognitive crisis because they are the norm. There, racial identity is determined along a continuum of color without sharp borders.

7. See Merleau-Ponty 1962, esp. part 1. See also the elucidation of this concept in Weiss 1998, chap. 1.

8. See also Grosz 1994 for an excellent explanation and development of the concept of body image, esp. chaps. 3 and 4.

9. Gordon 1995, 117ff. Gordon argues that romanticizing and exoticizing racial others (as in "I just *love* black people") is like animal loving in that it seeks an object that has consciousness without judgment, that can know it is loved but be incapable of understanding or judging the one who loves.

10. There are numerous insightful analyses of racism in *Days of Obligation*; see esp. chap. 1.

11. I learned this because he has written a novel based on his experience of our relationship.

Chapter 8

1. This is Georgia Warnke's helpful gloss on the view of vision held by Mead and Habermas. See Warnke 1993, 305.

2. Hirschfeld describes his experiments and reports their results in chapters 4, 5, and 6 of *Race in the Making*.

Chapter 9

1. For balanced critiques of the movie, see Bird 1996. The movie champions one group of Indians by demonizing another group, portraying the latter as a bad Indians in the same one-dimensional fashion as old Westerns often portrayed all Indians. *Dances with Wolves* also replays a "going native" transformative narrative in which Europeans shed their enculturated, deformed subjectivities to return to an original and moral nobility, a narrative that values native culture primarily as an instrument for white enhancement.

2. For a critique of the way racism survives in these movies, see Wiegman 1995, esp. chap. 4.

3. This is not to deny that working-class and poor whites are treated badly by, for example, police and the courts. I was involved in protesting a police brutality case in Atlanta in 1977 in which a white working-class Vietnam-era veteran, Benny McQurter, was murdered by police when put in a choke hold outside a bar. McQurter lived in the poorest white section of Atlanta, the kind of neighborhood where people sliced up hotdogs lengthwise to serve as their breakfast meat. McQurter's whiteness did not save his life, but police brutality has caused the deaths of many more black and brown people than white. I learned this lesson clearly in the student movement of the 1970s. Whenever I went to student demonstrations in those days in which the majority of the participants were white, the police would come, take pictures, handle their billy clubs for our observations, and stand back. When I went to student demonstrations—peaceful, legal demonstrations, by the way—in which the majority of the participants were African American, the police not only came, they charged. I witnessed young students beaten about their heads and genital areas with clubs for doing nothing more than peacefully picketing against racism. I well remember the hallway full of bloodstains and torn human hair after the police had taken the people they'd beaten off to jail and charged them with "resisting arrest." Though whites and especially poor whites do face police brutality in this country, there is no equality in the level of police violence directed against white communities versus non-white ones.

4. As this book goes to press, the playing of "Dixie" at sports events is being challenged and may soon end at the University of Mississippi.

5. Gilroy's more recent book, *Against Race* (2000), has been disappointing to many of his readers, including me, for seeming to return to the idea that all identitites entail not only abjectification of others but also rigid conformism.

Chapter 10

1. Jorge Gracia, Pablo DeGreiff, Eduardo Mendieta, Paula Moya, Susan Sanchez-Casal and Angelo Corlett gave me substantive help with the arguments of this chapter, for which I am extremely grateful.

2. I refused to accept a five-year full scholarship to graduate school at the University of Michigan, a scholarship that I had not applied for but that the (white Anglo) graduate director in the philosophy department applied for on my behalf and then urged me to accept. It's not that refusing this makes me a moral hero, but refusing it was a means to avoid being burdened by moral guilt. So I don't believe that such refusals require superlative moral qualities.

3. Jorge Gracia, personal communication, December 1998.

4. "Disparities Grow in SAT Scores of Ethnic and Racial Groups," *Chronicle of Higher Education*, Sept. 11, 1998, A42. Emphasis added.

5. I am very aware of the paradoxical way this question is raised (since in a project of deracialization one shouldn't refer to people by their color), and of other paradoxes with the categories I've used at times in this chapter (e.g., the use of "black" when I have argued that it is oppressive). It is impossible to avoid all such paradoxes while maintaining clarity about which groups one is trying to pick out. All I can hope to have done is to problematize all such categories, and increase our self-reflectiveness about them.

6. And it is no less true for theories of Latino identity that the differences of racializing practices must receive serious attention. On another point, I realize that it is odd to launch an argument about an Anglo/Latino divide using the example of Brazil, but in this context, the division between Anglophone "developed" North America and non-Anglophone "developing" Latin America (thus including Brazil as well as others) is the key conflict.

7. For example, it is sometimes assumed that the possibility of self-determination is hopelessly compromised if a group or person has genealogical or other such ties to an outside group, especially the outside group from which one wants to be autonomous. It is this logic that sometimes polices any feminist or anti-heterosexist sentiments within nationalist movements on the grounds that feminism and gay liberation originate outside this culture. Of course feminism and gay liberation do not originate simply in, for example, the West, but the point is that this shouldn't matter in any case. Solidarity across gender or sexual lines does not threaten a movement for self-determination unless one presumes the necessity of political purity and community homogeneity.

Chapter 11

1. The use of terms such as "antiblack racism," used for example by Gordon (1995), helpfully specifies the kind of racism one is discussing and leaves open the possibility that there are other forms of racism.

2. Some give the figure of destroyed businesses as 2700; see Chang 1993, 101–18.

3. The issue of who counts as an immigrant has some variability. On the most extreme definition, only those peoples indigenous to North America would *not* count as immigrant, which would cover American Indians and some Latinos. In more common usage, "immigrants" refers to more recent arrivals. Thus Asian American and Latino families who have lived in the United States for multiple generations are no more "immigrant" than the German American and Anglo-American families here.

4. This surely explains the jockeying for position among the Democrats and Republicans for African American and Latino voters, respectively. If those groups unite with opposing sectors of the white majority, white majority rule is ensured.

5. It is also distinguished from "indigenism," or the view that only those peoples indigenous to a land have moral rights to its occupation.

6. Just to give one example, there is an 80 point difference between blacks and whites in mean SAT scores, even when both come from families making $70,000 or more, and similar cases apply to Puerto Ricans and other groups.

Chapter 12

1. Recent work that refutes the myth that Latin America is nonracist because it is pro-mestizo includes Wade 1993 and Appelbaum et al. 2003.

2. Latinos in the Florida of the 1950s were generally classified as "almost white" or as "black" depending on their color. But most lived in Miami and Tampa, which were even then cosmopolitan cities very different from the Deep South cities in northern Florida and other southern states. The biggest source of ostracism for Latinos then, as now, was language. Today, the many dark-skinned Latinos who have moved to southern Florida are ostracized not only by white Anglos but by African Americans as well for their use of Spanish. Anglos of all colors ridicule the sound of the language, share jokes about un-comprehending sales clerks, and commiserate across their own racial and ethnic differences about the "difficulties" of living in a bilingual city. The experience of Latinos in the United States makes it very clear that so-called racial features never operate alone to determine identity but are always mediated by language, culture, nationality, and sometimes religion.

3. For a moving and insightful literary description of this situation, see Nella Larsen's brilliant novel, *Quicksand*.

4. Although in the United States, the internal rule of hypodescent (where an offspring of a mixed union is identified with the lower status parent), has made most African American communities open and accepting of difference.

5. For example, it seems likely that the problems Israeli feminists are having in gaining acceptance for a reproductive rights agenda has to do not only with the close association between the Israeli state and Judaism, but also because the state's self-understood legitimation requires the reproduction of an ethnic identity.

6. Notice that, as Minh-Ha points out, no whites applied to become black.

7. Just as feminist historians have countered the usual assessment of the Renaissance, arguing that in this period women's situation actually worsened, so that there was no renaissance for women, so it has been argued that the Enlightenment offered nothing for those peoples of the world newly colonized. These epoch-dividing categories reflect the perspectives of the dominant.

8. "Self-consciousness exists in itself and for itself, in that, and by the fact that it exists for another self-consciousness; that is to say, it *is* only by being acknowledged or 'recognized'" (Hegel 1967, 229).

Bibliography

Aboulafia, Mitchell. 1986. *The Mediating Self: Mead, Sartre, and Self-Determination*. New Haven, Conn.: Yale University Press.

Acuña, Rodolfo. 1988. *Occupied America: A History of Chicanos*. 3rd ed. New York: Harper Collins.

Adorno, Theodor. 1988. *Minima Moralia: Reflections from Damaged Life*. London: New Left Books.

Adorno, Theodor, and Max Horkheimer. 1987. *Dialectic of Enlightenment*. Translated by John Cumming. New York: Continuum.

Albó, Xavier. 1995. "Our Identity Starting from Pluralism in the Base." Translated by Michael Aronna. In *The Postmodernism Debate in Latin America*. Edited by John Beverley, Michael Aronna, and José Oviedo. Durham, North Carolina: Duke University Press. Pp. 18–33.

Alcoff, Linda Martín. 1993. "On Mastering Master Discourses." *American Literary History* (summer): 335–46.

———. 1995. "Democracy and Rationality: A Dialogue with Hilary Putnam." In *Women, Culture, and Development*, edited by Martha Nussbaum and Jonathan Glover. New York: Oxford University Press.

———. 1996a. "The Problem of Speaking for Others." In *Who Can Speak? Authority and Critical Identity*, edited by Judith Roof and Robyn Wiegman. Chicago: University of Illinois Press.

———. 1996b. *Real Knowing: New Versions of the Coherence Theory*. Ithaca, N.Y.: Cornell University Press.

———. 2000. "Philosophy Matters: A Review of Recent Work in Feminist Philosophy." *SIGNS: Journal of Women in Culture and Society* 25, no. 3: 841–82.

———. 2004. "Against Post-Ethnic Futures" *Journal of Speculative Philosophy*, Vol. 18, No. 2, 99–117.

———, and Eduardo Mendieta, eds. 2002. *Identities: A Reader*. Malden, Mass.: Blackwell.

Allen, Amy. 1999. *The Power of Feminist Theory : Domination, Resistance, Solidarity*. Boulder, Colo.: Westview Press.

Allen, Anita. 1994. "Recent Racial Constructions in the U.S. Census." Paper presented at the conference "Race: Its Meaning and Significance," Rutgers University, November.

Althusser, Louis. 1971. *Lenin and Philosophy and Other Essays*. Translated by Ben Brewster. New York: Monthly Review Press.

Anzaldúa, Gloria. 1987. *Borderlands/La Frontera*. San Francisco: Spinsters/Aunt Lute.

Appelbaum, Nancy P., Anne S. Macpherson, and Karin Alejandra Rosemblatt, eds. 2003. *Race and Nation in Modern Latin America*. Chapel Hill: University of North Carolina Press.

Appiah, Anthony. 1992. *In My Father's House: Africa in the Philosophy of Culture*. New York: Oxford University Press.

Babbitt, Susan E. 1996. *Impossible Dreams: Rationality, Integrity, and Moral Imagination* Boulder, Colo.: Westview Press.

Baldwin, James. 1988. "A Talk to Teachers." In *The Graywolf Annual 5: Multicultural Literacy*, ed. Rick Simonson and Scott Walker. Saint Paul, Minn.: Graywolf Press.

Bannerji, Himani. 1994. *Thinking Through: Essays on Feminism, Marxism, and Anti-racism*. Toronto: Women's Press.

Barber, Benjamin. 1995. *Jihad vs. McWorld: How Globalism and Tribalism Are Reshaping the World*. New York: Ballantine.

Barrera, Mario. 1979. *Race and Class in the Southwest: A Theory of Racial Inequality*. South Bend, Ind.: University of Notre Dame Press.

Barry, Tom, Beth Wood and Deb Preusch. 1983. *Dollars and Dictators: A Guide to Central America*. New York: Grove Press.

Bartky, Sandra. 1991. *Femininity and Domination: Studies in the Phenomenology of Oppression*. New York: Routledge.

Battersby, Christine. 1998. *The Phenomenal Woman: Feminist Metaphysics and the Patterns of Identity*. New York: Routledge.

Bauer, Nancy. 2001. *Simone de Beauvoir, Philosophy, and Feminism*. New York: Columbia University Press.

Bell, Linda, ed. 1983. *Visions of Women*. Clifton, N.J.: Humana Press.

Bender, Leslie and Daan Braveman. 1995. *Power, Privilege, and Law: A Civil Rights Reader*. St. Paul, Minnesota: West Publishing Company.

Benhabib, Seyla, and Drucilla Cornell, eds. 1987. "Introduction: Beyond the Politics of Gender." In *Feminism as Critique: On the Politics of Gender*. Minneapolis: University of Minnesota Press.

Benhabib, Seyla, Judith Butler, Drucilla Cornell, and Nancy Fraser. 1995. *Feminist Contentions: A Philosophical Exchange*. New York: Routledge.

Berman, Paul. 1996. "In Defense of Reason." *New Yorker*, September 4, 94.

Bernstein, Richard J. 1971. *Praxis and Action: Contemporary Philosophies of Human Activity*. Philadelphia: University of Pennsylvania Press.

Berry, Bernita C. 1995. "'I Just See People': Exercises in Learning the Effects of Racism and Sexism." In *Overcoming Racism and Sexism*, edited by Linda A. Bell and David Blumenfeld, 45–51. Lanham, Md.: Rowman and Littlefield.

Bhabha, Homi. 1984. "Of Mimicry and Man." *October* 28: 125–33.

———. 1994. *The Location of Culture*. New York: Routledge.

Bird, Elizabeth S., ed. 1996. *Dressing in Feathers: The Construction of the Indian in American Popular Culture*. Boulder. Colo.: Westview Press.

Boone, Elizabeth Hill, and Walter Mignolo, eds. 1994. *Writing Without Words: Alternative Literacies in Mesoamerica and the Andes*. Durham, N.C.: Duke University Press.

Bordo, Susan. 1987. *The Flight to Objectivity: Essays on Cartesianism and Culture*. New York: State University of New York Press.

———. 1993. *Unbearable Weight: Feminism, Western Culture, and the Body*. Berkeley: University of California Press.

———. 1997. *Twilight Zones: The Hidden Life of Cultural Images from Plato to O.J.* Berkeley: University of California Press.

Boyarin, Daniel, and Jonathan Boyarin. 1995. "Diaspora: Generation and the Ground of Jewish Identity." In *Identities*, edited by Kwame Anthony Appiah and Henry Louis Gates. Chicago: University of Chicago Press.

Braidotti, Rosi. 1994. *Nomadic Subjects.* New York: Columbia University Press.

Brennan, Teresa. 1992. *The Interpretation of the Flesh: Freud and Femininity.* New York: Routledge.

———. 1993. *History after Lacan.* New York: Routledge.

Brimelow, Peter. 1995. *Alien Nation: Common Sense about America's Immigration Disaster.* New York: Random House.

Brison, Susan. 1997. "Outliving Oneself: Trauma, Memory, and Personal Identity." In *Feminists Rethink the Self*, edited by Diana Tietjens Meyers. Boulder, Colo.: Westview Press.

———. 2002. *Aftermath: Violence and the Remaking of a Self.* Princeton, N.J.: Princeton University Press.

Brown, Wendy. 1995. *States of Injury: Power and Freedom in Late Modernity.* Princeton, N.J.: Princeton University Press.

Bulkin, Elly, Minnie Bruce Pratt, and Barbara Smith. 1984. *Yours in Struggle: Three Feminist Perspectives on Anti-Semitism and Racism.* Brooklyn, N.Y.: Long Haul Press.

Burbach, Roger and Patricia Flynn. 1984. *The Politics of Intervention: The United States in Central America.* New York: Monthly Review Press.

Butler, Judith. 1987. "Variations on Sex and Gender: Beauvoir, Wittig, and Foucault." In *Feminism as Critique: On the Politics of Gender*, edited by Seyla Benhabib and Drucilla Cornell, 128–42. Minneapolis: University of Minnesota Press.

———. 1990. *Gender Trouble: Feminism and the Subversion of Identity.* New York: Routledge.

———. 1993. *Bodies That Matter: On the Discursive Limits of "Sex."* New York: Routledge.

———. 1997. *The Psychic Life of Power: Theories in Subjection.* Stanford, Calif.: Stanford University Press.

Cabral, Amilcar. 1973. "Identity and Dignity in the Context of the National Liberation Struggle." In *Return to the Source*, 9–25. New York: Monthly Review Press.

Camper, Carol, ed. 1994. *Miscegenation Blues: Voices of Mixed Race Women.* Toronto: Sister Vision Press.

Castells, Manuel. 1997. *The Power of Identity.* Vol. 2 of *The Information Age: Economy, Society and Culture.* Oxford: Blackwell.

Chakrabarti, Arindam. 1994. "Telling as Letting Know." In *Knowing from Words: Western and Indian Philosophical Analysis of Understanding and Testimony.* Vol. 230, Synthese Library: Studies in Epistemology, Logic, Methodology, and Philosophy of Science. Edited by Bimal Krishna Matilal and Arindam Chakrabarti. Dordrecht: Kluwer Academic Publishers.

Chang, Edward T. 1993. "America's First Multiethnic 'Riot'." In *The State of Asian America: Activism and Resistance in the 1990s*, edited by Karin Aguilar-San Juan, 101–18. Boston: South End Press.

Chock, Phyllis Pease. 1985. "Culturalism: Pluralism, Culture, and Race in the *Harvard Encyclopedia of American Ethnic Groups*." In *(Multi) Culturalism and the Baggage of "Race."* Special Issue. *Identities: Global Studies in Culture and Power* 1, no. 4 (April): 301–24.

Chomsky, Noam. 1993. *Year 501: The Conquest Continues*. Boston: South End Press.

Code, Lorraine. 1995. *Rhetorical Spaces: Essays on Gendered Locations*. New York: Routledge.

Colapietro, Vincent M. 1989. *Peirce's Approach to the Self: A Semiotic Perspective on Human Sexuality*. Albany: State University of New York Press.

Combahee River Collective. 1979. "A Black Feminist Statement." In *Capitalist Patriarchy and the Case for Socialist Feminism*, edited by Zillah R. Eisenstein, 362–72. New York: Monthly Review Press.

Coniff, Michael L. *Black Labor on a White Canal*. Pittsburgh: University of Pittsburgh Press, 1985; and Walter LeFeber *The Panama Canal: The Crisis in Historical Perspective* Oxford: Oxford University Press, 1990.

Corlett, J. Angelo. 2003. *Race, Racism, and Reparations*. Ithaca, N.Y.: Cornell University Press.

Cornell, Drucilla. 1995. *The Imaginary Domain: Abortion, Pornography, and Sexual Harassment*. New York: Routledge.

Cruz, José E. 1998. *Identity and Power: Puerto Rican Politics and the Challenge of Ethnicity*. Philadelphia: Temple University Press.

Crystal, David. 1997. *English as a Global Language*. Cambridge: Cambridge University Press.

Cuomo, Chris J. 1998. *Feminism and Ecological Communities: An Ethic of Flourishing*. New York: Routledge.

Daly, Mary. 1978. *Gyn/Ecology: The Metaethics of Radical Feminism*. Boston: Beacon Press.

———. 1984. *Pure Lust: Elemental Feminist Philosophy*. Boston: Beacon Press.

Darity, William A., Jr., Jason Dietrich, and Derrick Hamilton. 2003. "Bleach in the Rainbow: Latin Ethnicity and Preference for Whiteness." Paper delivered at the Globalizing Ethnic Studies Conference, Brown University, March.

Davidson, Arnold. 2001. *Historical Epistemology and the Formation of Concepts*. Cambridge, Mass.: Harvard University Press.

Dávila, Arlene. 2001a. *Latinos, Inc.: The Marketing and Making of a People*. Berkeley: University of California Press.

———. 2001b. "The Latin Side of Madison Avenue: Marketing and the Language That Makes Us 'Hispanics.'" In *Mambo Montage: The Latinization of New York*, edited by Augustín Laó-Montes and Arlene Dávila. New York: Columbia University Press, 411–24.

Davis, Angela. 1998. "Surrogates and Outcast Mothers; Racism and the Reproductive Politics in the Nineties." In *The Angela Y. Davis Reader*, edited by Joy James, 210–21. Malden, Mass.: Blackwell.

Dawson, Michael C. 1994. *Behind the Mule: Race and Class in African-American Politics*. Princeton, N.J.: Princeton University Press.

de Alba, Alicia Gaspar. 1998. "Born in East L. A.: An Exercise in Cultural Schizophrenia." In *The Latino Condition: A Critical Reader*, edited by Richard Delgado and Jean Stefancic. New York: New York University Press, 226–29.

de Beauvoir, Simone. 1989. *The Second Sex*. Translated by H. M. Parshley. New York: Random House.

de Lauretis, Teresa. 1984. *Alice Doesn't*. Bloomington: Indiana University Press.

———. 1986. "Feminist Studies/Critical Studies: Issues, Terms, Contexts." In *Feminist Studies/Critical Studies*, edited by Teresa de Lauretis. Bloomington: Indiana University Press, 1–19.

———. 1990. "Upping the Anti (sic) in Feminist Theory." In *Conflicts in Feminism*, edited by Marianne Hirsch and Evelyn Fox Keller. New York: Routledge, 255–70.

———. 1994. *The Practice of Love: Lesbian Sexuality and Perverse Desire*. Bloomington: Indiana University Press.

Deleuze, Gilles, and Félix Guattari. 1983. *Anti-Oedipus*. Translated by Robert Hurley, Mark Seem, and Helen R. Lane. Minneapolis: University of Minnesota Press.

———. 1986. *Kafka: Toward a Minor Literature*. Translated by Dana Polan. Minneapolis: University of Minnesota Press.

———. 1987. *A Thousand Plateaus: Capitalism and Schizophrenia*. Translated by Brian Massumi. Minneapolis: University of Minnesota Press.

Delgado, Richard. 1995. *The Rodrigo Chronicles: Conversations about America and Race*. New York: New York University Press.

———. 1998. "The Black/White Paradigm: How Does It Work?" In *The Latino Condition*, edited by Richard Delgado and Jean Stefancic, 369–75. New York: New York University Press.

Derricotte, Toi. 1997. *The Black Notebooks: An Interior Journey*. New York: W. W. Norton.

Derrida, Jacques. 1978. *Spurs*. Translated by Barbara Harlow. Chicago: University of Chicago Press.

———. 1982a. "Choreographies." *Diacritics* 12: 66–76.

———. 1982b. *Margins of Philosophy*. Translated by Alan Bass. Chicago: University of Chicago Press.

———. 1989. "Women in the Beehive." In *Men in Feminism*, edited by Alice Jardine and Paul Smith, 189–203. New York: Routledge.

Descombes, Vincent. 1980. *Modern French Philosophy*. New York: Cambridge University Press.

Dicker, Susan. 1966. *Languages in America: A Pluralist View*. (Bilingual Education and Bilingualism, 42). Philadelphia: Multilingual Matters Limited.

Dingwaney, Anuradha, and Lawrence Needham. 1996. "The Difference That Difference Makes." *Socialist Review* 26, nos. 3 and 4.

Domínguez, Virginia R. 1997. *White by Definition: Social Classification in Creole Louisiana*. New Brunswick, N.J.: Rutgers University Press.

Donovan, Josephine. 1985. *Feminist Theory: The Intellectual Traditions of American Feminism*. New York: Ungar.

D'Orso, Michael. 1996. *Like Judgment Day: The Ruin and Redemption of a Town Called Rosewood*. New York: Berkley Publishing Co.

Du Bois, W. E. B. 1999. *Black Reconstruction in America 1860–1880*. New York: Free Press.

Dunn, Robert G. 1998. *Identity Crises: A Social Critique of Postmodernity*. Minneapolis: University of Minnesota Press.

Dussel, Enrique. 1985. *Philosophy of Liberation*. Translated by Aquilina Martinez and Christine Morkovsky. Maryknoll, N.Y.: Orbis.

———. 1995. *The Invention of the Americas: Eclipse of 'the Other' and the Myth of Modernity*. Translated by Michael D. Barber. New York: Continuum.

Echols, Alice. 1983. "The New Feminism of Yin and Yang." In *Powers of Desire: The Politics of Sexuality*, edited by Ann Snitow, Christine Stansell, and Sharon Thompson, 439–59. New York: Monthly Review Press.

———. 1984. "The Taming of the Id: Feminist Sexual Politics, 1968–1983." In *Pleasure and Danger: Exploring Female Sexuality*, edited by Carole S. Vance, 50–72. Boston: Routledge and Kegan Paul.

———. 1989. *Daring to Be Bad: Radical Feminism in America 1967–1975*. Minneapolis: University of Minnesota Press.

Eco, Umberto. 1976. *A Theory of Semiotics*. Bloomington: Indiana University Press.

———. 1979. *The Role of the Reader*. Bloomington: Indiana University Press.

Eisenstein, Hester. 1983. *Contemporary Feminist Thought*. Boston: G. K. Hall.

Elbaum, Max. 2002. *Revolution in the Air: Sixties Radicals turn to Lenin, Mao, and Che.* New York: Verso.

Elshtain, Jean Bethke. 1995. *Democracy on Trial.* New York: Harper Collins, 1995.

Encarnación, Omar G. 2000. "Tocqueville's Missionaries: Civil Society and the Promotion of Democracy." *World Policy Journal*, vol. xvii, no. 1 (June), 9–18.

——. 2003. *The Myth of Civil Society: Social Capital and Democratic Consolidation in Spain and Brazil.* New York: Palgrave.

Eze, Emmanuel Chukwudi. 2001. *Achieving Our Humanity: The Idea of a Postracial Future.* New York: Routledge.

——, ed. 1997. *Race and the Enlightenment.* Cambridge, Mass.: Blackwell.

Fanon, Frantz. 1963. *The Wretched of the Earth.* Translated by Constance Farrington. New York: Grove Press.

——. 1967. *Black Skin, White Masks.* Translated by Charles Lam Markmann. New York: Grove Press.

Fausto-Sterling, Anne. 1986. *Myths of Gender: Biological Theories about Women and Men.* New York: Basic Books.

Feder, Ellen K., Mary C. Rawlinson, and Emily Zakin. 1997. *Derrida and Feminism: Recasting the Question of Woman.* New York: Routledge.

Ferguson, Ann. 2005. "Butler, Sex/Gender, and a Postmodern Gender Theory." *Feminist Interventions in Ethics and Politics: Feminist Ethics and Social Theory* edited by Barbara S. Andrew, Jean Keller, and Lisa H. Schwartzman. Lanham, Md.: Rowman and Littlefield. 59–73.

Fernandez, Carlos A. 1992. "La Raza and the Melting Pot: A Comparative Look at Multiethnicity." In *Racially Mixed People in America*, edited by Maria P. P. Root. Newbury Park, Calif.: Sage.

Firestone, Shulamith. 1970. *The Dialectic of Sex: The Case for Feminist Revolution.* New York: William Morrow.

Flores, Juan. 1996. "Pan-Latino/Trans-Latino: Puerto Ricans in the 'New Nueva York.'" *CENTRO: Journal of the Center for Puerto Rican Studies* 8, nos. 1 and 2.

——. 2000. *From Bomba to Hip Hop: Puerto Rican Culture and Latino Identity.* New York: Columbia University Press.

Flores, Juan, and George Yudice. 1990. "Buscando América: Languages of Latino Self-Formation." *Social Text* 24: 57–84.

Flores, William V., and Rina Benmayor. 1997. *Latino Cultural Citizenship: Claiming Identity, Space and Rights.* Boston: Beacon Press.

Foner, Philip S., and Herbert Shapiro. 1991. *American Communism and Black Americans: A Documentary History 1930–1934.* Philadelphia: Temple University Press.

Fosl, Catherine. 2002. *Subversive Southerner: Anne Braden and the Struggle for Racial Justice in the Cold War South.* New York: Palgrave Macmillan.

Foucault, Michel. 1970. *The Order of Things: An Archaeology of the Human Sciences.* Translated by A. Sheridan. New York: Random House.

——. 1972. *The Archaeology of Knowledge.* Translated by A. M. Sheridan Smith. New York: Pantheon Books.

——. 1978. *The History of Sexuality.* Vol. 1. Translated by Robert Hurley. New York: Random House.

——. 1979. *Discipline and Punish: The Birth of the Prison.* Translated by Alan Sheridan. New York: Random House.

——. 1980. "Two Lectures." In *Power/Knowledge: Selected Interviews and Other Writings 1972–1977.* Edited by Colin Gordon, translated by Colin Gordon, Leo Marshall, John Mepham, Kate Soper. New York: Pantheon.

———. 1983. "Why Study Power? The Question of the Subject." In *Beyond Structuralism and Hermeneutics: Michel Foucault,* by Hubert L. Dreyfus and Paul Rabinow. 2nd ed. Chicago: University of Chicago Press.

———. 1984. "Nietzsche, Genealogy, History." In *The Foucault Reader,* edited by Paul Rabinow. New York: Pantheon.

———. 1986. *Death and the Labyrinth: The World of Raymond Roussel.* London: Athlone Press.

———. 1988. "The Concern with Truth." In *Politics, Philosophy, Culture,* edited by Lawrence D. Kritzman. New York: Routledge, 255–67.

———. 2000a. "The Subject and Power." In *Power: Essential Works of Foucault 1954–1984,* edited by James D. Faubion. New York: New Press.

———. 2000b. "Truth and Power." In *Power: Essential Works of Foucault 1954–1984,* edited by James D. Faubion. New York: New Press.

Fox Piven, Francis. 1995. "Globalizing Capitalism and the Rise of Identity Politics." *Socialist Register:* 102–16.

Frankenberg, Ruth. 1993. *White Women, Race Matters: The Social Construction of Whiteness.* Minneapolis: University of Minnesota Press.

Franklin, John Hope. 1989. *Race and History.* Baton Rouge: Louisiana State University Press.

Fraser, Nancy. 1997. *Justice Interruptus: Critical Reflections on the "Postsocialist" Condition.* New York: Routledge.

———. 2000. "Rethinking Recognition." *New Left Review* 3 (May-June): 107–20.

Fraser, Nancy, and Axel Honneth. 2003. *Redistribution or Recognition? A Political-Philosophical Exchange.* Translated by Joel Golb, James Ingram, and Christiane Wilke. London: Verso.

Freud, Sigmund. 1962. *The Ego and the Id.* Translated by Joan Riviere, edited by James Strachey. New York: W. W. Norton.

———. 1995. *Basic Writings of Sigmund Freud (Psychopathology of Everyday Life, the Interpretation of Dreams, and Three Contributions to the Theory of Sex).* Edited by A. A. Brill. New York: Modern Library.

Friedan, Betty. 1996. "Children's Crusade: A Gathering Heralds a Shift Toward a New Paradigm." *New Yorker,* June 3, 5–6.

Frye, Marilyn. 1983. *The Politics of Reality: Essays in Feminist Theory.* Trumansburg, N.Y.: Crossing Press.

———. 1992. *Willful Virgin: Essays in Feminism.* Freedom, Calif.: Crossing Press.

Fuss, Diana. 1989. *Essentially Speaking: Feminism, Nature and Difference.* New York: Routledge.

Gadamer, Hans-Georg. 1991. *Truth and Method.* 2nd ed. Translated by Joel Weinsheimer and Donald G. Marshall. New York: Crossroad Press.

Galeano, Eduardo. 1967. *Guatemala: Occupied Country.* New York: Monthly Review Press.

———. 1973. *Open Veins of Latin America: Five Centuries of the Pillage of a Continent.* Translated by Cedric Belfrage. New York: Monthly Review Press.

Gallagher, Charles. 1994. "White Reconstruction in the University." *Socialist Review* 94, nos. 1 and 2: 165–88.

Gatens, Moira. 1991. *Feminism and Philosophy: Perspectives on Difference and Equality.* Bloomington: Indiana University Press.

Gates, Henry Louis, Jr. 1990. "The Master's Pieces: On Canon Formation and the African-American Tradition." *South Atlantic Quarterly* (Winter), pp. 89–113.

Gibbons, L. 1991. "Race against Time, Racial Discourse, and Irish History." *Oxford Literary Review* 13, nos. 1 and 2: 95–117.

Gilroy, Paul. 1993. *The Black Atlantic: Modernity and Double Consciousness.* Cambridge, Mass.: Harvard University Press.

———. 2000. *Against Race: Imagining Political Culture beyond the Color Line.* Cambridge, Mass.: Harvard University Press.

Gitlin, Todd. 1993. "From Universality to Difference: Notes on the Fragmentation of the Idea of the Left." *Contention* 2 (winter).

———. 1995. *The Twilight of Common Dreams: Why America Is Wracked with Culture Wars.* New York: Henry Holt.

Glazer, Nathan. 1983. *Ethnic Dilemmas: 1964–1982.* Cambridge Mass.: Harvard University Press.

Glazer, Nathan, and Daniel Patrick Moynihan. 1970. *Beyond the Melting Pot: The Negroes, Puerto Ricans, Jews, Italian, and Irish of New York City.* 2nd ed. Cambridge Mass.: MIT Press.

———, eds. 1975. *Ethnicity: Theory and Experience.* Cambridge, Mass: Harvard University Press.

Glissant, Edouard. 1999. *Caribbean Discourse: Selected Essays.* Translated by J. Michael Dash. Charlottesville: University Press of Virginia.

Goldberg, David Theo. 1993. *Racist Cultures: Philosophy and the Politics of Meaning.* Oxford: Basil Blackwell.

Gooding-Williams, Robert. 1995. "Comments on Anthony Appiah's 'In My Father's House.'" Paper presented at the American Philosophical Association Central Division Meetings, Chicago, April.

———. 1998. "Race, Multiculturalism, and Democracy." *Constellations* 5, no. 1 (March): 18–41.

Gordon, Lewis. 1995. *Bad Faith and Antiblack Racism.* Atlantic Highlands, N.J.: Humanities Press.

Gossett, Thomas F. 1965. *Race: The History of an Idea in America.* New York: Schocken.

Gould, Stephen Jay. 1993. "American Polygeny and Craniometry: Blacks and Indians as Separate, Inferior Species." In *The Racial Economy of Science: Toward a Democratic Future,* edited by Sandra Harding, 84–115. Bloomington: Indiana University Press.

Gramsci, Antonio. 1971. *Selections from the Prison Notebooks.* Edited by Q. Hoare and G. N. Smith. London: Lawrence and Wishart.

Gregory, Steven, and Roger Sanjek, eds. 1994. *Race.* New Brunswick, N.J.: Rutgers University Press.

Grosfoguel, Ramón, and Chloé S. Georas. 1996. "The Racialization of Latino Caribbean Migrants in the New York Metropolitan Area." *CENTRO: Journal of the Center for Puerto Rican Studies* 8, nos. 1 and 2: 199.

Grosz, Elizabeth. 1990. *Jacques Lacan: A Feminist Introduction.* New York: Routledge.

———. 1994. *Volatile Bodies.* Bloomington: Indiana University Press.

———. 1995. *Space, Time, and Perversion: Essays on the Politics of Bodies.* New York: Routledge.

Guillamin, Colette. 1995. *Racism, Sexism, Power, and Ideology.* New York: Routledge.

Guinier, Lani, and Gerald Torres. 2002. *The Miner's Canary: Enlisting Race, Resisting Power, Transforming Democracy.* Cambridge, Mass.: Harvard University Press.

Habermas, Jürgen. 1987. *Philosophical Discourses of Modernity.* Translated by Frederick Lawrence. Cambridge, Mass.: MIT Press.

Hacker, Andrew. 1995. *Two Nations: Black and White, Separate, Hostile, Unequal.* 2nd ed. New York: Ballantine.

Hall, Stuart. 1987. "Minimal Selves." In *Identity,* edited by Lisa Appignanesi. London: ICA Document 6.

———. 1990. "Cultural Identity and Diaspora." In *Identity: Community, Culture, Difference*, edited by Jonathan Rutherford. London: Lawrence and Wishart, 222–37.

———. 1996. "New Ethnicities." In *Stuart Hall: Critical Dialogues in Cultural Studies*, edited by David Morley and Kuan-Hsing Chen. London: Routledge, 441–49.

Halperin, David. 1995. *Saint Foucault: Toward a Gay Hagiography*. New York: Oxford University Press.

Hampton, Fred. 1970. "You Can Murder a Liberator, but You Can't Murder Liberation." In *The Black Panthers Speak*, edited by Philip S. Foner. Philadelphia: J. P. Lippincott.

Haney López, Ian F. 1996. *White by Law: The Legal Construction of Race*. New York: New York University Press.

———. 1998. "Race and Erasure: The Salience of Race to Latinos/as." In *The Latino Condition*, edited by Richard Delgado and Jean Stefancic, 180–95. New York: New York University Press.

Hardin, C. L. 1984. "A New Look at Color." *American Philosophical Quarterly* 21, no. 2 (April): 125–34.

Harding, Sandra, ed. 1993. *The Racial Economy of Science: Toward a Democratic Future*. Bloomington: Indiana University Press.

Harrington, Michael L. 1996. *Traditions and Changes: The University of Mississippi in Principle and in Practice*. 2nd ed. New York: McGraw-Hill.

Harris, Cheryl I. 1995. "Whiteness as Property." In *Critical Race Theory: The Key Writings That Formed the Movement*, edited by Kimberlé Crenshaw, Neil Gotanda, Gary Peller, and Kendall Thomas, 276–91. New York: New Press.

Hartsock, Nancy. 1985. *Money, Sex, and Power: Toward a Feminist Historical Materialism*. Boston: Northeastern University Press.

Haskin, Frederic J. 1913. *The Panama Canal*. Garden City, N.Y.: Doubleday.

Haslanger, Sally. 2000. "Feminism and Metaphysics: Negotiating the Natural." In *The Cambridge Companion to Feminist Philosophy*, edited by Miranda Fricker and Jennifer Hornsby, 102–26. Cambridge: Cambridge University Press.

Haywood, Harry. 1976. *Negro Liberation*. Chicago: Liberator Press.

———. 1978. *Black Bolshevik: Autobiography of an Afro-American Communist*. Chicago: Liberator Press.

Hegel, G. W. F. 1953. *Reason in History*. Translated by Robert S. Hartman. Indianapolis: Bobbs-Merrill.

———. 1971. *Hegel's Philosophy of Mind*. Translated by William Wallace and A. V. Miller. Oxford: Oxford University Press.

———. 1975. *Philosophy of Right*. Translated by T. M. Knox. London: Oxford University Press.

———. 1977. *The Phenomenology of Spirit*. Translated by A. V. Miller. Oxford: Oxford University Press.

Heidegger, Martin. 1962. *Being and Time*. Translated by John Macquarrie and Edward Robinson. New York: Harper and Row.

Herrnstein, Richard J., and Charles Murray. 1994. *The Bell Curve: Intelligence and Class Structure in American Life*. New York: Free Press.

Hirschfeld, Lawrence A. 1996. *Race in the Making: Cognition, Culture, and the Child's Construction of Human Kinds*. Cambridge, Mass.: MIT Press.

Hobbes, Thomas. 1839. "Elements of Philosophy (*De Corpore*)." In *The English Works of Thomas Hobbes*, Vol. 1, edited by W. Molesworth. N.p.: John Bohn.

Hobsbawm, Eric. 1996. "Identity Politics and the Left." *New Left Review* (May/June): 38–47.

Hochschild, Jennifer L. 1996. *Facing Up to the American Dream*. Princeton, N.J.: Princeton University Press.

Holliman, Daniel, and Robert A. Brown. 1997. "'A Nation within a Nation': Racial Identity, Self-Help, and African American Economic Attitudes at the End of the Twentieth Century." Paper delivered at the annual meeting of the American Political Science Association, Washington, D.C.

Hollinger, David A. 1995. *Post-ethnic America: Beyond Multiculturalism.* New York: Harper Collins.

hooks, bell. 1984. *Feminist Theory: From Margin to Center.* Boston: South End Press.

Horkheimer, Max. 1972. *Critical Theory: Selected Essays.* Translated by Matthew J. O'Connell and others. New York: Seabury Press.

Hudson, Hosea. 1972. *Black Worker in the Deep South: A Personal Record.* New York: International Publishers.

Hughes, Robert. 1993. *The Culture of Complaint: The Fraying of America.* New York: Oxford University Press.

Huntington, Samuel P. 1998. *The Clash of Civilizations and the Remaking of World Order.* New York: Simon and Schuster.

———. 2004. *Who Are We? The Challenges to America's National Identity.* New York: Simon and Schuster.

Husserl, Edmund. 1950. *Ideen zu reinen Phänomenologie und Phänomenologischen Philosophie.* Edited by Walter Biemel. The Hague: Martins Nijhoff.

Ignatiev, Noel, and John Garvey. 1996. *Race Traitor.* New York: Routledge.

Irigaray, Luce. 1985a. *Speculum of the Other Woman.* Translated by Gillian C. Gill. Ithaca, N.Y.: Cornell University Press.

———. 1985b. *This Sex Which Is Not One.* Translated by Catherine Porter. Ithaca, N.Y.: Cornell University Press.

Jay, Martin. 1973. *The Dialectical Imagination: A History of the Frankfurt School and the Institute of Social Research, 1923–1950.* Boston: Little, Brown.

Johnson, Kevin R. 1999. *How Did You Get to Be Mexican? A White/Brown Man's Search for Identity.* Philadelphia: Temple University Press.

Johnson, Mark. 1987. *The Body in the Mind: The Bodily Basis of Meaning, Imagination, and Reason.* Chicago: University of Chicago Press.

Jones Correa, Michael. 1998. *Between Two Nations: The Political Predicament of Latinos in New York City.* Ithaca, N.Y.: Cornell University Press.

Jordan, Winthrop. 1968. *White over Black: American Attitudes toward the Negro 1550–1812.* Baltimore: Penguin Books.

Joseph, Gloria. 1981. "The Incompatible Menage à Trois: Marxism, Feminism, and Racism." In *Women and Revolution,* edited by Lydia Sargent. Boston: South End Press.

Jurist, Elliot L. 2002. *Beyond Hegel and Nietzsche: Philosophy, Culture, and Agency.* Cambridge, Mass.: MIT Press.

Kanpol, Barry, and Peter McLaren, eds. 1995. *Critical Multiculturalism.* New York: Bergin and Garvey.

Kaplan, Caren. 1987. "Deterritorializations: The Rewriting of Home and Exile in Western Feminist Discourse." *Cultural Critique* (spring): 187–98.

Katz, Judith. 1978. *White Awareness: Handbook for Anti-racism Training.* Norman: University of Oklahoma Press.

Kelley, Robin D. G. 1997. *Yo' Mama's Disfunktional: Fighting the Culture Wars in Urban America.* Boston: Beacon Press.

Kerouac, Jack. 1998. "On the Road Again." *New Yorker,* June 22 and 29.

Kim, Elaine H. 1993. "Between Black and White: An Interview with Bong Hwan Kim." In *The State of Asian America: Activism and Resistance in the 1990s,* edited by Karin Aguilar-San Juan, 71–100. Boston: South End Press.

Kim, Elaine H. and Eui-Young Yu. 1995. *East to America: Korean American Life Stories.* New York: New Press.

King, Anthony D., ed. 2000. *Culture, Globalization and the World-System: Contemporary Conditions for the Representation of Identity.* Minneapolis: University of Minnesota Press.

Klor de Alva, Jorge, and Cornel West. 1996. "Our Next Race Question: The Uneasiness between Blacks and Latinos." *Harper's*, April, 55–63.

Kockelmans, Joseph. 1967. "Some Fundamental Themes of Husserl's Phenomenology." In *Phenomenology: The Philosophy of Edmund Husserl*, edited by Joseph Kockelmans. Garden City, N.Y.: Doubleday, 24–36.

Kojève, Alexandre. 1969. *Introduction to the Reading of Hegel: Lectures on the Phenomenology of Spirit.* Edited by Allan Bloom and translated by James H. Nichols Jr. Ithaca, N.Y.: Cornell University Press.

Kristeva, Julia. 1981a. "Oscillation between Power and Denial." In *New French Feminisms*, edited by Elaine Marks and Isabelle de Courtivron. New York: Schocken.

———. 1981b. "Woman Can Never Be Defined." In *New French Feminisms*, edited by Elaine Marks and Isabelle de Courtivron. New York: Schocken.

———. 1984. *Revolution in Poetic Language.* Translated by Margaret Walker. Introduction by Léon S. Roudiez. New York: Columbia University Press.

———. 1986. *The Kristeva Reader.* Edited by Toril Moi. New York: Columbia University Press.

Kruks, Sonia. 2001. *Retrieving Experience: Subjectivity and Recognition in Feminist Politics.* Ithaca, N.Y.: Cornell University Press.

Lacan, Jacques. 1966. *Écrits.* Paris: Seuil.

LaCapra, Dominick. 1994. *Representing the Holocaust.* Ithaca, N.Y.: Cornell University Press.

Laclau, Ernesto, ed. 1994. *The Making of Political Identities.* London: Verso.

Lakoff, George. 1987. *Women, Fire, and Dangerous Things: What Categories Reveal about the Mind.* Chicago: University of Chicago Press.

Lakoff, George, and Mark Johnson. 1999. *Philosophy in the Flesh: The Embodied Mind and Its Challenge to Western Thought.* New York: Basic Books.

Langer, Lawrence. 1991. *Holocaust Memories: The Ruins of Memory.* New Haven, Conn.: Yale University Press.

Larsen, Nella. 1993. *Quicksand.* New Brunswick, N.J.: Rutgers University Press.

Las Casas, Bartolomé de. 1999. *In Defense of the Indians.* Translated and edited by Stafford Poole, C. M. Dekalb: Northern Illinois University Press.

Le Dœuff, Michéle. 1991. *Hipparchia's Choice: An Essay Concerning Women, Philosophy, Etc.* Translated by Trista Selous. Oxford: Blackwell.

Lee, Sharon M. 1993. "Racial Classifications in the U.S. Census: 1890–1990." *Ethnic and Racial Studies*, Volume 16, Number 1, January: 75–94.

Leon-Portilla, Miguel, ed. 1990. *The Broken Spears: The Aztec Account of the Conquest of Mexico.* 2nd ed. Boston: Beacon Press.

Levin, David Michael, ed. 1993. *Modernity and the Hegemony of Vision.* Berkeley: University of California Press.

———. 1997. *Sites of Vision: The Discursive Construction of Sight in the History of Philosophy.* Cambridge, Mass.: MIT Press.

Livingstone, Frank B. 1993. "On the Nonexistence of Human Races." In *The Racial Economy of Science: Toward a Democratic Future*, edited by Sandra Harding, 131–41. Bloomington: Indiana University Press.

Lloyd, Genevieve. 1984. *The Man of Reason: "Male" and "Female" in Western Philosophy.* Minneapolis: University of Minnesota Press.

Locke, Alain. 1992. *The New Negro*. New York: Simon and Schuster.

Loomba, Ania. 1998. *Colonialism/Postcolonialism*. London: Routledge.

Lorde, Audre. 1984. "Age, Race, Class, and Sex." In *Sister Outsider*. Trumansberg, N.Y.: Crossing Press.

Louie, Miriam Ching Yoon. 2001. *Sweatshop Warriors: Immigrant Women Workers Take on the Global Factory*. Cambridge, Mass.: South End Press.

Lowe, Lisa. 1996. *Immigrant Acts: On Asian American Cultural Politics*. Durham, N.C.: Duke University Press.

Lukács, Georg. 1971. *History and Class Consciousness: Studies in Marxist Dialectics*. Translated by Rodney Livingstone. Cambridge, Mass.: MIT Press.

Lyman, Stanford. 1994. *Color, Culture, Civilization: Race and Minority Issues in American Society*. Chicago: University of Illinois Press.

Lyons, Oren. 1992. "The American Indian in the Past." In *Exiled in the Land of the Free: Democracy, Indian Nations, and the U.S. Constitution*, 13–42. Edited by Oren Lyons, John Mohawk, Vine Deloria Jr., Laurence Hauptman, Howard Berman, Donald Grinde Jr., Curtis Berkey, and Robert Venables. Santa Fe, N.M.: Clear Light Publishers.

Marable, Manning. 1996. *Speaking Truth to Power: Essays on Race, Resistance, and Radicalism*. Boulder, Colo.: Westview Press.

Marcuse, Herbert. 1969a. *An Essay on Liberation*. Boston: Beacon Press.

———. 1969b. *Eros and Civilization: A Philosophical Inquiry into Freud*. London: Sphere Books.

Marmon Silko, Leslie. 1994. "Fences Against Freedom." *Hungry Mind Review*, no. 31, Fall: 9, 20, 58–59.

Marshall, Gloria A. 1993. "Racial Classifications: Popular and Scientific." In *The Racial Economy of Science: Toward a Democratic Future*, edited by Sandra Harding, 116–27. Bloomington: Indiana University Press.

Martin, Biddy. 1982. "Feminism, Criticism, and Foucault." *New German Critique*, 27: 3–30.

Martin, Biddy, and Chandra Talpade Mohanty.1986. "Feminist Politics: What's Home Got to Do with It?" In *Feminist Studies/Critical Studies*, edited by Teresa de Lauretis. Bloomington: Indiana University Press, 191–212.

Martinez, George A. 1998. "Mexican Americans and Whiteness," in *The Latino Condition*, edited by Richard Delgado and Jean Stefancic. New York: New York University Press, 175–79.

Martinez, Elizabeth. 1998. "Beyond Black and White: The Racisms of Our Time" in *The Latino Condition*, edited by Richard Delgado and Jean Stefancic. New York: New York University Press, 466–77.

Mato, Daniel. 1997. "Problems in the Making of Representations of All-Encompassing U.S. Latino–'Latin' American Transitional Identities." *Latino Review of Books* 3, nos. 1–2, (spring/fall).

McClymer, John. 1982. "The Americanization Movement and the Education of the Foreign-Born Adult, 1914–1925." In *American Education and the European Immigrant: 1880–1940*, edited by Bernard Weiss. Champaign: University of Illinois Press.

Mead, George Herbert. 1934. *Mind, Self, and Society From the Standpoint of a Social Behaviorist*. Chicago: University of Chicago Press.

———. 1982. *The Individual and the Social Self: Unpublished Work of George Herbert Mead*. Edited by David L. Miller. Chicago: University of Chicago Press.

Medina, José. 2003. "Identity Trouble: Disidentification and the Problem of Difference." *Philosophy and Social Criticism* 29, no. 6: 657–82.

Menocal, Maria Rosa. 2002. *The Ornament of the World: How Muslims, Jews, and Christians Created a Culture of Tolerance in Medieval Spain*. Boston: Little, Brown.

Merleau-Ponty, Maurice. 1962. *Phenomenology of Perception*. Translated by Colin Smith. London: Routledge and Kegan Paul.

——. 1964. *Signs*. Translated by Richard C. McCleary. Chicago: Northwestern University Press.

——. 1968. *The Visible and the Invisible*. Translated by Alphonso Lingis. Evanston, Ill.: Northwestern University Press.

Mignolo, Walter. 1995. *The Darker Side of the Renaissance: Literacy, Territoriality, and Colonization*. Ann Arbor: University of Michigan Press.

——. 2000. *Local Histories/Global Designs: Coloniality, Subaltern Knowledges, and Border Thinking*. Princeton, N.J.: Princeton University Press.

Mills, Charles. 1994. "Non-Cartesian Sums: Philosophy and the African-American Experience." *Teaching Philosophy* 17: no. 3: 223–43. Reprinted in Charles Mills, *Blackness Visible: Essays on Philosophy and Race*. Ithaca, N.Y.: Cornell University Press.

——. 1997. *The Racial Contract*. Ithaca, N.Y.: Cornell University Press.

Minh-ha, Trinh T. 1991. *When the Moon Waxes Red*. New York: Routledge.

Mohanty, Satya. 1997. *Literary Theory and the Claims of History*. Ithaca, N.Y.: Cornell University Press.

Moi, Toril. 1999. *What Is a Woman? And Other Essays*. Oxford: Oxford University Press.

Moraga, Cherríe. 1983. "La Guerra." In *This Bridge Called My Back: Writings by Radical Women of Color*, edited by Cherríe Moraga and Gloria Anzaldua. New York: Kitchen Table Press, 27–34.

——. 1986. "From a Long Line of Vendidas: Chicanas and Feminism." In *Feminist Studies/Critical Studies*, edited by Teresa de Lauretis. Bloomington: Indiana University Press, 173–90.

"More Gender Trouble: Feminism Meets Queer Theory." 1994. Special issue. *differences* 6 (summer/fall).

Morrison, Toni. 1998. "Home." In *The House That Race Built*, edited by Wahneema Lubiano. New York: Random House.

Mosley, Albert G. 1999. "Negritude, Nationalism, and Nativism: Racists or Racialists?" In *Racism*, edited by Leonard Harris. Amherst, N.Y.: Humanity Books.

Moya, Paula M. L. 2002. *Learning From Experience: Minority Identities, Multicultural Struggles*. Berkeley: University of California Press.

Nancy, Jean-Luc. 2000. *Being Singular Plural*. Translated by Robert D. Richardson and Anne E. O'Bryne. Stanford, Calif.: Stanford University Press.

Nelson, Lynn Hankinson. 1990. *Who Knows: From Quine to a Feminist Empiricism*. Philadelphia: Temple University Press.

Nussbaum, Martha. 1997. *Cultivating Humanity: A Classical Defense of Liberal Education*. Cambridge, Mass.: Harvard University Press.

Oboler, Suzanne. 1995. *Ethnic Labels, Latino Lives: Identity and the Politics of (Re)Presentation in the United States*. Minneapolis: University of Minnesota Press.

Okihiro, Gary. 1994. *Margins to Mainstreams: Asians in American History and Culture*. Seattle: University of Washington Press.

——. 1995. "Comparing Colonialism and Migrations, Puerto Rico and the Philippines." Paper delivered at Duke University, February 17–19.

Oliver, Kelly. 1995. *Womanizing Nietzsche: Philosophy's Relation to the "Feminine."* New York: Routledge.

Olsen, Joel. 2001. "The Democratic Problem of the White Citizen." *Constellations* 8, no. 2 (June): 163–83.

Omi, Michael, and Howard Winant. 1986. *Racial Formations in the United States: From the 1960s to the 1980s*. New York: Routledge.

Oquendo, Angel R. 1998. "Re-imagining the Latino/a Race." In *The Latino Condition: A Critical Reader*, edited by Richard Delgado and Jean Stefancic. New York: New York University Press.

Ortner, Sherry, and Harriet Whitehead, eds. 1981. *Sexual Meanings: The Cultural Construction of Gender and Sexuality*. New York: Cambridge University Press.

Palmer, Richard E. 1969. *Hermeneutics: Interpretation Theory in Schleiermacher, Dilthey, Heidegger, and Gadamer*. Evanston, Ill.: Northwestern University Press.

Panikkar, Raimundo. 1988. "What Is Comparative Philosophy Comparing?" In *Interpreting Across Boundaries: New Essays in Comparative Philosophy*, edited by G. J. Larson and E. Deutsch, 116–36. Princeton, N.J.: Princeton University Press.

Parker, Pat. 1999. "For the White Person Who Wants to Know How to Be My Friend." In *An Expanded Edition of Movement in Black*, 99. Ithaca, N.Y.: Firebrand Books.

Parkes, Henry Bamford. 1969. *A History of Mexico*. 3rd ed. Boston: Houghton Mifflin.

Peirce, Charles Sanders. 1940. "The Fixation of Belief." In *The Philosophy of Peirce*, edited by Justus Buchler. London: Routledge and Kegan Paul.

———. 1931–1958. *Collected Papers*, Vols. 1–8. Cambridge, Mass.: Harvard University Press.

Peller, Gary. 1995. "Race Consciousness." In *After Identity: A Reader in Law and Culture*, edited by Dan Danielsen and Karen Engle. New York: Routledge.

Perea, Juan. 1998. "The Black/White Binary Paradigm of Race" in *The Latino Condition*, edited by Richard Delgado and Jean Stefancic. New York: New York University Press, pp. 359–68.

Perera, Victor. 1993. *Unfinished Conquest: The Guatemalan Tragedy*. Berkeley: University of California Press.

Piper, Adrian M. S. 1992–93. "Xenophobia and Kantian Rationalism." *Philosophical Forum* 24, nos. 1–3 (fall-spring): 188–232.

———. 1992. "Passing for White, Passing for Black." *Transition* 58: 5–32.

Prashad, Vijay. 2000. *The Karma of Brown Folk*. Minneapolis: University of Minnesota Press.

Quiñones, Ernesto. 2000. *Bodega Dreams*. New York: Random House.

Rahman, Abdur. 1983. *Intellectual Colonization*. New Delhi: Vikas.

Ramirez, Deborah A. 1998. "It's Not just Black and White Anymore," in *The Latino Condition* edited by Richard Delgado and Jean Stefancic. New York: New York University Press, pp. 478–87.

Ramos, Juanita. 1995. Latin American Lesbians Speak on Black Identity—Violeta Garro, Minerva Rosa Pérez, Digna, Magdalena C., Juanita. In *Black Women's Diasporas*. Vol 2 of *Moving beyond Boundaries*, edited by Carole Boyce Davies. New York: New York University Press.

Ramos, Samuel. 2004. "Profile of Man and Culture in Mexico." Translated by Peter G. Earle. In *Latin American Philosophy for the 21st century: The Human Condition, Values, and the Search for Identity*. Edited by Jorge J.E. Gracia and Elizabeth Millán-Zaibert. Amherst, New York: Prometheus Books. Excerpted from *Profile of Man and Culture in Mexico*. Translated by Peter G. Earle. Austin: University of Texas Press, 1962, 281–85.

———. 1986. "Toward a New Humanism." In *Latin American Philosophy in the Twentieth Century: Man, Values, and the Search for Philosophical Identity*. Edited and translated by Jorge J.E. Gracia. Amherst, New York: Prometheus Books. Excerpted from Samuel Ramos, *Hacia un nuevo humanismo*. Mexico City: Fondo de Cultura Económica, 1962, 69–77.

Rapaport, Herman. 1993. "Time's Cinders." In *Modernity and the Hegemony of Vision*, edited by David Michael Levin, 218–33. Berkeley: University of California Press.

Rich, Adrienne. 1977. *Of Woman Born*. New York: Bantam.

———. 1979. *On Lies, Secrets, and Silence*. New York: Norton.

———. 1986. "Notes toward a Politics of Location." In *Blood, Bread, and Poetry*. New York: Norton Publishing House.

Ricoeur, Paul. 1992. *Oneself as Another*. Translated by Kathleen Blamey. Chicago: University of Chicago Press.

Riley, Denise. 1983. *War in the Nursery: Theories of the Child and Mother*. London: Virago.

———. 1988. "Am I That Name?" *Feminism and the Category of "Women" in History*. Minneapolis: University of Minnesota Press.

Rodriguez, Clara E. 1989. *Puerto Ricans Born in the U.S.A.* Boston: Unwin Hyman.

———. 2000. *Changing Race: Latinos, the Census, and the History of Ethnicity in the United States*. New York: New York University Press.

Rodriguez, Richard. 1983. *Hunger of Memory*. New York: Bantam.

———. 1992. *Days of Obligation: An Argument with My Mexican Father*. New York: Viking Books.

Root, Maria P. P. 1992. "Within, Between, and Beyond Race." In *Racially Mixed People in America*, edited by Maria P. P. Root. Newbury Park, Calif.: Sage.

———, ed. 1996. *The Multiracial Experience: Racial Borders as the New Frontier*. Thousand Oaks, Calif.: Sage.

Rorty, Richard. 1998. *Achieving Our Country: Leftist Thought in Twentieth-Century America*. Cambridge, Mass.: Harvard University Press.

———. 1999. *Philosophy and Social Hope*. New York: Penguin Books.

Rosaldo, Renato. 1985. "Assimilation Revisited." Stanford Center for Chicano Research. Working Paper Series no. 9 (July), Stanford, California.

———. 1993. *Culture and Truth: The Remaking of Social Analysis*. Boston: Beacon Press.

———. Forthcoming. "Identity Politics: An Ethnography by a Participant." In *Identity Politics Reconsidered*, edited by Linda Martín Alcoff, Michael Hames-Garcia, Satya Mohanty, and Paula Moya. New York: Palgrave.

Rubin, Gayle. 1975. "The Traffic in Women: Notes on the 'Political Economy' of Sex." In *Toward an Anthropology of Women*, edited by Rayna R. Reiter, 157–210. New York: Monthly Review Press.

Said, Edward. 2001. *Power, Politics, and Culture: Interviews with Edward Said*. Edited by Gauri Viswanathan. New York: Pantheon.

———. 2004. *Humanism and Democratic Criticism*. New York: Columbia University Press.

Sanjek, Roger. 1994. "The Enduring Inequalities of Race." In *Race*, edited by Steven Gregory and Roger Sanjek. New Brunswick, N.J.: Rutgers University Press.

Santiago-Valles, Santiago. 1996. "Policing the Crisis in the Whitest of the Antilles." *CENTRO: Journal of the Center for Puerto Rican Studies* 8, nos. 1 and 2: 43–55.

Sartre, Jean-Paul. 1956. *Being and Nothingness: A Phenomenological Essay on Ontology*. Translated by Hazel E. Barnes. New York: Pocket Books.

———. 1991. *The Intelligibility of History*. Vol. 2 of *Critique of Dialectical Reason*. Translated by Quintin Hoare. London: Verso.

Scheman, Naomi. 1983. "Individualism and the Objects of Psychology." In *Discovering Reality: Feminist Perspectives on Epistemology, Metaphysics, Methodology, and Philosophy of Science*, edited by Sandra Harding and Merrill B. Hintikka, 225–44. Dordrecht, Holland: Reidel.

Scheman, Naomi. 1993. *Engenderings: Constructions of Knowledge, Authority, and Privilege*. New York: Routledge.

Schiller, Nina Glick. 1995. "The Dialectics of Race and Culture." Editor's foreword to *(Multi) Culturalism and the Baggage of "Race."* Special issue. *Identities: Global Studies in Culture and Power* 1, no. 4 (April): iii–iv.

Schlesinger, Jr., Arthur M. 1992. *The Disuniting of America: Reflections on a Multicultural Society.* New York: W.W. Norton.

Schott, Robin. 2002. "Resurrecting Embodiment: Toward a Feminist Materialism." In *A Mind of One's Own,* edited by Louise M. Antony and Charlotte Witt, 319–34. 2nd ed. Boulder, Colo.: Westview Press.

Schrift, Alan. 2001. "Judith Butler: Une nouvelle existentialiste?" *Philosophy Today* (spring): 12–23.

Schutte, Ofelia. 1993. *Cultural Identity and Social Liberation in Latin American Thought.* Albany: State University of New York Press.

———. 2000. "Cultural Alterity: Cross-Cultural Communication and Feminist Theory in North-South Contexts." In *Decentering the Center: Philosophy for a Multicultural, Postcolonial, and Feminist World,* edited by Uma Narayan and Sandra Harding, 47–66. Bloomington: Indiana University Press. First published in *Hypatia* 13, no. 2 (spring 1998).

Senna, Danzy. 1998. *Caucasia.* New York: Penguin.

Seshadri-Crooks, Kalpana. 2000. *Desiring Whiteness: A Lacanian Analysis of Race.* New York: Routledge.

Shapin, Steven. 1994. *A Social History of Truth: Civility and Science in Seventeenth-Century England.* Chicago: University of Chicago Press.

Shapiro, Gary. 1993. "In the Shadows of Philosophy: Nietzsche and the Question of Vision." In *Modernity and the Hegemony of Vision,* edited by David Michael Levin, 124–42. Berkeley: University of California Press.

Shorris, Earl. 1992. *Latinos: A Biography of the People.* New York: W.W. Norton and Company.

Simons, Margaret A. 1979. "Racism and Feminism: A Schism in the Sisterhood." *Feminist Studies* 5, no. 2 (summer): 384–401.

Smith, Barbara. 1983. Introduction to *Home Girls: A Black Feminist Anthology,* edited by Barbara Smith, xix–lvi. New York: Kitchen Table Press.

Smith, Paul. 1988. *Discerning the Subject.* Minneapolis: University of Minnesota Press.

Snitow, Ann. 1990. "A Gender Diary." In *Conflicts in Feminism,* edited by Marianne Hirsch and Evelyn Fox Keller. New York: Routledge.

Solomon, Robert C. 1983. *In the Spirit of Hegel: A Study of G. W. F. Hegel's "Phenomenology of Spirit."* New York: Oxford University Press.

Spivak, Gayatri. 1987. *In Other Worlds: Essays in Cultural Politics.* New York: Methuen.

———, with Ellen Rooney. 1989. "In a Word. Interview." *differences* 1, no. 2 (summer): 124–54.

Stannard, David E. 1992. *American Holocaust: The Conquest of the New World.* Oxford: Oxford University Press.

Steele, C. M., and Aronson, J. 1995. "Stereotype threat and the intellectual test performance of African-Americans." *Journal of Personality and Social Psychology,* 69, 797–811.

Steele, Meili. 1997. *Theorizing Textual Subjects: Agency and Oppression.* Cambridge: Cambridge University Press.

Storr, Anthony. 1989. *Freud.* New York: Oxford University Press.

Stubbs, Marcia, and Sylvan Barnet, eds. 1966. *The Little, Brown Reader.* 7th ed. New York: Longman Publishing Group.

Suro, Roberto. 1999. *Strangers among Us: Latino Lives in a Changing America.* New York: Random House.

Takagi, Dana Y. 1992. *The Retreat from Race: Asian-American Admissions and Racial Politics.* New Brunswick, N.J.: Rutgers University Press.

Takaki, Ronald. 1990. *Iron Cages: Race and Culture in 19th Century America.* New York: Oxford University Press.

———. 1993. *A Different Mirror: A History of Multicultural America.* New York: Oxford University Press.

———. 1994. *From Different Shores: Perspectives on Race and Ethnicity in America*, Second edition. New York: Oxford University Press.

Taylor, Charles. 1985. *Philosophy and the Human Sciences: Philosophical Papers* 2. Cambridge: Cambridge University Press.

———. 1989. *Sources of the Self: The Making of Modern Identity.* Cambridge, Mass.: Harvard University Press.

Taylor, Paul C. 2003. *Race: A Philosophical Introduction.* New York: Polity Press.

Tchen, Jack Kuo Wei. 1999. *New York Before Chinatown: Orientalism and the Shaping of American Culture 1776–1882.* Baltimore: Johns Hopkins Press.

Todorov, Tzvetan. 1984. *The Conquest of America: The Question of the Other.* Translated by Richard Howard. New York: Harper and Row.

Tomasky, Michael.1996. *Left for Dead: The Life, Death and Possible Resurrection of Progressive Politics in America.* New York: Free Press.

Toro, Luis Angel. 1998. "Race, Identity, and 'Box Checking': The Hispanic Classification in OMB Directive No. 15." In *The Latino/a Condition*, A Critical Reader, Edited by Richard Delgado and Jean Stefancic. New York: New York University Press, pp. 52–59.

Torres-Saillant, Silvio. 1992. "Western Discourse and the Curriculum (The Uniting of Multicultural America)." *Punto 7 review: A Journal of Marginal Discourse* 2.2 : 107–167. Reprinted in *Impact: A Journal of Open Mind* 1.1 (1993): 7–64.

———. 2000. "Diasporic Disquisitions: Dominicanists, Transnationalism, and the Community." Dominican Studies Working Papers Series 1. New York: CUNY Dominican Studies Institute, pp. 1–41.

Uribe, Armando. 1975. *The Black Book of American Intervention in Chile.* Translated by Jonathan Casart. Boston: Beacon Press.

Valadez, Jorge M. 2001. *Deliberative Democracy, Political Legitimacy, and Self-Determination in Multicultural Societies.* Boulder, Colo.: Westview Press.

Vasconcelos, José. 1979. *The Cosmic Race, La raza Cósmica: A Bilingual Edition.* Translated by Didier T. Jaén. Baltimore: Johns Hopkins University Press.

Wade, Peter. 1993. *Blackness and Race Mixture: The Dynamics of Racial Identity in Colombia.* Baltimore: Johns Hopkins University Press.

Warnke, Georgia. 1987. *Gadamer: Hermeneutics, Tradition, and Reason.* Stanford, Calif.: Stanford University Press.

———. 1993. "Ocularcentrism and Social Criticism." In *Modernity and the Hegemony of Vision*, edited by David Michael Levin, 287–308. Berkeley: University of California Press.

———. 1999. *Legitimate Differences: Interpretation in the Abortion Controversy and Other Public Debates.* Berkeley: University of California Press.

Weinsheimer, Joel C. 1985. *Gadamer's Hermeneutics: A Reading of Truth and Method.* New Haven, Conn.: Yale University Press.

Weir, Allison. 1996. *Sacrificial Logics: Feminist Theory and the Critique of Identity.* New York: Routledge.

Weiss, Gail. 1998. *Body Images: Embodiment as Intercorporeality.* New York: Routledge.

West, Cornel. 1982. *Prophesy Deliverance!* Philadelphia: Westminster Press.

———. 1994. *Race Matters.* New York: Vintage Books.

Wiegman, Robyn. 1995. *American Anatomies: Theorizing Race and Gender*. Durham, N.C.: Duke University Press.

Williams, Gregory Howard. 1995. *Life on the Color Line: The True Story of a White Boy Who Discovered He Was Black*. New York: Penguin.

Williams, Patricia J. 1997. *Seeing a Color-Blind Future: The Paradox of Race*. New York: Farrar, Straus, and Giroux.

Winant, Howard. 1994. *Racial Conditions: Politics, Theory, Comparisons*. Minneapolis: University of Minnesota Press.

Wittig, Monique. 1992. *The Straight Mind and Other Essays*. Boston: Beacon Press.

Wood, Allen W. 1990. *Hegel's Ethical Thought*. Cambridge: Cambridge University Press.

Wu, Frank. 2002. *Yellow: Race in America beyond Black and White*. New York: Basic Books.

Young, Iris Marion. 1990. *Throwing Like a Girl*. Bloomington: Indiana University Press.

——. 1998. "Unruly Categories: A Critique of Nancy Fraser's Dual Systems Theory." In *Theorizing Multiculturalism: A Guide to the Current Debate*, edited by Cynthia Willett. Malden, Mass.: Blackwell.

——. 2000. *Inclusion and Democracy*. Oxford: Oxford University Press.

Zack, Naomi. 1993. *Race and Mixed Race*. Philadelphia: Temple University Press.

——. 1994. "Race and Philosophic Meaning." APA *Newsletter on Philosophy and the Black Experience* (spring).

Zea, Leopoldo. 1988–1989. "Identity: A Latin American Philosophical Problem." *Philosophical Forum* 20 (fall-winter): 33–42.

Index